Thinking Clearly about Psychology
Volume 1: Matters of Public Interest

Thinking Clearly about Psychology

Volume 1   Matters of Public Interest   *Dante Cicchetti and William M. Grove, editors*

Volume 2   Personality and Psychopathology   *William M. Grove and Dante Cicchetti, editors*

Thinking Clearly about Psychology

Volume 1: Matters of Public Interest

Edited by Dante Cicchetti
and William M. Grove

Essays in honor of Paul E. Meehl

University of Minnesota Press
Minneapolis   Oxford

Published by the University of Minnesota Press
2037 University Avenue Southeast, Minneapolis MN 55414
Printed in the United States of America on acid-free paper

Library of Congress Cataloging-in-Publication Data

Thinking clearly about psychology.
Includes bibliographical references and index.
Contents: v. 1. Matters of public interest
—v. 2. Personality and psychopathology.
1. Psychology, Clinical. 2. Psychology. I. Meehl,
Paul E. (Paul Everett), 1920– . II. Cicchetti,
Dante. III. Grove, William M.
RC467.T43   1991   150   90-15474
ISBN 0-8166-1891-7 (v. 1)
ISBN 0-8166-1918-2 (set)

A CIP catalog record for this book is available from the British Library

Contents

Contents of Volume 2

Personality and Abilities

Methodology

Psychopathology

Introduction

Dante Cicchetti and
William M. Grove

Everything that can be thought at all can be thought clearly.
Everything that can be said can be said clearly.

(Wittgenstein, *Tractatus*, 4.116)

The contributions of Paul E. Meehl can best be summarized by the 1989 citation of the Gold Medal Award for Life Achievement in Psychology, which he received from the American Psychological Association. "He has had a lasting impact on modern psychology through the clarity of his thinking and the elegance of his writing" (Lykken, 1990, p. 656).

This book has two aims: to express the contributors' appreciation for the stimulation and example offered by Paul Everett Meehl, psychologist, methodologist, and philosopher; and to reflect on some topics close to Paul's heart. Finding topics that interest Paul is no great feat. Paul's range of interests is remarkable, a source of wonderment to students and colleagues alike. After discussing paradoxes of confirmation in the philosophy of science, one discovers the next day that Paul can argue with equal depth of understanding about the intricacies of psychoanalytic theory, or the implications of gaps in the fossil record for the theory of evolution.

Paul's career has been Minnesotan in character as well as in location. He is a native, and he did his undergraduate work at the university. He received his Ph.D. there, studying individual differences with D. G. Paterson, learning with B. F. Skinner, and clinical psychology with Starke Hathaway, his advisor and an author of the Minnesota Multiphasic Personality Inventory (MMPI) to which Paul contributed one of the most theoretically interesting scales in work that led to his dissertation. He joined the Minnesota psychology faculty immediately upon obtaining his Ph.D., beginning his meteoric rise in academia. He embodied the scientist-practitioner model before it had been formulated. He was psychoanalyzed (not one of his more Minnesota-like activities!), and saw ten to fifteen hours of patients per week while conducting research on latent learning in the rat with Kenneth MacCorquodale, all while acting as Psychology Department chair-

viii DANTE CICCHETTI AND WILLIAM M. GROVE

man. Concurrently, he undertook work on the clinical-statistical prediction controversy. After being turned down by two publishers (they said it wouldn't sell!), he placed his book on the subject with the University of Minnesota Press, with which he has maintained a close relationship. The book, *Clinical versus Statistical Prediction*, promptly sold out eight printings and became a true classic in psychology.

Meanwhile, Paul became ever more interested in psychodiagnosis, which for him has never been the mere assignment of rubrics of convenience, but, rather, the detection of latent internal states (such as schizotypal personality organization). He was a firm believer in the reality of psychiatric disease entities when super-operationist and behaviorist colleagues pronounced them to be pseudo-scientific or even meaningless. Resurgence in the 1970s of American interest in descriptive psychopathology, diagnosis, and genetics simply brought the profession back to where Paul had the good sense to stay all along, as can be seen by rereading his presidential address to the American Psychological Association.

Probing the quantitative implications of categorical models of psychiatric illness (and applying his considerable mathematical talents) in the 1960s, Paul developed his taxometric methods to detect, through highly fallible indicators, a latent genotypic group of individuals at risk for schizophrenia. Always the consummate clinician, this mathematical work was paralleled by Paul's development of the Schizotypy Checklist, another classic circulated in photocopy around the country's clinical psychology programs.

Somehow Paul still found time to pursue interests in personality theory, voter behavior, philosophy of science (he was a founder of the Minnesota Center for Philosophy of Science) and psychological methodology, forensic psychology (he long co-taught a course in the area with contributor Carl Malmquist), and the reconciliation of Lutheran beliefs with psychological findings. Few people could be more aptly called a Renaissance man.

In seeking to produce a volume that reflects the richness of Paul's contributions, we were daunted by the number of his areas of involvement. While the contributors to these volumes address many of the fields that Paul has tilled, covering all the areas of his expertise would have resulted in an encyclopedia. To bring order to this embarrassment of riches, we have placed the contributions in two volumes. The first contains a personal note by Paul's long-time friend Bill Schofield, followed by chapters from David Lykken, W. Grant Dahlstrom, and Leonard G. Rorer on the "State of Psychology." Paul directed attention to this area throughout his career, and his hopes as well as disappointments emerge in this excerpt from his recent autobiography.

While I don't suppose any of us had the crazy idea that psychology was practically on the threshold of becoming like chemistry or physics, these exciting developments did make it reasonable to think that it wouldn't be

very many years before a large integrative job between the clinic, the
laboratory, and the mental testing room would be accomplished. It didn't
turn out to be that way . . . we have settled for more modest theoretical
aspirations, and even with that resetting of sights, the record of
psychology as a cumulative quantitative science, especially in the
"soft" areas, cannot be considered impressive." (Meehl, 1989, p. 382)

Volume 1 then turns to philosophy, a field that Paul, by his own description,
considers to be commensurate with his personal predilection for the theoretical
over the empirical. Without the contributions of Paul Feyerabend, Sir Karl
Popper, and Adolf Grünbaum, the volume would have fallen far short of capturing Paul's investment in fields other than psychology. In fact, it is Paul's incorporation of philosophy into his approach to psychological investigations that has
resulted in such thought-provoking treatises.

Being a neo-Popperian in the philosophy of science, I am myself quite
comfortable in engaging in speculative formulations completely
unsubstantiated by data. . . . I am not an inductivist. To "justify"
concocting a theory, all one needs is a problem, plus a notion . . . of
how one might test one's theory." (Meehl, 1972, p. 12)

Following the philosophical pieces are chapters by Lewis R. Goldberg, David
Faust, Benjamin Kleinmuntz, and Robyn M. Dawes on "Clinical versus Statistical Prediction." This topic is a fitting conclusion to Volume 1 because it is an
area of Paul's work that has, perhaps, generated the most interest as well as mis-
understanding. According to Paul:

Both theoretical and empirical considerations suggest that we would be
well advised to concentrate effort on improving our actuarial techniques
rather than on the calibration of each clinician for each of a large
number of different prediction problems. How should we meanwhile be
making our decisions? Shall we use our heads, or shall we follow the
formula? Mostly we will use our heads, because there just isn't any
formula, but suppose we have a formula, and a case comes along in
which it disagrees with our heads? Shall we then use our heads? I
would say, yes—provided the psychological situation is as clear as a
broken leg; otherwise, very *very* seldom. (Meehl, 1957, p. 273)

Volume 2 begins with essays directed to "Personality and Abilities," yet another area where Paul's ideas have been at the forefront.

If all the thousands of clinical hours currently being expended in
concocting clever and flowery personality sketches from test data could
be devoted instead to scientific investigation . . . , it would probably
mean a marked improvement in our net social contribution. (Meehl,
1956, p. 272)

Ten chapters, the largest of any topical section in this volume, reflect the work that has been generated since Paul's comment over 30 years ago. Contributors to this area include B. F. Skinner, Auke Tellegen, Jane Loevinger, Paul H. Blaney, Brendan A. Maher, Jerry S. Wiggins, Harrison G. Gough, George S. Welsh, Lloyd G. Humphreys, and Thomas J. Bouchard, Jr.

Paul is widely known and respected for his contributions to psychometric theory, and his opinion on "methodology" serves as an appropriate introduction to that section of Volume 2.

> While many concepts in psychology are unfortunately quite vague or foggy so that to set forth a purported operational definition of the concept would really amount to pseudoscientific pretentiousness . . . , this does not excuse us from trying to be as precise, explicit, and clearheaded as we can about that very conceptual fuzziness. (Meehl, 1973, p. xiii)

Contributions by Judy Garber and Zvi Strassberg, Robert R. Golden, I. I. Gottesman and M. McGue, and William M. Grove provide current insights into methodological considerations.

Volume 2 concludes with essays on "Psychopathology" by David M. Buss, Dante Cicchetti and Douglas Barnett, Carl P. Malmquist, Leonard L. Heston, Joseph Zubin, Richard Feldman, and Suzanne Salzinger, and William G. Iacono. Paul's long-term belief in the importance of examining complex pathways and multiple factors, including neurobiological and genetic/biochemical ones, in the etiology of psychopathology emerges in this statement.

> For many psychotherapists everything that is wrong with anybody is attributable either to having a battle-ax mother, being raised on the wrong side of the tracks, or having married the wrong mate. It is dangerous to be the parent or spouse of a mentally ill person because you will almost certainly get blamed for it, even if he was patently abnormal before you met him and his family tree abounds with food fadists, recluses, perpetual-motion inventors, suicides, and residents of mental hospitals. Part of this attitude springs from the two related ideas that if it were the case that genes had something to do with aberrated behavior, then 1) psychotherapy could not "work," and 2) the psychodynamics we think we understand about mental patients would have to be abandoned. (Meehl, 1973, p. 273)

These introductory quotes provide some insight into the depth and breadth of Paul Meehl. The editors came to know Paul when they were graduate students in psychology at Minnesota. Grove moved to Minnesota specifically with the hope of studying with him. Will's professional, as well as personal, development was enhanced greatly through this mentorship. Although Paul did not function as Cicchetti's sole research mentor, the intellectual stimulation and personal support provided by Paul throughout Dante's training resulted in a life-long impact on his development. These two separate descriptions of the effect of knowing Paul Meehl reflect an influence that supersedes the bounds of the classroom or laboratory to a more personal and enduring relationship.

When we found out (from our mutual friend, Paul's wife and indefatigable collaborator, Dr. Leslie Yonce) that each wanted to prepare a volume in honor of Paul, we joined forces. The work was actually completed in secret because Paul's distaste for any public show of approbation for him is quite strong.

As editors, we have been extraordinarily fortunate. First, Paul inspires such regard (both professional and personal) that very few prospective contributors passed up the invitation. Second, they are a brilliant group whose work needs little editing or introduction. Third, we had the aid and support of Leslie Yonce, surreptitiously helping us find contributors from old addresses on Paul's correspondence, encouraging us always, advising us frequently. This book would not have been possible without her.

References

Lykken, D. T. (1990). Gold Medal Award for Life Achievement in the Applications of Psychology. *American Psychologist, 45*, 656–657.

Meehl, P. E. (1954). *Clinical versus statistical prediction*. Minneapolis: University of Minnesota Press.

Meehl, P. E. (1956). Wanted—A good cookbook. *American Psychologist, 11*, 263–272.

Meehl, P. E. (1957). When shall we use our heads instead of the formula? *Journal of Counseling Psychology, 4*, 268–273.

Meehl, P. E. (1972). Specific genetic etiology, psychodynamics and therapeutic nihilism. *International Journal of Mental Health, 1*, 10–27.

Meehl, P. E. (1973). *Psychodiagnosis: Selected papers*. Minneapolis: University of Minnesota Press.

Meehl, P. E. (1989). Autobiography. In G. Lindzey (Ed.), *History of psychology in autobiography*, Vol. 8, (pp. 337–389). Stanford: Stanford University Press.

An Appreciation
William Schofield

When one has been privileged, as I have, to enjoy nearly forty-five years of association with a man who has achieved worldwide renown, and when that association has ranged from graduate school days to senior faculty status, it is difficult to sift and order the myriad recollections to convey the warts and wonders of a remarkable personality as seen in evolving perspective. Paul Meehl and I were briefly graduate students together, sharing instruction by such Minnesota "founding fathers" as Richard Elliott, Donald Paterson, William Heron, Charles Bird, and Miles Tinker. Later, briefly, he was my teacher, but for over four decades he has been my esteemed colleague, warm friend, and good neighbor.

In his first year of graduate school Meehl established active intellectual exchange with advanced students who included such notables as Robert Harris, William Estes, and Howard Hunt. Harris and Hunt were advisees of Starke Hathaway and undoubtedly had some influence on Meehl's decision to migrate for his minor studies to the medical school and University Hospital complex, with Starke as his major advisor.

This "drift" was a response in part to a long-standing interest pattern. As an undergraduate, Meehl had been drawn to law, medicine, and psychology, and deciding on a field for graduate study was not easy. It was perhaps the relative strength and national visibility of the three programs at Minnesota at that time that contributed to Paul's ultimate choice—a most fortunate one for psychology! However, with the decision to study psychology, his special interest in medicine and law persisted. More about that later.

Meehl completed his graduate studies, received his degree in 1945, and, not surprisingly, was immediately appointed to an assistant professorship on the psychology faculty where he began his truly meteoric career. He was promoted to associate professor with tenure in 1948 and was made a full professor in 1952, at the age of 32.

He began early to build a reputation as a teacher, with initial experience as instructor in introductory courses in general psychology and laboratory psychology, moving on later to advanced courses in personality theory, psychodiagnosis, psychotherapy, systems of psychology, philosophical problems of psychology, and forensic psychology. I recall vividly the occasion on which I heard him specify very succinctly his view of the requirements to be a good teacher or to write a good book—"brains, facts, and passion." It has been evident to all who have known him, studied or worked with him, or read him that he has consistently brought this triad to his scholarly endeavors.

Intensity has been an enduring characteristic. Meehl has never settled for a superficial study of any subject that has caught his attention or that he has viewed as substantively related to his enduring focal interest—human behavior. After completion of his formal graduate studies, he regularly attended for some seven years a series of classes in mathematics and logic, a natural progression from his undergraduate minor in biometry. Still later, from 1964 to 1966, he audited classes in the Law School of the university. Evidence of the depth of his scholarly interests is found in his appointment to professorial rank in the Law School (1967) and the Department of Philosophy (Center for Philosophy of Science) in 1969. Acknowledgment of his seminal contributions to psychology, and of the catholicity of his scholarly pursuits, came with the university's highest faculty recognition—appointment as a Regents' Professor in 1968.

From the beginning of his academic career at Minnesota, Meehl has held joint rank in the Department of Psychiatry in the Medical School. This has fed his consistent interest in neurology and medicine. His occasional informal memos to selected colleagues informed us that he was reading the *New England Journal of Medicine*, as well as psychiatry journals. However, he was trained as a clinical psychologist and his dedication to that field was expressed in formal study, e.g., a course in electroencephalography, and separate workshops on the Rorschach technique with Samuel Beck and Bruno Klopfer, and on graphology with Werner Wolff—all in the same year, 1947.

His "immersion" and dedication to the role of teacher has been reflected further in the vivacity and generosity with which he has sought to share the gleanings from his studies with his colleagues. Thus, his return from his Rorschach studies found him ready to effectively disabuse many of his clinical colleagues of a superficial prejudice against the projective method in personality study.

Similarly, his drive for truth found him ready to challenge Minnesota's rather apparent anti-Freudian atmosphere and to arrive at his own appraisal of psychoanalytic theory and practice. This meant a study in depth of original sources. It meant also the experience of personal psychoanalysis and of supervised psychoanalytic practice. And it means that he takes occasional satisfaction in being able to correct some of his orthodox Freudian medical colleagues for their misperceptions of the evolution and specifics of psychoanalytic theory. Continued study and an open mind has meant a change over time in his evaluation of the validity of various psychoanalytic tenets (Meehl, 1983b).

A passion for study, for scholarship, for getting to the accessible truth of a matter—and a consistent rejection of "either-or" or "nothing but" simplification have led him to a penetrating analysis of subjects of less than popular appeal to many of his colleagues, or on which they carried a comfortable prejudice. His study of projective techniques has been mentioned in this vein. Similar was his interest in extrasensory perception, expressed primarily by exegesis of the implications of the concept for psychology and by his penetrating analysis of the methodological criteria for any critical experiments (Meehl & Scriven, 1956; Meehl, 1962).

Of course, with his seminal work of 1954, *Clinical vs. Statistical Prediction*, calling into serious question the validity and especially the efficiency of clinical judgment as applied to many decisions, Meehl aroused at least the anxiety and defenses, if not the animosity, of many clinical psychologists whose day-to-day activity (and income) rested on the assumption that clinical judgments were both valid and reliable (Meehl, 1954). In his balanced appraisal of the evidence at hand, he was not being untrue to his basic *professional* identity as a clinical psychologist; rather, he was exercising the full range of his knowledge and experience, fulfilling the idealized role of scientist-practitioner as endorsed by his graduate program and his mentors.

Contrary to the understandable perception by many of Meehl as an intellectual who is absorbed only by philosophical subtleties and statistical esoteria, his colleagues have had the opportunity to appreciate his concern for very practical and political issues. Thus among Minnesotans, he was one of the first to publicly acknowledge the failure, at least in part, of the so-called Boulder model for the preparation of clinical psychologists to achieve its goals. He argued that the department either should acknowlege openly a disinterest in the preparation of practitioners or should provide a second track (and possibly a professional degree) for those students whose career aspirations were not academic (Meehl, 1971). This was one of the rare instances in which Meehl's triad—brains, facts, and passion—did not persuade his colleagues. However, their respect for his powers of representation and his fairness in dealing with complex issues was reflected in his appointment as department chairman (1951–57).

One of Meehl's lesser known intellectual investments flowed naturally from his profound sensitivity to the human dilemma, his philosophical predilections, and the frequent course by which truly large minds are led ultimately to grapple with ultimate questions. He contributed as a consultant to a program whereby carefully selected ordained Lutheran pastors were supported for doctoral study of psychology, so that they might become key resource persons in assisting clergy toward more sensitive and appropriate work as pastoral counselors. Parallel to this practical program, the Missouri Synod of the Lutheran Church designed a program for scholarly inquiry into "the problem of man as he is viewed in theology, psychology, and psychiatry." A committee of scholars met for a month in 1956 and again, briefly, in 1957 to draft an overview of the essential concepts of these three fields and to point up compatibilities and points of divergence. Appropriately, Meehl served as chair of the group. In the final product of their work, a book entitled *What, Then, Is Man?* (Meehl, et al., 1958), he is acknowledged as sole author of seven of the thirteen chapters, as co-author of one chapter, and as author of three of the five appendixes. In reading these chapters (e.g., "Tensions between Psychology and Theology," or "Valid and Displaced Guilt, and Their Relation to Psychological Health and Spiritual Condition") one is impressed by the astute manner in which he drew upon his extensive knowledge of psychology, psychiatry, medicine, formal logic, the philosophy of science, theological concepts generally, church history, and Christian doctrine in particular. In characteristic fashion, with this endeavor as with other periods of intense study, Meehl shared certain of his thoughts and experiences with his selected colleagues in the department of psychology. This was not a function of any zeal to convert to a belief, but, rather, an expression of a constant motive to stimulate toward thought, especially in areas in which he might have reason to believe that some of his colleagues were comfortably thought-less. In this intellectual sharing, Paul has been unique among his colleagues. I look back with appreciation to memoranda—some brief and hand-drafts, some lengthy and typewritten—in which he has called attention to matters forensic, economic, political, and historical (Meehl, 1970, 1977, 1983a).

Paul's avocational interests show the same passionate pursuit that has been the hallmark of his academic contributions—study in depth. Playing the familiar game of "Personalities" with him was always a challenge. Once he became "it," he would hold forth for a very long time by relying on his knowledge of the German General Staff in World War I, the succession of the early popes, or the early Olympic champions in the pole vault! In earlier days, he played poker with characteristic enthusiasm and more than average success—a talent attributable at least in part to his attention to detail and his remarkable memory. Colleagues have learned not to challenge his recollection of specific dates or the magnitude of reported correlations.

A special opportunity for intensive and extensive direct research collaboration with Paul came with the mounting of a major project that was formally titled "The Skilled Clinician's Assessment of Personality." It began its official history in June 1956, upon word of funding by the Ford Foundation for nearly a quarter of a million dollars. Paul was clearly the instigator and major architect of the research proposal leading to the grant. The protocol was extensively reflective of his interest and abundant knowledge of personality theory, personality nomenclature, psychiatric nosology, psychometric theory, and psychotherapy. As principal investigator, his erudition in these subjects, critical to the research goals, was consistently demonstrated over the seven-plus years of the project. (The Ford grant was followed by NIMH support.) The formal minutes of meetings of the core research group (Meehl, Schofield, B. C. Glueck, M.D., and Walter Stud-diford) and the volumes of formal memoranda exchanged by the members are clear testament to both the extent and cruciality of Paul's contributions. His gift for penetrating analyses and parceling out of conceptual complexities, his sensitivity to subtleties and capacity to see implications that had escaped our perceptions, his willingness to explicate fully, both orally and in writing, to ensure the clarity of his theses—these were a source of continued awe, appreciation, and stimulation for the "Fordites." Over the span of the project Paul brought equal thought, fact, and intensity to problems ranging from the drafting of instruction for Q-sort-ratings to development of a methodology for descriptive labeling of factor-analytically derived personality dimensions. I have particular recall of the early debates between the "lumpers" and the "splitters" as we developed a structural matrix for the phenotypic description of personality (Meehl, et al., 1962; Glueck, et al., 1964). Repeatedly Paul would bring an incisive dialectic to bear to convince the "lumpers" that a substantive difference existed where they initially perceived a semantic equivalence. On those rare occasions when he was outvoted, he was always graciously flexible, always respectful of the views of those who differed with him.

From its inception until the 1950s, Minnesota psychology was remarkably atheoretical. More than any other faculty member, Paul Meehl persuaded the department away from its "dust bowl empiricism" toward a faculty and curriculum that more fully represented the perspectives and problems of modern psychology. He did this while bringing credit to the department through the recognition he received nationally as a theoretician-researcher-clinician of the very first order. His colleagues took pride in his many honors: American Psychological Association's (APA) Distinguished Scientific Contributor Award, 1958; election to the presidency of the APA, 1962; election to the American Academy of Arts and Sciences, 1965; APA's Division of Clinical Psychology Distinguished Contributor Award, 1967; APA's Division of Experimental Clinical Psychology Distinguished Scientist Award, 1976; The Bruno Klopfer Distinguished Contribution Award of the Society of Personality Assessment, 1979—all of these capped with his election to the National Academy of Science in 1987. In 1990, he was named the first incumbent of the Hathaway-Meehl Chair in Clinical Psychology.

With this opportunity to acknowledge my appreciation of Paul Meehl as a man of rare and exceptional talent, a complex and extraordinary personality, I must recognize the vital role played by his wives—Alyce M. Roworth (1941–deceased 1972), and Leslie J. Yonce (1973–). With patience, tolerance, and devotion, Alyce and Leslie have provided the seclusion and guarded the privacy and solitude he has required for his studies, accepting with graciousness and good humor the burdens of protecting a man at his work.

This is the Paul Meehl I have been privileged to know—to study with, to learn from, to work with, and occasionally to ponder with. A great and restless mind—a polymath whose catholicity of interests, fired by a passion for understanding, has meant always a study in depth. A restless mind, endowed by a talent for analysis and explication that has led to a sweeping away of webs of abstruseness and a replacement with clearly articulated conceptual structures. A restless mind passionately committed to the search for truth and constrained by the ineffableness of some philosophical questions and the essential open-endedness of science to suspend judgment.

I can sum up best by citing an ethic quoted by Paul in one of his papers: "It is wrong always, everywhere, and for anyone, to believe anything whatsoever upon insufficient evidence."*

References

Glueck, B. C., Meehl, P. E., Schofield, W., and Clyde, D. J. (1964). The quantitative assessment of personality. *Comprehensive Psychiatry, 5*:15–23.

Meehl, P. E. (1954). *Clinical versus statistical prediction: A theoretical analysis and a review of the evidence.* Minneapolis: University of Minnesota Press.

Meehl, P. E. (1962). Parapsychology. *Encyclopedia Britannica, 17*:267–269.

Meehl, P. E. (1970). Psychology and the criminal law. *University of Richmond Law Review, 5*:1–30.

Meehl, P. E. (1971). A scientific, scholarly, nonresearch doctorate for clinical practitioners: Arguments pro and con. In R. R. Holt (Ed.), *New horizon for psychotherapy: Autonomy as a profession* (pp. 37–81). New York: International Universities Press.

Meehl, P. E. (1977). The selfish voter paradox and the thrown-away vote argument. *American Political Science Review, 71*:11–30.

Meehl, P. E. (1983a). Consistency tests in estimating the completeness of the fossil record: A neo-Popperian approach to statistical paleontology. In J. Earman (Ed.), *Minnesota studies in the philosophy of science: Vol. X, Testing scientific theories* (pp. 413–473). Minneapolis: University of Minnesota Press.

Meehl, P. E. (1983b). Subjectivity in psychoanalytic inference: The nagging persistence of Wilhelm Fliess's Achensee question. In J. Earman (Ed.), *Minnesota studies in the philosophy of science: Vol. X, Testing scientific theories* (pp. 349–411). Minneapolis: University of Minnesota Press.

Meehl, P. E., Klann, R., Schmieding, A., Breimeier, K. & Schroeder-Slomann, S. (1958). *What, then, is Man?* St. Louis: Concordia Publishing House.

Meehl, P. E., Schofield, W., Glueck, B. C., Studdiford, W. B., Hastings, D. W., Hathaway, S. R., and Clyde, D. J. (1962). *Minnesota-Ford Pool of Phenotypic Personality Items, August 1962 Edition.* Minneapolis: University of Minnesota Press.

Meehl, P. E., & Scriven, M. J. (1956). Compatibility of science and ESP. *Science, 123*:14–15.

---

*From W. K. Clifford, *The Ethics of Belief*, cited in "Tensions between psychology and theology," in *What, Then, Is Man?*, Concordia Publishing House, St. Louis, Mo. 1958.

The State of Psychology

What's Wrong with
Psychology Anyway?
David T. Lykken

When I was an undergraduate at Minnesota in 1949, the most exciting course I took was Clinical Psychology, open to seniors and graduate students and taught by the dynamic young star of the psychology faculty, Paul Everett Meehl. In 1956, back at Minnesota after a postdoctoral year in England, the first course I ever tried to teach was that same one; Meehl, now Chair of the Department, wanted more time for other pursuits. Like most new professors of my acquaintance, I was innocent of either training or experience in college teaching, and I shall never forget the trepidation with which I took over what had been (but, alas, did not long remain) the most popular course in the psychology curriculum.

Years later, Paul asked me to contribute a few lectures to a new graduate course he had created called Philosophical Psychology. Sitting in class that first year, I experienced again the magic of a master teacher at work. Meehl's varied and extraordinary gifts coalesce in the classroom—the penetrating intellect, astonishing erudition, the nearly infallible memory, the wit and intellectual enthusiasm, the conjurer's ability to pluck the perfect illustration from thin air . . . I recall one class that ended late while Paul finished explaining some abstruse philosophical concept called the Ramsey Sentence. I have long since forgotten what a Ramsey Sentence is, and I doubt if fifty people in the world besides Paul and, perhaps, Ramsey himself think the concept is exciting. But Meehl had those students on the edge of their seats, unwilling to leave until they had it whole.

The present paper is a distillation of the three lectures I have been contributing to Paul's Philosophical Psychology. I offer it here in fond respect for the man who has been my teacher and friend for nearly forty years.

I shall argue the following theses:

(I) Psychology isn't doing very well as a scientific discipline and something seems to be wrong somewhere.

3

(II) This is due partly to the fact that psychology is simply harder than physics or chemistry, and for a variety of reasons. One interesting reason is that people differ structurally from one another and, to that extent, cannot be understood in terms of the same theory since theories are guesses about structure.

(III) But the problems of psychology are also due in part to a defect in our research tradition; our students are carefully taught to behave in the same obfuscating, self-deluding, pettifogging ways that (some of) their teachers have employed.

Having made this diagnosis, I will suggest some home remedies, some ways in which the next generation could pull up its socks and do better than its predecessors have done. Along the way I shall argue that research is overvalued in the Academy and that graduate students should not permit themselves to be bullied into feeling bad about the fact that most of them will never do any worthwhile research.

For reasons that escape me, students have said that they tend to find these illuminating discussions depressing in some way. The first lecture, focusing on the defects of the research tradition, is a particular downer, so I'm told. I think this attitude is shortsighted. By taking a frank look at ourselves and making an honest assessment of our symptoms and defects, it is possible, I think, to see some of the apparent and correctable reasons for these problems.

I. Something Is Wrong with the Research Tradition in Psychology

It is instructive to attempt to follow the progress of a research idea from its germination in the mind of a psychological scientist until it finally flowers (if it ever does) within the pages of an archival journal. If the budding idea seems to its parent to be really promising, the almost invariable first step is to write it up in the form of a grant application directed most commonly to one of the federal agencies. Writing grant applications is laborious and time-consuming, and there is no doubt that many research ideas begin to seem less viable during the course of this process and are aborted at this early stage.

A. Most Grant Applications Are Bad

Applications directed to the National Institute of Mental Health are routed to an appropriate Research Review committee consisting of 10 or 12 established investigators with broadly similar interests who meet for several days three times each year to consider submissions and make recommendations for funding. Although all committee members are nominally expected to read the entire set of applications (and a few probably do this), the review committees depend largely on the reports of those two or three members who have been assigned principal responsibility for the given proposal. The Institute gets good value from these peer review committees whose members, not wishing to appear foolish or uninformed before their peers at the tri-annual meetings, invest many (uncompensated) hours before each meeting studying their assigned subset of applications and composing well-considered critiques and recommendations. At the meetings, proposals are carefully discussed and evaluated before the committee votes. Of all the applications received by NIMH in a given year, only about 25% are considered promising enough to be actually funded.

B. Most Manuscripts Submitted to the Journals Are Bad

Archival scientific journals also depend upon the peer review system. The editors of most psychological journals do a preliminary screening, returning at once those manuscripts that are the most obviously unacceptable, and then send out the remainder to two or more referees selected for their expertise on the topic of the given paper. Like most academic psychologists of my advanced age, I have refereed hundreds of papers for some 20 journals over the years and can attest that it is a dispiriting business. My reviews tended to be heavily burdened with sarcasm evoked by the resentment I felt in having to spend several hours of my time explicating the defects of a paper which one could see in the first ten minutes' reading had no hope of contributing to the sum of human knowledge. I became troubled by the fact that it was possible for me thus to assault the author's *amour propre* from the safety of the traditional anonymity of journal referees, and I began to sign my reviews and have done so unfailingly these past 15 years or so. While I continue to be critical, I find that I am very careful to be sure of the grounds for my comments, knowing that the author will know who is talking. It seems to me, in this age of accountability, that authors *ought* to know who has said what about their work and, moreover, that journal readers ought to be able to learn in a footnote which editor or reviewers decided that any given article should have been published.

In any case, whether the reviews are signed or not, the effect of this peer review process is that from 60 to 90% of articles submitted to journals published by the American Psychological Association are rejected.

C. Most Actually Published Research Is Bad

In their 1970 *Annual Review* chapter on Memory and Verbal Learning, Tulving and Madigan reported that they had independently rated each of 540 published articles in terms of its "contribution to knowledge." With "remarkable agreement," they found that they had sorted two-thirds of the articles into a category labeled:

"utterly inconsequential." The primary function these papers serve is to give something to do to people who count papers instead of reading them. Future research and understanding of verbal learning and memory would not be affected at all if none of the papers in this category had seen the light of day. (Tulving & Madigan, 1970, p. 441)

About 25 percent of the articles were classified as:

"run-of-the-mill" . . . these articles also do not add anything really new to knowledge . . . [such articles] make one wish that at least some writers, faced with the decision of whether to publish or perish, should have seriously considered the latter alternative. (p. 442)

Only about 10 percent of the entire set of published papers received the modest compliment of being classified as "worthwhile." Given that memory and verbal learning was then a popular and relatively 'hard' area of psychological research, attracting some of the brightest students, this is a devastating assessment of the end product.

Hence, of the research ideas generated by these psychologists, who are all card-carrying scientists and who liked these ideas well enough to invest weeks or months of their lives working on them, less than 25% of 40% of 10% = 1% actually appear to make some sort of contribution to the discipline.

D. Most Published Articles Are Not Read Anyway

Garvey and Griffith (1963) found that about half the papers published in APA journals have fewer than 200 readers (not all of whom are edified). Two-thirds of these papers are never cited by another author. Somewhat surprisingly, the same thing is true even in physics: Cole and Cole (1972) found that half the papers in physics journals are never cited. Even articles in *Physical Review*, generally considered one of the most prestigious journals, do not always make much of a splash; 50% are cited once or never during the three years after they appear.

When he was at Minnesota years ago, B. F. Skinner used to say that he avoided reading the literature since it only "poisons the mind." In psychology, what other researchers are doing is seldom useful to one's self except perhaps as something to refute or, more rarely, as a bandwagon to climb up on. One does not have to actually read the literature until it is time to start writing one's paper. Lindsey (1978) and Watson (1982) have cited the long publication lags typical of social science journals as evidence that psychologists do not need to know what their colleagues are doing; we do not fear being 'scooped' because it is so unlikely that anyone else would be prospecting in the same area.

E. Theories in Psychology Are Like Old Soldiers: They Are Not Refuted or Replaced—They Don't Die—They Only Fade Away

Like a good scientific theory, this simile of Paul Meehl's has sufficient verisimilitude to continue to be useful. The exciting theoretical developments of my student days—the work of Hull, Spence, and Tolman, to focus just on one then-active area—have sunk into obscurity. In the hard sciences, each generation stands upon the shoulders of its predecessors, the bones of the Elder Giants become part of the foundation of an ever-growing edifice. The great names of psychology's comparatively recent past are respected mainly as intrepid explorers who came back empty-handed. There is no edifice, just this year's ant hill, most of which will be abandoned and washed away in another season.

In the 1940s and '50s, there was a torrent of interest and research surrounding the debate between the S-R reinforcement theorists at Yale and Iowa City and the S-S expectancy theorists headquartered at Berkeley. As is usual in these affairs, the two sides produced not only differing theoretical interpretations but also different empirical findings from their rat laboratories, differences that ultimately led Marshall Jones to wonder if the researchers in Iowa and California might not be working with genetically different animals. Jones obtained samples of rats from the two colonies and tested them in the simple runway situation. Sure enough, when running time was plotted against trial number, the two strains showed little overlap in performance. The Iowa rats put their heads down and streaked for the goal box, while the Berkeley animals dawdled, retraced, investigated, appeared to be making "cognitive maps" just as Tolman always said they did. But by 1965 the torrent of interest in latent-learning had become a backwater and Jones's paper was published obscurely (Jones & Fennel, 1965).

A brilliant series of recent studies of goal-directed behavior in the rat (Rescorla, 1987) demonstrates with elegant controls that the animal not only learns to emit the reinforced response in the presence of the discriminative stimulus but it also learns which response leads to which reward. When one of the reinforcers is devalued (e.g., by associating that type of food pellet with the gastric upset produced by lithium chloride), the rate of that response falls sharply while the animal continues to emit responses associated with different reinforcers. In 1967 these findings would have seemed much more important, embarrassing as they are for the Hull-Spence type of theory. However, in 1987, although these studies were ingenious and produced clear-cut results, they are the results that any layperson might expect and they do not have the surplus value of seeming to contribute to some growing theoretical structure.

The present state of knowledge in psychology is very broad but very shallow. We know a little bit about a lot of things. There are many courses in the psychology curriculum, but few have real prerequisites. One can read most psychology texts without first taking even an introductory course. But the range or scope of the field is very great so that there will be a majority of people at every APA convention with whom I share few if any scientific interests.

F. Research in Psychology Does Not Tend to Replicate

Charles Darwin once pointed out that, while false theories do relatively little harm, false facts can seriously retard scientific progress. As Mark Twain put it, somewhere, it is not so much what we don't know that hurts us, as those things we do know that aren't so. Weiner and Wechsler (1958), in a similar vein, remark that "the results that are the most difficult to explain are the ones that are not true" (p. ix). Every mature psychologist knows from experience that it is foolish to believe a new result merely on the basis of the first published study, especially if the finding seems unusually important or provocative. Within the narrow circles of our particular fields of interest, many of us learn that there are certain investigators who stand out from the herd because their findings can be trusted.

There is a lot of talk currently about actual dishonesty in research reporting. We were all quite properly scandalized by the Cyril Burt affair when his official biographer concluded that at least most of the subjects in Burt's widely cited study of monozygotic twins reared apart were as fictitious as the two female collaborators whose names Burt signed to his reports of this alleged research (Hearnshaw, 1979). But the problem of the unreplicability of so many findings in the psychological literature involves something more subtle and more difficult to deal with than deliberate chicanery. In amost every study, the investigator will have hoped to find a certain pattern of results, at the very least an orderly, self-consistent pattern of results. The processes of planning, conducting, and analyzing any psychological experiment are complicated, frequently demanding decisions that are so weakly informed by any ancillary theory or established practice as to seem essentially arbitrary. As the investigator makes his or her way through this underbrush, there is the ever-beckoning lure of the desired or expected outcome that tends to influence the choices made at each step.

Selective error-checking is perhaps the simplest and most innocent example of the problem. If the worst sin researchers committed was to re-score or re-calculate results that come out 'wrong,' while accepting at once those results that fit with expectations, a significant number of unreplicable findings would appear in the journals. To illustrate some of the subtler sources of distortion, let us consider a couple of real-life examples (see also Gould, 1978).

(1) Marston's Systolic Blood Pressure Lie Detector Test

Before the First World War, psychologist William Moulton Marston discovered what he thought to be Pinocchio's nose, an involuntary physiological reaction that all human beings display when they are deliberately lying but never when they are telling the truth. Marston's specific lie response was a transitory increase in systolic or peak blood pressure following the (allegedly deceptive) answer. When World War I broke out, the National Research Council appointed a committee to assess the validity of Marston's test as a possible aid in the interrogation of suspected spies. The committee consisted of L. T. Troland of Harvard, H. E. Burtt of Ohio State, and Marston himself. According to Marston (1938), a total of 100 criminal cases were examined in the Boston criminal court and the systolic blood pressure test led to correct determinations in 97 of the 100 cases.

Marston later invented the comic-strip character "Wonder Woman," with her magic lasso that makes men tell the truth. During the 1930s his picture was to be found in full-page magazine advertisements using the lie detector to "prove" that Gillette blades shave closer and more comfortably. For these reasons, we might be skeptical of Marston's scientific claims. But Troland and Burtt were respected psychologists, and Father Walter Summers, chair of the Psychology Department at Fordham, was not a man to be suspected of exaggeration. Summers (1939) invented a lie detector based on an entirely different principle and claimed that his method had proved 100% accurate on a long series of criminal cases. But both Marston and Summers were wrong. Neither method has been taken seriously during the last 50 years and both of the "specific lie responses" they claimed to have discovered are commonly shown by innocent people while truthfully denying false accusations. It is impossible now to discover how it was that the hopes of these enthusiastic investigators became transmuted into false proofs. Their "studies" are not described in detail, the raw data are not available for re-analysis, we do not even know how they established in each case which of the criminal suspects were in fact lying and which were not.

(2) The "Neural Efficiency Analyzer" Scandal

A simple flash of light produces in the brain a complex voltage waveform known as an event related potential (ERP), lasting about half a second after the flash. The ERP can be easily recorded from EEG electrodes attached to the scalp. Because the ERP is weak in comparison with the random background brain-wave activity, a large number of flashes must be presented to obtain an adequate ratio of signal to noise. ERPs to simple stimuli vary in form from person to person but are quite stable over time, and the ERPs of monozygotic twins are very similar in shape. In 1965 John Ertl and William Barry, at the University of Ottawa, reported correlations of − .88 and − .76 between Wechsler IQ and ERP latency in samples of college students (Barry & Ertl, 1966). If IQ depends primarily upon the speed with which the brain responds to stimulation then, since IQ scores are not perfectly reliable and certainly contain some variance associated with differences in prior learning, a direct, culture-free measure of native intelligence could not be expected to correlate with IQ test scores more strongly than this.

Impressed by this work, the Educational Records Bureau obtained from the Ford Foundation a grant of $414,000 for a follow-on study (in the 1960s, $414,000 amounted to real money). The study subjects were 1,000 elementary school children in Mt. Vernon, NY, preschoolers, first- and seventh-graders. At the start of the school year, an ERP was obtained by Ertl's method from each child. In addition, five basic mental abilities were measured by conventional tests. At the end of the year, teacher's ratings, grades, and scores on standardized achievement tests were also collected. The latencies of the various ERP components showed no relationship whatever to any of the intelligence or achievement variables. Hundreds of correlations were computed and they formed a tight Gaussian distribution centered on zero with an SD of about .15 (Davis, 1971).

This large study was a debacle, an utter waste of everybody's time and the Ford Foundation's money, and it should have been avoided. It *would* have been avoided if the team of investigators had included a psychologist trained at Minnesota because he (she) would have been deeply suspicious of those original findings and would have insisted on doing a quick, inexpensive pilot study to find out whether Ertl's remarkable IQ correlations could be replicated in New York.

(3) Perceptual Disorders in Schizophrenia

In 1968, while on sabbatical leave in London, I came upon a remarkable article in the *American Journal of Psychiatry*. A psychiatrist named Bemporad (1967) reported a striking perceptual anomaly in schizophrenic patients. The study was distinguished by Bemporad's exemplary use of separate groups of chronics, acutes (many of these actually tested in the hospital emergency room upon admission), and, most interestingly, a group of previously psychotic patients tested in remission. Thus, one could apparently conclude not only that the phenomenon was not just a consequence of long-term hospitalization but also that it was not merely an effect of psychotic state per se since it appeared almost as strongly among the remitted patients.

Bemporad employed three of the Pseudo-Isochromatic Plates published by the American Optical company and widely used for the assessment of color blindness. These plates are composed of an apparently random pattern of colored dots or circles of various sizes and hues. In each plate a dotted figure or numeral (e.g., "86") can be discerned by a person with normal color vision because the dots making up the figure are of a hue different from the background dots or circles. Because these figural dots or circles are matched for saturation with their neighbors, persons incapable of distinguishing the hues cannot perceive the pattern. Bemporad reasoned that the primitive inability to organize component parts into an integrated perceptual whole, which had been reported for schizophrenics by previous authors, might reflect itself in this test since the perception of the number patterns requires the subject to impose a gestalt upon a set of circles having no common boundary.

Bemporad showed three of the plates, one at a time, to his subjects, asking them only to tell what they saw in each plate. His 20 control subjects made only 2% errors on the three cards, while the chronic, acute, and recovered schizophrenics made 97%, 78%, and 65% errors, respectively.

Because I was currently doing research involving schizophrenic patients at a London hospital, it was easy to arrange a partial replication of the Bemporad study. We thought we might improve slightly on his test simply by using 10 of the pseudo-isochromatic plates, including the 3 that Bemporad employed, and by administering another, easy plate as the first one seen by each subject. The easy plate contained the figure "12" outlined by closely spaced dots that differed both in hue and saturation from the background; it is included in the set as a demonstration plate or as a check for possible malingering. By beginning with this easy sample, we made sure that each subject understood the task (some of these patients, after all, might have been recently shown ink blots and asked, "Tell me what you see."). We tested 18 schizophrenic patients, some chronic and some in the acute phase of their first admission. We also tested 12 hospital nurses as our control group. All of the subjects were male. The control group was an unnecessary indulgence since we already knew that normal people could see the figures and the only point of our study was to determine whether the Bemporad phenomenon was genuine. British psychiatrists were stricter in their diagnostic practices than American psychiatrists in the 1960s; if the schizophrenic brain had difficulty imposing a gestalt on dotted figures, most of our 18 patients should have made numerous errors on our expanded test.

Our replication required no research grant or fancy preparations. The data were easily collected in a week's time. The results were easily summarized; 29 of the 30 subjects tested correctly identified the figures in all ten plates. The single exception was a patient with specific red-green color blindness who made characteristic errors. While we were never able to account for Bemporad's findings, we could certainly conclude that his empirical generalization was false. This failure to replicate was described in a short note and submitted to the *American Journal of Psychiatry*. After several months, a rejection letter was received from the editor together with an impassioned seven-page critique of my three-page note by an anonymous referee, obviously Bemporad himself.

I then suggested to the editor that it seemed a poor policy to permit an author whose work had failed to replicate to decide whether to publish the report of that failure. The editor agreed and submitted our note to "an altogether neutral referee and a very wise man" who agreed that our study proved the Bemporad phenomenon to be a figment. However, he too recommended against publication of the note on what still seem to me to have been curious grounds. "I doubt whether the readers of the *APA Journal* have even heard of 'Bemporad's phenomenon' any more than I did. . . . So far as I know the original paper has now been forgotten and the new notice which it receives can only give the item new life."

This is, I guess, the "let sleeping dogs lie" principle of editorship and may help account for the fact that, while many psychological research findings do not in fact replicate, comparatively few reports of specific failures to replicate can be found in the journals.

G. Science Is Supposed to Be a Cumulative Endeavor But Psychologists Build Mostly Castles in the Sand

Anyone who reads the recent book *What is Intelligence? Contemporary Viewpoints on its Nature and Definition* edited by Sternberg and Detterman (1986), in which 25 experts responded to the question posed in the title, could easily conclude that there are about as many different conceptions of "intelligence" as the number of experts. This was also true back in 1921 when the same question was asked of an earlier group of experts. Comparing the two symposia, separated by 65 years, we find scarcely more concensus among experts today than in 1921. . . . Shouldn't we expect by now something more satisfying than [this] welter of diverse and contradictory opinions? . . . Where are indications of cumulative gains of research, converging lines of evidence, and generally accepted definitions, concepts, and formulations? (Jensen, 1987, pp. 193–194)

One of the central concepts of psychology—the paradigmatic concept of differential psychology—is intelligence, a topic of great theoretical and practical interest and research for more than a century, the only psychological trait that can boast its own exclusive journal. Yet, in 1987, the leading modern student of intelligence finds it necessary to lament the lack of real cumulative progress in that core area.

Suppose that with some magic Time Machine we could transport Linus Pauling back to the day in 1925 when he had his final oral examination for the Ph.D. in Chemistry at Cal Tech. Our Time Machine will restore his youthful vigor but will permit him to retain all the new things that he has learned, through his own research and that of others, in the 60-plus years since he was examined for his doctorate. Imagine the wonders with which he could regale his astonished professors! Many of the most important developments—the quantum theoretical aspects, for example—would be beyond their understanding. Just a partial description of the technology that is now available in the chemical laboratory would be likely to induce ecstatic seizures in at least some committee members. Those professors of the flapper era would look upon their bright-eyed student as if he were a visitor from some advanced civilization on another planet—as indeed he would be.

Contrast this fantasy now with its psychological equivalent. Let us put Paul Meehl in the Time Machine and send him back to his final oral at Minnesota in 1945. What could he amaze his committee with? What wonders of new technology, what glistening towers of theoretical development, could he parade before their wondering eyes? Shall we tell them the good news about biofeedback? How about the birth and death, without issue, of the Theory of Cognitive Dissonance? What James Olds discovered about pleasure centers in the brain would be exciting, but most of the substantial work that followed would have to be classified as neuroscience rather than psychology.

They will be interested to learn that Hull is dead and that nobody cares anymore about the "latent learning" argument. He could tell them now that most criminals are not helpless victims of neuroses created by rejecting parents; that schizophrenia probably involves a biochemical lesion and is not caused by battle-ax mothers and bad toilet training; that you cannot fully understand something as complex as language by the simple principles that seem to account for the bar-pressing behavior of rats in a Skinner box. In other words, there are some things we know now that many professional psychologists did not know 45 years ago. But it was the professionals who had managed to convince themselves of such odd notions in the first place—their neighbors would have known better. I am sure that each of you could, with some effort, generate a short list of more interesting and solid findings (my own list, not surprisingly, would include some of my own work), but it is a depressing undertaking because one's list compares so sadly with that of any chemist, physicist, or astronomer. Can we blame it on our youth? Think of the long list of astonishing discoveries produced in our coeval, genetics, with just a fraction of our person-power.

H. Cargo-Cult Science

In his lively autobiography, the late Nobel laureate Richard Feynman (1986) expressed the view that much of psychological research is "Cargo-cult science":

> In the South Seas there is a cargo cult of people. During the war, they saw airplanes land with lots of good materials, and they want the same thing to happen now. So they've arranged to make things like runways, to put fires along the sides of the runways, to make a wooden hut for a man to sit on, with two wooden pieces on his head like headphones and bars of bamboo sticking out like antennas—he's the controller—and they wait for the airplanes to land. They're doing everything right. The form is perfect. It looks just the way it looked before. But it doesn't work. No airplanes land. So I call these things cargo cult science, because they follow all the apparent precepts and forms of scientific investigation, but they're missing something essential, because the planes don't land.

Summary

It is hard to avoid the conclusion that psychology is a kind of shambling, poor relation of the natural sciences. As the example of genetics shows us, we cannot reasonably use our relative youth as an excuse—and at age 100 we are a little long in the tooth to claim that with a straight face anyway. Psychologists in the American Association for the Advancement of Science have been trying recently to get *Science* to publish a psychological article now and then. The editors reply that they get lots of submissions from psychologists but they just are not as interesting as all the good stuff they keep getting from the biochemists, the space scientists, the astronomers, and the geneticists.

Moreover, *Science*, like its British counterpart, *Nature*, is a relatively fast-publication journal where hot, new findings are published, findings that are of general interest and that other workers in the field will want to know about promptly. But psychologists seldom have anything to show and tell that other psychologists need to know about promptly. We are each working in a different part of the forest, we are not worried that someone else will publish first, and we do not need to know what others have found because ours is not a vertical enterprise, building on what has been discovered previously.

Most of us realize that we do not really have to dig into the journals until we are ready to write up our own work for publication and need some citations to make our results seem more relevant and coherent. Our theories have a short half-life and they just die in the larval stage instead of metamorphosing into something better. Worse yet, our experiments do not replicate very well and so it is hard to be sure what to theorize about.

II. Why? What Has Gone Wrong with Psychology's Research Tradition?

A. Are Psychologists Dumber Than Physicists or Biologists?

Many years ago W. S. Miller administered the advanced form of his Analogies test to graduate students in various disciplines at the University of Minnesota. Ph.D candidates in psychology ranked with those in physics and math and higher than those in most other fields. Graduate Record Examination scores of students applying now for graduate work in psychology are still very high.

Every now and then an eminent 'hard' scientist decides to devote his later years to fixing up psychology. Donald Glaser, who won a Nobel Prize for inventing the bubble-chamber, became a psychologist and sank into obscurity. More recently, Crick, of Double Helix fame, has started theorizing about the function of dreams. I predict that the Freudian theory will outlive the Crickian. We are probably not actually dumber than scientists in the more progressive disciplines

(I wish I could really be sure of this), and it seems doubtful that the problems of psychology can be attributed to a failure to attract bright young researchers. One cannot be sure how long that is going to hold true (or even if it's true now) because the competition for really bright, energetic young minds is fierce.

B. Psychology Is More Difficult, More Intractable, Than Other Disciplines

(1) It Is Hard to See the Forest for the Trees

Everybody is at least an amateur psychologist since we all exemplify the system in question and we each need to understand and predict behavior, our own and that of others; for most of us this imperative is stronger than our need to understand the genes or the stars. This constant intimacy with the raw material of our science is often helpful in the sense of doing armchair experiments or as a source of ideas but, on balance, it is more of a hindrance. Scientists must be able to idealize and oversimplify, to escape from the particular to the general and, often, to sneak up on a complicated problem by successive approximations. The atomic model of Thompson and Bohr, for example, served physics well for many years and probably made possible the new knowledge and the new concepts which ultimately proved that model to be grossly oversimplified. If Thompson and Bohr had known some of what is now known about leptons and quarks and so on, if they had been required to operate in the murk of all these forbidding complexities, they might never have been able to make any progress. The same thing is true in biology. It was important for nineteenth-century biologists to be able to think of the cell as a simple little basic unit of protoplasm with relatively simple functions and properties. If they had been forced to realize that the average cell does more complicated chemistry every day than the Dupont Corporation, it might have been very inhibiting.

When one looks at the heavens on a clear night, it is interesting to contemplate the fact that only a few hundred stars are visible to the naked eye at any given time and place, only about 6,000 in the entire celestial sphere. Moreover, only a few really bright stars are present and they combine in our perception as the great constellations. The constancy of shape of these starry patterns and their regular apparent movement from east to west was the beginning of astronomy. If we had had the eyes of eagles, there would have been millions of visible stars in the night sky, perhaps too many for us to be able to distinguish clear patterns. The north star, Polaris, essential to the ancient navigators, is easily located by any child; the lip of the Big Dipper points it out. Could a child with eagle's eyes find Polaris so easily with hundreds of distractor stars visible in the intervening space which seems empty to the human eye? Now we speak in a familiar way about island universes in their billions, each containing billions of suns, about pulsars and quasars and black holes. It is possible that these great achievements of human understanding would have been impeded and delayed if our vision had been clearer so that the true complexity of the heavens had been more thrust upon us.

Good scientists need to be capable of a kind of tunnel vision, to be able to ignore even obvious difficulties long enough for their vulnerable newborn ideas to mature sufficiently to be able to survive on their own. This is difficult for psychologists because we live inside an exemplar of the object of study and we cannot help having some idea of how complicated these mechanisms are. Doing physics is like map-making from a helicopter, you can begin with a bird's-eye view, zoom in later to look at the details; doing psychology is more like making a map on the Lewis and Clarke expedition, right down there in the mud among the trees and the poison ivy.

(2) Experimental Control Is Very Difficult

We cannot breed human subjects like pea plants or treat them like laboratory animals. Moreover, behavior—including mental events—is exquisitely sensitive to countless influences which the chemist or physicist can safely ignore, e.g., whether the experimenter is smiling or sober, male or female, attractive or homely. An old study whose source I have forgotten took advantage of the fact that the same instructor taught two sections of the same course in different rooms. In one classroom, for some reason, there was a faint but distinct odor of peppermint in the air. It was arranged to administer the final examination to half of each class in the peppermint room and half in the room that smelled only of chalk. Those students who were tested in the rooms where they had heard the lectures scored significantly better than their transplanted classmates.

C. Psychology Seeks to Understand the Workings of the Most Complicated Mechanism in the Known Universe

Psychology is the study of behavioral and mental events which, in turn (we assume), are determined by physico-chemical processes in the brain and nervous system. The brain is the most complex mechanism we know of, and its complexity results in large part from the brain's ability to modify itself structurally as the result of learning or experience. The digital computer is a man-made mechanism that shares this remarkable capacity for progressive structural elaboration.

(1) Parametric versus Structural Properties

Both brains and computers are delivered from the factory with a certain standard hardware that is determined by the blueprint, in the case of computers, or by the species plan, in the case of brains. Both mechanisms share the property of almost unlimited structural modifiability.

Entities or mechanisms that have the same structure can be described in terms of the same set of laws. These laws, which we can think of as transfer-functions or equations relating stimulus input to response output, will contain various constants or parameters. Different systems sharing the same structure can be compared with respect to these parameters, but comparing systems that differ structurally is like comparing apples and oranges. You *can* compare apples and oranges, of course, but you have to know what you are doing and be clear about what you are not doing. We will come back to apples and oranges in a minute.

Computers change or elaborate their structure by being programmed; brains elaborate their structure through experience and learning (sometimes called "programming"). When the structure of a system gets elaborated, so too does the set of laws necessary to describe its functioning. Two Apple computers both running the software called "Lotus 123" are still structurally alike, still can be described in terms of the same laws or the same theory, still can be compared with respect to various parameters. But two computers running different software are to that extent structurally different, march to different laws, and each one will have idiosyncratic characteristics that are not even defined for the other.

The people who study computers and brains have rather parallel divisions of labor. Computers have "hardware experts" while brains have "neuroscientists." The people who write the most sophisticated computer software must have some understanding of the hardware also; they have to understand the laws of the hardware which determine how the structure can be elaborated. They are alike in this respect to some developmental psychologists and to people who study sensation and perception, conditioning and memory and cognitive processing. Finally, the people who use these sophisticated software packages, like *Lotus 123* and *FORTRAN* and *PASCAL*, do not need to know much about the hardware but they must know the rules of the software they are using. Their analogues, I guess, are the personality and clinical and social psychologists. And the big question is, since we have all developed within a broadly similar society, with broadly similar patterns of experience, are we all running roughly similar software packages?

If you use the package called *Word Perfect* for word processing, and *Framework* for spreadsheets, and *PASCAL* for number-crunching, whereas I am using *WordStar* and *Lotus 123* and *FORTRAN*, then our computers may look alike but they won't act alike; you will not understand mine nor I yours. To the extent that our brains are running different programs, no one nomothetic psychological theory is going to be able to account for all of us.

Now, of course, we are always comparing people with one another in a million ways. If we can compare people, sort them out on some dimension, give them each a score, does that not mean that they must be comparable, i.e., structurally isomorphic, i.e., similar systems understandable in terms of the same laws and theory? This brings us back to the apples and oranges. We can compare them in a million ways too—which is heavier or softer or tastes better and so on. When we stop to think about it, many of the most interesting of human psychological traits are similar to these kinds of comparisons of apples and oranges—I call them "impact traits."

(2) Impact Traits

An impact trait can be defined only in terms of the impact that the person has on his or her environment, usually the social environment. If you were kidnapped by Martians and studied in their space ship laboratory, they could not assess your Social Dominance or your Interpersonal Attractiveness because those are not so much features of your bodily mechanism or your brain as they are properties of your impact upon other human beings. We can fairly reliably rank-order people for leadership, sales ability, teaching ability, ability to be a good parent—all impact traits—but we do not really expect that the people who get the same rank will achieve that rank in exactly the same way. There are many different ways of being good or bad at each of these things. Just because we can rank people on some dimension does not mean that there is some isomorphic entity or process in each of their brains that determines their score. There are also various ways of achieving any given score on the WAIS. Until it has been shown that g is determined by some unidimensional brain process, the possibility remains open that IQ is an impact trait too.

We can compare apples, oranges, and cabbages using a theory of, say, Produce which contains all the generalities that apply to vegetable foodstuffs. We can compare apples and oranges in terms of a larger set of generalizations which we might call the theory of Fruit. The theory of Apples is richer and more detailed than the theory of Fruit and the theory of MacIntosh Apples is richer yet. The greater the structural similarity between the entities under study, the richer will be the set of generalities that holds true across all members of the set and the more specific will be the predictions we can make about particular entities in the set.

(3) The Nomothetic-Idiographic Issue

It is possible that the general laws of psychology will comprise a relatively small set, that there just are not that many nomologicals that apply across people in general. Perhaps the developmental psychologists will turn out to be better off in this respect; maybe we are most like one another in the ways in which we learn to be qualitatively different from one another. Perhaps the only way to predict individual behavior with any precision or in any detail is idiographically, one individual at a time studied over months or years. To the extent that this is so, perhaps Psychology is really more like History than it is like Biology.

A natural scientist is not embarrassed because he cannot look at a tree and predict which leaves will fall first in the autumn or the exact path of the fall or where the leaf will land. Maybe individual lives are a lot like falling leaves; perhaps there is a very limited amount one can say about the individual case, based on a knowledge of leaves in general or people in general, without detailed, idiographic study of that particular case and even then it is hard to know how the winds will blow from one day to the next.

Maybe psychology is like statistical mechanics in the sense that we can make confident statements only about the means and variances of measurements on groups of people. We can say pretty confidently, for example, that at least 70% of the variance in IQ is related to genetic variation and that people with IQs of 90 are unlikely to get through medical school. We cannot say that two people with the same IQ must be alike in some part of their brains or that they will achieve comparable success, and we cannot say that a person with an IQ of 140 is going to do something outstanding or useful in the world—that depends on which way the winds blow. We can say that social conservatism, as measured by Tellegen's Traditionalism scale, has most of its stable variance determined by genetic factors. We can say that most of those Americans who favor mandatory testing for AIDS or who admire Oliver North and call the Contras "Freedom Fighters" would get high scores on Traditionalism, but once we start risking individual predictions we get into trouble. Some Traditionalists see the Contras as ordinary mercenaries, Col. North as a troublemaker, and are very nervous about any governmental interference in private lives.

(4) Radical Environmentalism

There are some highly regarded scientists—Leon Kamin, Richard Lewontin, Stephen J. Gould—who believe that our twin research here at Minnesota is immoral, that any findings which seem to indicate that psychological diversity is in any way determined by genetic diversity are either invalid and incompetent or else fraudulent (like the Cyril Burt affair) or both, and that investigators pursuing this sort of research are old-fashioned Social Darwinians at best and probably fascists and racists at worst. These "Anties" have been careful not to assert any specific alternative position that the opposition could criticize; it is easier and safer just to hide in the bushes and snipe at the enemy's breastworks and outposts. If we could capture one of these Anties and put him on the rack and make him say what he really believes, I think it would have to be some sort of Radical Environmentalism doctrine, perhaps along the following lines.

Psychological differences within species of the lower animals are strongly genetic in origin, every dog breeder knows that. A basic postulate of evolutionary theory is that intra-specific variability has been essential to ensure that the species can adapt to environmental change. Behavioral variation has undoubtedly been as important as morphological variability in the evolution of the other mammals. But somewhere in the course of human evolution, probably coincident with the development of human culture, the rules changed. Behavioral variation due to learning and experience began to take the place of variation due to genetic differnces until, finally, cultural variation has replaced genetic variation entirely, in the special case of *homo sapiens*. Unlike dogs or chimps or pigeons, every normal human infant is equipped with a large, almost infinitely plastic brain right off the shelf, all of these brains being made from identical blueprints and specifications. Thus, for our species alone, evolution of the genetic material has achieved a plateau from which the only subsequent evolution will be cultural; phylogeny has ended and ontogeny is all.

If the evolution of the microcomputer continues at its present pace, we might see such a thing happen there. So far it has been useful and adaptive to have available many different sizes and types of computer for use in different applications. New and better designs have made their predecessors rapidly obsolete. One day soon, however, there may come along an Apple or an IBM-PC that is so powerful, so fast, so versatile that hardware development will stop because additional refinements are unnecessary. The only differences then between your computer and mine will reside in the software that we happen to be running.

I think the extreme form of this Radical Environmentalist position is plainly wrong, but there is certainly a large measure of truth in the idea that the proximal cause of much human psychological individuality is learning and experience. If nomothetic theory building requires structural isomorphism within the mechanisms being theorized about—and surely it does, since the point of theory building is to infer what that structure *is*—then the future of personality, clinical, and social psychology depends upon whether the varieties of individual experience produce similar structural elaborations. If our different learning histories yield software packages that differ qualitatively, structurally, from person to person, then perhaps Allport (1961) was right and the core nomothetic theory will be limited to some very general propositions, mostly about learning and development.

Reverting to the computer analogy, there are structural similarities among software programs that might permit a general theory that goes some distance beyond just the structure of the initial hardware. Each of a dozen very different programs may require a subroutine for sorting data, in alphabetical or numerical order, and these sorting subroutines are likely to be quite similar across programs. No doubt there are psychological subroutines which most of us learn and which create reasonably similar structures that will yield reasonably general laws. This would lead to numerous, independent microtheories, each describing software commonalities, held loosely together by a single nomothetic macrotheory concerned with the hardware.

Al Harkness has pointed out to me that many computers come equipped with "read-only" memories or ROMs, innate software packages which serve, among other things, to get the hardware up and running. ROMs enhance the computer-brain analogy by permitting us to talk about innate fears and other instincts, the native ability of the human (but, perhaps, not the chimpanzee) brain to deal with complex linguistic relationships, and the rather extensive pre-programming that seems to guide child development. Inexperienced goslings show no alarm when a silhouette of a flying goose is passed over head but run fearfully for cover when the same silhouette is passed backward, which makes it resemble a hawk. This implies the innate existence of the same sort of connections or associations that the goslings will later acquire through learning.

In other words, the human brain (and the brains of most "lower" animals) comes equipped not only with hardware capable of elaborate programming but also with certain important aspects of programming already in place. Since we know that there are individual differences in the hardware itself, it seems likely that our ROMs, too, are not always identical, one to another. And it should be emphasized that the brain's ROMs, while perhaps they cannot be erased or written over, can be written around or circumvented. Thus, the incest taboo, which inhibits sexual interest in persons with whom we were reared, whether in a family or in a kibbutz, is not always effective (individual differences) and could doubtless be overcome in most cases if, for some reason, one wished to do so.

(5) Typologies

It is possible that, with respect to personality structure broadly construed, each human individual can usefully be considered to belong to several independent types or taxa and that the laws or theories of these several taxa can be used, alone or in combination, to predict the behavior of that individual in different situations. That is, there may be subroutines (or even ROMs) shared only among the members of a given type.

A type or taxon can be defined as a set of homeomorphic entities. Therefore, a single set of nomologicals, a single theory, will approximately describe all members of a type. For our purposes, it will be useful to modify this definition slightly: we shall define a type as a set of entities that share structural components, i.e., subroutines, that are homeomorphic. Therefore, those aspects of the behavior of these entities which are determined by the structural components that they have in common will be describable in the terms of a single theory. Thus, all radio receivers belong to one type of electronic instrument, all transmitters to another type, and all two-way radios belong to both types. The "kleptomaniac" and the primary psychopath are two quite different subtypes of the weak taxon "criminal."

Since human development begins with a set of homeomorphic entities that differ only parametrically, by what mechanism do people develop structural components shared with other members of the same type? One important insight of modern behavior genetics (one that *would* have impressed Meehl's Ph.D. committee) is that genes influence complex psychological characteristics indirectly, by influencing the kinds of environment the individual experiences or seeks out (e.g., Plomin, DeFries, & Loehlin, 1977; Scarr & McCartney, 1983). The child's temperament and other innate predispositions help to determine how other people will react to him or her, what sorts of experiences he or she will have, and what imprint these experiences will leave behind. To an important extent—just how important we do not yet know—the brain writes its own software. Since the hardware of the human computer is homeomorphic, since individual differences at the beginning of development are parametric rather than structural then, to the extent that gene-environment covariation is important in development, it is more likely that the structural elaborations wrought by self-selected experience will retain some of that original homeomorphism.

One unique feature of our species is that much of the experience that shapes us is vicarious, derived from stories we hear and probably also stories we make up in our own heads. Much of the primitive person's knowledge of the world comes from stories, traditional myths and experiences related by others. Books and television provide our own children with an almost unlimited range of vivid quasi-experiences which play an important role in shaping their world-view, their knowledge, and probably too their attitudes and personality. Because most of this rich library of vicarious experience is provided cafeteria-style, the opportunity for a modern child's nature to determine its nurture is greatly expanded.

The "cafeteria" metaphor for human experience misleadingly suggests that selections are made stochastically when clearly choices made early on tend to influence choices made later. Because of differences in temperament and native ability, Bill eschews most vicarious experience in favor of active adventure outdoors; Bob is fascinated by science fiction and later by real science; George is addicted to adventure programs; Paul, who is precocious, discovers pornography. What began as mere parametric differences must often lead to real differences in structure. Since human nature is so obviously complicated, perhaps the most we can reasonably hope for is that the varieties of human software packages will be classifiable into a manageable number of homeomorphic types within each of which some rules hold that do not hold across groups or types. (And it is relevant to note that we now have powerful analytic methods for detecting latent taxa in psychometric data, viz., Meehl & Golden, 1982.)

Summary of the Structural vs. Parametric Variation Issue

All sciences have as their objects of study collections of entities or systems, and the job of the science is to describe the behavior of these entities and, ultimately, to develop a theory about the structure of the different types of entities so that their behavior can be deduced from the theory of their structure. This job is relatively easier when the entities are all structurally alike, or when they can be sorted into classes or types within which there is structural similarity. Thus, all atoms of a given isotope of any element are structurally alike; thus, one microtheory fits all exemplars of a given isotope and, moreover, one macrotheory contains the features common to all the microtheories.

The same is true for molecules, the next higher level of organization, although now there are many more types which it is convenient to sort into classes—acids, bases, nucleotides, etc.—and into classes of classes—polypeptides, proteins, etc. And so we can go upward in the hierarchy—organellae, cells, tissues, organs, mammals, primates—seeking to classify these increasingly complex entities into types that share sufficient structural homeomorphism so that a single structural description, a single microtheory, can provide a usefully general and adequate account of all members of the type or class.

The step from neuroanatomy and neurophysiology to psychology, like the step from computer hardware to software, is a very large and different kind of step from any preceding steps lower in the hierarchy. Entities that are extensively modifiable in structure, whose hardware is designed for structural modification or elaboration, are something *sui generis*, without parallel in science or in engineering. Entities in which the hardware helps to write the software are without parallel at all. We can certainly aspire to create reasonably conventional scientific theories about the hardware, about how the brain's structure can be modified. If it turns out to be true that most individuals within a common culture have been modified in reasonably similar ways, or if they can be classified into a manageable number of reasonably homeomorphic types, then we can have at least crude theories—Produce or Fruit theories, perhaps Apple or even MacIntosh theories—about aspects of the elaborated organism, about personality, interests, and intelligence. We must simply keep trying and find out how far we can go.

D. Psychology So Far Has Lacked Good Paradigms

We talked earlier about the long publication lags in social science journals and the suggestion that we countenance this because we are all digging in separate places on the beach, looking for different things; we do not need to know how anyone else is doing—or what they are doing—and we do not fear that anyone else will scoop us because we know that no one else is hunting where we are or for the same thing—i.e., we lack paradigms. In gold mining, a paradigm consists in the discovery of a deposit, a seam, so that people can get to work, all the technicians who know how to dig, to timber a tunnel, to build sluices for treating the ore, and so on.

Heinrich Schliemann was a paradigm maker; he figured out where to dig for the ruins of the ancient city of Troy. Based on his pathfinding, an army of archaeologists could start doing useful work, had whole careers laid out before them. Many good doctoral dissertations were made possible by Schliemann's essential first steps. It is important to understand that just having the tools for research, for digging, is not enough. You can be smart and well trained, bright-eyed and bushy-tailed, but if you do not know where to dig, you may end up in a dry hole or a mud hole. The hot paradigms currently are, of course, in molecular biology. Any psychology graduate student has the option of transferring to one of those areas where one could have almost total certainty of spending one's career doing useful work identifying codon sequences on the ninth chromosome or etc. The paradigms are there, it is just a matter of digging.

Paradigm-makers are few and far between in every science. In psychology there have been a few—Freud, Skinner, Pavlov, and Piaget, to list some important examples—and there have also been some pseudo paradigm-makers or false prophets—Jung, Hull, and Kohler, for example, able and intrepid adventurers who had the bad luck to return empty-handed (and also Freud, Skinner, Pavlov, and Piaget from another point of view, i.e., implicitly or explicitly they claimed too much).

E. Too Many Go into Research Who Do Not Have a True Vocation

(1) Fact: Most Meaningful Research Is Done by an Elite Handful

a) Price's Inverse Square Law. In a 1963 book called *Little Science, Big Science*, Derek de Sola Price pointed out that, going back into the nineteenth century, rates of scientific publication have followed, approximately, an "inverse square law" in the sense that the number, N, of scientists producing k papers is approximately proportional to $1/k^2$. This means that for every 100 authors who produce one paper, 25 will produce two, 11 will write three papers, 6 will write four, and so on (1 of the 100 will manage as many as ten papers). This model suggests that about 50% of all scientific papers are produced by about 10% of the scientists— and we're including as "scientists" not all the graduates or Ph.D.s but only those who have published at least one paper. The modal lifetime number of publications for Ph.D. psychologists is zero.

b) Publication by Psychologists. Out of 20,000 first authors in APA journals over a five-year span, Garvey's APA study found that only 5% appear twice in that five years; less than 2% average one appearance per year—i.e., only about 400 authors publish once per year in APA journals. Using a different data set, George Miller found a similar result, namely that most of the lasting work in psychology was done by a core group of about 400 individuals. Myers (1970) found that half of all authors of articles in psychological journals were cited once or less over the next six years.

(2) The Ortega Hypothesis

Jose Ortega y Gasset, a Spanish philosopher who died in 1955, described the world of science as a kind of beehive:

> For it is necessary to insist upon this extraordinary but undeniable fact: experimental science had progressed thanks in great part to the work of men astoundingly mediocre, and even less than mediocre. That is to say,

modern science, the root and symbol of our actual civilization, finds a place for the intellectually commonplace man and allows him to work therein with success. In this way the majority of scientists help the general advance of science while shut up in the narrow cell of their laboratory, like the bee in the cell of its hive, or the turnspit at his wheel. (Cole & Cole, 1972)

In their interesting *Science* paper, the Coles point out that the common view accords with Ortega's, that science is an ant hill or termite colony kind of enterprise, with multitudes of anonymous workers each contributing essential efforts. Another version from Lord Florey, a past-president of the Royal Society:

Science is rarely advanced by what is known in current jargon as a "breakthrough"; rather does our increasing knowledge depend on the activity of thousands of our colleagues throughout the world who add small points to what will eventually become the splendid picture, much in the same way the Pointillistes built up their extremely beautiful canvasses.

Any large city works, to the extent that it does work, on this principle of the termite colony. So does the world of business and commerce under the free enterprise system. The postulate of free enterprise economists is that this is the only way that the world of commerce can work at all effectively.

Cole & Cole (1972) investigated whether this description actually fits the enterprise of physics by examining the patterns of citations of other researchers in papers published in the physics journals in 1965. They discovered that, at least in 1965, 80% of citations were to the work of just 20% of physicists. They took a "representative" sample of 84 university physicists, got their "best" paper published in 1965, looked at the 385 authors whom these 84 cite. Sixty percent of the cited authors were from the top nine physics departments, 68% had won awards on the order of the Nobel Prize or election to the National Academy of Sciences, 76% were prolific publishers. "Eminent" physicists, as defined by more than 23 citations of their papers in the 1965 *Physical Review*, cited authors who were themselves eminent; they averaged 175 citations per year in *Science Citation Abstracts*. Even non-eminent authors (those with few citations, few publications) cite mainly this same set of eminent authors.

This situation is the same but more so in psychology where less than 20% — perhaps more like 5 or 10% — carry the load.

It may be that modern physics and psychology are nontypical sciences in this respect. I think it could be argued that modern biology, or at least some of its branches, does fit the Ortega model, perhaps not his emphasis on "mediocrity" but at least his idea of the busy beehive. Maybe the paradigm idea is really central here. Theoretical physics in the 1960s was running low on paradigms. The experimentalists were turning up all these strange new particles, showing that the old theories were inadequate, but no new ideas had surfaced. I remember hearing one of the Minnesota physicists say that he was going into administration because the situation in physics was just too chaotic, everyone milling about, scratching their heads, not knowing which way to go.

I think that the elitism that emerges from de Solla Price's and the Coles' analyses should be tempered a bit this way: only a handful of scientists have whatever it takes to be paradigm-makers, to know where to dig. Many more may be perfectly qualified to do good work, useful work, once a paradigm is available.

(3) Serendipity Is Emergenic

It may be that being a good researcher, in the sense of paradigm maker, is an "emergenic" trait (Lykken, 1982; Li, 1987), the result of a particular configuration of independent traits all of which have to be present or present in a certain degree to yield the result. Having a fine singing voice, for example, is an emergenic trait. Being a great violinist or pianist probably requires high scores on several quasi-independent traits; there are lots of people with a good ear or fast reflexes or deep musical insight or good manual dexterity, but one has to have all of these to play at Carnegie Hall. I would guess that successful paradigm-making may be a multiplicative function of brains x energy x creativity x arrogance x daring x ??? and perhaps the relative weighting of the components is different for different fields of study. *Chutzpah* is probably a necessary ingredient in many situations; if you don't sell your ideas, they won't make any waves. Barbara McKlintock is a case in point. Her Nobel Prize was awarded for work done many years earlier which had not been noticed because she did not sell it. Someone else realized, retrospectively, that she had really pioneered in a currently hot area and did the selling, belatedly, for her.

In fact, I think that what we call genius is probably emergenic. In the biographies of most people of genius — people like Gauss or Shakespeare or Ramanujan, Mozart or Benjamin Franklin or Mark Twain — it seems apparent, first, that they were innately gifted. We have no idea at all what sort of early experience or training could turn an ordinary lump of clay into people like these. Yet, second, the genius does not run in families. The parents, sibs, or offspring of these supernovae usually do not show similar talents, even allowing for regression to the mean. This might indicate that the qualities of genius comprise a configuration of independent, partially genetic characteristics, all of which must be present to produce the result. The first-degree relatives may have some of the components or more than an average amount of all of them, but, as any poker-player knows, being dealt the Ace, King, Queen, Jack of spades plus the nine of diamonds is qualitatively different from being dealt a royal flush in spades. I don't think you have to be a Gauss to be a paradigm-maker, but I do think that the principle may be similar.

(4) Research Is Over-Valued, Especially in the Academy

There is more pay, more prestige, more freedom, more job security for academics who are successful researchers or who at least manage to publish frequently.

a) Meehl's "Seven Sacred Cows of Academia." Among these (regrettably unpublished) fallacious postulates is the proposition that a good university-level teacher must be a productive scholar. The two activities are competitive more than they are complementary. It takes much the same kind of intelligence, thought, reading, and insight—not to mention clock hours—to prepare a good lecture as to write a good article or plan a good experiment. (A really good researcher is likely to be a good teacher only because he/she has these abilities and is the kind of person who won't do something at all without doing it well.) Think about people like Isaac Asimov and Carl Sagan, Walter Munn and Gardner Lindzey, or the late Kenneth MacCorquodale. Munn and Lindzey wrote outstanding textbooks, MacCorquodale was a splendid teacher, Asimov and Sagan have helped millions of people to understand science a little better. All were fine scholars and good communicators, all of them might have made less of a contribution if they had allocated more of their energies trying to do original research.

b) Teaching and Public Service. These two avenues through which an academic can justify his or her paycheck are at least as important as research, at least as demanding of very similar abilities. Most research discoveries will be made by someone else if you do not do it; e.g., if Watson and Crick hadn't worked so hard on the double helix of DNA, Linus Pauling would have had it in a few more months. Much useful research is not really very brilliant, the only mystery is why one didn't think of it sooner. Yet it must be said that many bright and knowledgeable people never seem to think of these things or, if they do, don't do anything about it, or can't seem to discriminate between the more- and less-promising ideas that they do have and tend to follow up the wrong ones.

Is it better to turn up even a real nugget of new truth (which many would-be researchers never achieve) or to save a marriage, cure a phobia, teach a really stimulating course, influence legislation by persuasive testimony, plant some important ideas in the minds of students, policy-makers, or laypersons?

Over the past ten years or so, I have spent about one-third of my professional time educating the public about the "lie detector": One does not need specialized knowledge to see that most of the claims of the lie detector industry are nonsense and sheer wishful thinking. Senator Sam Ervin, untrained in psychology, realized at once that the polygraph test is a form of "20th Century witchcraft." Yet most people, including many psychologists, cannot see it until someone points it out. Let's say that I am a Grade B researcher: i.e., nothing wholly trivial or flagrantly wrong, some product that is genuinely useful, nothing really great. If I spend about one-third of my time on polygraph-related matters, that means one-third less production of Grade B research. In exchange, however, quite a few innocent persons who might have gone to prison because they failed polygraph tests were found innocent, quite a few bad guys who might have escaped prison because they had passed "friendly" polygraph tests are in prison. Where there was virtually no scientific criticism of the lie detector on which legislators, lawyers, and judges could draw, now there is a book and more than 40 articles and editorials and these criticisms have been cited in several state supreme court decisions banning polygraph evidence because of its inaccuracy. Minnesota and Michigan now ban the use of the polygraph on employees; I was the only scientific witness to testify on behalf of both bills. A bill for a similar federal statute was passed by the House of Representatives in 1986, in part because of my testimony, and will likely become law in 1988.

Any Grade B psychologist could have done these things and it demands no great personal sacrifice since it is mostly fun to do; I lay no claim to be either a genius or a saint. The point is that this sort of public service work is more useful and valuable than most Grade B research (and *all* research of Grades C through Z). One suspects that most of you young psychologists would be able to find a way to make a similar *pro bono* use of your abilities and training at some time in your careers. One hopes that more of you will seize the opportunity when it comes along and not be hindered by any silly notion that it is nobler in the mind to publish some dingbat paper instead.

c) Research Has Visibility. One reason research is overvalued is that it gets the glory, its fruits are tangible and public—you can count the books and articles and you know who wrote them. Great teaching or brilliant clinical work goes relatively unrecognized. But we do not have to passively accept this state of affairs. If you think you have a knack for teaching, for example, do not hesitate to cultivate it, work at it, give it everything you've got. If your knack develops into a real skill it will be recognized and rewarded, especially if the consumer movement finally reaches the Academy and students start demanding competent teaching. If you shirk developing your teaching skills, however, because you're too busy writing Grade C papers, then both you and your institution will be the poorer.

III. Some Things We Are Doing Wrong That We Have Only to Stop Doing

Mark Twain once told of an elderly lady, feeling poorly, who consulted her physician. The doctor told her that she could be restored to health if she would give up cussing and drinking whiskey and smoking cigars.

"But, Doctor!", said the lady, "I don't do any of those things!" Well, there you have it. She had neglected her bad habits. She was like a ship floundering at sea with no ballast to throw over-board!

We psychologists are in a much happier position than this lady, for we have an abundance of bad habits. Surrounded by difficulties and complexities, we have invented comforting "Cargo Cult" rituals, adopted scientistic fads, substituted pedantry for substance, jargon for common sense, statistical analysis for human judgment. The examples we shall have space for here are only illustrative; our bad habits are legion and every one that we throw overboard will make us feel and function better.

A. Use of Scientistic Jargon

When I was serving my time on an NIMH research review committee and was assigned to be primary reviewer for a dumb proposal, I found that it was usually sufficient just to translate the author's proposal into ordinary language. "No, is that really what he plans to do? Why that's dumb!" Graduate students planning dissertation projects could save themselves later grief by following this rule: Using only language understandable by an intelligent layperson, state your hypothesis, the ancillary hypotheses necessary for your experiment to be a test of that hypothesis, and your predictions. If, stripped of jargon, such a prospectus fails to sound sensible and promising, forget it. Many examples of how social scientists, including some of the most eminent, tend to dress up banal ideas in jargon can be found in Andreski's *The Social Sciences as Sorcery*. I take as my moral for this sermon an excellent phrase of Hans Eysenck's: eschew meretricious and obfuscating sesquipedalianism.

Psychologists, and their psychiatric cousins, are susceptible not only to fads of jargon but to fads of methodology, research techniques, experimental designs, even variables chosen less because of their relevance to some important problem than because they are currently in vogue. In the field of psychopathology research, for example, structured interviews and "research diagnostic criteria" are now a *sine qua non* even though they may not be appropriate to one's application. Most current research on the psychopathic personality, for example, defines the target population in terms of *DSM-III*'s category of Anti-Social Personality although (in my opinion, at least) any group thus defined will be hopelessly heterogeneous, excluding some genuine Cleckley psychopaths while including many persons who are not true primary psychopaths at all. The slavish adoption of *DSM-III* classification has purchased an overall increment in diagnostic reliability at the cost of much specific diagnostic validity.

Some scientific rituals are all right in themselves and mischievous only when they are used as a substitute for thoughtful analysis of one's particular problem. The older psychiatric literature contains many meaningless, uncontrolled studies of various treatment procedures. When it was realized that many patients get better spontaneously, the idea of an untreated control group was invented. Then someone noticed the placebo effect; it became necessary to let the control patients think they were being treated (e.g., with some drug) when they were not. Finally, someone realized that the clinician rating the patient's improvement also could be influenced by knowing who was on the real drug—hence, the "double-blind" design. This simple, sensible approach would not have taken so long to invent if the people then doing psychiatric research had more of the kind of talent that research requires.

Once invented, the double-blind design became ritualized; as long as your study was double-blind, it must be okay. Example: The financier, Dreyfus, after much psychoanalysis and other psychiatric treatment, discovered that the well-known anti-seizure drug, Dilantin, cured his particular problem (Dreyfus, 1981). Dreyfus financed research on Dilantin's applications in psychiatry. Much money was spent giving unselected psychiatric patients Dilantin according to a double-blind design; the results were essentially negative. But who could imagine that any one drug would produce useful effects in all or most patients? Surely the sensible thing to do in this case would be to look for other people with complaints like those Dreyfus had and try the drug on them. Use of a ritualized procedure seems to blind some investigators, depriving them of common sense.

Another common and dangerous fad is the tendency to take up counter-intuitive research findings and then generalize them to the point where they are not only counter-intuitive but false. Perfectly respectable research has demonstrated that honest eyewitnesses are frequently mistaken. Yet, if the witness had a clear view of a woman's face and he identified her as his wife, his testimony has very strong probative value. It has been shown that psychiatric predictions concerning the "dangerousness" of patients or of criminal suspects are frequently in error. Nonetheless, if a twice-convicted rapist, on bail awaiting trial for a third offense, is charged with rape by yet a fourth victim, it is reasonable for the Court, even without psychiatric assistance, to conclude that this individual is dangerous and to refuse bail on the new charge. Common sense tells us that some kinds of identifications are more certain than others, that predictions can be made more confidently in some cases than in others. One of Meehl's classic papers (1957) provides an elegant analysis of this problem. It is the Cargo Cult mentality, when someone cites a "research finding," which leads us to renounce common sense and embrace foolishness. We should throw it overboard.

B. Over-Reliance on Significance Testing: The Favorite Ritual

Researchers often do not know what they are looking for or what will turn up—but one goal always beckons, namely, a p-value less than .05, since that is what it takes to get a publication. Pursuit of statistical significance has become the tail that wags the dog.

I once was outside reviewer on a dissertation from a Canadian university, a rather interesting-sounding study of autonomic responses of psychopaths, neurotic offenders, and normals. I found it impossible to determine how the study came out, however, because there were *75 pages* of ANOVA tables, 4th order interactions, some of them "significant" and discussed at wearying length. I suggested that the candidate should be passed since he clearly had been taught to do this by his faculty but that perhaps some of the faculty ought to be defrocked.

(1) The Null Hypothesis Is (Almost) Always False

A professor at Northwestern spent most of 1967 flipping a coin 300,000 times, finding 50.2% heads, significant at the .01 level. At about the same time, Meehl and I did our unpublished "Crud Factor" study. We had available from the University's Student Counseling Bureau computerized responses to an "After High School, What?" questionnaire that had been administered to 57,000 Minnesota high-school seniors. We cross-tabulated all possible pairs of 15 categorical variables on this questionnaire and computed Chi-square values. All 105 Chi-squares were significant and 96% of them at p less than 10^{-6}. Thus, we found that a majority of Episcopalians "like school" while only a minority of Lutherans do (52% vs. 45%). Fewer ALC Lutherans than Missouri Synod Lutherans play a musical instrument. Episcopalian high-school students are more likely to be male than is the case for Baptists.

Fourteen of the 18 scales of the *California Psychological Inventory* (CPI) were developed empirically, by selecting items which differentiated various criterion groups (Gough, 1987). There is no general factor that runs through all of these scales or any substantive theory that predicts them all to be interrelated. Yet the mean of the absolute values of the 144 intercorrelations is about .4. In psychology, everything is likely to be related at least a little bit to everything else, for complex and uninteresting reasons. Therefore, any investigator who makes a directional prediction (A is positively correlated with B, Group X has more Z than Group Y does) has a 50:50 chance of confirming it just by gathering enough N — no matter how fatuous or lunatic his/her theory might be (Meehl, 1967).

Bill Oakes (1975) has pointed out that this may not be as serious a problem for genuinely experimental designs in which groups are truly randomly assigned to treatment and control conditions. In correlational designs (e.g., Anxiety *vs.* Anality) or in comparisons between self-selected groups (e.g., normals *vs.* schizophrenics), one is asking if one variable is related to some other pre-existing variable and, for psychology, the answer seems always to be "Yes; at least a little bit, although perhaps not for the reason you think." In a true experiment with random assignment, one is asking whether one's experimental treatment affects most of the experimental group with respect to the measured dependent variable and in the same way, and the answer to that question can be "No." Oakes cites an Office of Economic Opportunity study in which 13,000 experimental subjects received two hours per day of special instruction in reading and mathematics for one school year. Compared to 10,000 untreated controls, there was no significant difference in the achievement gains over the year.

But difference scores, like these achievement gains, are notoriously unreliable. If the achievement tests had a reliability of .8 and if, say, the one-year retest stability of the scores for the untreated students was about .7, then the reliability of the difference or gain scores could have been on the order of .3. Then 90% of the variance of both distributions of gain scores might be error variance so that even large samples could fail to detect a true difference between them. I think that the only way a psychologist is likely to fail to refute the null hypothesis with really large samples is by using unreliable measures (which, of course, is easy for a psychologist to do!). And if the null hypothesis is always false, then refuting a null hypothesis is a very weak test of a theory and not in itself a justification for publishing a paper.

(2) Statistically Significant Findings Are Frequently Misleading

I once published an article (Lykken, 1968) examining the claim of another author that a "frog response" on the Rorschach test is evidence that the responder unconsciously believes in the "cloacal theory of birth." That author reasoned that one who believes impregnation occurs *per os* and parturition *per anus* might see frogs on the Rorschach and also be disposed toward eating disorders. A group of patients who had given frog responses were found to have many more references to eating disorders in their charts than a control group of patients without frog responses. The Chi-square was highly significant. We have already seen why we need not feel the least compulsion to accept this theory on the basis of this outcome, but must we not at least admit that an empirical fact has been demonstrated, viz., this connection between frog responding and eating problems?

Remembering that false facts tend to be more mischievous than false theories, let us ask what is the "fact" that this study seems to have demonstrated. The notion of a valid empirical finding is grounded in the idea of replication. Because this author's result achieved the .01 level of significance, we say that, if this experiment were to be repeated exactly hundreds of times, then we should be willing to bet $99 to $1 that the grand mean result will be non-zero and at least in the direction found by the first author. But not even he could repeat the same experiment exactly, not even once. The most we could do, as readers, is to repeat the experiment as the author described it, to follow his *experimental recipe*; I call this process "operational replication." But neither he nor we know whether he has adequately described all the conditions that pertained in his first study and that influenced the outcome. If our operational replication fails, the most likely explanation will be that his experimental recipe was incomplete. And his original significance test provides no quantitative estimate of the likelihood that our operational replication will succeed.

If an operational replication is successful, we still cannot be certain that "Rorschach frog responding is associated with eating disorders." Such an empirical generalization leaps far ahead of the facts in hand. These facts are that patients of the type he studied, who give what he calls frog responses when the Rorschach is administered the way he did it, are likely to have an excess of eating disorders, defined as he defined them, listed in the ward notes of the nurses who worked in his hospital. If we are dissatisfied with the limitations of all these particularities, then we do a "constructive replication." In a constructive replication, we deliberately ignore the first author's recipe and focus solely on the generalization in which he and we are interested. We design our own test of that hypothesis, select our own patients, administer the Rorschach as we think it should be given, define "frog responding" and "eating disorders," and assess the latter, in whatever way seems sensible to us. Only by constructive replication can we reasonably hope to compel respect for any claim we make of having demonstrated a generalizable empirical difference or relationship.

A significance test is like a license on a car; you have to have one before you drive to the APA convention, but only an idiot would invest in an old wrecker just because it has a valid license plate. R. A. Fisher himself made a similar point to the British Society for Psychical Research (Fisher, 1929); significance testing may make a finding more intriguing but it takes replication (constructive replication) to make it believable.

(3) Ways of Staying Out of "Significant" Trouble

a) Make Range, Rather Than Merely Directional, Predictions When we test the null hypothesis, that the difference or correlation is actually zero, against the usual weak, directional hypothesis, that the difference or correlation is, say, positive, then even if our theory is quite wrong our chances of refuting the null hypothesis increase with the size of the sample, approaching $p = 0.5$; that is, the bigger and more expensive the experiment, the more likely it is to yield a false result, a seeming but undeserved confirmation of the theory. If our theory were strong enough to make a point prediction (e.g., the correlation is 0.50), then this situation would be happily reversed. The larger our sample and the more precise our measurements, the more stringent would be the test of our theory. Psychological theories may never be able to make point predictions, but at least, like say the cosmologists, we ought to be able to squeeze out of our theories something more than merely the prediction that A and B are positively correlated.

If we took our theories seriously and made the effort, we should be able to make rough estimates of parameters sufficient to say, e.g., that the correlation ought to be greater than .40 but not higher than .80. Then, at least we should be able to claim that the better the experiment the tougher the test of the theory.

Suppose that a very large and careful experiment yields a correlation within the predicted range; what are the odds of this happening even if our theory is wholly false? I know of no general way to quantify this problem beyond saying that the odds are substantially less than the customary value of 50:50. There are no firm and heaven-sent criteria, only informed human judgment applied to the particulars of this case. If the theory does logically lead to the given range prediction, using auxiliary hypotheses that seem reasonably robust, and if the experiment was truly a tough test, then we must respect the theory *a posteriori* more than the frog response result compelled us to respect the theory of cloacal birth.

b) Multiple Corroboration. Any theory worth thinking about should be rich enough to generate more than one testable prediction. If one makes five reasonably independent predictions and they all are confirmed experimentally, one can claim p less than $(0.5)^5$ or less than about 4 chances in 100 of doing that well accidentally.

c) Comparing Alternative Models. As Sir Karl Popper has pointed out, we should not aspire to show that our theory is valid but, rather, that it possesses more "verisimilitude" than any current competitor and therefore deserves interim allegiance until something better comes along. That is, for any theory, if our tests are sufficiently searching and stringent, the theory must ultimately fail. A more constructive approach, therefore, is to apply equally stringent tests to existing alternative models and to focus subsequent research and development on the model or models that fit the data best. This is the approach of modern biometrical genetics (e.g., Jinks & Fulker, 1970; Eaves, 1982) and of structural-modeling specialists (e.g., Bentler & Bonett, 1980; Cudeck & Browne, 1983).

In most areas especially of "soft" psychology, it is rare for a proponent of a theory to give explicit systematic attention to possible alternative explanations of a data set. Showing that one's theory is compatible with the trend of one's data is, as we have seen, only weak corroboration for the theory. Showing that our theory fits the data better than all plausible alternative models, on the other hand, is strong corroboration, strong enough in fact to establish our theory squarely in the catbird seat until such time as a new and more plausible competitor is advanced by someone else.

Example: I have proposed that the primary psychopath is the frequent, but not inevitable, product of a typical environmental history imposed upon a child who is at the low end of the normal distribution of genetic fearfulness or harmavoidance (Lykken, 1957, 1984). In a mental maze task where certain errors are specifically punished, we know that psychopaths avoid errors punished by loss of money (quarters) but do not avoid errors punished by a painful shock. That such findings can be predicted from my theory is encouraging, but the fact that they cannot be predicted by rival hypotheses (e.g., the hypoarousal model or the disinhibition model) is considerably more significant.

d) The Multi-Trait, Multi-Method Matrix (Campbell & Fiske, 1959). We know we ought to distrust most alleged measures of particular traits (e.g., "anxiety" tests), and we also know that method variance accounts for much of the common variance in psychological research. Therefore, we can construct a tougher hurdle for our hypothesis by using several measures of each trait and several methods of measurement. We should also include in the matrix measures of other possible traits that might be producing spurious findings. For example, intelligence tends to be correlated with everything so one should make sure that one's finding that A correlates with B is not just because both A and B are loaded on IQ. The objective is to show that the common factor measured by one's four measures of X correlates with the common factor measured by the several tests of Y even after the co-variance produced by Z (e.g., IQ) has been removed. Example: One can reasonably wonder whether many of the interesting findings obtained in research on Kohlberg's (1984) Stages of Moral Development would remain if verbal intelligence had been partialed out in each case.

e) The Two-Phase Experiment and Overlapping Replication. In programmatic research, which is generally the best kind of research for several reasons, we can use the technique of sequential, overlapping replication. Each successive study replicates the most interesting new findings of the previous experiment and also extends them in new directions or tests some new hypotheses. In the initial attack on a new problem, we can use the Two-Phase Experiment. Phase 1 is the discovery phase, the pilot study, in which we find out for ourselves how the land lies. Since we are not trying to impress or convince anyone else, we include only such refinements and controls as we ourselves believe to be necessary to evaluate the hypothesis. If we decide after running three subjects that some aspect of our set-up should be changed, we change it and roll on. If our planned method of analysis of the data yields mostly noise, we feel free to seek a different method that will yield an orderly result. If Phase 1 produces interesting findings and if, in our judgment, we can now design a full-scale experiment that will yield the same findings, then we move on to Phase 2, the proof or verification phase, the elegant experiment designed to convince others (e.g., journal referees) that our findings are valid.

Assuming that our judgment is good, the Phase 2 experiment will always be better designed and more likely to produce useful results because of what we have learned in Phase 1. If Phase 1 does not work out, we will not feel so committed to the project that we will struggle to wring some publishable but unreplicable findings out of it. Muller, Otto, and Benignus (1983) discuss these and other useful strategies in a paper written for psychophysiologists but equally valuable for workers in other research areas.

Reichenbach's distinction between the *Context of Discovery* (e.g., the pilot study) and the *Context of Verification* (e.g., the Phase 2 study) is a useful one, especially for psychologists. Since we should be honestly humble about how little we know for sure, it behooves us to be open and relatively loose in the context of discovery. Just as there are few hypotheses than we can claim as proven, so are there relatively few that we can reasonably reject out of hand. Extrasensory perception is a good example. Having worked for years with hundreds of pairs of adult twins, hearing so many anecdotes of apparent telepathic communication between them, which usually occur in moments of stress or crisis, I am inclined to believe in telepathy — as an individual but not as a scientist. That is, I would be happy to invest of my time and the government's money in what I thought was a promising telepathy experiment. But to compensate for this openness in the context of discovery, we must be tough-minded in the context of verification. Since no one has yet succeeded in capturing telepathy in the laboratory, in discovering a paradigm that yields consistent, reproducible results, telepathy remains just an intriguing hypothesis which no one should believe in *qua* scientist.

(4) The Bottom Line

The best single rule may be Feynman's principle of total scientific honesty. Feynman says:

> If you're doing an experiment, you should report everything that you think might make it invalid — not only what you think is right about it [but] other causes that might possibly explain your results. . . . Details that could throw doubt on your interpretation must be given if you know them. . . . If you make a theory, for example, you must also put down all the facts that disagree with it . . . you want to make sure, when explaining what it fits, that those things it fits are not just the things that gave you the idea for the theory but that the finished theory makes something else come out right, in addition. (Feynman, 1986)

This is not nearly so easy as it seems since it is natural to become infatuated with one's own ideas, to become an advocate, to be a much gentler critic of one's own work than one is of others'. Many of us are able to tear other people's research limb from limb while we smile upon our own like an indulgent parent. In fact, I think one *should be* protective at first until the toddler at least can stand erect. But before one lets the little devil out into the neighborhood, one must learn to look at it as critically as others will.

Conclusions

In my junior year in college, I was led to change my major from Chemical Engineering to Psychology by the brilliant teaching of Kenneth MacCorquodale and Paul Meehl and by my discovery, in W. T. Heron's course in Learning Theory, that I was already at the cutting edge of development of this slow-blooming young science. I have never regretted that decision, for there is nothing I would rather have been—that I could have been—than a psychologist. I am a rough carpenter rather than a finisher or cabinetmaker and there is need yet for rough carpentry in Psychology's edifice. This is a field in which there remain many simple yet important ideas waiting to be discovered and that prospect is alluring. I would rather pan for gold dust on my own claim than climb the executive ladder at the *Glitter Mining Company*.

When we exclude those parts of our enterprise that are really neuroscience or genetics or applied statistics, it has to be admitted that psychology is more like political science and economics than it is like the physical or biological sciences and that those colleges which permit undergraduates to "satisfy the science requirement" by taking a few courses in psychology are helping to sustain the scientific illiteracy of the educated segment of society. We can take (rather weak) comfort in the fact that, if our discipline were as mature as physics is, then psychology would probably be recognized as more difficult than physics. It is certainly harder to be a psychological researcher now than it was to do research in physics in Faraday's time.

The brain-computer analogy seems to me to be provocative and genuinely useful, clarifying the relationship among the traditional sub-areas of psychology and illuminating the deep waters of the nomothetic-ideographic problem. It may even be that the new academic Departments of Computer Science will evolve a structure that foreshadows that of future Departments of Psychology.

It is important that we recognize, acknowledge, and root out the Cargo Cult aspects of our enterprise, the scientistic rituals and related bad habits by means of which we have sought to emulate the form, but not the substance, of the hard sciences. Some of the most pernicious of these bad habits involve rituals of statistical inference. My prescription would be a limited moratorium on directional tests of significance. From now until the Year 2000, let us say that research reports submitted to psychological journals must include either tests of range, rather than mere directional, predictions or else systematic comparisons of alternative hypotheses. I think these latter, more powerful techniques are potentially within our grasp, but they are new and harder than the nearly futile null hypothesis testing to which we have become addicted. If my idiosyncratic and sometimes overstated critique does nothing else, I hope it illustrates at least that Psychology is truly better situated than Mark Twain's ailing lady who had no bad habits she could jettison in order to regain her health.

References

Allport, G. W. (1961). *Pattern and growth in personality*. New York: Holt, Rinehart and Winston.
Andreski, S. (1972). *Social sciences as sorcery*. London: Andre Deutsch.
Barry, W. M., & Ertl, J. P. (1966). In F. G. Davis (Ed.) *Modern educational developments: Another look*. New York: Educational Records Bureau.

Bemporad, P. E. (1967). Perceptual disorders in schizophrenia. *American Journal of Psychiatry, 123*, 971–975.

Bentler, P. M., & Bonett, D. G. (1980). Significance tests and goodness of fit in the analysis of covariance structure. *Psychological Bulletin, 88*, 588–606.

Campbell, D. P., & Fiske, D. W. (1959). Convergent and discriminant validation by the multitrait-multimethod matrix. *Psychological Bulletin, 56*, 81–105.

Chalke, F. C. R., & Ertl, J. P. (1965). Evoked potentials and intelligence. *Life Sciences, 4*, 1319–1322.

Cole, J., & Cole, S. (1972). The Ortega hypothesis. *Science, 178*, 368–375.

Cudeck, R., & Browne, M. W. (1983). Cross-validation of covariance structures. *Multivariate Behavioral Research, 18*, 147–167.

Davis, F. B. (1971). *The measurement of mental capability through evoked potential recordings.* Greenwich, CT: Educational Records Bureau.

Dreyfus, J. (1981). *A remarkable medicine has been overlooked: With a letter to President Reagan.* New York: Simon & Schuster.

Eaves, L. J. (1982). The utility of twins. In E. Anderson, W. A. Hauser, J. K. Penry, & C. F. Sing (Eds.), *Genetic basis of the epilepsies* (pp. 249–276). New York: Raven Press.

Feynman, R. (1986). *Surely you're joking, Mr. Feynman!* New York: Bantam Books.

Fisher, R. A. (1929). The statistical method in psychical research. *Proceedings of the Society for Psychical Research, 39*, 189–192.

Garvey, X., & Griffith, Z. (1963). *Reports of the project on scientific exchange in psychology.* Washington, D. C.: American Psychological Association.

Gould, S. J. (1978). Morton's ranking of races by cranial capacity. *Science 200*, 503–509.

Gough, H. G. (1987). *California Psychological Inventory: Administrator's Guide.* Palo Alto, CA: Consulting Psychologists Press.

Hearnshaw, L. S. (1979). *Cyril Burt: Psychologist.* London: Hodder & Stoughton.

Jensen, A. R. (1986). In R. Sternberg & D. Detterman (Eds.), *What is intelligence? Contemporary viewpoints on its nature and definitions.* Norwood, NJ: Ablex Publishing Corp.

Jinks, J. L., & Fulker, D. W. (1970). A comparison of the biometrical genetical, MAVA, and classical approaches to the analysis of human behavior. *Psychologial Bulletin, 73*, 311–349.

Jones, M. B., & Fennel, R. S. (1965). Runway performance in two strains of rats. *Florida Academy of Sciences, 28*, 289–296.

Kohlberg, L. (1984). *The psychology of moral development.* New York: Harper & Row.

Lewontin, R. C., Rose, S., & Kamin, L. J. (1984). *Not in our genes: Biology, ideology, and human nature.* New York: Pantheon.

Li, C. C. (1987). A genetical model for emergenesis. *American Journal of Human Genetics, 41*, 517–523.

Lindsey, D. (1978). *The scientific publication system in social science.* San Francisco: Jossey-Bass.

Lykken, D. T. (1957). A study of anxiety in the sociopathic personality. *Journal of Abnormal and Social Psychology, 55*, 6–10.

Lykken, D. T. (1968). Statistical significance in psychological research. *Psychological Bulletin, 70*, 151–159.

Lykken, D. T. (1982). Research with twins: The concept of emergenesis. *Psychophysiology, 19*, 361–373.

Lykken, D. T. (1984). Psychopathic personality. In R. J. Corsini (Ed.), *Encyclopedia of Psychology, Vol. 2.* New York: Wiley.

Marston, W. M. (1938). *The lie detector test.* New York: R. R. Smith.

Meehl, P. E. (1957). When shall we use our heads instead of the formula? *Journal of Consulting Psychology, 4*, 268–273.

Meehl, P. E. (1967). Theory testing in psychology and physics: A methodological paradox. *Philosophy of Science, 34*, 103–115.

Meehl, P. E. (1978). Theoretical risks and tabular risks: Sir Karl, Sir Ronald, and the slow progress of soft psychology. *Journal of Consulting and Clinical Psychology, 4*, 806–834.

Meehl, P. E., & Golden, R. (1982). Taxometric methods. In P. Kendall & J. Butcher (Eds.), *Handbook of research methods in clinical psychology* (pp. 127–161). New York: Wiley.

Meehl, P. E., & Rosen, A. (1955). Antecedent probability and the efficiency of psychometric signs, patterns, or cutting scores. *Psychological Bulletin, 52*, 194–216.

Muller, K. E., Otto, D. A., & Benignus, V. A. (1983). Design and analysis issues and strategies in psychophysiological research. *Psychophysiology, 20*, 212–218.

Myers, C. R. (1970). Journal citations and scientific eminence in contemporary psychology. *American Psychologist, 25*, 1041–1048.

Oakes, W. F. (1975). On the alleged falsity of the null hypothesis. *The Psychological Record, 25*, 265–272.

Plomin, R., DeFries, J. C., & Loehlin, J. C. (1977). Genotype-environmental interactions and correlations in the analysis of human behavior. *Psychological Bulletin, 84*, 309–322.

Popper, K. R. (1962). *Conjectures and refutations*. New York: Basic Books.

Rescorla, R. A. (1987). A Pavlovian analysis of goal-directed behavior. *Amerian Psychologist, 42*, 119–129.

Scarr, S., & McCartney, K. (1983). How people make their own environments: A theory of genotype-environmental effects. *Child Development, 54*, 424–435.

Summers, W. G. (1939). Science can get the confession. *Fordham Law Review, 8*, 334–354.

Tulving, E., & Madigan, G. (1970). Memory and verbal learning. In *Annual Review of Psychology, Vol. 29*.

Watson, J. S. (1982). Publication delays in natural and social-behavioral science journals: An indication of the presence or absence of a scientific paradigm? *American Psychologist, 37*, 448–449.

Weiner, A. S., & Wechsler, I. B. (1958). *Heredity of the blood groups*. New York: Grune & Stratton.

Psychology as a Historical Science: Meehl's Efforts to Disentangle Science B from Science A

W. Grant Dahlstrom

Prologue: On a late winter evening Paul and I were leaving the campus and walking westward on University Avenue toward the Meehls' apartment for dinner and good talk when Paul suddenly grabbed my arm and pointed up ahead: "Dahlstrom, you see that old geezer walking along up there? Well, let me tell you what he's going to do. I predict that in about two minutes he will stop dead, turn to his right facing north, and then for a couple minutes he'll do like this!" Paul raised his right hand, extended his index finger, and began stabbing the air repeatedly with a rhythmic motion like the head of a strutting turkey. "How in the world can you know that?" I asked. Paul told me, "Just wait. You'll find out."

Sure enough, as we continued our walk we could see him slow down, stop, and turn to face the street. Then, just as Paul had predicted, the old man raised his right hand and began that peculiar pecking motion in the air with his index finger extended. He was just completing his strange repetitive gesturing and was turning west again by the time we came up to him on the sidewalk. "Do you recognize the guy?" Paul asked me. The small bent man was indeed familiar: the person who ran an elevator in one of the main buildings on the Minnesota campus. Anyone who was naïve enough or lazy enough to take the elevator up to the third or fourth floor of this building would have vivid memories of the ride he would give you.

With both a door and a gate to close and a hand-controlled lever to raise or lower the elevator car, this old gentleman had worked out at each successive floor a series of careful checking, rechecking, and re-rechecking of these closings—first outside door, then inside gate, then outside door again, with further checking of the inner gate—interspersed with false starts up or down, followed by more runs through his checking routines to the utter distraction of anyone unwise enough to have entered his elevator. One wondered: Were his dreams filled with nightmares of someone finding a door ajar and stepping out into space for a fatal fall down the elevator shaft? What anxieties must he have experienced to have developed so elaborate a set of neurotic rituals about the doors and gate to his car! Even the poorest student of Psychology 1 could have diagnosed his condition: an almost paralyzing obsessive-compulsive neurosis.

But why the halt along the way home from work? Why the odd gesture made over and over toward the busy traffic along University Avenue? As the old man walked away from us, I waited for an explanation. Although Paul had not seen him do this more than two or three times, Paul had recognized who he was and, remembering the elevator rituals, had realized both what the man was doing and why he could expect him to do it again, this time in the cold wind of a Minnesota evening. The place where he stopped was across the street from the University Baptist Church with its high banks of windows made up of scores of small panes of glass. In another characteristic compulsive ritual he had fallen into a pattern of stopping to count the panes each evening as he came opposite the facade of the church.

To confound me with his clinical acumen Paul used a typological assignment—obsessive-compulsive neurosis—together with knowledge about a key correlate of that particular type—the rigid running-off of a compulsive ritual. (It is interesting that this was not one of the subset of identifiers used to assign him to that typological category in the first place.) In addition to checking and counting—like endless rounds of hand-washing, quirky aversions, or senseless and distracting thoughts, all defining features of this type—the specific ritual that Paul had predicted had another feature characteristic of such behavioral patterns: lack of any functional significance in the real world. This aspect of bizarreness, peculiarity, or oddness had helped to identify it as a predictable element in this poor man's repertoire of compulsions. With a very small sample of the behavior itself and his prior acquaintance with his neurotic style of operating the elevator, Paul could risk his dramatic prediction without an actuarial table but with little probability of being wrong.

* * * * *

In an invited paper in the *American Scientist*, Stephen Jay Gould (1986) summarized evolution's intellectual impact on science during the century during which the Society of the Sigma Xi had existed by highlighting the steps Darwin had taken to establish both the scientific credentials of geology and evolutionary biology and the legitimacy of their claims to full membership in the domain of science. Even though most of the findings did not derive from experimental interventions or yield a basis for clearcut predictions, Darwin was able to demonstrate the soundness and respectability of the basic techniques of these sciences. Gould's retrospective account of Darwin's approach provides an excellent framework within which to review Meehl's efforts to establish psychology as an equally worthy claimant to such membership, and to demonstrate the comparability in the requisite steps needed to add psychology to the list of historical sciences.

In the course of his exploration of Darwin's long and difficult struggle to gain acceptance for evolutionary concepts and methods, Gould takes a side excursion to reflect on the recent "reforms" of the core curriculum at Harvard. In the new format students must make a choice among course requirements from lists of either Science A (experimental-predictive) or Science B (historical), with a not-so-subtle implication of second-class status inherent in this distinction. Like astronomy, paleontology, or geology, the psychology of personality has all too often been viewed as less than scientific because it fails to meet the arbitrary criterion of the hard sciences: "repeatability under common conditions." In several key papers Paul Meehl has addressed this same issue and has pinpointed the essential differences between the hard sciences and the subject matter and methods of psychology. It is worthwhile to review the common points in his efforts and the earlier struggles in evolutionary theory, as summarized by Gould, to appreciate more fully the contributions that Meehl has made to personology as a branch of psychology and to the field of personality assessment and research.

"Hard" vs. "Soft" Science

Although they have much in common—e.g., objectivity, systematic observations, careful teasing apart of variables, prediction as the crucial test of soundness, and, above all, a willingness to change accepted ideas—"hard" science, with its inductive bent and rigorous experimenting, stands in sharp contrast to the "soft" versions, which rely more heavily on hypothetico-deductive methods. A recurring risk of these latter procedures is a lapse into mere description or, worse, an idle substitution of names for unobservable variables. The subject matter of the soft sciences may become, thus, either trivial or unobservable. According to Gould, in order to escape the dilemmas posed by the puniness of humankind's power to manipulate in any direct experimentation the monumental forces in geological processes or to bring about in the laboratory the kinds of structural alterations in living organisms of concern to evolutionary biologists, Darwin advanced two broad methodological approaches which result in making a science of history possible. Gould refers to these key scientific methods that Darwin employed as the *uniformitarian assumption* and *inferring history from its results*.

In the former method the historical scientist must work "with observable, gradual, small-scale changes" that are ongoing now and thus available for study (and perhaps even for direct manipulation); then by smooth extrapolation over appropriately long spans of time both the processes and the results from these observations and/or experiments may be insightfully applied to all of history. (In using this method, however, it is overly simplistic to exclude the occasional catastrophic event that can drastically alter the otherwise smoothly accumulating impacts of the much more typical small-scale processes, as Gould himself has so vividly portrayed in several of his essays [Gould, 1977, 1980] for *Natural History Magazine.*)

In his use of this approach, Darwin personally carried out detailed studies of the rate of soil-churning by earthworms and used the data that he gathered as a basis for extrapolation to estimate the long-term results on the topography of the British Isles. He also utilized observations made on rates of the growth of reefs by slow accretion of the shells of corals to explain different patterns of island formation and employed the results obtained from generations of selective breeding records in animal husbandry to account for biological changes over much longer time spans. A more contemporary example would be the short-term shifts that have been documented in the predominant wing color of moths as the specific requirements for successful camouflage from predators undergo gradual change owing to pollution in the moths' environment.

Gould also cautions that an inflexible application of the backward extrapolation in time of even well-documented small-scale processes may fail to account for some outcomes that have resulted from rare but massive effects of some catastrophic events in geological or biological history. Current issues in biological evolution which involve such interruptions in continuously cumulative processes focus, for example, on the ways in which massive extinctions of certain species may have come about on a wholesale, worldwide scale. Appeals to the occurrence of collisions of our planet Earth with a comet or a meteor, along with the resulting atmospheric changes that in turn would destroy food supplies or alter climate, are examples of ways in which the uniformitarian assumption would have to be augmented to account for very dramatic exceptions to the gradual processes more typical of the history of our world.

Darwin's second broad method is an even more complex mode of analysis, one which relies upon a "concilience of inductions" (a phrase that Gould borrows from William Whewell). If the key to the first method is careful observation or experimentation on contemporary processes in which reliance may be placed on traditional statistical methods of estimating the likelihood of a given event from a set of causal factors (i.e., Gaussian probability), then the essential characteristic of the second approach is the way to estimate the likelihood of a set of causal factors given a particular event (i.e., Bayesian inverse probability). This latter challenge of assigning prior probabilities to explain particular outcomes lies at the very heart of "doing" historical science.

As Gould (1986, 1987) summarizes this second method, data from many sources are insightfully joined in an effort to reconstruct the most likely antecedents to a particular present state of affairs. Organization of these data involves the judicious use of taxonomies, pathologies, and metrics to reveal "iterated patterns and diverse paths of causal ordering." For example, after some understanding has been gained about the way that various geographic, geologic, and biologic processes sequentially interacted to bring about the requisite isolation of a breeding population to give rise to some species of migratory birds, it may take only one more addition to such a concilience to account for the unbelievable ranges of migration of some of these world travelers. That is, knowledge of the dynamic processes of plate tectonics which give rise to vast but incredibly slow drifting of continental masses may then be introduced to account for the present-day pattern of pole-to-pole migration of some of these species. If their breeding grounds and feeding ranges were at one time in close proximity, it is a reasonable surmise that selective survival rates of the longer distance flyers among these populations could easily match the slow rate of drift as the distance separating these two vital areas increased to our present-day magnitudes. In such a formulation, of course, the rate, amount, and direction of continental drift is determined by smooth extrapolation from contemporary rates that are themselves based on changes observed in present-day studies. Thus, by a conjoint application of both of Darwin's methods the scientist of history can achieve a reconstruction of the processes and events that vastly antedate the time period within which any one scientist can make empirical observations.

The esssential role of measurement in both methodological approaches is obvious, providing as it does the crucial precision needed to document the presence and quantify the rates of the small-scale changes in the former approach and to generate the data that are required to specify the taxonomic groups as well as to identify and distinguish the deviations in the latter. More often misunderstood here is the role played by the taxonomic categories in the all-important task of "separating basic or essential homologies from closely similar analogies" among the phenomena under investigation. The assertion is often made that in the early efforts to devise ways of quantifying the data in any area of science only very crude categories may be available, but that as the science matures, these "typological" schemas give way to accurate measurements of dimensions and continua. To the contrary, as Gould emphasizes, accurate taxonomic classification is developed and elaborated (based on increasingly precise measurement techniques) to provide the means by which the scientist is able to capture the "histories of development." That is, the careful ordering in a sound classification system "reflects the historical pathway, pure and simple" of the objects of study as they have evolved over time. Thus, the scaling of various dimensions, together with the instruments required to measure them, must proceed, but such advances do not serve to replace a parallel development of accurate typological distinctions. Of even greater utility is the evidence provided by contrasting the well-adapted taxons with the "imperfections, oddities and deviations" that result from nature's own experiments. These errors are key elements in the historical scientist's effort to reconstruct various sequences of cascading events that occur

Table 1. Mayr's Causal Framework

	Subject Matter	
Causal Time Scale	Biological Evolution	Human Development
Proximate	Processes in life of any one organism (Development)	Processes in development of any one person (Personology)
Ultimate	Processes in the development of that species (Systematics)	Processes in the development of humankind (Sociobiology)

as complex processes interact over innumerable occasions but which are no longer accessible for direct study.

In his 1986 Sigma Xi paper Gould documented these methodological approaches as central aspects of Darwin's careful articulation of data and emphasized insightful reconstruction of geological and biological processes in Darwin's successful effort to place historical sciences solidly in the domain of science in general. A review and examination of the writings and research of Paul Meehl reveal an impressive degree of correspondence between Darwin's approaches to evolutionary processes extended over eons of time and the methods that Meehl has employed in the comparable task of analyzing complex historical processes in the life-course of single individuals. The challenges are the same, only the phenomena and the time-scale differ.

In discussing this basic difference in time-scale, the taxonomist Ernst Mayr (1961) has noted for the biological sciences the methodological similarities in the two orders of scale. He refers to them as the ultimate-causal scale (or large-time frame) and proximate-causal scale (the time frame within the life-span of particular individual organisms). In Mayr's view knowledge of the processes and events in each time frame are complementary in any final accounting for the facts of evolution. If sociobiology can be viewed as dealing with the processes that have operated in the ultimate-causal scale to give rise to modern humans, then personology can be understood as working within Mayr's proximate-causal scale. (See Table 1.)

Meehl's Program

The elements in Meehl's systematic assault on the difficulties of understanding human personality and psychopathology are: insightful causal ordering, taxometric sophistication, and psychometric precision. In the course of his elaboration of each of these different aspects of his formulation, Meehl has tried to make clear the differences between the methods of research applied in the hard sciences (those domains of study that employ what Gould has termed "billiard ball" models in their explanatory schemas) and the techniques demanded by the more complex phenomena of psychology, especially personology (Meehl, 1967a, 1970a, 1970b, 1978). In these papers Meehl has repeatedly tried to distinguish the crucial differences between the two kinds of scientific endeavor (Science A and Science B in the Harvard terminology) and the difficulties that psychologists encounter when they slavishly follow the physical science model.

At times, however, readers of Meehl's writings on these topics have been struck with what seem to be basic contradictions. That is, while strongly endorsing actuarial over clinical methods of making predictions about various psychopathological states (Meehl, 1954, 1956, 1957, 1986), preferring data from more objective test instruments rather than relying on projective personality assessment methods (Meehl, 1945a, 1945b, 1946, 1950), as well as viewing favorably the therapeutic benefits to be gained by Ellis's Rational Emotive Treatment (RET) and various behavior modification interventions (1975a)—positions ususally characterized as hard-headed, tough-minded, and strongly empirical in orientation—Meehl nevertheless is an equally devoted student of Freudian psychoanalysis, in both its theoretical and practical formulations.

In the credence and support that he gives to basic Freudian psychodynamic formulations it seems clear that Meehl is concerned with those long-term effects of the historical processes in the individual personality that take place over the course of a lifetime from which only large-scale results are available for study in an adult. (Psychoanalytic explorations of remote memories have often been called "psychic diggings" in an archaeology of the mind [Sulloway, 1979].) The micro-dynamics of behavior therapy, on the other hand, can be viewed as providing data on those small-scale changes that are available for study and that can then be appropriately generalized (i.e., extended "by smooth extrapolation") to the countless encounters that a person may have with differing stimulus situations, to his or her widely varying responses, and to the complex patterns or schedules of reinforcing events that transpire in such a lifetime. Accordingly, it should be clear that these two formulations are not basically contradictory but that both in fact are needed in combination in order to apply to human life histories the uniformitarian methodology that proved to be so powerful in Darwin's hands. (See Table 2.)

In addition, the general psychoanalytic model can be seen as providing examples of those kinds of large-scale "catastrophic" events in the historical development of personality (e.g., traumatic assaults, losses, or fixations in emotional development) which may be used to account for dramatic departures from the patterns of effects to be expected from the day-to-day accumulation of long series

Table 2. Methods of a Science of History

Darwin's Approaches	Meehl's Approaches

I. *Uniformitarian Assumption*

Darwin's Approaches	Meehl's Approaches
Small-scale changes demonstrating the basic processes	Short-term effects of behavior modification or RET
Smooth extrapolation over entire course of period	Extrapolation over the life-time of the adult
Exceptions: catastrophes (e.g., effects of comets or asteroids colliding with earth)	Traumatic losses, fixations

II. *Inferring History from Its Results*

Construction of taxonomies

Based on kind, extent, & amount of similarity	Search methods for latent clinical taxons
Accurate taxons separate homologies from analogies	Distinguish borderline vs. schizotype

Capture the histories of development in taxons

Imperfections, oddities, deviations reflect experiments carried out by nature	Occurrence of actual schizophrenic breakdown
Bases for a theory of causal ordering over a complex and contingent history	Sequence:
	Major gene defect
	Anhedonia (schizotaxia)
	Schizotypic personality
	Schizophrenogenic mothering (or other situational stressors)
	Schizophrenic psychosis

Employ a "concilience of inductions" (Whewell)

Formulate a pathway of potential transformations	Source of gene
	1. Mother
	2. Father
	Other personality traits
	1. Introversion
	2. Anxiety
	Life Events
	1. Parental loss
	2. Marital quality

of reinforcing events. An appropriate fusion of the theoretical concepts from both approaches would serve well to begin a reconstruction of the complexities of human personality and psychopathology.

Another example of such apparent contradictions in Meehl's formulations is given in an addendum to his penetrating and exhaustive explication of the difficulties that he saw in the way of making "progress" in psychology (Meehl, 1978). Here he reported a conversation about a problem that Thomas Bouchard had found in an early draft of that paper. Professor Bouchard had noted that Meehl had espoused a number of very hard-headed requirements of falsifiability laid down by Sir Karl Popper for sound scientific theories and yet Meehl seemed to endorse a general psychoanalytic view of personality dynamics. Bouchard had brought to Meehl's attention what seemed to him to be a basic disparity in his formulation. He was puzzled that Meehl could simultaneously embrace such apparently incompatible approaches to psychological theory and research as Popper's rigorous criteria of acceptable scientific theory and the untestable formulations of psychodynamics, particularly a Freudian version. In his answer to Professor Bouchard, Meehl followed the same general line of his thesis in the paper: falsifiability need not rest solely on those techniques that are available to us at the moment — although the needed evidence may not yet be in, it may not always be impossible to obtain.

Earlier in the 1978 paper Meehl had employed another of Darwin's major methodological distinctions when he elaborated on the imprecision we all face when we try to assign probability levels to some of our well-entrenched beliefs. This kind of endeavor is based on diverse evidence and involves "both practical and theoretical inference" employed in a logical network, in other words, a concilience of inductions. As Meehl notes, "nobody knows how to state the manner or degree in which various lines of evidence converge on a certain conjecture as having high (Popperian) verisimilitude" (1978, p. 831). The questions here require the application of inverse probability rather than the more usual lines of statistical inference. That is, in contrast to studies that are carried out to prove that a significant impact has resulted from some particular experimental or therapeutic manipulation (a difference appraised by means of the more traditional hypothesis-testing statistical models of Sir Ronald Fisher), in the task of synthesizing various sorts of information into a theoretical formulation, Bayesian approaches are needed (Mosteller & Wallace, 1984). Hence historical reconstructions as exemplified in the application of psychoanalytic models are a different kind of scientific endeavor (Meehl, 1970b) than the procedures that are brought into play when applying the technology of some behavioral intervention and demonstrating its impact on a particular set of responses under investigation at the moment. However, when properly done, both are equally scientific, as Gould so convincingly documented in his 1986 discussion of Whewell's concilience of inductions. It is this kind of creative construction which Meehl had in mind when he contrasted what a psychologist (clinician) can do that clearly distinguishes his capabilities from that of the actuary (Meehl, 1960, 1967b).

What this creative synthesis of a causal sequence involves is a method of weighing the evidence as it accumulates in a growing understanding of the complex processes that interact to determine the development of human personality over the course of a lifetime. It is a reflection of the primitive state of both our theories and our data that (as Meehl noted) we can do so little in the way of scaling our beliefs about the development of either personality types or forms of psychopathology. Eventually we will be in a position to synthesize our findings into conciliences of inductions and assign various degrees of belief, perhaps using units along a scale of likelihood. One such scale was proposed by the mathematician Alan Turing, expanding on the ideas advanced by Venn (1888/1962). Turing's proposals were then elaborated and synthesized by his colleague I. J. Good (1950). The Turing scale employs the "natural ban," a logarithmic unit with fractional units ("decibans") reflecting "the smallest change in weight of evidence that is directly perceptible in human intuition" (Hodges, 1983, p. 197).

It is in this arena of debate about methods for combining data into accurate conciliences of inductions about personality processes that the measurement of basic parameters in human behavior becomes crucial. Also it is in this context that the recent discussions about Meehl's sobering diagnosis of the "causes" for slow progress in "soft" psychology, together with his prescriptions for a cure of this paresis in our field, that the contrasting positions on falsifiability of psychological theory taken by Popper and by Lakatos (Serlin & Lapsley, 1985; Dar, 1987) become most relevant. That is, if and when our science of personology reaches sufficient maturity, it will then become crucial that determinations of various parameter values be made with "satisfactory precision" to enable investigators to choose among alternative theoretical formulations. Then falsifiability will become a much more essential feature of our theories and precision will be demanded of our psychometric instruments. However, if Meehl's formulations are correct, before we reach such maturity in our theories we will have to have a sophisticated taxonomy of personological and psychopathological classes within which to conduct our investigations. As matters now stand, we lack the all-important classificatory schemata, the classification methods, and the proper identification and measurement of the variables themselves that interact within each of our types and syndromes. We now suffer severe challenges to our ability even to replicate one another's research findings because of confusions that result from such a chaotic state of affairs. It will undoubtedly be some time before personologists and psychopathologists team up to remedy this lack of a taxonomic framework and to carry out the related tasks of elaborating the details of our personality systematics (Dahlstrom, 1972a).

Even though we lack the bases we need for constructing deciban scales of degree of certitude about the relevant psychological processes involved in personological development, Paul Meehl, in several of his most important papers, has already provided us with an excellent preliminary framework of theory on one particular form of psychopathology (schizophrenia) that can serve as a model for the many other formulations that we will need to further a science of human personality and psychopathology.

Path of Causal Ordering

In his presidential address to the American Psychological Association in St. Louis, Meehl (1962) demonstrated for our field the way that a sophisticated concilience of inductions can be marshaled to make psychological sense out of a welter of evidence and observations over a wide range of disciplines. In this address he elaborated a psychodynamic formulation in which he drew upon findings from such diverse fields as psychogenetics, neurobiology, clinical psychiatry, analytically oriented psychotherapy, and family dynamics to reconstruct an elaborate "complex and contingent history" of the events that lead to the timing and appearance of a schizophrenic psychosis in an adult individual. (See Figure 1.)

In its barest outline the sequence is:

(1) A major gene defect which manifests itself as an alteration (schizotaxia) in the central nervous system of the afflicted individual is transmitted at conception to an offspring.

(2) This CNS defect either seriously impairs (dyshedonia) or completely limits (anhedonia) the person's experience of the usual kinds and sources of pleasure.

(3) In addition, the thought processes of the afflicted individual show various forms of errors of reasoning and logic (cognitive slippage).

(4) With little or no experience of enjoyment to offset the buffeting of the pains and frustrations that modern life brings to everyone in this world (especially for an individual with difficulties in thinking who is trying to interact with people), the individual develops a pattern of personality organization (schizotypy) that characteristically renders him or her avoidant of social contacts.

(5) This pattern of interpersonal relationships, although handicapping, is not as seriously pathological as the development of a psychotic disorganization (schizophrenia).

(6) Although it may be indefinitely postponed if the individual is emotionally buffered, schizophrenia may be triggered, sooner or later, by various kinds of situational stressors.

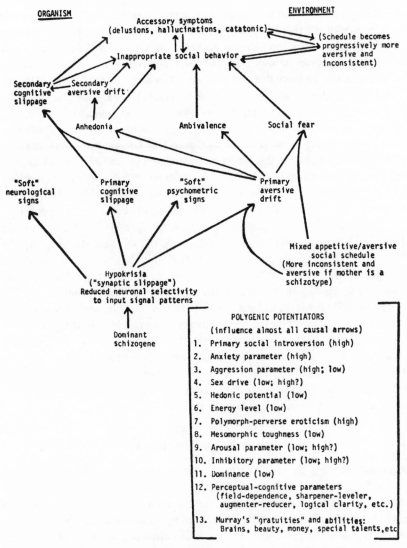

ORGANISM

ENVIRONMENT

Accessory symptoms
(delusions, hallucinations, catatonic)

(Schedule becomes
progressively more
aversive and
inconsistent)

Inappropriate social behavior

Secondary
cognitive
slippage

Secondary
aversive drift

Anhedonia   Ambivalence   Social fear

"Soft"
neurological
signs

Primary
cognitive
slippage

"Soft"
psychometric
signs

Primary
aversive
drift

Mixed appetitive/aversive
social schedule
(More inconsistent and
aversive if mother is a
schizotype)

Hypokrisia
("synaptic slippage")
Reduced neuronal selectivity
to input signal patterns

Dominant
schizogene

POLYGENIC POTENTIATORS

(influence almost all causal arrows)

1. Primary social introversion (high)
2. Anxiety parameter (high)
3. Aggression parameter (high; low)
4. Sex drive (low; high?)
5. Hedonic potential (low)
6. Energy level (low)
7. Polymorph-perverse eroticism (high)
8. Mesomorphic toughness (low)
9. Arousal parameter (low; high?)
10. Inhibitory parameter (low; high?)
11. Dominance (low)
12. Perceptual-cognitive parameters
    (field-dependence, sharpener-leveler,
    augmenter-reducer, logical clarity, etc.)
13. Murray's "gratuities" and abilities:
    Brains, beauty, money, special talents,etc

Figure 1. Causal chains in schizophrenia, minimum complexity (Meehl, 1972b.
Reproduced with permission from the *International Journal of Mental Health*.)

This sequence of etiological stages that Meehl proposed had different pathways of potential transformation which provided several crucial implications for the prophylaxia, therapeusis, and prognosis of schizophrenia (Meehl, 1972a, 1972b, 1977). For example, the schizophrenic disorder would run in families, but if a given child failed to get the major gene for schizotaxia, then he or she would be free of the risk of developing schizophrenia. If the schizotaxic condition does develop in a given individual, then schizotypy might be the best that he or she could expect in the way of emotional adjustment; however, schizophrenia was by no means an inevitable consequence (Meehl & Golden, 1978). The timing and degree of disorganization that the individual would manifest during the acute breakdown would also depend upon other personological characteristics, many of them also genetically transmitted (e.g., social introversion or susceptibility to high anxiety arousal), listed in Figure 1 as polygenetic potentiators.

Of equal importance in this set of transformation pathways would be the particular parent who was the carrier of the major gene. The quality of the emotional support provided by a mother who was herself free of the schizotaxic deficiency would likely be very different from the mothering the child could expect if she were schizotypic in her own personality organization. In Meehl's view this major difference in the early childhood experiences of the affected offspring (Meehl, 1975b) would lead to important differences in the likelihood and timing of a schizophrenic disorder. That is, were the father the source of the defective gene the most probable situation would be that the mother in such a family would herself be unusually maternal and protective (since she was the sort of woman who was attracted to a schizotypic man) and thus any of her children showing the schizotaxic limitations would in turn benefit from these supportive and protective tendencies as well. While a schizotypic mother might help precipitate an early overt schizophrenic psychosis in her schizotypic offspring, a warm and supportive mother might help delay any psychotic disorganization for years or even for the lifetime of that individual. (See Table 2.)

Taxonomies and Nosologies

The causal ordering sketched out in the 1962 paper not only brought together material from a variety of scientific disciplines (coordinating structures and processes at the cellular, neuroanatomical, and behavioral levels of organization) but it served to highlight the essential role played by valid and workable taxonomies and nosologies. Both personological types and clinical syndromes were utilized in Meehl's formulation of the cascading events contributing to the final appearance of a manifest schizophrenic psychosis. Meehl has made several important contributions to the methods of discovery and elaboration of both systems of categories: personological types and nosological syndromes.

In an invited address to the Canadian Psychological Association, Meehl (1959b) made a strong defense of the scientific legitimacy of psychiatric nosological categories *provided they are employed in a skillful manner*. As he noted at that time:

When the indicators of membership in the class constitute a long list, none of which is either necessary or sufficient for the class membership, the descriptive information which is conveyed by the taxonomic name has a 'statistical-disjunctive' character. That is, when we say that a patient belongs to category X, we are at least claiming that he displays indicators a or b or c with probability p (and separate probabilities p_a, p_b, and p_c). This may not seem very valuable, but considering how long it would take to convey to a second clinician the entire list of behavior dispositions whose probability of being present is materially altered by placing a patient in category X, we see from the standpoint of sheer economy even a moderately good taxonomic system does something for us. (1959b, p. 113)

The way in which this economy can work was illustrated in the episode described in the prologue and has been elaborated in considerable detail in several other of Meehl's writings, particularly in his 1962 paper that was discussed above.

In that presentation, Meehl developed a crucial distinction in personological taxonomies: the essential difference between classes of predisposition and classes of psychopathological disorder. Individuals with different personality organization are vulnerable or susceptible to different patterns of emotional breakdown, an issue also elaborated in Dahlstrom (1972a) in the distinction between personological "species" and "syndromes." In Meehl's discussion, the full-blown disorder (schizophrenia) requires the pre-existing condition (schizotypy), but the presence of the predisposition does not necessarily or inevitably lead to a breakdown into the pathological condition. Even more important, the psychological indicators of these two kinds of personality pattern are likely to be very different, both quantitatively and qualitatively (Golden & Meehl, 1979).

In disentangling these two kinds of classificatory systems (in many ways analogous to the distinctions that are currently embedded in the groupings on Axis I and Axis II in the American Psychiatric Association's *Diagnostic and Statistical Manual [DSM-III]* [1980]), Meehl and his colleagues have introduced an array of conceptual and methodological refinements of great importance. Although the attributes of both the predisposition and the disorder itself are assumed to be present during the height of an acute episode of the pathological condition, the features of the former are all too likely to be masked or obscured by the latter. In fact, the predispositional classes or taxa are usually characterized as "latent" and thus require search methods of considerable subtlety and complexity to discern their presence before the actual manifestation of the pathological condition. In addition, since the disorder awaits very special circumstances to bring out the latent susceptibility (conditions which in particular individuals may, in fact, never come about in their lifetimes), the eventual validational evidence may be extremely difficult (or impossible) to collect under the usual circumstances of research on human psychopathology (Meehl & Golden, 1978). Thus, while the assessment measures that are developed against the available criteria of psychological disorders (such as the basic clinical scales of the MMPI) are likely to contain contributions of both predispositional attributes and psychopathological states (Dahlstrom, 1972b), the difficulties in disentangling such variances are formidable.

In place of these test-based procedures for the identification of schizotypic individuals, Meehl (1964) assembled a checklist of an elaborate set of clinical observations together with the means of noting and recording these "signs" in a systematic way during the course of routine assessment and treatment contacts with clients and patients. Judicious application of these indicators makes it possible to identify and follow up in appropriate research designs individuals with high probability of subsequent breakdown in some form of schizophrenic psychosis. Meehl (1965; Meehl & Golden, 1982) has also proposed several strategies for the identification of personological types when no clear-cut indicator is known. These taxometric search procedures employ data analytic methods designed to detect patterns of covariation among core personality measures that differ mathematically from one personality to another in distinctive ways. That is, systems of variables relate one to another in one way for Type P, say, but show a different pattern of interrelationships in Types Q, R, S, or T. Potentially useful type indicators are those parameters which can be used to form subgroups of research subjects within which these patterns of interrelationship are maximally uniform or homogeneous.

Meehl and his colleagues have reported three fairly successful empirical efforts to demonstrate the effectiveness of these search methods for "latent clinical taxa" based on data from the MMPI. Two of these exploratory efforts did in fact have an external (non-test) personological indicator—biological gender—but were carried out as if that information were not in fact available (Golden & Meehl, 1973; Meehl, Lykken, Burdick, & Schoener, 1969). A third study focused on the core construct of schizotypic personality (Golden & Meehl, 1979) and yielded results that corresponded to an impressive degree with a set of MMPI scores reported many years before by Peterson (1954). Peterson's data were obtained from individuals who had originally been given a wide array of different nosological assignments on their first contact with a Veterans Administration psychiatric service but who were all later correctly identified as manifesting a schizophrenic disorder. These search procedures proposed by Meehl (1979) have not as yet been employed in any systematic way to develop a larger taxonomy of personological subgroups comparable to the judgmentally formed groupings on Axis II in the DSM-III. These approaches hold high promise for application to such problems in the future.

Psychometric Precision

In order to capitalize upon such distinctions, accurate methods are also needed to distinguish between nosological classes or syndromes as well as between predispositional types. Psychological tests of various kinds have offered promise in these important tasks but, in Meehl's view, have not lived up to early expectations (Meehl, 1972b). However, if they were employed properly, they could serve to enhance the construct validity of our psychopathological categories (Cronbach & Meehl, 1955) and further refine the taxonomic structures for both personality types and nosological syndromes. Proper development and application of psychometric methods, however, must be carried out in a context of appropriate theory. Meehl's formulations provide us with a general guideline or framework for psychometric scales as they are developed and applied to taxometric issues.

This framework in broad outline involves several points. Each member of a personality type can be considered to be an identifiable system of interacting variables. Members of one type may differ from members of other types either in the basic parameter settings (traits) on the basis of which the variables (states) interrelate or in the number and kind of variables comprising the system, or both (Dahlstrom, 1972a). Within this framework there are three basic kinds of psychometric tasks:

(1) determination of the most probable taxon membership of an individual being assessed (which may be facilitated by data provided by also carrying out the next task);

(2) establishing the value of each of an array of parameters in the system characteristic of that individual (i.e., assessing his or her basic traits or stable attributes);

(3) appraising the momentary level or value of each of the variables in the system over a series of occasions (in order to plot the pattern of interconnections among these various states of the individual under study).

It is likely that each of these measurement tasks will require different kinds of psychological scales and that each of these kinds of instruments will, in turn, need differing scaling methods.

Similarly, it can be assumed that each personality type has idiosyncratic susceptibilities to particular stressors and when the dynamic system of such a type is under stress, it will manifest features of psychopathology characteristic of that type. That is, personality types furnish predispositional frameworks within which various forms of disorder can be understood, predicted, and perhaps prevented or ameliorated.

For both types and syndromes, then, various psychometric issues in the area of personology can be clarified in terms of the different measurement roles that the psychological scales may play in this same broad framework that derives from Meehl's theoretical perspectives. Accurate taxon assignment and precise measurement of states during the course of a disorder, as well as any alteration in parameter settings resulting from the disorder, constitute psychometric challenges in psychopathological nosology equal to the challenges they pose in the assessment of personological types.

Little agreement has yet to appear in the area of personology about the range of variables that operate as different states in various personality systems, but considerable attention has been devoted lately to anger, depression, and, most notably, anxiety. Tuma and Maser (1985) edited a lengthy volume on *Anxiety and the anxiety disorders* covering from several perspectives the three general issues noted above in regard to taxometrics: disorders of anxiety as a psychopathological syndrome (how to determine whether a given disorder is a member of this particular class in a psychiatric nosology); anxiety as a trait (the parameter settings under which various individuals operate that determine when and to what extent they become anxious); and anxiety as a state (at any given time the level of anxiety aroused in an individual).

Tellegen (1985), in his contribution to the Tuma and Maser volume, developed in some detail a distinction between structured and unstructured approaches to scale construction. In the former, he included both "rational" scaling and the external (or outside) correlate approach because both methods are designed to implement the measurement of constructs that have already been defined. For Tellegen, the unstructured approach includes internal (inductive) methods such as exploratory factor analysis. External keying relies heavily upon the differences to be discovered between self-report characteristics of each of two (or more) groups of subjects and is called a structured approach in that the subject groups have already been defined as the bases for selecting component items and appraising the psychometric power of the tentative scale so constructed. The unstructured internal approach utilizes intercorrelations among item sets to locate and organize clusters of items that are reflecting the same sources of variation among respondents. The first requires items that are relatively unrelated to each other but which are all sensitive to different segments of the (often complex) basis for the original segregation of those postulated contrasting groups. The second approach does not work well unless a large number of items all share heavy components of a single source of variance.

Within the framework of Meehl's taxometric formulation, however, it should be clear that these methods that Tellegen discussed in the context of research on anxiety do not constitute so much a rivalry of alternative tactics in psychometric scaling as they involve different measurement tasks. That is, most of the scale work employing external criterion groups has had as its essential task (whether fully articulated or not) that of discovering the most accurate bases for assigning individuals to taxa.

On the other hand, scaling based on the (unstructured) inductive methods of cluster or factor analysis (or structured methods based on face validity or other prior considerations of content) has much more often been devoted to the task of discovering and/or assessing traits or tracking the vicissitudes of various states. Although often characterized as competing methods of scale construction which would be expected to yield psychometric scales serving the same measurement tasks with differing degrees of precision, it may be more accurate to view these approaches as providing quite different, but equally valuable, psychometric instruments.

Thus, in a scale that has been criterion-keyed against the item endorsements obtained from separate groups of subjects, the information provided by any given difference in item endorsement frequency (the basic datum of this method of scale construction) can be most accurately characterized as an increment to the probability that a given subject belongs to one group (or a drop in the probability that he or she belongs in some other group). Of course, that is precisely the issue in taxon classification. The less that any given item duplicates the informational contributions already made to this classification by other items in the "scale," the more useful that item can be to the classificatory task. The value of the scale, per se, rests on the inherent construct validity of the taxon (type or syndrome). Several of Meehl's early articles were devoted to the ways that such scales could be improved in the precision of their "taxon" assignment or diagnostic accuracy by means of corrections for biasing response styles unrelated to such criterion classifications or taxon memberships (McKinley, Hathaway, & Meehl, 1948; Meehl, 1945b, 1950; Meehl & Hathaway, 1946) or ways that the conjoint use of several such measures could be capitalized on to improve such classifications (Meehl, 1946, 1959a; Meehl & Dahlstrom, 1960; Meehl & Rosen, 1955).

Similarly, in the internal scaling of items to form scales that are either homogeneous in regard to content (face validity in self-reports of some experienced state) or to some trait (a stable parameter linking various attributes and situational features), the task is not taxon assignment, per se, but the establishment of some quantity or quality in the personological system. The parameters, of course, may serve as taxon indicators and facilitate taxon assignment; but this may be only one role that such instruments can play.

Summary

Gould ends his 1986 Sigma Xi review by noting the ways by which students of human behavior may in turn benefit from the proper use of Darwin's methods of doing historical science. We do indeed seem to be in urgent need of such enlightenment and changes in perspective. Until psychologists come to accept the fundamental differences in theory building and in the methodology of research inherent in intellectual enterprises of Science A and Science B, progress will be impeded and the contributions of psychological investigators will fail to cumulate into a proper edifice of understanding. Many of Paul Meehl's most thoughtful and insightful writings have been devoted to the task of disentangling these two major forms of scientific endeavor and articulating the requisite conceptual tools, methodological approaches, and measurement techniques that we must employ in a sophisticated attack on the difficult challenges we face in personology. If our future investigators and theory-builders pay proper attention to his pioneering efforts, these penetrating analyses will pay off handsomely in real gains for our science.

References

American Psychiatric Association. (1980). *Diagnostic and statistical manual of mental disorders (DSM-III)*. Washington, DC: APA.

Cronbach, L. J., & Meehl, P. E. (1955). Construct validity in psychological tests. *Psychological Bulletin, 52,* 281–302.

Dahlstrom, W. G. (1972a). *Personality systematics and the problem of types.* Morristown, NJ: General Learning Press.

Dahlstrom, W. G. (1972b). Whither the MMPI? In J. N. Butcher (Ed.), *Objective personality assessment.* New York: Academic Press.

Dar, R. (1987). Another look at Meehl, Lakatos, and the scientific practices of psychologists. *American Psychologist, 42,* 145–151.

Golden, R. R., & Meehl, P. E. (1973). *Detecting latent clinical taxa, IV: An empirical study of the maximum covariance method and the normal minimum chi-square method using three MMPI keys to identify the sexes* (Report No. PR-73-2). Minneapolis: University of Minnesota, Research Laboratories of the Department of Psychiatry.

Golden, R. R., & Meehl, P. E. (1979). Detection of the schizoid taxon with MMPI indicators. *Journal of Abnormal Psychology, 88,* 217–233.

Good, I. J. (1950). *Probability and the weighing of evidence.* London: Charles Griffin & Co., Ltd.

Gould, S. J. (1977). *Ever since Darwin: Reflections in natural history.* New York: Norton.

Gould, S. J. (1980). *The panda's thumb: More reflections in natural history.* New York: Norton.

Gould, S. J. (1986). Evolution and the triumph of homology, or why history matters. *American Scientist, 74,* 60–69.

Gould, S. J. (1987). Darwinism defined: Sifting fact from theory. *Discover, 8,* 64–70.

Hodges, A. (1983). *Alan Turing: The enigma.* New York: Simon & Schuster.

Mayr, E. (1961). Cause and effect in biology. *Science, 134,* 1501–1506.

McKinley, J. C., Hathaway, S. R., & Meehl, P. E. (1948). The MMPI: VI. The K scale. *Journal of Consulting Psychology, 12,* 20–31.

Meehl, P. E. (1945a). The dynamics of structured personality tests. *Journal of Clinical Psychology, 1,* 296–303.

Meehl, P. E. (1945b). An investigation of a general normality or control factor in personality testing. *Psychological Monographs, 59* (4, Whole No. 274).

Meehl, P. E.. (1946). Profile analysis of the MMPI in differential diagnosis. *Journal of Applied Psychology, 30,* 517–524.

Meehl, P. E. (1950). Configural scoring. *Journal of Consulting Psychology, 14,* 165–171.

Meehl, P. E. (1954). *Clinical versus statistical prediction: A theoretical analysis and a review of the evidence.* Minneapolis: University of Minnesota Press.

Meehl, P. E. (1956). Clinical versus actuarial prediction. *Proceedings of the 1955 Invitational Conference on Testing Problems*. Princeton: Educational Testing Service.

Meehl, P. E. (1957). When shall we use our heads instead of the formula? *Journal of Counseling Psychology, 4*, 268–273.

Meehl, P. E. (1959a). A comparison of clinicians with five statistical methods of identifying psychotic MMPI profiles. *Journal of Counseling Psychology, 6*, 102–109.

Meehl, P. E. (1959b). Some ruminations on the validation of clinical procedures. *Canadian Journal of Psychology, 13*, 102–128.

Meehl, P. E. (1960). The cognitive activity of the clinician. *American Psychologist, 15*, 19–27.

Meehl, P. E. (1962). Schizotaxia, schizotypy, schizophrenia. *American Psychologist, 17*, 827–838.

Meehl, P. E. (1964). *Manual for use with checklist of schizotypic signs*. Minneapolis: University of Minnesota, Psychiatric Research Unit.

Meehl, P. E. (1965). *Detecting latent clinical taxa by fallible quantitative indicators lacking an accepted criterion* (Report No. PR-65-2). Minneapolis: University of Minnesota, Research Laboratories of the Department of Psychiatry.

Meehl, P. E. (1967a). Theory-testing in psychology and physics: A methodological paradox. *Philosophy of Science, 34*, 103–115.

Meehl, P. E. (1967b). What can the clinician do well? In D. N. Jackson & S. Messick (Eds.), *Problems in human assessment*. New York: McGraw-Hill.

Meehl, P. E. (1970a). Nuisance variables and the ex post facto design. In M. Radner & S. Winokur (Eds.), *Minnesota studies in the philosophy of science, Vol. IV. Analyses of theories and methods of physics and psychology*. Minneapolis: University of Minnesota Press.

Meehl, P. E. (1970b). Some methodological reflections on the difficulties of psychoanalytic research. In M. Radner & S. Winokur (Eds.), *Minnesota studies in the philosophy of science. Vol. IV. Analyses of theories and methods of physics and psychology*. Minneapolis: University of Minnesota Press.

Meehl, P. E. (1972a). A critical afterword. In I. I. Gottesman & J. Shields (Eds.), *Schizophrenia and genetics: A twin study vantage point*. New York: Academic Press.

Meehl, P. E. (1972b). Specific genetic etiology, psychodynamics, and therapeutic nihilism. *International Journal of Mental Health, 1*, 10–27.

Meehl, P. E. (1975a). Control and counter-control: A panel discussion. In T. Thompson & W. S. Dockens (Eds.), *Applications of behavior modification*. New York: Academic Press.

Meehl, P. E. (1975b). Hedonic capacity: Some conjectures. *Bulletin of the Menninger Clinic, 39*, 295–307.

Meehl, P. E. (1977). Specific etiology and other forms of strong influence: Some quantitative meanings. *Journal of Medicine and Philosophy, 2*, 33–53.

Meehl, P. E. (1978). Theoretical risks and tabular asterisks: Sir Karl, Sir Ronald, and the slow progress of soft psychology. *Journal of Consulting and Clinical Psychology, 46*, 806–834.

Meehl, P. E. (1979). A funny thing happened to us on the way to the latent entities. *Journal of Personality Assessment, 43*, 564–581.

Meehl, P. E. (1986). Causes and effects of my disturbing little book. *Journal of Personality Assessment, 50*, 370–375.

Meehl, P. E., & Dahlstrom, W. G. (1960). Objective configural rules for discriminating psychotic from neurotic MMPI profiles. *Journal of Consulting Psychology, 24*, 375–387.

Meehl, P. E., & Golden, R. R. (1978). Testing a single dominant gene theory without an accepted criterion variable. *Annals of Human Genetics, 88*, 217–233.

Meehl, P. E., & Golden, R. R. (1982). Taxometric methods. In P. C. Kendall & J. N. Butcher (Eds.), *Handbook of research methods in clinical psychology*. New York: Wiley.

Meehl, P. E., & Hathaway, S. R. (1946). The K factor as a suppressor variable in the MMPI. *Journal of Applied Psychology, 30*, 525–564.

Meehl, P. E., Lykken, D. T., Burdick, M. R., & Schoener, G. R. (1969). *Identifying latent clinical taxa, III: An empirical trial of the normal single-indicator method, using MMPI scale 5 to identify the sexes* (Report No. PR-69-1). Minneapolis: University of Minnesota, Research Laboratories of the Department of Psychiatry.

Meehl, P. E., & Rosen, A. (1955). Antecedent probability and the efficiency of psychometric signs, patterns, and cutting scores. *Psychological Bulletin, 52,* 194–216.

Mosteller, F., & Wallace, D. L. (1984). *Applied Bayesian and classical inference: The case of the Federalist papers.* (2nd ed.) New York: Springer-Verlag.

Peterson, D. R. (1954). The diagnosis of subclinical schizophrenia. *Journal of Consulting Psychology, 18,* 198–200.

Serlin, R. C., & Lapsley, D. K. (1985). Rationality in psychological research: The good-enough principle. *American Psychologist, 40,* 73–83.

Sulloway, F. J. (1979). *Freud, biologist of the mind: Beyond the psychoanalytic legend.* New York: Basic Books.

Tellegen, A. (1985). Structures of mood and personality and their relevance to assessing anxiety, with an emphasis on self-report. In A. H. Tuma & J. Maser (Eds.), *Anxiety and the anxiety disorders.* Hillsdale, NJ: Lawrence Erlbaum Associates.

Tuma, A. H., & Maser, J. D. (Eds.), (1985). *Anxiety and the anxiety disorders.* Hillsdale, NJ: Lawrence Erlbaum Associates.

Venn, C. (1962). *The logic of chance.* (4th ed.) New York: Chelsea. (Original work published 1888.)

Some Myths of Science in Psychology

Leonard G. Rorer

I am going to discuss scientific methodology as I understand it to be widely taught, although not necessarily practiced, in psychology today. I will first discuss logical empiricism, on which the methodology is presumably based, and describe some of the reasons for its rise and success and for its abandonment. Then I will examine the claim that psychological theories are tested by means of the hypothetico-deductive method and null-hypothesis significance tests. I will argue that the hypothetico-deductive method is fatally flawed and that both theory testing and null-hypothesis significance testing should be abandoned. I will conclude by arguing that Bayesian formulations provide a better way of thinking about scientific research and the growth of knowledge, and that they are more descriptive of the conduct of science in psychology as well.

Logical Empiricism

Historical Background and Overview

As science and mathematics emerged from the Middle Ages, they were seen as

Preparation of this paper was supported, in part, by Grant MH-39077 from the National Institute of Mental Health.

Earlier versions of parts of this paper have been presented to the Society of Multivariate Experimental Psychology; as colloquia at Miami University and the Universities of Manitoba, Toledo, and Hawaii at Manoa; as an invited address to the Cincinnati Psychological Association; and as a keynote address to the First North American Personal Construct Network Conference.

This paper has benefited from the comments and criticisms of William F. Chaplin, Lewis R. Goldberg, William M. Grove, Sarah E. Hampson, Bobbie G. Hopes, Oliver P. John, Richard C. Sherman, and William B. Stiles, all of whose contributions are gratefully acknowledged.

ways of glorifying God by describing the wonders of His universe. Ultimately the problem scientists had with this view was that the church, rather than science, was the final authority. During the last half of the nineteenth century, scientists had another problem: Although engineering and manufacturing were making great strides, science, including mathematics, physics, and medicine, made comparatively little progress.

Around the turn of the century there were dramatic changes in all these disciplines. Frege (1950/1884) and Whitehead and Russell (1913) profoundly changed our ideas about the nature of logic, and showed that much of what had passed as logic had, in fact, been illogical on its own terms. An explosion of new developments in mathematics followed. Relativity theory rescued physics from the morass of ether drift and provided the foundation for modern theoretical physics. Until about 1900 one's chances of survival were somewhat better if one did not go to a physician, but in the early parts of this century bloodletting and the unaseptic practices that had been at the root of much iatrogenic illness were replaced by the first stunning achievements of experimental medicine.

A group of philosophers took as their task the explication of the changes that had taken place. The key to the triumphs of science, they claimed, was to be found in a change in the philosophy of science, a change that simultaneously (a) asserted the independence of science from religion by declaring the latter to be meaningless metaphysical speculation, and (b) protected science from the quagmires of entelechies, ether drift, absolute time and motion, humors of the blood, and the like by banishing them to the same metaphysical swamp. Through much of the first half of this century the new group cited the achievements in mathematics, logic, physics, and medicine as evidence for the correctness of their position. With such seeming successes they were able to overthrow the old order and exert an influence on philosophy that, for its swiftness and impact, was unprecedented. Other philosophical positions fell into a relative obscurity from which they have only recently emerged (Polkinghorne, 1983). Led by Moritz Schlick, the group called themselves "Der Wiener Kreis" or "The Vienna Circle," and they called their philosophy first logical positivism and then logical empiricism. They met in Vienna during the 1920s, and then many of them emigrated to this country during the rise of the Nazis in the 1930s.

During the 1940s and '50s the group was to a considerable extent responsible for the demise of the position that they had constructed, although others contributed. Schools of thought that have an impact as profound as that of logical empiricism do not expire on a certain date, but it is common to cite Carnap's (1936–37) paper as the beginning of the end, and it seems safe to say that the death knell had been rung by the mid-1960s.

The demise of logical empiricism left a void. Although it was clear that empiricism was no longer tenable, it was not clear what to put in its place. That situation has been changing, and the past ten years have seen the formulation of a number of alternatives that seem to provide a middle ground between the excesses of positivism and the excesses that positivism was designed to avoid.

But what of psychology? The success of empirical scientists such as Helmholtz and Binet provided a solid basis for the adoption of Watsonian behaviorism (the psychological counterpart of logical positivism) and the overthrow of Titchnerian introspectionism. Psychoanalysis has always claimed to be empirically based. The 1930s saw a keen rivalry between Hullian and Tolmanian learning theories, and the beginning of the successes of empirical test construction. The 1940s saw the rise of Skinnerian behaviorism as the successor to Watson and the challenger to Hull and Tolman. The publication of Sigmund Koch's masters thesis in the *Psychological Review* in 1941 is often cited as the point at which psychology adopted logical empiricism as not only its dominant, but as its only empirical and methodological position—just a few years after the start of its demise in philosophy. With the ascendancy of behavior modification in the 1950s, the victory of logical empiricism in psychology was complete. Hardly a dissenting voice was to be heard. Ironically, one of the few was that of Sigmund Koch (1977). It was to be another 25 years before psychologists would hear the first faint calls for a return to a consideration of consciousness and for the inclusion of mental events as a legitimate field of study. Recently, the number of papers reflecting discontent with the empiricist position has been rising.

With this background, I will describe (a) the basic features of what was first called logical positivism and then logical empiricism, and (b) the influence of this position on research methodology in psychology. First, some caveats. Logical empiricism was a school of philosophy, not the work of a single individual. No two philosophers agree with each other on all points, and, as I have already indicated, members of the group changed their minds over time, so it is not possible to state *the* position of logical empiricism. It is only possible to state some points that are generally taken to be central to that position. It is similarly impossible to state *the* critique of logical empiricism. There are many; not all are included.

The Meaning Criterion

The program of the logical empiricists was to give a reconstructive account of science with the goal of developing prescriptions that would avoid the scientific errors of the nineteenth century and establish scientific method, rather than religious contemplation or divine guidance, as the source of true knowledge. The touchstone for separating science from religion, phantasy, and other metaphysical issues, and for protecting against useless entities such as humors and ether drift, was the meaning criterion. The attempt to formulate a satisfactory criterion of meaningfulness occupied a leading position on the empiricists' research agenda, and the formulation evolved throughout the life of the program.

At first, a statement was meaningful to the extent that it was directly testable (positivism); this was later relaxed to allow for statements that were at least indirectly confirmable (empiricism). The intent was to avoid statements that were in principle untestable because of their very form, statements that were framed so as to make the evaluation of their truth status impossible. If I assert that my watch runs because of the work of invisible blue devils whose presence can in no way be detected, then, according to the meaning criterion, I have made a statement that is meaningless because of its logical form. It is a pseudo-statement, which may have poetic or pictorial, but not empirical, meaning. The goal of the empiricists, then, was to formulate rules to demarcate scientific (meaningful) statements from nonscientific (meaningless) ones. It follows from the definition that there is no meaningful question that is, in principle, unanswerable. Seemingly unanswerable questions are pseudo-questions: How far is up? What is the meaning of life?

There are several problems with this position. First and foremost, the empiricists were never able to formulate an acceptable line of demarcation. It is now generally acknowledged that it is not possible to write a set of rules that will separate science from nonscience. If the criterion is sufficiently strict to exclude all metaphysical or theological statements, then it also excludes some recognized scientific laws or theories (e.g., all persons are mortal); if it is liberalized to admit the desired scientific theories, then some metaphysical and theological statements are admitted also (Schlagel, 1979). Science is an abstract concept and, as with all such concepts, cannot be defined explicitly, but only implicitly and prototypically.

Second, philosophers today would tend to separate questions of meaningfulness from those of truth value. Statements that are understandable, that is, not garbled or self-contradictory, would be considered meaningful even though it might not be possible to specify any way in which one might determine their truth value. The empiricists' distinction between statements that are scientifically meaningful in contrast to those that have pictorial, poetic, or emotive meaning has been dropped. Although philosophers differ about which statements they consider meaningful, the criteria are something other than simply whether the logical or empirical truth value of the statement can be ascertained.

Hypothetico-Deductive Systems and Operational Definitions

Scientific theories were to be interpreted calculi, which means that they were to be stated in a logically defined system with a minimum number of postulates or axioms from which theorems could be deduced by logical operations specified within the system. Terms in the theory were to be tied to terms in the observation language by means of operational definitions. The latter constituted the interpretation or instantiation of the logical system. The theory was then tested by deducing theorems according to the logical tenets of the theory, translating these logical assertions into observation statements via operational definitions, and then comparing the deductions with empirical observations (Bridgman, 1927, 1945). If the observation statements matched, the theory was said to be confirmed; if they did not, then the theory was said to be disconfirmed.

Much of the empiricists' research program was focused on the logical problems encountered in trying to give an acceptable formulation of operational definitions. Basically, the problem was that a term in the theory was being defined in two ways (Suppe, 1977). On the one hand, it was supposed to be defined solely by its logical relation to other terms in the theory. On the other hand, its meaning or empirical content came from the operational definitions. But if the empirical findings were allowed to contribute to the definition of the term, then it was no longer defined solely by its logical relations; and it was not possible to have two terms, one of which was purely logical and the other purely observational, if the two terms were definitionally linked.

This aspect of the empiricists' program also received a staggering blow with the publication of Gödel's incompleteness theorem in 1931. Essentially, Gödel's theorem states that no logical system that includes the axioms of arithmetic can be both consistent and complete; if the system is consistent (that is, does not contain contradictory statements), then it must contain statements whose truth value cannot be determined. Hence, the observation language will contain statements whose truth value cannot be determined. In other words, Gödel showed that it was logically impossible to have a hypothetico-deductive system of the kind envisioned by the empiricists.

Foundationist Epistemology

A critical aspect of the hypothetico-deductive system was the assumption that there existed a factual basis against which the logically constructed theories could be tested. Given the restriction of intersubjective testability, the empiricists assumed that it was possible to accumulate factual information in a theory-free manner, and that these theory-free observations could be used to test competing theories. In retrospect it seems strange that a philosophical movement developing during the 1920s should have ignored the lessons of introspectionism, which had been rejected precisely because it had shown phenomenological reports to be so tainted by experience as to be useless as a data base. Of course, the members of the Vienna Circle were physicists and philosophers, but how are we to account for the psychologists?

Although it seems clear now that we must acknowledge factual relativity, namely, that what we observe is at least in part determined by the theories we hold, Kuhn's 1962 book, which documented factual impermanence historically, constituted the first effective attack on this premise. Kuhn was followed by Paul

Feyerabend (e.g., 1970), whose witty accounts of the history of science destroyed the claims that scientific progress had been based on an accumulation of objective facts that had been the basis for the acceptance or rejection of scientific theories. Feyerabend has espoused a radical, anarchist epistemology, arguing that facts are accepted for sociopolitical, not rational, reasons. By his account, "anything goes" in trying to gain acceptance of one's theories. The process is an argumentative and political, not a rational or reasoned, one. One should study rhetoric, not logic. I would like to be convinced that he is wrong, but I am not. Even though it may be possible to state rational rules of behavior, history does not support the contention that scientists always follow them, though they may come closer than nonscientists. Logical empiricism provides an example of a position that was accepted as much for psychological, sociological, and political, as for logical, reasons.

To sum up the current position, it is generally acknowledged that facts are not independent of theories, from which it follows that science cannot be an accumulation of facts on the basis of which theories are inductively derived and against which theories are then tested. Rather, theories are invented, often for reasons that are later rejected. If logically consistent, theories are incomplete; and if complete, they are inconsistent. Scientific theories cannot be demarcated from nonscientific ones. Theories are neither true nor false, but have varying degrees of verisimilitude and utility, and are held or believed or accepted for many reasons other than their empirical or factual support.

Phenomenalism (Observationism) and Physicalism

With a few exceptions the positivists grounded their position on an epistemological phenomenalism. The only reality was a sense datum. Ontological questions were metaphysical. Because we have access only to sense data, it was not meaningful to discuss what was beyond that. Given that one can know nothing beyond what one's senses reveal, what check does one have on the veridicality of one's perceptions or statements? Very little. So little, in fact, that the position was open to the charge that it was solipsistic. In addition it was unduly restrictive. So positivism was replaced by empiricism, which was based on a physicalism that allowed for reports of physical objects, subject to the constraint of intersubjective testability. Truth was to be determined by the convergence of observational reports. Meaningfulness demanded that one's statements pertain to objects or events that others could corroborate by making their own observations. In the distinction proposed by MacCorquodale and Meehl (1948), there could be no hypothetical constructs, only intervening variables. Thus, mentalisms were to be avoided.

It is difficult (for me at least) to understand why psychologists, who study the limitations of perceptual processes, including illusions such as the phi phenom-

enon, and who study the nonoptimal properties of human information processing, would want to define reality in terms of "observables." What is one to make
of a magic show, for heaven's sake? Is that really reality? Most scientists would
now agree that science is not, and cannot be, limited to that which is immediately
perceivable; it must include constructs and theories referring to inferred entities,
states, and processes, which provide causal explanations of events.

If the world as we immediately encounter it in experience were self-
explanatory, there would be no . . . problem—everything would be
intelligible and explainable from mere observations. But since in fact
the manifest behavior of phenomena requires explanations in terms of
unobservable entities and processes, such as atoms, minds, neurons,
etc., to supplement the limitations of observation, it is natural to assume
that these entities have some reality. Moreover, it seems quite egocentric
to restrict reality . . . to what is observed, especially as human beings
appeared on the cosmic scene only very recently. (Schlagel, 1979, p.
15)

In psychology there seems to be a growing acceptance of the idea that it makes
sense to assume that, or to act as if, there is a world out there, even if one can't
prove that there is and one can only know about it imperfectly. This amounts to
accepting a realist ontology and a constructivist epistemology (e.g., Leary, 1984;
Manicas & Secord, 1984; Mulaik, 1984). One may argue for a realist ontology
on pragmatic grounds, "for example, that realism makes what we do in science
more intelligible[,] rather than on grounds that we know realism to be true" (Mulaik, 1984). Although the realist position strikes most of us as reasonable, there
are problems in establishing it (e.g., Laudan, 1984).

Explanation

For the empiricists an event could be explained if it could be instantiated as a
particular instance of a general law. Under this covering law model, as it was
called, an event can be considered to be explained only if it can be (or could have
been) predicted. Explanation, for the realist or the structuralist, is not subsump-
tion under a general law; rather, it is the description of the causal structure (or
system) and its boundary conditions at the time of the event. Thus, it is possible
to explain events that it would not have been possible, even in principle, to have
predicted, because systems do not operate under closure. Although the past is
determined, and therefore explainable, the future is not predictable "because the
complexly related structures and systems of the world are constantly being re-
configured" (Manicas & Secord, 1983, p. 403).

There is a fundamental difference here between the empiricists' empirical
laws based on regularities among observable events (e.g., negatively accelerated
learning curves), and structural descriptions of the systems involved (e.g., the

mental processes of the organism). In the logical empiricists' account, the former were explanations of causal relations, whereas in the realists' account "such a 'law' has no explanatory power whatsoever" (Manicas & Secord, 1983, p. 403). In the logical empiricists' account the latter were meaningless and could have no explanatory or causal status, whereas in the realists' account the latter constitute a causal explanation (but see Robinson, 1984, and the rejoinder by Manicas & Secord, 1984).

Causality

Wittgenstein followed Hume in rejecting causality, asserting that each state of affairs is independent of every other state of affairs. "We *cannot* infer the events of the future from those of the present." "Superstition is nothing but belief in the causal nexus" (quoted by Schlagel, 1979). Because causality refers to the relations among real events, it follows from the empiricists' phenomenalism that causality could not be part of a system that recognized only contingent regularities. The world, rather, was represented by phenomenological accounts in the observation language ("the pointer is at 3"), and these accounts were joined by logical connectives such as material implication. Relations, including causal relations, held among propositions, which constituted a representation of reality, not among events, which are ultimately unknowable.

(To those who have been taught that experimental research is superior to observational or correlational research because only experimental research establishes causal relations, this exposition of the logical empiricists' rejection of causality may seem puzzling or incongruous; yet, it is the case that the rationalizations of most experimental methodologists in psychology are at variance with the philosophical position on which they are purportedly based.)

Manicus and Secord (1983) contrasted the phenomenalism of the logical empiricists with realism, under which entities such as atoms and mental states are accorded real status and causal efficacy. Given a certain structure, then, *ceteris paribus*, certain events must occur because that is the nature of the system. The properties of structures are causal properties that exist and operate in the world. The *ceteris paribus* clause is to acknowledge that, with the exception of the universe, there is no closed system (as far as we know), so that any particular event is complexly and multiply determined. Thus, in accounting for a particular event one must know the structure of the entities or systems involved, and, in addition, one must know the state of the system and of the other systems that were impinging on the system at that time. Another way of saying this is that one must know both the structure and the boundary conditions of the system at the time of the event (Meehl, 1977).

If this kind of structural or systems account is given in the context of a constructionist epistemology, there might be more than one causal account of an event, because more than one construction of an event or entity would be possible.

More Recent Positions

Post Empiricism

The demise of logical empiricism left a vacuum that was for a time filled by the logical analysis or *Weltanschauungen* school which held that, given there could be no ultimate justification for knowledge, any knowledge claim was as good as any other. Each of us is entitled to our own world view, and one person's reality is just as valid and real as anyone else's reality. Philosophy was to be descriptive, not prescriptive; its goal was simply to analyze, clarify, and understand. Clearly, this was not a satisfactory position for most psychologists, who wanted a clear demarcation between science and nonscience (and between sense and nonsense), and who, therefore, reacted by clinging to logical empiricism, in spite of its increasingly obvious problems.

In the last ten years there have been a number of attempts to provide alternatives somewhere between the extremes of the logical empiricist and *Weltanschauungen* positions. Realism (Manicas & Secord, 1983, 1984), constructionism (Gergen, 1985), and functionalism (Block, 1980) have all had recent proponents in psychology.

Pancritical Rationalism

Bartley (1984) has provided another alternative, referred to variously as comprehensively critical rationalism or pancritical rationalism. Crediting Popper with the initial insight, Bartley pointed out that all Western philosophies have been authoritarian, in that they have all relied on some ultimate authority as the final justification for knowledge. In the case of the rationalists it was the intellect; in the case of religion it is the word of god; and in the case of the logical empiricists it was sense data. The problem with the empiricists' requirement that all knowledge be justifiable knowledge is that the criterion itself cannot be justified (Weimer, 1979), with the result that logical empiricism ultimately required a leap of faith or commitment that is no different from that of religion. Whereas many religious theoreticians accept faith as the ultimate basis for their religious beliefs, the whole goal of logical empiricism was to do away with such unfounded beliefs in science. Empiricism said, in effect, that you must accept on faith the premise that you must not accept beliefs on faith.

Bartley's solution to the logical empiricists' dilemma was to separate justification and criticism, which have been fused in modern philosophies, and to reject the requirement for justification while retaining a commitment to criticism. However, the commitment to criticism is itself open to criticism; it is not accepted as an act of faith.

The philosophical questions that would have to be asked within such a program would show a striking structural change [from logical empiricism]. The traditional demand for justification . . . would not legitimately arise. And if it arose in fact, the philosopher would have to reply: " . . . I have no guarantees."

If he wanted to be a little clearer, he might elaborate: "Some of the beliefs I hold may in fact be true; but since there are no guarantees or criteria of truth, no ways of definitely deciding, I can never know for sure whether what I believe to be true is in fact so." For such a philosopher, a different question would become important: *How can our intellectual life and institutions be arranged so as to expose our beliefs, conjectures, policies, positions, sources of ideas, traditions, and the like—whether or not they are justifiable—to maximum criticism, . . . ?* (Bartley, 1984, p. 113)

Thus, Bartley abandoned the empiricists' quest for certainty. The effect is to replace the line of demarcation, which no one had been able to formulate, with a gradation from speculative to well-established knowledge, from that which is held tentatively to that which is held with great conviction. Reasonable people may disagree about the reasonableness of a particular knowledge claim, and we cannot know that what seems well established today may not be questioned tomorrow.

Without the burden of the empiricists' demand for justifiable knowledge, one is free, within the framework of pancritical rationalism, to argue for the reasonableness of realism. The advantage of a realist, as opposed to a constructionist, ontology is that the structures of the world will place limitations on the possible findings of scientists, thereby providing the kind of safeguards that the empiricists were seeking via their meaning criterion. The difference is that the limitation is not absolute, because under a constructionist epistemology one may have different representations of the same reality.

When thinking about the empiricists' attempts to develop their system, I am often reminded of the idea, expressed in *The Caine Mutiny* (Wouk, 1951), that the navy was designed by geniuses to be run by idiots. In a sense, that is what the empiricists were trying to do for science. One of the consequences of pancritical rationalism is that there is no longer any rule by which one can determine whether a piece of research is a good one. We cannot be assured that we have produced a worthwhile piece of research just because we followed the procedures in our textbook of experimental methods and performed some statistical significance tests. Nor can we reject a study just because it did not follow such rules. The burden is on each investigator to provide a persuasive presentation of the relevance of his or her findings to the conclusion that he or she wishes to make. That freedom and responsibility seem to frighten some people.

This completes my admittedly incomplete summary of the rise and fall of logical empiricism. I will now turn to a consideration of experimental methodology in psychology. The question is, can the corroboration and refutation of theories by means of the hypothetico-deductive method and null-hypothesis significance testing stand without the supporting structure of logical empiricism? I will argue that they cannot.

The Paradoxes of Theory Testing

The standard description of scientific method in psychology is in terms of the hypothetico-deductive method and null-hypothesis testing procedures. I am first going to summarize that description, and then explain some of the fallacies in it.

We start with a substantive theory, T, from the axioms of which we deduce hypotheses, H_1. We test the theory by testing the hypotheses, using the null-hypothesis procedure. We cast our substantive hypothesis, H_1, in a form that concerns a difference between two groups. In order to make the example accord with current practice, I'll assume that H_1 is directional, I'll call the groups E for experimental and C for control, and I'll make H_1: $E > C$. The hypothesized difference can be the result of some treatment that we administer to the E but not the C group (e.g., a drug or a class), the result of some prior treatment that has been received by E but not C (e.g., daily intake of nicotine), or the result of natural group differences (e.g., sex). In the first case we refer to the procedure as an experiment; in the latter two cases we call the procedure observational or correlational.

In psychology we do not test our hypothesis directly. Instead, we set up another hypothesis, a statistical hypothesis, H_0, of no difference.[1] If we can reject H_0, we will accept H_1, our substantive hypothesis. Otherwise we will accept H_0 and reject H_1. If there were no errors of sampling or measurement, this step would be straightforward, but there are errors of both sampling and measurement, so we strive to protect ourselves against them by adopting a statistical procedure that (we are taught) will make it unlikely that we will reject H_0 (and thereby accept H_1) because of these errors. Our index of "likeliness" is a ratio of variances, σ_B^2/σ_W^2, and by suitable assumptions (often questionable) we assign probabilities to the values of this ratio.

Maximum-Likelihood Considerations

The probability that we obtain in this way, the probability of the datum given that the null hypothesis is true [$p(D|H_0)$] (Pollard & Richardson, 1987), is a number in which no one is interested. Given that it is highly unlikely that the values of any parameter are equal in any two groups, we know that the null hypothesis is false; therefore, we are calculating a hypothetical value based on a premise we do not believe. What we really want to know is the probability that our substantive hypothesis, H_1, is true, given the outcome of the experiment $[p(H_1|D)]$. The number we have calculated tells us nothing about that; its purpose is solely to accept H_0 within a certain range and to reject H_0 outside that range.

Consider the problem from a Bayesian point of view. We want to know which of our hypotheses, H_0 or H_1, is more likely, given the experimental outcome. To do this, we consider the hypothesized distribution for H_0 and H_1 and ask, "Under which distribution is the observed outcome more likely?" When our statistics books present this problem, under the topic of power analyses, they always draw the picture as if there were two competing point estimates with normal distributions around them. There aren't. There is one point estimate, 0, and we can draw the usual normal probability distribution around this value to allow for sampling and measurement errors. But our substantive hypothesis is merely a directional one; it says that every value greater than 0 has equal probability. If we draw this, it is a rectangular distribution going from 0 to infinity in some cases, or to 100% in others.[2] Thus, it is possible to have a value in the rejection region for H_0, even though the probability of that outcome may be greater under H_0 than under H_1. However, using null-hypothesis procedures, we would reject H_0, accept H_1, and thereby confirm our theory, even though the outcome favors H_0. It can be shown that for any probability for H_0, no matter how small, there can be a likelihood ratio favoring H_0 (Edwards, Lindman, & Savage, 1963). Some decision procedure!

Rozeboom (1960), Lykken (1968), and others have delivered stinging attacks against the logic of null-hypothesis procedures. I am not going to reproduce those arguments here, except to note Rozeboom's (1960) observation that psychologists do not accept or reject theories on the basis of null-hypothesis significance tests. Our acceptance of a theory has more to do with the conceptual coherence of the theory, and that, in turn, depends on the extent to which it accounts for generally accepted facts and fits in with our background information and general world view (e.g., Kuhn, 1962; Lakoff, 1987; Murphy & Medin, 1985). I now turn to the logic of null-hypothesis procedures in the context of hypothetico-deductivism.

Meehl's Paradox

The following exposition follows that of Swoyer and Monson (1975), from whom the examples are taken. To protect ourselves against a Type I error, namely rejecting H_0 when it is true, we set the probability of a Type I error at a low value, say .05 or .01. Given fixed μ and σ, Type I errors can be reduced by improving the logical structure of our experiment, by using better experimental techniques,

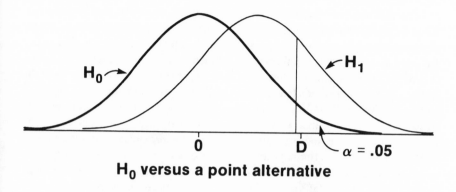

H₀ versus a point alternative

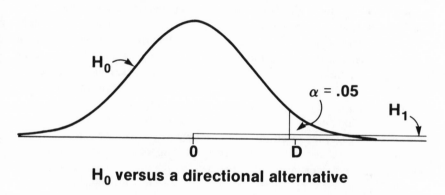

H₀ versus a directional alternative

Figure 1. Null hypothesis versus point hypothesis compared to null hypothesis versus directional hypothesis.

or by increasing the sample size. For example, if the success rates in the two conditions are C = 50% and E = 75%, and if the probability of this difference is .5, then 10 times as many subjects will reduce the probability to .05, and 100 times as many will get it below .001.

But we run two risks. The other, that of accepting H_0 when it is false, is called, reasonably enough, a Type II error. Type II errors can be reduced in the same ways as Type I errors. If we take the example above and assume that $p = .05$ for C = 50% and E = 75%, then with 10 times as many subjects we need only an 8% difference, and with 10,000 times as many subjects only .25% to achieve the same probability level. As N approahces infinity, the difference needed for significance approaches 0. In other words, as precision and power increase, there is a greater range of experimental outcomes that will reject H_0 and confirm H_1.

Let's look at the logic of what we have done. First of all, H_0 is almost certainly false, because it is highly unlikely that the values of any parameter are exactly the same in any two groups, so it is fairly silly to test H_0 in the first place. The only real question is whether our experiment is sufficiently precise to be able to detect whatever difference there is. Given that there is a difference, the probability that it is in the predicted direction is .5, even assuming that the theory has no verisimilitude. Therefore, as the precision and power of our experiment increase, the probability that we will find a significant difference approaches .5. Thus, any theory whatsoever could be confirmed approximately half the time.

Many psychologists find this counterintuitive, so let me put it another way. In the example above, the difference between the two groups could range from -100% to $+100\%$. Half of these possible outcomes are in the predicted direction. Therefore, given a sufficiently powerful experiment we will detect a difference in the predicted direction approximately half the time. Hence we will reject H_0, accept H_1, and by implication confirm T approximately half the time, even if T is false. Hardly a stringent test of T. When one considers that a theory only needs a box score of slightly more successes than failures to be considered a hot topic for further research in order to resolve the controversy, and when one takes into account that there is a bias to publish positive outcomes, it should make one more than a little uneasy about the state of our published experimental research.

Furthermore, if we fail to reject H_0, there is no logical basis for accepting 0 rather than our obtained value. Under the Fisherian framework, which assumes no prior knowledge, the result that we have obtained is the best estimate of the population value. Under a Bayesian framework it might make sense to continue to accept 0 as the best estimate, if we had a very high prior probability for 0; but if we had a high prior probability for 0 (or, more precisely, $p[0|T]$), it would make no sense to conduct the experiment in the first place.

Contrast the above approach with a different one. Instead of simply specifying a difference in a given direction, our theory predicts that the difference will be 25%. We set 95% confidence intervals on 25% and agree to reject H_1 if the observed value falls outside these limits. In contrast to the earlier example, increased precision now results in a smaller and smaller set of values that will lead to acceptance of H_1. If the results are exactly as in the above example, then the 95% confidence bounds for $p = .5$ are from -50% to $+100\%$. With 100 times as many subjects, and with the same sample variances, the interval is from 17.25% to 32.5%, and with 10,000 times as many subjects it is from 24.25% to 25.75%. Thus, as power and precision increase, the theory must survive a much more stringent test in order to survive; whereas in the earlier example as power and precision increased, the theory had to undergo a progressively less stringent test in order to survive.

Meehl (1967) has pointed out that the former null-hypothesis procedure is the one used in psychology, whereas the latter point-prediction procedure is the one used in physics, and he has speculated that the difference in the experimental procedures adopted by the two disciplines may have something to do with their relative rates of scientific progress. "I believe that the almost universal reliance on merely refuting the null hypothesis as the standard method for corroborating substantive theories in the soft areas [of psychology] is a terrible mistake, is basically unsound, poor scientific strategy, and one of the worst things that ever happened in the history of psychology" (Meehl, 1978, p. 817).

To question this traditional experimental approach has often been taken as tantamount to suggesting that psychology should not be scientific, but Meehl is clearly not proposing that psychology should be less scientific. Quite the contrary. He is challenging null-hypothesis procedures on the grounds that they lead to a nonrigorous science. He argues that we must eliminate null-hypothesis procedures in order to make psychology more, not less, scientific.

In an attempt to salvage conventional statistical tests, Serlin and Lapsley (1985) have proposed a modified procedure that involves the use of indecision zones. To claim significance an investigator would have to find an effect significantly greater than some minimum effect size stipulated in advance as constituting practical significance. This procedure would partly resolve the paradox, because increasing precision would not lead to increasing rejection of H_0 if the difference between the groups was less than the stipulated effect size.

Mayo (1985), while agreeing with the critique presented here, has suggested an alternative rationale for conducting conventional statistical tests: "the primary function of statistical tests in science is neither to decide how to behave nor to assign measures of evidential strength to hypotheses. Rather, tests provide a tool for using incomplete data to *learn* about the process that generated it . . . by providing a *standard* for distinguishing differences between observed and hypothesized results due to accidental or trivial errors from those due to systematic or substantively important discrepancies" (p. 493).

I now turn from the logic of null-hypothesis testing procedures to the logic of the hypothetico-deductive system itself.

The Hypothetico-Deductive Method

The Logic of Theory Confirmation

The form of a hypothetico-deductive system, $T \supset H$, and $H \supset D$, is that of material implication, for which there are two valid forms of argument, modus ponens and modus tollens. These are, respectively, $T \supset D$, T, $\therefore$ D, and $T \supset D$, $\overline{D}$ $\therefore$ $\overline{T}$. In words, if the theory is true, then the datum will be observed; and, if the datum is not observed, then the theory is not true. There are also two invalid forms of argument. The one in which we are interested is known as affirming the consequent: $T \supset D$, D, $\therefore$ T. There are at least a couple of ways of seeing the invalidity of this argument. The easiest for me is to think in terms of Venn diagrams. If T then D is equivalent to asserting that T is a subset of D. Thus, whenever we find a T we know that it is also a D, but the reverse does not hold: A D is not necessarily a T. Another way of demonstrating the fallacy is to note that there are numerous theories that could predict the outcome, so that finding the outcome cannot be construed as confirming any one more than another, unless we consider likelihood ratios, $P(D|H_1)/P(D|H_2)$, of the probability of the datum given each of the hypotheses.

Now, consider our experimental methodology once more. When our data fall outside the prescribed confidence bounds and we reject H_0, we are correctly using modus tollens. But when we accept H_1 and interpret this as confirming our theory, we are committing the logical error of affirming the consequent. As a matter of elementary logic, a positive outcome cannot be construed as confirming a theory.

Salmon (1973) has provided entertaining examples of paradoxes that arise when one attempts to construe positive outcomes as confirming a theory. For example, if one asserts that "All swans are white," then it follows that "If something is nonwhite, then it is a nonswan." The latter is confirmed by finding any nonwhite nonswan, such as a raven—or a piece of coral. W. M. Grove (personal communication, November 23, 1988) noted that Meehl has argued that such paradoxes of confirmation result from the attempt to formalize scientific inference by means of the propositional calculus, and suggested that the paradoxes would disappear if one used predicate logic instead.

If all of this has not convinced you to dump hypothetico-deductivism, then maybe the following will. Ignore the fact that a theory can never be confirmed and suppose that it could be. Now, any evidence that confirms T also confirms any conjunction of the theory with another statement, such as "Rorer is a genius." Therefore, every time you obtain a positive outcome and interpret it as confirming your theory you are simultaneously confirming that I am a genius. Doesn't that give you pause?

There are other logical difficulties, and logicians have labored to devise constraints that would prevent the kind of example I have just given. If you want to slug your way through the formalisms, see Glymour (1980), whose article is titled "Hypothetico-Deductivism Is Hopeless," and Rozeboom (1982), whose rejoinder is titled "Let's Dump Hypothetico-Deductivism for the Right Reasons." I know of only one published dissenting response to these articles. Waters (1987) has argued that the problem lies not with hypothetico-deductivism, but rather with classical logic, and that we could salvage hypothetico-deductivism by replacing classical logic with relevance logic. It is not clear why we would want to do that.

Duhemian Dilemmas

Ironically, an important work containing severe problems for the hypothetico-deductive method was published early in this century, before the formation of the Vienna Circle. Written in French, it remained in obscurity until the 1950s. In his 1978 critique, Meehl noted that Duhem (1914/1954) had pointed out that we can never test a theory (T) in isolation. Rather, we test it in conjunction with auxiliary hypotheses (A), and we test it under certain experimental conditions (C), so that the logical situation is really $(T \cdot A \cdot C) \supset D$, i.e., if the theory is true and the auxiliary hypotheses are true and the experimental conditions hold, then we will observe the datum. If we fail to observe the datum, we have not thereby refuted T, but rather the conjunction $(T \cdot A \cdot C)$. We can account for the finding by concluding that any one of them is false, and we all know what happens in psychology: Given a negative outcome, the proponents of a theory tend to argue that the experiment did not constitute an adequate test of the theory either because it made unacceptable auxiliary assumptions, or because there were flaws in the experimental procedures (e.g., the diagnoses were not made correctly, the subjects weren't really anxious, the test was not an adequate measure of the construct, or the outcome can be accounted for by certain demand conditions to which the subjects responded). As Meehl (1978) and others have pointed out, theories in psychology are like old soldiers: They never die; they just fade away.

When we combine Meehl's paradox, that precise methods bias null-hypothesis procedures against the false but approximately correct null hypothesis, and Bayesian analyses showing that null-hypothesis procedures are biased against H_0, with the Duhemian dilemmas, showing that even if negative outcomes are obtained they will not be interpreted as having an impact against the theory, we can see that most research in psychology is irrelevant to testing any theory at all, because there is no way in which the theory will be rejected. If you doubt this, there is an experiment you can try. The next time you propose to do a theory-testing study, ask yourself if you will give up the theory if the results do not come out as you predicted.

Serlin and Lapsley (1985) responded to Meehl by appealing to the theories of Lakatos. Lakatos and Laudan replaced Kuhn's paradigms with research programs and research traditions, respectively (see Gholson & Barker, 1985, for a summary and references). Lakatos identified a research program as a succession of theories with a unifying core commitment, surrounded by a protective belt of auxiliary theories. As long as a research program is expanding, that is, producing new theories, it is appropriate that the core should be protected. In Lakatos's view, it is even possible that a program might have more failures than successes and still be expanding. Thus, Serlin and Lapsley (1985) argued that there was nothing wrong with the fact that theories in psychology are not rejected on the basis of negative research results.

Dar (1987) responded to Serlin and Lapsley (1985) by pointing out that Lakatos had explicitly sided with Meehl in his critique of research programs in psychology, and had expressed the opinion that most new theories in psychology were merely *ad hoc* adjustments to old theories and, therefore, contained no new empirical content. Lakatos described these psychology programs as degenerating rather than expanding.

Lakatos's and Laudan's contributions are important. Research programs or research traditions must be allowed to make some mistakes. With rare exceptions the essence of a theory is not threatened by an individual study. Whether a research program or tradition is expanding or degenerating depends on whether it is making empirical, and Laudan would include conceptual, contributions, and it is often not easy to say whether a program is making such contributions. However, that does not constitute a defense against either Meehl's critique of null-hypothesis testing procedures or Duhemian deficiencies in the hypothetico-deductive method in psychology. In fact, Lakatos's and Laudan's descriptions constitute a further indictment, because they make it clear that decisions concerning the acceptability of a theory are not made simply, or even primarily, on the basis of a theory-testing ritual.

Salmon's Paradoxes

Salmon (1975) began by noting that the term "confirm" is used ambiguously to refer to either an absolute or a relative level of confirmation. If we say that a theory is highly confirmed in the first sense, we are saying that it is part of the established body of knowledge; we believe it to be true with a high degree of certainty. If we say that a theory has been highly confirmed in the second sense, we are saying that its degree of confirmation has been greatly increased by some piece of evidence. An experiment may highly confirm a theory in the second sense without the theory being confirmed in the first sense, and vice versa.

Salmon argued that, in describing the results of experiments, "confirm" is used more frequently in its second or incremental (he called it relevance) sense than in its first or absolute sense. When we say that a test confirmed a hypothesis, we would normally be taken to mean that the result made the hypothesis relatively more certain, rather than that the result made the hypothesis absolutely certain. Following Salmon, I will use the concept of confirmation in its incremental (relevance) sense. Salmon (1975) noted that Carnap had shown that the incremental concept of confirmation has some highly counterintuitive properties.

> Suppose, for instance, that two scientists are interested in the same hypothesis h, and they go off to their separate laboratories to perform tests of that hypothesis. The tests yield two positive results, i and j.

Table 1. Salmon's (1975) Chess Tournament Example

	Local	Out of Town	P(M)
Junior	MWW	MM	3/5
Senior	MM	WWW	2/5
P(M)	3/5	2/5	1/2

Note: M = man; W = woman

Result

c(hle) = 1/2	c(h|e·l) = 3/5	I(l,h,e) = 1/10
	c(h|e·j) = 3/5	I(j,h,e) = 1/10
	c(h|e·l=j) = 1/3	I(l·j,h,e) = −1/6

Each of the evidence statements is positively relevant to h [i.e., each incrementally confirms h] in the presence of common background information e. Each scientist happily reports his positive finding to the other. Can they now safely conclude that the net result of both tests is a confirmation of h? The answer, amazingly, is no! As Carnap has shown, two separate items of evidence can each be positively relevant to a hypothesis, while their conjunction is negative to the very same hypothesis. (Salmon, 1975, p. 14)

Consider the following example from Salmon (1975). Ten chess players participate in a chess tournament. Some of them are local players and some are from out of town; some are junior players and some are seniors; some are men (M) and some are women (W). Their distribution is given in Table 1. Assume that they each have an equal probability of winning. Let e be the background evidence, l the evidence that a local player wins, j the evidence that a junior wins, and h the hypothesis that a man wins. Using c to represent confirmation in the absolute (prior) sense, and I to indicate confirmation in the incremental sense, we have the result shown in the table. "In . . . words, l confirms h and j confirms h but l · j disconfirms h" (Salmon, 1975, p. 15; the notation has been changed). That is, the information that a local player won increases the probability that a man won, and the information that a junior player won increases the probability that a man won, but the information that the winner was both a local and a junior player decreases the probability that a man won.

Similarly, it can be shown that a piece of evidence that confirms each of two hypotheses individually may disconfirm either their conjunction or their disjunction. For those who prefer concrete examples, the latter says that it is possible for a physician to obtain test results that confirm the hypothesis that Jones has viral pneumonia, and that also confirm the hypothesis that Jones has bacterial pneumonia, but that disconfirm the hypothesis that Jones has pneumonia. (An example is given in Salmon, 1975.)

Psychologists are more used to this paradox with respect to correlation. Amount of treatment may be positively related to improvement for women and for men, but negatively related to improvement for men and women combined. For a discussion and analysis of reversal paradoxes, see Messick and van de Geer (1981).

Aside from the entertainment value of such examples, they have devastating significance when combined with the Duhemian dilemmas. Duhem noted that we are always testing a conjunction of hypotheses, and Carnap has shown that a result disconfirming a conjunction can nevertheless confirm each of the conjuncts, in this case the auxiliary hypotheses and the hypothesis of interest, and that it is also possible for a positively confirming test result to disconfirm each of the hypotheses separately. Thus, there is no way to get from our experimental result to a statement about the confirmation of the hypotheses of interest. Salmon (1975) observes, "Carnap has provided a number of examples that . . . seem to make a shambles of confirmation; why do they not also make a shambles of science itself?" (p. 27). On the basis of further analyses he concludes, "Recognition of the basic inadequacy of the hypothetico-deductive schema does no violence to the logic of science; it only shows that the methods of science are more complex than this oversimplified schema" (p. 35). His further conclusion is that some sort of Bayesian formulation is required.

Think Bayesian!

In our search for knowledge we operate on the basis of hunches or conjectures. Call them theories, if you will. Within a theory-testing paradigm, the goal of a research program is to determine the probability that one's theory is true, or, alternatively, the probability one is willing to assign to its being true. Whatever one's initial probability, Bayes's Theorem tells us how to revise it on the basis of the experimental result. If T stands for theory and D stands for data, then a simple form of Bayes's Theorem is $P(T|D) = P(D|T)P(T)/P(D)$. Under the hypothetico-deductive model $(PD|T) = 1$, so the equation reduces to $P(T|D) = P(T)/P(D)$. However, in psychology we know that we never have hypotheses that are deduced from theories—loosely reasoned would be the most charitable description that most of them deserve—so $P(D|T) < 1$. One of the advantages of Bayes's Theorem is that it gives us a way of taking this fact into account.

Note that Bayes's Theorem gives us a way of explicating Meehl's paradox in rather straightforward fashion. If our prediction is simply that two things differ in a given direction, then P(D) is large, approaching .5 with exemplary experimental rigor. If, on the other hand, the evidence is unlikely in the absence of the theory, as when we have made a point prediction such as "The score will be 104," or "The difference will be -3," then the denominator will be small and we will get a nice boost in our posterior probability if we achieve the predicted result. We can also see why setting confidence intervals (104 ± 7 or $-3 \pm .2$) is a big improvement over simply making a directional hypothesis, but not as good as a point prediction. Predicting an ordinal result among several variables is similarly a much stronger procedure than simply predicting differences. The general principle is to make the denominator, P(D), as small as possible. This allows us to see quite simply and directly what is wrong with much psychological research. When a theory does not make any novel predictions, but only purports to explain what we already know (e.g., a *post hoc* explanation of a previous experimental finding), then P(D) approaches P(D|T), so the net boost that a positive outcome can give to P(T) is negligible. To put it another way, if the evidence was expected, it can hardly give much support to the theory under which it was expected.

Serious questions can be raised concerning the extent to which evidence can make any theory more probable in the abstract. What evidence may be able to do is to make one theory more likely than another (Edwards, 1965). Likelihood ratios, based on Bayes's Theorem, tell us how to adjust our initial beliefs concerning the relative likelihood of the two theories. Thus, if the journals would publish likelihood ratios instead of probability levels, then each reader would be able to make appropriate adjustments in his or her prior beliefs.

Edwards, Lindman, and Savage (1963), Fischhoff and Beyth-Marom (1983), Overall (1969), and Pitz (1978, 1980) have all described procedures for testing hypotheses within a Bayesian framework. These Bayesian procedures would make us think about our initial beliefs and the impact of our data on those beliefs, rather than about the probability of our outcome under a hypothesis, H_0, that we know to be false.

If we are willing to abandon the theory-testing paradigm, then we are probably more interested in Bayes's Theorem in its continuous form than in its discrete form. In this form we get a better description of the process of constant revision that characterizes much scientific research. Suppose we carry out an investigation in which our initial estimate (hypothesis, if you will) of the outcome is 7, and we obtain a value of 12. What should we do now? If our initial belief was a strong one, that is, if our probability was all packed into a narrow range around 7, say 7 ± 2, and if the data from the experiment were not very strong, that is, if the distribution has only a slight peak at 12 and a wide or diffuse dispersion, then we might revise our initial estimate only a little bit, say to 8 or 8.5. On the other hand, if our initial estimate was pretty much a shot in the dark, that is, our probability was quite diffuse, and the results of the experiment were strong, that is, packed tightly in a narrow distribution around 12, then we might shift our estimate most of the way to 12. The entire range of intermediate cases is possible.

I am arguing that we should give up the notion of theory testing in favor of successive revision, and that even if we were to do nothing more than to follow the informal kind of procedure I have described, we would be many steps ahead of our present pseudo-rigorous null-hypothesis theory-testing procedures. Formal Bayesian analyses would provide more precision.

Objections to using Bayes's Theorem have usually centered on assigning values to P(T), on the grounds that the same outcome can lead two investigators to different conclusions—one to accept and one to reject the theory—if they started with radically different priors for P(T). First, we should note that this objection is based on the overly simplistic notion, carried over from the hypothetico-deductive model, that theories are accepted or rejected, rather than held with some degree of belief. Given the latter, more appropriate formulation, it has been shown that the evidence will rather quickly constrain any two investigators to come to the same conclusion, no matter how divergent their initial views, if they follow Bayes's Theorem (e.g., Edwards, Lindman, & Savage, 1963). The problem, as psychological research has shown, is that people do not follow Bayes's Theorem, in that they are not nearly as constrained by the data as they should be—a case of "my mind's made up; don't confuse me with facts."

Second, we should note that scientists do start with different views. Far from being a shortcoming, it is an advantage of Bayesian analysis that it allows us to take these different prior probabilities into account. Differences in initial probabilities explain how reviewers can come to different conclusions conerning the same body of evidence. For example, those who for social or ideological reasons adopt a strong hypothesis of equality of intelligence for all racial groups will require strong evidence for any value other than 0 as the difference between two groups. A geneticist who observes that there is some difference on almost any attribute for groups whose gene pools are at least partially segregated would put a much lower prior probability on 0, and would, therefore, be more swayed by data suggesting a value other than 0. There are additional factors, including the evaluation of the evidence, that are relevant here (e.g., Fischhoff & Beyth-Marom, 1983), but the point is that Bayes's Theorem gives us a way of describing and understanding at least some of the bases for differences in interpretations of the same data.[3]

Let's evaluate all this by checking it against what must be considered one of the most famous experiments of this century, the first test of the special theory of relativity. It was widely believed at the time that light traveled in a straight line. The special theory predicted that light might travel in other than a straight line, specifically, that its course could be changed by a gravitational field. The theory, therefore, predicted that stars would appear to be displaced when viewed in such a way that light rays from the stars would have to pass very close to the sun. Observers noted the apparent position of several stars during an eclipse of the sun. Although there was variation in their reports, it was agreed that the results indicated that there had been an apparent deflection in the position of the stars. Note that this experiment meets the criteria that I have set forth. Two theories made differing predictions. The predicted outcome had low prior probability, because it was strongly believed that light would not bend. Thus, although the theory was given a low prior probability, it was able to gain credibility almost instantly.

Now let's see how this experiment would be evaluated in psychology. First, it should be noted that it would not even be accepted as an experiment, because no subjects or objects were randomly assigned to conditions; it would be pejoratively described as "merely observational." Second, because it was merely observational, it would be claimed that no causal inferences could be made on the basis of the results. Third, no statistics were done to assign probability values to the data. And fourth, there were no controls on the demand conditions for the observers who were not blind to the significance of their observations. Clearly not a publishable piece of research. And yet this is the experiment that probably changed our thinking more radically than any other in this century.

More recently the theory of the double helix was accepted because it provided conceptual coherence and understanding by describing a structure that explained known phenomena, not because it lead to hypotheses that were confirmed at some level of statistical probability, or because it stated a law from which particular instances could be deduced.

Summary

Logical empiricism was a complete philosophy of science, an elegant system including ontological, epistemological, and methodological positions. Ontological questions were metaphysical. First phenomenalism (verifiability) and then physicalism (intersubjective testability) provided the epistemological basis. Theories were to be tested, and explanations were to be provided, by means of the hypothetico-deductive method.

Psychologists adopted the epistemology and the methodology, but not the ontology, and added null-hypothesis testing procedures. Previous critiques, which have focused on one or another of these elements, have not had much impact in psychology. The critiques of the epistemology and the methodology have appeared in the philosophical literature and are not widely known to psychologists. To the extent that they are known, they may have had little impact because they failed to provide alternatives. The critiques of null-hypothesis testing procedures, which have appeared in the psychological literature, may have had little impact because psychologists still believe that science progresses by testing theories, and they do not know any other way to do that.

I have attempted to increase the impact of these critiques by assembling them in one place to show that the whole system is flawed, and by offering alternatives that better describe the actual practice of science.

Pragmatism offers a reasonable basis for adopting an ontological realism, a position that I believe is implicitly held by most scientists. Pancritical rationalism, by abandoning the impossible search for certainty, allows for degrees of knowledge and belief, in accord with the subjective experience of most psychologists, while simultaneously maintaining a commitment to the critical perspective that distinguishes science from religion. We all know that theories are not accepted or abandoned in toto on the basis of critical tests. They are modified and developed, and are held, perhaps with little conviction, until a more compelling theory is presented. Bayesian procedures provide a means for making these adjustments and for describing our changing degrees of belief.

Ten specific points and recommendations follow:

1. No one has yet been able to formulate a generally acceptable line of demarcation between science and nonscience. If you are looking for a rule to tell you if something is scientific, welcome to the company of Ahab and Demosthenes.

2. There are viable alternatives to logical postivism, which has been shown to be untenable. Pancritical rationalism is one of them.

3. Concepts cannot be operationalized. It is in the nature of hypothetical constructs that they have no explicit definition and no infallible indicator (MacCorquodale & Meehl, 1948).

4. Hypothetico-deductivism *is* hopeless. Lakatosian and Laudanian formulations provide more helpful ways of conceptualizing research programs.

5. Null-hypothesis significance testing is not *the* method of science. It's not even a very good method. We should stop teaching it, and we should stop reporting meaningless and misleading probability levels in our journals.

6. We do not explain a phenomenon by showing that it can be predicted as a special instance of a general law. We explain it by describing the structure of the system of which it is a part. There is no statistical test for that.

7. A causal explanation of a particular event combines a description of the system with a description of the boundary conditions of the system at the time of the event. Controlled experiments have no privileged status in providing information relevant to providing a causal explanation of an event.

8. Theories are not accepted or rejected, they are held with differing degrees of belief.

9. Psychological research does not test theories. If we would abandon the pretense of testing theories, then our journal articles could report our best estimate of the magnitude of the effect being studied. The determination of whether that effect is significant depends on pragmatic and theoretical, not statistical, considerations.

10. Bayesian formulations provide a more helpful way of describing and thinking about research methodology.

Notes

1. I am using the designation null hypothesis to refer to a hypothesis of zero effect. Some authors (e.g., Fowler, 1985; Gravetter & Wallnau, 1985) have used the designation null hypothesis to refer to a directional hypothesis as well as a hypothesis of no difference, e.g., H_0: $\mu \leq 0$; H_1: $\mu > 0$. Others (e.g., Fowler, 1985) have used the designation null hypothesis to refer to nonzero effects. The logic of the argument is unchanged in these cases.

2. When I present this, a common reaction is, "We don't really mean that; we just don't bother to specify H_1 more precisely." I agree. The procedure we teach and claim to use doesn't say what we mean.

3. *No* methodology or epistemology is without logical problems. It is possible to construct examples that pose serious difficulties for the Bayesian, or any other, position. Such problems are beyond the scope of this paper.

References

Bartley, W. W., III. (1984). *The retreat to commitment* (2nd ed.). New York, NY: Knopf.

Block, N., (Ed.). (1980). *Readings in philosophy of psychology.* Vols. 1, 2. Cambridge, MA: Harvard University Press.

Bridgman, P. W. (1927). *The logic of modern physics.* New York, NY: Macmillan.

Bridgman, P. W. (1945). Some general principles of operational values. *Psychological Review, 52,* 246–249.

Carnap, R. (1936, 1937). Testability and meaning. *Philosophy of Science, 3,* 419–471 and *4,* 1–40.

Dar, R. (1987). Another look at Meehl, Lakatos, and the scientific practices of psychologists. *American Psychologist, 42,* 145–151.

Duhem, P. (1954). *The aim and structure of physical theory* (2nd ed.), (P. P. Wiener, Trans.). Princeton, NJ: Princeton University. (Original work published 1914.)

Edwards, W. (1965). A tactical note on the relation between scientific and statistical hypotheses. *Psychological Bulletin, 63,* 400–402.

Edwards, W., Lindman, H., & Savage, L. J. (1963). Bayesian statistical inference for psychological research. *Psychological Review, 70,* 193–242.

Feyerabend, P. K. (1970). Against method: Outline of an anarchistic theory of knowledge. In M. Radner & S. Winokur (Eds.), *Minnesota studies in the philosophy of science: Vol. IV. Analyses of theories and methods of physics and psychology.* Minneapolis: University of Minnesota Press.

Fischhoff, B., & Beyth-Marom, R. (1983). Hypothesis evaluation from a Bayesian perspective. *Psychological Review, 90,* 239–260.

Fowler, R. L. (1985). Testing for substantive significance in applied research by specifying nonzero effect null hypotheses. *Journal of Applied Psychology, 70,* 215–218.

Frege, G. (1950). *The foundations of arithmetic* (J. L. Austin, Trans.). New York, NY: Philosophical Library. (Original work published 1884.)

Gergen, K. J. (1985). The social constructionist movement in modern psychology. *American Psychologist, 40*, 266–275.

Gholson, B., & Barker, P. (1985). Kuhn, Lakatos, and Laudan: Applications in the history of physics and psychology. *American Psychologist, 40*, 755–769.

Glymour, C. (1980). Hypothetico-deductivism is hopeless. *Philosophy of Science, 47*, 322–325.

Gödel, K. (1962). *On formally undecidable propositions.* New York, NY: Basic Books. (Original work published 1931.)

Gravetter, F. J., & Wallnau, L. B. (1985). *Statistics for the behavioral sciences.* St. Paul, MN: West Publishing Co.

Koch, S. (1941a). The logical character of the motivation concept. I. *Psychological Review, 48*, 15–38.

Koch, S. (1941b). The logical character of the motivation concept. II. *Psychological Review, 48*, 127–154.

Koch, S. (1977, August). *Vagrant confessions of an asystematic psychologist: An intellectual autobiography.* Paper presented at the meeting of the American Psychological Association, San Francisco, CA.

Kuhn, T. W. (1962). *The structure of scientific revolutions.* Chicago: University of Chicago Press.

Lakoff, G. (1987). *Women, fire, and dangerous things: What categories reveal about the mind.* Chicago, IL: University of Chicago Press.

Laudan, L. (1984). Discussion: Realism without the real. *Philosophy of Science, 51*, 156–162.

Leary, D. L. (1984). Philosophy, psychology, and reality. *American Psychologist, 39*, 917–919.

Lykken, D. T. (1968). Statistical significance in psychological research. *Psychological Bulletin, 70*, 151–159.

MacCorquodale, K., & Meehl, P. E. (1948). On a distinction between hypothetical constructs and intervening variables. *Psychological Review, 55*, 95–107.

Manicas, P. T., & Secord, P. F. (1983). Implications for psychology of the new philosophy of science. *American Psychologist, 38*, 339–413.

Manicas, P. T., & Second, P. R. (1984). Implications for psychology: Reply to comments. *American Psychologist, 39*, 922–926.

Mayo, D. G. (1985). Behavioristic, evidentialist, and learning models of statistical testing. *Philosophy of Science, 52*, 493–516.

Meehl, P. E. (1967). Theory testing in psychology and physics: A methodological paradox. *Philosophy of Science, 34*, 103–115.

Meehl, P. E. (1977). Specific etiology and other forms of strong influence: some quantitative meanings. *The Journal of Medicine and Philosophy, 2*, 33–53.

Meehl, P. E. (1978). Theoretical risks and tabular asterisks: Sir Karl, Sir Ronald, and the slow progress of soft psychology. *Journal of Consulting and Clinical Psychology, 46*, 806–834.

Messick, D. M., & van de Geer, J. P. (1981). A reversal paradox. *Psychological Bulletin, 90*, 582–593.

Mulaik, S. A. (1984). Realism, pragmatism, and the implications of the new philosophy of science for psychology. *American Psychologist, 39*, 919–920.

Murphy, G. L., & Medin, D. L. (1985). The role of theories in conceptual coherence. *Psychological Review, 92*, 289–316.

Overall, J. E. (1969). Classical statistical hypothesis testing within the context of Bayesian theory. *Psychological Bulletin, 71*, 285–292.

Pitz, G. F. (1978). Hypothesis testing and the comparison of imprecise hypotheses. *Psychological Bulletin, 85*, 794–809.

Pitz, G. F. (1980). Using likelihood ratios to test imprecise hypotheses. *Psychological Bulletin, 87*, 575–577.

Polkinghorne, D. (1983). *Methodology for the human sciences: Systems of inquiry.* Albany, NY: State University of New York Press.

Pollard P., & Richardson, J. T. E. (1987). On the probability of making type I errors. *Psychological Bulletin, 102,* 159–163.

Robinson, D. N. (1984). The new philosophy of science: A reply to Manicas and Secord. *American Psychologist, 39,* 920–921.

Rozeboom, W. W. (1960). The fallacy of the null-hypothesis significance test. *Psychological Bulletin, 67,* 416–428.

Rozeboom, W. W. (1982). Let's dump hypothetico-deductivism for the right reasons. *Philosophy of Science, 49,* 637–647.

Salmon, W. C. (1973). Confirmation. *Scientific American, 228*(5), 75–83.

Salmon, W. C. (1975). Confirmation and relevance. In G. Maxwell & R. H. Anderson (Eds.), *Minnesota studies in the philosophy of science: Vol. VI: Induction, probability, and confirmation* (3–36). Minneapolis, MN: University of Minnesota Press.

Schlagel, R. H. (1979, September). *Revolution in the philosophy of science: Implications for method and theory in psychology.* Paper presented at the meeting of the American Psychological Association, New York.

Serlin, R. C., & Lapsley, D. K. (1985). Rationality in psychologyical research: The good-enough principle. *American Psychologist, 40,* 73–83.

Suppe, F. (1977). *The structure of scientific theories* (2nd ed.). Urbana, IL: University of Illinois Press.

Swoyer, C., & Monson, T. C. (1975). Theory confirmation in psychology. *Philosophy of Science, 42,* 487–502.

Waters, C. K. (1987). Relevance logic brings hope to hypothetico-deductivism. *Philosophy of Science, 54,* 453–464.

Weimer, W. B. (1979). *Notes on the methodology of scientific research.* Hillsdale, NJ: Erlbaum.

Whitehead, A. N., & Russell, B. (1913). *Principia Mathematica* 3 vol. Cambridge: Cambridge University Press.

Wouk, H. (1951). *The Caine mutiny.* Garden City, NY: Doubleday.

Philosophy

Gods and Atoms:
Comments on the Problem of Reality
Paul Feyerabend

In his important and influential paper "Empiricism, Semantics and Ontology" Rudolf Carnap[1] ties the use of abstract entities to linguistic frameworks and distinguishes between external questions, i.e., questions about the choice of a framework, and internal questions, i.e., questions concerning the truth and falsehood of the statements which are formulated within a certain framework. External questions, he says, are decided in a practical way, by testing the efficiency of a given framework. Internal questions are either questions of logic or of empirical accuracy. Quine[2] "espouse[s] a more thorough pragmatism." By this he means that external and internal questions are to be treated in the same way and that ontological questions "are on a par with questions of natural science." Both Quine and Carnap assume that frameworks are well defined, that the act of accepting them can be "rationalised" in the sense that it becomes a conscious decision based on clearly formulated principles and that existence is always understood to be framework dependent.

Knowledge claims, scientific knowledge claims included, violate these three assumptions. Entities which today are assigned to different traditions often merged (cf. the role of a continually active creator-god in Newton's universe), entities disappeared from neglect, not from a rational calculation of efficiencies, and realists make their existence independent of what people think about them. In the present paper I shall examine this last assumption in somewhat greater detail.

It is now generally admitted that modern science owes its existence and its features to specific and highly idiosyncratic historical circumstances. The Greeks had the mathematics and the intelligence to develop the theoretical views that arose in the sixteenth and seventeenth centuries — yet they failed to do so. "Chinese Civilization had been much more effective than the European in finding out about Nature and using natural knowledge for the benefit of mankind for fourteen centuries or so before the scientific revolution" and yet this revolution occurred in "backward" Europe.[3] It needed a special mental attitude inserted into a particular social structure combined with a unique sequence of accidents to divine, formulate, check, and establish basic physical and cosmological laws.[4]

Scientific realists assume that what *was found* in this idiosyncratic and culture-dependent way (and is, therefore, formulated and explained in idiosyncratic and culture-dependent terms) *exists* independently of the circumstances of its discovery: there were nuclei long before the scintillation screen and mass spectroscopy; they obeyed the laws of quantum theory long before those laws were written down and they will continue to do so when the last human being has disappeared from earth: we can cut the way from the result without losing the result. I shall call this assumption the separability assumption (SA for short).

The separability assumption is plausible. The behavior of things discovered seems indeed to be independent of the vagaries of the process of discovery. The discovery of America was the result of political machinations set in motion by false beliefs and erroneous estimates, and it was misread by the great Columbus himself—but this did not affect the properties of the American continent. On the other hand, the assumption is also part of nonscientific traditions. According to Greek common sense (sixth and fifth centuries B.C.) Homer and Hesiod did not create the gods, they merely enumerated them and described their properties. The gods had existed before and they were supposed to live on, independently of human wishes and mistakes.[5] The Greeks, too, thought they could cut the way from the result without losing the result. Does it follow that our world contains particles and fields side by side with demons and gods?

It does not, scientific realists say, because gods do not fit into a scientific world view.[6] But if the entities postulated by a scientific world view can be assumed to exist independently of it, then why not gods? True, few people now believe in gods and those who do only rarely offer acceptable reasons—but the assumption was that existence and belief are different things and that a new Dark Age for science would not obliterate atoms. Why should gods—whose Dark Age is now—be treated differently?

They must be treated differently, the champions of a scientific world view reply, because the belief in gods did not just disappear; it was removed by argument. Entities postulated by such beliefs cannot be said to exist separately. They are illusions, or "projections"; they have no significance outside the projecting mechanism.

But the Greek gods were not "removed by argument." The opponents of popular beliefs about the gods never offered reasons which, using commonly held assumptions, showed the inadequacy of the beliefs.[7] What we do have is a gradual social change leading to a new attitude, new standards, and new ways of looking at the world: history, not argument, undermined the gods.[8] And history cannot make things disappear, at least not according to the separability assumption. This assumption still forces us to admit the existence of the Homeric gods.

It does not so force us, scientific realists assert, because the belief in gods, though perhaps not removed by reason, never was a reasonable belief. Only entities postulated by reasonable beliefs can be separated from their history. I shall call this the modified separability assumption (MSA).

Now it is plausible to assume that the science of today will not look very reasonable to a scientist of the future. Those who believe in progress through qualitative changes certainly hold such a view. Speaking "objectively," i.e., preferring the better account to the worse and postulating, with the progressivists, that science can only improve, we ought to admit that present-day physics is unreasonable and not a good basis for ontological inferences: gods do not exist—but atoms do not exist either.

The point can be made in a different way, and without any appeal to progress. Making reasonability a measure of separable existence means assuming that we know reasonable procedures which, given any entity, can establish its existence or show it to be a chimera. Scientific practice does not agree with this assumption. Birds are said to exist because we can see them, catch them, hold them in our hands. The procedure is useless in the case of alpha-particles and the criteria used for identifying alpha-particles do not help us with distant galaxies or with the neutrino. Quarks, for a time, were a doubtful matter partly because the experimental evidence was controversial (and note that "being controversial" here means different things for different kinds of experiment), partly because new criteria were needed for entities allegedly incapable of existing in isolation ("confinement").[9] We can measure temperature with a thermometer—but this does not get us very far. The temperature in the center of the sun cannot be measured with any known instrument, and the temperature in interstellar space was not even defined before the arrival of the second law of thermodynamics. Similarly, the criteria of acceptability for beliefs change with time, situation, and the nature of the beliefs. To say that gods do not exist because they cannot be found by experiment is, therefore, as foolish as the remark, made by some nineteenth-century physicists and chemists, that atoms do not exist because they cannot be seen. However, postulating history-independent atoms because this increases testability[10] means introducing special concepts, not special things. Result: neither SA nor MSA can make us accept atoms but deny gods.[11] *Scientific entities* (and, for that matter, all entities) *are projections and thus tied to the theory, the ideology, the culture that postulates and projects them.* The assertion that some things are independent of research, or history, *belongs to special projecting mechanisms* that "objectivize" their ontology: it is not valid outside the historical stage that contains the mechanisms.

With this I come to the last and apparently most decisive argument for atoms and against gods. Gods—and this now means the Homeric gods as well as the omnipotent creator-god of Christianity—were not only moral, but also physical powers. They made thunderstorms, earthquakes, floods; they broke the laws of nature to produce miracles; they could raise the sea and stop the sun in its course. But such events are now either rejected or accounted for by physical causes, and remaining lacunae are being swiftly closed by research. Thus projecting the theoretical entities of science, we remove gods from their position of power and, as the more fundamental entities obey time-invariant laws, show that they never existed.

This apparently quite powerful argument assumes that the existence of scientific models for a process eliminates all other accounts. However, there are many scientists who do not share this assumption. Neurophysiology provides very detailed models for mental processes; yet the mind-body problem is being kept alive, both by scientists and by scientifically inclined philosophers. Some scientists even demand that we "put[] mind and consciousness in the driver's seat"[12] i.e., that we return to them the power they had before the rise of a materialistically inclined psychology. There is no reason why gods whose numinous aspects always resisted reduction should be treated differently, and, indeed, there are and always were scientists who see no conflict between their theories and the idea of a divinely guided universe.

Furthermore, the argument uses scientific facts and theories to remove nonscientific projections. Now science has this power of removal only if: (a) scientific projections are proper projections, i.e., can be separated from the process of projecting; (b) it can offer a coherent point of view, not merely a patchwork of incoherent guesses; and (c) this point of view is more acceptable than any alternative (i.e., nonscientific) story. But science as we know it does not satisfy any one of these conditions.

To start with, many entities of modern science depend on individual or collective actions by special projectors (complementarity): condition (a) is violated.[13] Even before that science permitted condition-independent projections only if its actual shape (which was a patchwork of partly incompatible, partly incomplete laws, models, theories, heuristic guesses, and experiments) was replaced by a smooth ideology. The idea that some disciplines can be "reduced" to others and that all major scientific results can "in principle" be obtained from elementary particle physics is part of this ideology, not independent support for it.[14] It can be, and frequently was saved by redefining subjects until they fit the reductionist ideology: biology *is* molecular biology. One admits the limitations of a procedure (botany, for example, does not belong to a biology defined in this way) but defuses the lacunae by calling them "unscientific." The "successes" (discovery of the structure of DNA, for example, and the ensuing explosion of molecular biology) that seem to support the move are not really decisive. They are a result of having followed a "path of least resistance": but who nowadays would assume that the world, i.e., the totality of "objective" things and processes, was built for the convenience of the experimenters?[15] Some decisive areas of divine activity such as thunderstorms and earthquakes are still far from providing the order which would give a semblance of plausibility to the (metaphysical) assertion that every process in the heavens and on earth is guided by the same small number of basic laws. There are promises, hopes, bald-faced claims—but there are no concrete results. Moreover, let us not forget that even basic physics, the alleged root of all reductions, is still divided into at least two principal domains, the world of the very large, tamed by Einstein's general relativity, and the quantum world, which itself is not yet completely united. "Nature likes to be compartmentalised" wrote Dyson,[16] describing this situation. "Subjective" elements such as feelings and sensations which form a further "compartment" are excluded from the natural sciences though they play a role in their acquisition and control. This means that the (unsolved) mind-body problem affects the very foundation of scientific research and that ethical difficulties such as the problem of the possible inhumanity of a relentless search for the truth are not even considered. I conclude that science has large lacunae, that its unity and comprehensiveness is a metaphysical hypothesis, not a fact, and that those of its projections that work come from isolated areas, have, therefore, only local relevance, and certainly not the destructive power habitually given to them.

Calling the unity of science a metaphysical hypothesis is not an objection against it—a science without metaphysics could not possibly bear fruit. This is shown by many instances of scientific practice. No interesting theory has ever had a clean bill of health. It is born refuted, beset by logical and mathematical difficulties which can last for centuries (example: the classical problem of planetary stability which Newton tried to solve by divine intervention, which Laplace solved by series developments that were later shown to be divergent so that an entirely new approach had to be invented) and often worse off, empirically, than less adventurous alternatives. Scientists in such circumstances try to look beyond experiments and the logical shape of a certain idea, i.e., they engage in metaphysics. Metaphysics is not the problem. The problem is if the idea that all scientific results form a unity which reflects objective properties of a research-independent world is a good metaphysical hypothesis. I don't think it is.

My reason is very simple. The fact that the experimental approach has led to certain results does not guarantee that these results are valid independently of it. If one considers the accidental and history-bound character of the ideas and the instruments that produce the results, this would be a rather absurd assumption to make. It is an accident that we are now in the middle of something called "Western Civilization"—and this accident is supposed to be a measure of reality? Besides, some of the most advanced theories teach us that decisive features of the world depend on the approach taken. Finally, the fact that we are dealing with historical accidents and the quantum analogy teaches us that entities despised by modern materialists (the Greek gods, the God of Christianity) played an important role in the lives of generations of people; regarding them as nonexistent means regarding these lives as inferior to the lives of a modern intellectual—not an attractive social attitude. Thus, the historicity of knowledge, the analogy of quantum theory and tolerance speak against the metaphysical hypothesis I mentioned above. What hypothesis shall we use in its stead?

Relativists suggest that we should relate all judgments concerning reality and existence to a socially given framework. This sounds attractive and at some time also sounded attractive to me. But there is a severe disadvantage: people can argue across frameworks and can argue their way out of frameworks. Understanding may be framework-bound for a time, but it is capable of building bridges into what a strict relativist would have to regard as sheer nonsense. There is another disadvantage: not all frameworks give pleasure to those who live in them (pleasure—in their terms). It needs a quite specific arrangement to lead to a viable culture, viable again meant in terms of those who live that way. Speaking evolutionary language we may say that some mutations survive while others struggle for a while and then disappear. Not that I regard survival as an absolute value—but the balance of joy and suffering certainly is a value found in many cultures. So we have not simply different *approaches*, we have different *responses* as well, which means we have a reality that I shall call Being that responds in different ways to different approaches. Approached with stern thoughts, mathematics, and increasing instrumentation, Being reacts with a material universe of great variety. Many defenders of science identify this universe, this "manifest reality" as I shall call it, with Being itself. This is a mistake which leads to the paradoxes created by the historicity of knowledge. Approached in a different way, Being reacts not only with divine beings but with a form of matter that is a seat of spiritual energies, animals that can change into gods and back and so on. Plutarch reports that one fine day the cry was heard "The great Pan is dead"—and dead he was because a new manifest reality, i.e., a new type of interaction between Being and those of its parts that had achieved a certain independence (forms of life, individuals, etc.) was about to arise. Being itself is unknowable—why? Because knowing it would enable us to predict history, which I do not think we can do. All we can say is that Being can become spiritual, and extremely material, that it is deus sive natura, only without the Spinozean conceptual constipation.

The way suggested by Carnap and Quine pays attention to the manner in which social conditions and individual efforts jointly determine the nature of our projections but without taking the responses of Being into account. We now say that scientists, being embedded in constantly changing social surroundings, used ideas and physical equipment to *manufacture* first, metaphysical atoms, then crude physical atoms, then complex systems of elementary particles out of material lacking all these features. Scientists, according to this account, are sculptors of reality—but sculptors in a rather unusual sense. They do not merely *act causally* upon physical systems (though they do that too, and rather energetically sometimes), they also *create semantic conditions* engendering strong inferences from known effects to novel projections and, conversely, from the projections to testable effects. We have here a dichotomy of descriptions similar to the one Bohr introduced in his analysis of the case of Einstein, Podolsky, and Rosen.[17] Every culture "posits" or "constitutes" entities that fit its beliefs, needs, expectations. The two principles with which I started my note (SA and MSA) belong to special constructions; they are not conditions (to be) satisfied by all constructions and they certainly are not a sound basis for epistemology. Altogether the dichotomy subjective/objective and the corresponding dichotomy between descriptions and constructions turn out to be much too naïve and simpleminded to guide our ideas about the nature and the implications of knowledge claims. And with this the sciences cease to be the only disciplines to be consulted in ontological matters.[18]

This does not mean that we can do without scientific know-how. We cannot. Our world is loaded with the material, intellectual, and ideological products of science and science-based technologies. We need to know how to deal with them, which means we still need scientists, engineers, scientifically inclined philosophers, sociologists — and so on. But the advice of these experts is much less grounded in "nature" than is generally assumed. It is not, therefore, easier to criticize — ideas, firmly believed, are harder than the hardest material. Far from merely stating what is already there, they create conditions of existence and a life adapted to these conditions. But the world they introduce is not a static system populated by thinking (and publishing) ants who, crawling all over its crevices, gradually discover its features without affecting them in any way. It is a dynamical and multifaceted Being which influences and reflects the activity of its explorers. It was once full of gods; it then became a drab material world and it can be changed again, if its inhabitants have the determination to take the necessary steps and the luck to receive an auspicious response.

Notes

1. *Revue Internationale de Philosophie, 4* 1950.

2. Two dogmas of empiricism. *Philosophical Review,* Jan. 1951.

3. J. Needham, *Science in traditional China.* Cambridge, MA: Harvard University Press / Hong Kong: The Chinese University Press, 1981, pp. 3 and 22ff.

4. Consider (Koyré's example) that in 1650, when Riccioli was working on his *Almagestum novum,* the Michelson experiment would have provided precise, conclusive, and irrefutable evidence for a stable earth. Also consider what would have happened if irregular curves such as von Koch's curve rather than unreal things such as circles and straight lines had become the paradigms of mathematical representation. See B. B. Mandelbrot, *The Fractal Geometry of Nature,* New York, 1977, for details.

5. For details and evidence see chapter 16 of my book *Against method,* revised edition, London, 1988.

6. This is true only if scientific results are interpreted in a special way and if more recent developments are disregarded.

7. Xenophanes' "argument" assumes that the battle has already been won and mocks those still

clinging to tradition; it did not play any part in the battle itself. See my essay Reason, Xenophanes and the Homeric gods, *The Kenyon Review,* Fall 1988.

8. The most obvious intellectual manifestations of the change were the opinions of writers such as Anaximander, Herakleitos, Xenophanes, and Parmenides who replaced the colorful notions of common sense by abstract and impoverished concepts. They affected history not by the power of their ideas (though they and their modern admirers claim that they did) but because of concurrent tendencies toward abstraction and generalization. Without any help from philosophers "words . . . [had] become impoverished in content, they had become one sided and empty formulae" (K. v. Fritz, *Philosophie und Sprachlicher Ausdruck bei Demokrit, Platon und Aristoteles,* Neudruck Darmstadt 1966, 11). The process started in Homer (example in my note Putnam on incommensurability, *The British Journal for the Philosophy of Science,* 1987), becomes prominent in Hesiod, obvious in the Ionian philosophers of nature. In politics abstract groups replaced neighborhoods as the units of political action (Cleisthenes), in economics money succeeded barter, armies no longer reflected local hierarchies, life as a whole moved away from personal ties and concrete dependencies, and terms involving such relations either lost in content or disappeared. Small wonder that arguments involving highly theoretical notions were not at once laughed out of court. They did not change history; they got a hearing because history had prepared the way.

9. A. Pickering, *Constructing quarks,* University of Chicago Press, 1984, chapter 4. The experiments used the Millikan-arrangement. G. Holton, *Historical studies in the physical sciences,* Vol. ix, R. McCormich, L. Pyenson, and R. S. Turner (Eds.), Johns Hopkins University Press, 1978, pp. 161ff., shows how Millikan and Ehrenhaft, using different versions of this arrangement and evaluating their data in different ways, got different results for the charge of the electron: in practice an experimental setup is a heap of equipment wrapped in an often very complex ideological blanket. Pickering, *Isis, 72,* 1981, describes the blanket in the case of quarks.

10. I did this in an essay published in 1964 and reprinted as chapter 11 of Vol. I of my *Philosophical Papers,* Cambridge, 1981, especially pp. 201ff.

11. By "gods" I always mean the gods described in the Homeric epics and accepted by Greek common sense down to the fifth and fourth centuries B.C., i.e., specific entities whose relation to experience and social practice is known to some extent (for details and literature see again chapter 16 of *Against method* as well as part 1, chapter 4, Seeing the gods, in R. L. Fox, *Pagans and Christians,* New York, 1986). The arguments about the triune God of Nicaean Christianity differ in details, but not in their general outline. Note, incidentally, that Christian theoreticians did not deny the existence of the pagan gods but declared them to be demons: St. Paul. I *Cor.* x, 20. For the Jews the pagan gods simply did not exist: Y. Kaufman, *The Religion of Israel,* New York, 1973, 20, 230. Thus the ontological chauvinism of the ancient Jews exceeded that of the early Christians and approached the chauvinism of modern agnostic scientists.

12. R. Sperry, *Science and moral priority,* Westport, Conn. 1985, p. 32.

13. Bohr's idea of complementarity which brought order into the confusing situation of the quantum mechanics of Heisenberg and Schroedinger was highly speculative — but it was on the right track. It became more solid in the course of a process that included the argument of Einstein, Podolsky and Rosen, Bell's critique of von Neumann's proof, Bell's theorem and the experiments designed to test it, the so-called delayed choice experiments, and, mathematically, the transition from the Hilbert Space formalism to algebraic quantum mechanics. As a result of these developments we can no longer say "molecules exist" — period but we must say that given certain conditions, molecules are the best way of describing what happens. For details see the literature given in the next footnote.

14. For a detailed criticism in the case of chemistry with illustrations from other fields, see Hans Primas, *Chemistry, quantum mechanics and reductionism,* Springer, Berlin, 1981; a brief and less formal account is H. Primas, Kann Chemie auf Physik reduziert werden? *Chemie in unserer Zeit 19,* 1985, 109–119; 160–169. The special case of physical laws is dealt with by N. Cartwright, *How the laws of physics lie,* Clarendon Press, Oxford, 1983.

15. "The great success of Cartesian method and the Cartesian view of nature is in part a result of a historical path of least resistance. Those problems that yield to the attack are pursued most vigorously, precisely because the method works there. Other problems and other phenomena are left behind, walled off from understanding by the commitment to Cartesianism. The harder problems are not tackled, if for no other reason than that brilliant scientific careers are not built on persistent failure. So the problems of understanding embryonic and psychic development and the structure and function of the central nervous system remain in much the same unsatisfactory state they were fifty years ago, while molecular biologists go from triumph to triumph in describing and manipulating genes." R. Levins and R. Lewontin, *The dialectical biologist*, Harvard University Press, Cambridge, 1985, pp. 2ff. "The insufficiency of all biological experimentation, when confronted with the vastness of life, is often considered to be redeemed by recourse to a firm methodology. But definite procedures presuppose highly limited objects." E. Chargaff, *Heraclitean fire*, The Rockefeller University Press, New York, 1978, 170.

16. *Disturbing the Universe*, Harper & Row, New York, 1979, p. 63.

17. Discussions with Einstein, quoted from J. A. Wheeler, W. H. Zurek (eds.) *Quantum theory and measurement*, Princeton University Press, Princeton, 1983, p. 42. Details in chapters i and iii of my book *Farewell to reason*, London, 1987. Quine, in a similar way, regards the creation of new entities as a semantic act having ontological consequences.

18. Interestingly enough even the American continent, which I used as an example to illustrate SA, was *manufactured* (in the sense just explained), not found. Columbus on his arrival interpreted coastlines, clima, populations as supporting his own belief that he had landed in East Asia. The existence of a new continent could be asserted only after a drastic reordering of inferences. Details in Edmondo O'Gorman's fascinating book *The Invention of America*, Indiana University Press, Bloomington, Indiana, 1961. In the arts it was Panofsky who, following Cassirer, emphasized the constructive ingredients of the "objective" features of our world: Die Perspektive als symbolische Form, *Vortraege der Bibliothek Warburg* 1924–1925, Leipzig/Berlin, 1927. This was a step in the right direction, but still unsatisfactory, because tied to the old opposition between constructions (which are imposed on a material not having the associated properties) and descriptions (which are abstracted from a material already in possession of the properties).

Of Clouds and Clocks:
An Approach to the Problem of
Rationality and
the Freedom of Man

Karl Raimund Popper

I

My predecessor, who in this hall gave the first Arthur Holly Compton Memorial Lecture a year ago, was more fortunate than I. He knew Arthur Compton personally; I never met him.[1]

But I have known of Compton since my student days in the nineteen-twenties, and especially since 1925 when the famous experiment of Compton and Simon[2] refuted the beautiful but short-lived quantum theory of Bohr, Kramers, and Slater.[3] This refutation was one of the decisive events in the history of quantum theory, for from the crisis which it created there emerged the so-called new quantum theory—the theories of Born and Heisenberg, of Schroedinger, and of Dirac.

It was the second time that Compton's experimental tests had played a crucial role in the history of quantum theory. The first time had been, of course, the discovery of the Compton effect, the first independent test (as Compton himself pointed out[4]) of Einstein's theory of light quanta or photons.

Years later, during the Second World War, I found to my surprise and pleasure that Compton was not only a great physicist but also a genuine and courageous philosopher; and further, that his philosophical interests and aims coincided with my own on some important points. I found this when, almost by accident, I got hold of Compton's fascinating Terry Lectures which he had published in 1935 in a book entitled *The Freedom of Man*.[5]

You will have noticed that I have incorporated the title of Compton's book,

This chapter was previously presented as The Arthur Holly Compton Memorial Lecture at Washington University, April 21, 1965. I thank Dante Cicchetti for reading the proofs of my contribution.

The Freedom of Man, into my own title today. I have done so in order to stress the fact that my lecture will be closely connected with this book of Compton's. More precisely, I intend to discuss the same problems which Compton discussed in the first two chapters of his book, and again in the second chapter of another book of his, *The Human Meaning of Science.*[6]

In order to avoid misunderstandings I must stress, however, that my lecture today is not mainly about Compton's books. It is rather an attempt to look afresh at the same ancient philosophical problems with which he grappled in these two books, and an attempt to find a new solution to these ancient problems. The sketchy and very tentative solution I am going to outline here seems to me to fit in well with Compton's main aims, and I hope—indeed I believe—that he would have approved of it.

II

The central purpose of my lecture is to try to put these ancient problems simply and forcefully before you. But first I must say something about the *clouds and clocks* which appear in the title of my lecture.

My clouds are intended to represent physical systems which, like gases, are highly irregular, disorderly, and more or less unpredictable. I shall assume that we have before us a schema or arrangement in which a very disturbed or disorderly cloud is placed on the left. On the other extreme of our arrangement, on its right, we may place a very reliable pendulum clock, a precision clock, intended to represent physical systems which are regular, orderly, and highly predictable in their behavior.

According to what I may call the common-sense view of things, some natural phenomena, such as the weather, or the coming and going of clouds, are hard to predict: we speak of the "vagaries of the weather." On the other hand, we speak of "clockwork precision," if we wish to describe a highly regular and predictable phenomenon.

There are lots of things, natural processes and natural phenomena, which we may place between these two extremes—the clouds on the left, and the clocks on the right. The changing seasons are somewhat unreliable clocks, and may therefore be put somewhere toward the right, though not too far. I suppose we shall easily agree to put animals not too far from the clouds on the left, and plants somewhat nearer to the clocks. Among the animals, a young puppy will have to be placed farther to the left than an old dog. Motor cars, too, will find their place somewhere in our arrangement, according to their reliability: a Cadillac, I suppose, is pretty far over to the right, and even more so a Rolls-Royce, which will be quite close to the best of the clocks. Perhaps farthest to the right should be placed the *solar system.*[7]

As a typical and interesting example of a cloud I shall make some use here of a cloud or cluster of small flies or gnats. Like the individual molecules in a gas, the individual gnats which together form a cluster of gnats move in an astonishingly irregular way. It is almost impossible to follow the flight of any one individual gnat, even though each of them may be quite big enough to be clearly visible.

Apart from the fact that the velocities of the gnats do not show a very wide spread, the gnats present us with an excellent picture of the irregular movement of molecules in a gas cloud, or of the minute drops of water in a storm cloud. There are, of course, differences. The cluster does not dissolve or diffuse, but it keeps together fairly well. This is surprising, considering the disorderly character of the movement of the various gnats; but it has its analogue in a sufficiently big gas cloud (such as our atmosphere, or the sun) which is kept together by gravitational forces. In the case of the gnats, their keeping together can be easily explained if we assume that, although they fly quite irregularly in all directions, those that find that they are getting away from the crowd turn back toward that part which is densest.

This assumption explains how the cluster keeps together even though it has no leader, and no structure—only a random statistical distribution resulting from the fact that each gnat does exactly what he likes, in a lawless and random manner, together with the fact that he does not like to stray too far from his comrades.

I think that a philosophical gnat might claim that the gnat society is a great society or at least a good society, since it is the most egalitarian, free, and democratic society imaginable.

However, as the author of a book on *The Open Society,* I would deny that the gnat society is an open society. For I take it to be one of the characteristics of an open society that it cherishes, apart from a democratic form of government, the freedom of association, and that it protects and even encourages the formation of free sub-societies, each holding different opinions and beliefs. But every reasonable gnat would have to admit that in his society this kind of pluralism is lacking.

I do not intend, however, to discuss today any of the social or political issues connected with the problem of freedom; and I intend to use the cluster of gnats not as an example of a *social* system, but rather as my main illustration of a cloud-like *physical* system, as an example or paradigm of a highly irregular or disordered cloud.

Like many physical, biological, and social systems, the cluster of gnats may be described as a "whole." Our conjecture that it is kept together by a kind of attraction which its densest part exerts on individual gnats straying too far from the crowd shows that there is even a kind of action or control which this "whole" exerts upon its elements or parts. Nevertheless, this "whole" can be used to dispel the widespread "holistic" belief that a "whole" is *always* more than the mere sum of its parts. I do not deny that it may sometimes be so.[8] Yet the cluster of gnats is an example of a whole that is indeed nothing but the sum of its parts—and in a very precise sense; for not only is it completely described by describing the movements of all the individual gnats, but the movement of the whole is, in this case, precisely the (vectorial) sum of the movements of its constituent members, divided by the number of the members.

An example (in many ways similar) of a biological system or "whole" which exerts some control over the highly irregular movements of its parts would be a picnicking family—parents with a few children and a dog—roaming the woods for hours, but never straying far from the family car (which acts like a center of attraction, as it were). This system may be said to be even more cloudy—that is, less regular in the movement of its parts—than our cloud of gnats.

I hope you will now have before you an idea of my two prototypes or paradigms, the clouds on the left and the clocks on the right, and of the way in which we can arrange many kinds of things, and many kinds of systems, between them. I am sure you have caught some vague, general idea of the arrangement, and you need not worry if your idea is still a bit foggy, or cloudy.

III

The arrangement I have described is, it seems, quite acceptable to common sense; and more recently, in our own time, it has become acceptable even to physical science. It was not so, however, during the preceding 250 years; the Newtonian revolution, one of the greatest revolutions in history, led to the rejection of the common-sense arrangement which I have tried to present to you. For one of the things which almost everybody[9] thought had been established by the Newtonian revolution was the following staggering proposition:

All clouds are clocks—even the most cloudy of clouds.

This proposition, "All clouds are clocks," may be taken as a brief formulation of the view which I shall call *"Physical determinism."*

The physical determinist who says that all clouds are clocks will also say that our common-sense arrangement, with the clouds on the left and the clocks on the right, is misleading, since *everything* ought to be placed on the extreme right. He will say that, with all our common sense, we arranged things *not according to their nature, but merely according to our ignorance.* Our arrangements, he will say, reflect merely the fact that we know in some detail how the parts of a clock work, or how the solar system works, while we do not have any knowledge about the *detailed* interaction of the particles that form a gas cloud, or an organism. And he will assert that, once we have obtained this knowledge, we shall find that gas clouds or organisms are as clock-like as our solar system.

Newton's theory did not, of course, tell the physicists that this was so. In fact, it did not treat at all of clouds. It treated especially of planets, whose movements it explained as due to some very simple laws of nature; also of cannonballs, and of the tides. But its immense success in these fields turned the physicists' heads; and surely not without reason.

Before the time of Newton and his predecessor, Kepler, the movements of the planets had escaped many attempts to explain or even to describe them fully. Clearly, they somehow participated in the unvarying general movement of the rigid system of the fixed stars; yet they deviated from the movement of that system almost like single gnats deviating from the general movement of a cluster of gnats. Thus the planets, not unlike living things, appeared to be in a position intermediate between clouds and clocks. Yet the success of Kepler's and even more of Newton's theory showed that those thinkers had been right who had suspected that the planets were in fact perfect clocks. For their movements turned out to be precisely predictable with the help of Newton's theory; predictable in all those details which had previously baffled the astronomers by their apparent irregularity.

Newton's theory was the first really successful scientific theory in human history; and it was tremendously successful. Here was real knowledge; knowledge beyond the wildest dreams of even the boldest minds. Here was a theory which explained precisely not only the movements of *all* the stars in their course, but also, just as precisely, the movements of bodies on earth, such as falling apples, or projectiles, or pendulum clocks. And it even explained the tides.

All open-minded men—all those who were eager to learn, and who took an interest in the growth of knowledge—were converted to the new theory. Most open-minded men, and especially most scientists, thought that in the end it would explain everything, including not only electricity and magnetism, but also clouds, and even living organisms. Thus physical determinism—the doctrine that all clouds are clocks—became the ruling faith among enlightened men; and everybody who did not embrace this new faith was held to be an obscurantist or a reactionary.[10]

IV

Among the few dissenters[11] was Charles Sanders Peirce, the great American mathematician and physicist and, I believe, one of the greatest philosophers of all time. He did not question Newton's theory; yet as early as 1892 he showed that this theory, even if true, does not give us any valid reason to believe that clouds are perfect clocks. Though in common with all other physicists of his time he believed that the world was a clock that worked according to Newtonian laws, he rejected the belief that this clock, or any other, was *perfect*, down to its smallest detail. He pointed out that at any rate we could not possibly claim to know from experience of anything like a perfect clock, or of anything even faintly approaching that absolute perfection which physical determinism assumed. I may perhaps quote one of Peirce's brilliant comments: "one who is behind the scenes" (Peirce speaks here as an experimentalist) " . . . knows that the most refined comparisons [even] of masses [and] lengths, . . . far surpassing in precision all other [physical] measurements, . . . fall behind the accuracy of bank accounts, and that the . . . determinations of physical constants . . . are about on a par with an upholsterer's measurements of carpets and curtains."[12] From this Peirce concluded that we were free to conjecture that there was a certain *looseness or imperfection* in all clocks, and that this allowed an *element of chance* to enter. Thus Peirce conjectured that the world was not only ruled by the *strict Newtonian laws*, but that it was also at the same time ruled by *laws of chance*, or of randomness, or of disorder: bylaws of statistical *probability*. This made the world an interlocking system of clouds and clocks, so that even the best clock would, *in its molecular structure,* show some degree of cloudiness. So far as I know Peirce was the first post-Newtonian physicist and philosopher who thus dared to adopt the view that to some degree *all clocks are clouds;* or in other words, that *only clouds exist,* though clouds of very different degrees of cloudiness.

Peirce supported this view by pointing out, no doubt correctly, that all physical bodies, even the jewels in a watch, were subject to molecular heat motion,[13] a motion similar to that of the molecules of a gas, or of the individual gnats in a cluster of gnats.

These views of Peirce's were received by his contemporaries with little interest. Apparently only one philosopher noticed them; and he attacked them.[14] Physicists seem to have ignored them; and even today most physicists believe that if we had to accept the classical mechanics of Newton as true, we should be compelled to accept physical determinism, and with it the proposition that all clouds are clocks. It was only with the downfall of classical physics and with the rise of the new quantum theory that physicists were prepared to abandon physical determinism.

Now the tables were turned. Indeterminism, which up to 1927 had been equated with obscurantism, became the ruling fashion; and some great scientists, such as Max Planck, Erwin Schroedinger, and Albert Einstein, who hesitated to abandon determinism, were considered old fogies,[15] although they had been in the forefront of the development of quantum theory. I myself once heard a brilliant young physicist describe Einstein, who was then still alive and hard at work, as "antediluvian." The deluge that was supposed to have swept Einstein away was the new quantum theory, which had risen during the years from 1925 to 1927, and to whose advent at most seven people had made a contribution comparable to that of Einstein.

V

Perhaps I may stop here for a moment to state my own view of the situation, and of scientific fashions. I believe that Peirce was right in holding that all clocks are clouds, to some considerable degree—even the most precise of clocks. This, I think, is a most important inversion of the mistaken determinist view that all clouds are clocks. I further believe that Peirce was right in holding that this view was compatible with the classical physics of Newton.[16] I believe that this view is even more clearly compatible with Einstein's (special) relativity theory, and it is still more clearly compatible with the new quantum theory. In other words, I am an indeterminist—like Peirce, Compton, and most other contemporary physicists; and I believe, with most of them, that Einstein was mistaken in trying to hold fast to determinism. (I may perhaps say that I discussed this matter with him, and that I did not find him adamant.) But I also believe that those modern physicists were badly mistaken who pooh-poohed as antediluvian Einstein's criticism of the quantum theory. Nobody can fail to admire the quantum theory, and Einstein did so wholeheartedly; but his criticism of the fashionable interpretation of the theory—the Copenhagen interpretation—like the criticisms offered by de Broglie, Schroedinger, Bohr, Vigier, and more recently by Lande, have been too lightly brushed aside by most physicists.[17] There are fashions in science, and some scientists climb on the bandwagon almost as readily as do some painters and musicians. But although fashions and bandwagons may attract the weak, they should be resisted rather than encouraged[18]; and criticism like Einstein's is always valuable: one can always learn something from it.

VI

Arthur Holly Compton was among the first who welcomed the new quantum theory and Heisenberg's new physical indeterminism of 1927. Compton invited Heisenberg to Chicago for a course of lectures which Heisenberg delivered in the spring of 1929. This course was Heisenberg's first full exposition of his theory, and his lectures were published as his first book a year later by the University of Chicago Press, with a preface by Arthur Compton.[19] In this preface Compton welcomed the new theory to whose advent his experiments had contributed by refuting its immediate predecessor[20]; yet he also sounded a note of warning. Compton's warning anticipated some very similar warnings by Einstein, who always insisted that we should not consider the new quantum theory—"this chapter of the history of physics," as Compton called it generously and wisely—as being "complete."[21] And although this view was rejected by Bohr, we should remember the fact that the new theory failed, for example, to give even a hint of the neutron, discovered by Chadwick about a year later, which was to become the first of a long series of new elementary particles whose existence had not been foreseen by the new quantum theory (even though it is true that the existence of the positron could have been derived from the theory of Dirac.[22]

In the same year, 1931, in his Terry Foundation Lectures (see note 5), Compton became one of the first to examine the human and, more generally, the biological[23] implications of the new indeterminism in physics. And now it became clear why he had welcomed the new theory so enthusiastically; it solved for him not only problems of physics but also biological and philosophical problems, and among the latter especially problems connected with ethics.

VII

To show this, I shall now quote the striking opening passage of Compton's *The Freedom of Man*:

> The fundamental question of morality, a vital problem in religion, and a subject of active investigation in science: Is man a free agent?
>
> If . . . the atoms of our bodies follow physical laws as immutable as the motions of the planets, why try? What difference can it make how great the effort if our actions are already predetermined by mechanical laws?[24]

Compton describes here what I shall call *"the nightmare of the physical determinist."* A deterministic physical clockwork mechanism is, above all, completely self-contained: in the perfect deterministic physical world there is simply no room for any outside intervention. Everything that happens in such a world is physically predetermined, including all our movements and therefore all our actions. Thus all our thoughts, feelings, and efforts can have no practical influence upon what happens in the physical world: they are, if not mere illusions, at best superfluous by-products ("epiphenomena") of physical events.

In this way, the daydream of the Newtonian physicist who hoped to prove all clouds to be clocks had threatened to turn into a nightmare; and the attempt to ignore this had led to something like an intellectual split personality. Compton, I think, was grateful to the new quantum theory for rescuing him from this difficult intellectual situation. Thus he writes, in *The Freedom of Man*:

> The physicist has rarely . . . bothered himself with the fact that if . . . completely deterministic . . . laws . . . apply to man's actions, he is himself an automaton."[25]

And in *The Human Meaning of Science* he expresses his relief:

> In my own thinking on this vital subject I am thus in a much more satisfied state of mind than I could have been at any earlier stage of science. If the statements of the laws of physics were assumed correct, one would have had to suppose (as did most philosophers) that the feeling of freedom is illusory, or if [free] choice were considered effective, that the statements of the laws of physics were . . . unreliable. The dilemma has been an uncomfortable one.[26]

Later in the same book Compton sums up the situation crisply in the words:

it is no longer justifiable to use physical law as evidence against human freedom.[27]

These quotations from Compton show clearly that before Heisenberg he had been harassed by what I have here called the nightmare of the physical determinist, and that he had tried to escape from this nightmare by adopting something like an intellectual split personality. Or as he himself puts it: "We [physicists] have preferred merely to pay no attention to the difficulties."[28] Compton welcomed the new theory which rescued him from all this.

I believe that the only form of the problem of determinism which is worth discussing seriously is exactly that problem which worried Compton: the problem which arises from a physical theory which describes the world as a *physically complete* or a *physically closed* system.[29] By a physically closed system I mean a set or system of physical entities, such as atoms or elementary particles or physical forces or fields of forces, which interact with each other—and *only* with each other—in accordance with definite laws of interaction that do not leave any room for interaction with, or interference by, anything outside that closed set or system of physical entities. It is this "closure" of the system that creates the deterministic nightmare.[30]

VIII

I should like to digress here for a minute in order to contrast the problem of physical determinism, which I consider to be of fundamental importance, with the far from serious problem which many philosophers and psychologists, following Hume, have substituted for it.

Hume interpreted determinism (which he called "the doctrine of necessity," or "the doctrine of constant conjunction") as the doctrine that "like causes always produce like effects" and that "like effects necessarily follow from like causes."[31] Concerning human actions and volitions, he held, more particularly, that "a spectator can commonly infer our actions from our motives and character; and even where he cannot, he concludes in general that he might, were he perfectly acquainted with every circumstance of our situation and temper, and the most secret springs of our . . . disposition. Now this is the very essence of necessity."[32] Hume's successors put it thus: our actions, or our volitions, or our tastes, or our preferences, are *psychologically* "caused" by preceding experiences ("motives"), and ultimately by our heredity and environment.

But this doctrine which we may call *philosophical or psychological* determinism is not only a very different affair from *physical* determinism, but it is also one which a physical determinist who understands what it is all about can hardly take seriously. For the thesis of philosophical determinism, that "like effects have like causes'' or that ''every event has cause,'' is so vague that it is perfectly compatible with physicial *in*determinism.

Indeterminism—or more precisely, physical indeterminism—is merely the doctrine that *not all* events in the physical world are predetermined with absolute precision, in all their infinitesimal details. Apart from this, it is compatible with practically any degree of regularity you like, and it does not, therefore, entail the view that there are ''events without causes,'' simply because the terms ''event'' and ''cause'' are vague enough to make the doctrine that every event has a cause compatible with physical indeterminism. While physical determinism demands complete and infinitely precise physical predetermination and the absence of *any* exception whatever, physical indeterminism asserts no more than that determinism is false, and that there are *at least some* exceptions, here or there, to precise predetermination.

Thus even the formula ''every observable or measurable *physical* event has an observable or measurable *physical* cause'' is still compatible with physical indeterminism, simply because no measurement can be infinitely precise: for the salient point about physical determinism is that, based on Newton's dynamics, it asserts the existence of a world of absolute mathematical precision. And although in so doing it goes beyond the realm of possible observation (as was seen by Peirce), it nevertheless is testable, in principle, with any desired degree of precision; and it actually withstood surprisingly precise tests.

By contrast, the formula ''every event has a cause'' says nothing about precision; and if, more especially, we look at the laws of psychology, then there is not even a suggestion of precision. This holds for a ''behaviorist'' psychology as much as for an ''introspective'' or ''mentalist'' one. In the case of a mentalist psychology this is obvious. But even a behaviorist may *at the very best* predict that, under given conditions, a rat will take 20 to 22 seconds to run a maze: he will have no idea how, by specifying more and more precise experimental conditions, he could make predictions which become more and more precise—and, *in principle, precise without limit.* This is so because behaviorist ''laws'' are not, like those of Newtonian physics, differential equations, and because every attempt to introduce such differential equations would lead beyond behaviorism into physiology, and thus ultimately into physics; so it would lead us back to the problem of *physical determinism.*

As noted by Laplace, physical determinism implies that every physical event in the distant future (or in the distant past) is predictable (or retrodictable) with any desired degree of precision, provided we have sufficient knowledge about the present state of the physical world. The thesis of a philosophical (or psychological) determinism of Hume's type, on the other hand, asserts even in its strongest interpretation no more than that any *observable* difference between two events is related by some as yet perhaps unknown law to some difference—an observable difference perhaps—in the preceding state of the world; obviously a very much weaker assertion, and incidentally one which we could continue to uphold even if most of our experiments, performed under conditions which are, *in appearance*, "entirely equal," should yield different results. This was stated very clearly by Hume himself. "Even when these contrary experiments are entirely equal," he writes, "we remove not the notion of causes and necessity, but . . . conclude, that the [apparent] chance . . . lies only in . . . our imperfect knowledge, not in the things themselves, which are in every case equally necessary [i.e., determined], tho' to appearance not equally constant or certain."[33]

This is why Humean philosophical determinism and, more especially, a psychological determinism lack the sting of physical determinism. For in Newtonian physics things really looked as if any apparent looseness in a system was in fact merely due to our ignorance, so that, should we be fully informed about the system, any appearance of looseness would disappear. Psychology, on the other hand, never had this character.

Physical determinism, we might say in retrospect, was a daydream of omniscience which seemed to become more real with every advance in physics until it became an apparently inescapable nightmare. But the corresponding daydreams of the psychologists were never more than castles in the air: they were Utopian dreams of attaining equality with physics, its mathematical methods and its powerful applications; and perhaps even of attaining superiority, by moulding men and societies. (While these totalitarian dreams are not serious from a scientific point of view, they are very dangerous politically[34]; but since I have dealt with these dangers elsewhere I do not propose to discuss the problem here.)

IX

I have called physical determinism a nightmare. It is a nightmare because it asserts that the whole world with everything in it is a huge automaton, and that we are nothing but little cogwheels, or at best sub-automata, within it.

It thus destroys, in particular, the idea of creativity. It reduces to a complete illusion the idea that in preparing this lecture I have used my brain to create *something new*. There was no more in it, according to physical determinism, than that certain parts of my body put down black marks on white paper: any physicist with sufficient detailed information could have written my lecture by the simple method of predicting the precise places on which the physical system consisting of my body (including my brain, of course, and my fingers) and my pen would put down those black marks.

Or to use a more impressive example: if physical determinism is right, then a physicist who is completely deaf and who has never heard any music could write all the symphonies and concertos written by Mozart or Beethoven, by the simple method of studying the precise physical states of their bodies and predicting where they would put down black marks on their lined paper. And our deaf phys-

icist could do even more: by studying Mozart's or Beethoven's bodies with sufficient care he could write scores which were never actually written by Mozart or
Beethoven, but which they would have written had certain external circumstances of their lives been different: if they had eaten lamb, say, instead of
chicken, or drunk tea instead of coffee.

All this could be done by our deaf physicist if supplied with a sufficient
knowledge of purely physical conditions. There would be no need for him to
know anything about the theory of music—though he might be able to predict
what answers Mozart or Beethoven would have written down under examination
conditions if presented with questions on the theory of counterpoint.

I believe that all this is absurd[35]; and its absurdity becomes even more obvious, I think, when we apply this method of physical prediction to a determinist.

For according to determinism, any theories—such as, say, determinism—are
held because of a certain physical structure of the holder (perhaps of his brain).
Accordingly we are deceiving ourselves (and are physically so determined as to
deceive ourselves) whenever we believe that there are such things as arguments or
reasons which make us accept determinism. Or in other words, physical determinism is a theory which, if it is true, is not arguable, since it must explain all
our reactions, including what appear to us as beliefs based on arguments, as due
to *purely physical conditions*. Purely physical conditions, including our physical
environment, make us say or accept whatever we say or accept; and a well-
trained physicist who does not know any French, and who has never heard of
determinism, would be able to predict what a French determinist would say in a
French discussion on determinism; and of course also what his indeterminist opponent would say. But this means that if we believe that we have accepted a theory like determinism because we were swayed by the logical force of certain arguments, then we are deceiving ourselves, according to physical determinism; or
more precisely, we are in a physical condition which determines us to deceive ourselves.

Hume saw much of this, even though it appears that he did not quite see what
it meant for his own arguments; for he confined himself to comparing the determinism of *"our judgements"* with that of *"our actions,"* saying that *"we have
no more liberty in the one than in the other."*[36]

Considerations such as these may perhaps be the reason why there are so many
philosophers who refuse to take the problem of physical determinism seriously
and dismiss it as a *"bogy."*[37] Yet the doctrine that *man is a machine* was argued
more forcefully and seriously in 1751, long before the theory of evolution became generally accepted, by de Lamettrie; and the theory of evolution gave the
problem an even sharper edge, by suggesting that there may be no clear distinction between living matter and dead matter.[38] And in spite of the victory of the
new quantum theory, and the conversion of so many physicists to indeterminism,
de Lamettrie's doctrine that man is a machine has today perhaps more defenders

than ever before among physicists, biologists, and philosophers; especially in the form of the thesis that man is a computer.[39]

For if we accept a theory of evolution (such as Darwin's) then even if we remain sceptical about the theory that life emerged from inorganic matter we can hardly deny that there must have been a time when abstract and nonphysical entities, such as reasons and arguments and scientific knowledge, and abstract rules, such as rules for building railways or bulldozers or sputniks or, say, rules of grammar or of counterpoint, did not exist, or at any rate had no effect upon the physical universe. It is difficult to understand how the physical universe could produce abstract entities such as rules, and then could come under the influence of these rules, so that these rules in their turn could exert very palpable effects upon the physical universe.

There is, however, at least one perhaps somewhat evasive but at any rate easy way out of this difficulty. We can simply deny that these abstract entities exist and that they can influence the physical universe. And we can assert that what do exist are our brains, and that these are machines like computers; that the allegedly abstract rules are physical entities, exactly like the concrete physical punch-cards by which we "program" our computers; and that the existence of anything nonphysical is just "an illusion," perhaps, and at any rate unimportant, since everything would go on as it does even if there were no such illusions.

According to this way out, we need not worry about the "mental" status of these illusions. They may be universal properties of all things: the stone which I throw may have the illusion that it jumps, just as I have the illusion that I throw it; and my pen, or my computer, may have the illusion that it works because of its interest in the problems which it thinks that it is solving — and which I think that I am solving — while in fact there is nothing of any significance going on except purely physical interactions.

You may see from all this that the problem of physical determinism which worried Compton is indeed a serious problem. It is not just a philosophical puzzle, but it affects at least physicists, biologists, behaviorists, psychologists, and computer engineers.

Admittedly, quite a few philosophers have tried to show (following Hume or Schlick) that it is merely a verbal puzzle, a puzzle about the use of the word "freedom." But these philosophers have hardly seen the difference between the problem of physical determinism and that of philosophical determinism; and they are either determinists like Hume, which explains why for them "freedom" is "just a word," or they have never had that close contact with the physical sciences or with computer engineering which would have impressed upon them that we are faced with more than a merely verbal puzzle.

X

Like Compton I am among those who take the problem of physical determinism seriously, and like Compton I do not believe that we are mere computing machines (though I readily admit that we can learn a great deal from computing machines—even about ourselves). Thus, like Compton, I am a *physical indeterminist*: physical indeterminism, I believe, is a necessary prerequisite for any solution of our problem. We have to be indeterminists; yet I shall try to show that indeterminism is not enough.

With this statement, *indeterminism is not enough,* I have arrived not merely at a new point, but at the very heart of my problem.

The problem may be explained as follows.

If determinism is true, then the whole world is a perfectly running flawless clock, including all clouds, all organisms, all animals, and all men. If, on the other hand, Peirce's or Heisenberg's or some other form of indeterminism is true, then sheer *chance* plays a major role in our physical world. *But is chance really more satisfactory than determinism?*

The question is well known. Determinists like Schlick have put it in this way: "freedom of action, responsibility, and mental sanity, cannot reach beyond the realm of causality: they stop where chance begins . . . a higher degree of randomness . . . [simply means] a higher degree of irresponsibility."[40]

I may perhaps put this idea of Schlick's in terms of an example I have used before: to say that the black marks made on white paper which I produced in preparation for this lecture were just the result of *chance* is hardly more satisfactory than to say that they were physically predetermined. In fact, it is even less satisfactory. For some people may be perhaps quite ready to believe that the text of my lecture can be in principle completely explained by my physical heredity, and my physical environment, including my upbringing, the books I have been reading, and the talks I have listened to; but hardly anybody will believe that what I am reading to you is the result of nothing but chance—just a random sample of English words, or perhaps of letters, put together without any purpose, deliberation, plan, or intention.

The idea that the only alternative to determinism is just sheer chance was taken over by Schlick, together with many of his views on the subject, from Hume, who asserted that "the removal" of what he called "physical necessity" must always result in "the same thing with *chance*. As objects must either be conjoin'd or not, . . . 'tis impossible to admit of any medium betwixt chance and an absolute necessity."[41]

I shall later argue against this important doctrine according to which the only alternative to determinism is sheer chance. Yet I must admit that the doctrine seems to hold good for the quantum-theoretical models which have been designed to explain, or at least to illustrate, the possibility of human freedom. This seems to be the reason why these models are so very unsatisfactory.

Compton himself designed such a model, though he did not particularly like it. It uses quantum indeterminacy, and the unpredictability of a quantum jump, as a model of a human decision of great moment. It consists of an amplifier which amplifies the effect of a single quantum jump in such a way that it may either cause an explosion or destroy the relay necessary for bringing the explosion about. In this way one single quantum jump may be equivalent to a major decision. But in my opinion the model has no similarity to any *rational decision*. It is, rather, a model of a kind of decision-making where people who cannot make up their minds say: "Let us toss a penny." In fact, the whole apparatus for amplifying a quantum jump seems rather unnecessary: tossing a penny, and deciding on the result of the toss whether or not to pull a trigger, would do just as well. And there are of course computers with built-in penny-tossing devices for producing random results, where such are needed.

It may perhaps be said that some of our decisions *are* like penny-tosses: they are snap-decisions, taken without deliberation, since we often do not have enough time to deliberate. A driver or a pilot has sometimes to take a snap-decision like this; and if he is well trained, or just lucky, the result may be satisfactory; otherwise not.

I admit that the quantum-jump model may be a model for such snap-decisions; and I even admit that it is conceivable that something like the amplification of a quantum-jump may actually happen in our brains if we make a snap-decision. But are snap-decisions really so very interesting? Are they characteristic of human behavior — of *rational* human behavior?

I do not think so; and I do not think that we shall get much further with quantum jumps. They are just the kind of examples which seem to lend support to the thesis of Hume and Schlick that perfect chance is the only alternative to perfect determinism. What we need for understanding rational human behavior — and indeed, animal behavior — is something *intermediate* in character between perfect chance and perfect determinism — something intermediate between perfect clouds and perfect clocks.

Hume's and Schlick's ontological thesis that there cannot exist anything intermediate between chance and determinism seems to me not only highly dogmatic (not to say doctrinaire) but clearly absurd; and it is understandable only on the assumption that they believed in a complete determinism in which chance has no status except as a symptom of our ignorance. (But even then it seems to me absurd, for there is, clearly, something like partial knowledge, or partial ignorance.) For we know that even highly reliable clocks are not really perfect, and Schlick (if not Hume) must have known that this is largely due to things such as friction — that is to say, to statistical or chance effects. And we also know that our clouds are not perfectly chance-like, since we can often predict the weather quite successfully, at least for short periods.

Thus we shall have to return to our old arrangement with clouds on the left and clocks on the right and animals and men somewhere in between.

But even after we have done so (and there are some problems to be solved before we can say that this arrangement is in keeping with present-day physics), even then we have at best only made room for our main question.

For obviously what we want is to understand how such nonphysical things as *purposes, deliberations, plans, decisions, theories, intentions,* and *values* can play a part in bringing about physical changes in the physical world. That they do this seems to be obvious, *pace* Hume and Laplace and Schlick. It is clearly untrue that all those tremendous physical changes brought about hourly by our pens, or pencils, or bulldozers can be explained in purely physical terms, either by a deterministic physical theory, or (by a stochastic theory) as due to chance.

Compton was well aware of this problem, as the following charming passage from his Terry Lectures shows:

> It was some time ago when I wrote to the secretary of Yale
> University agreeing to give a lecture on November 10 at 5 p.m. He had
> such faith in me that it was announced publicly that I should be there,
> and the audience had such confidence in his word that they came to the
> hall at the specified time. But consider the great physical improbability
> that their confidence was justified. In the meanwhile my work called me
> to the Rocky Mountains and across the ocean to sunny Italy. A
> phototropic organism [such as I happen to be, would not easily] . . .
> tear himself away from there to go to chilly New Haven. The
> possibilities of my being elsewhere at this moment were infinite in
> number. Considered as a physical event, the probability of meeting my
> engagement would have been fantastically small. Why then was the
> audience's belief justified? . . . They knew my purpose, and it was my
> purpose [which] determined that I should be there.[42]

Compton shows here very beautifully that mere physical indetermination is not enough. We have to be indeterminists, to be sure; but we also must try to understand how men, and perhaps animals, can be "influenced" or "controlled" by such things as aims, or purposes, or rules, or agreements.

This then is our central problem.

XII

A closer look shows, however, that there are *two* problems in this story of Compton's journey from Italy to Yale. Of these two problems I shall here call the first *Compton's problem,* and the second *Descartes's problem.*

Compton's problem has rarely been seen by philosophers, and if at all, only dimly. It may be formulated as follows: There are such things as letters accepting a proposal to lecture, and public announcements of intentions; publicly declared aims and purposes; general moral rules. Each of these documents or pronouncements or rules has a certain content, or meaning, which remains invariant if we translate it, or reformulate it. Thus *this content or meaning is something quite abstract*. Yet it can control—perhaps by way of a short cryptic entry in an engagement calendar—the physical movements of a man in such a way as to steer him back from Italy to Connecticut. How can that be?

This is what I shall call Compton's problem. It is important to note that in this form the problem is neutral with respect to the question whether we adopt a behaviorist or a mentalist psychology: in the formulation here given, and suggested by Compton's text, the problem is put in terms of Compton's *behavior* in returning to Yale; but it would make very little difference if we included such mental events as a volition, or the feeling of having grasped, or got hold of, an idea.

Retaining Compton's own behaviorist terminology, Compton's problem may be described as the problem of the influence of the *universe of abstract meanings* upon human behavior (and thereby upon the physical universe). Here "universe of meanings" is a shorthand term comprising such diverse things as promises, aims, and various kinds of rules, such as rules of grammar, or of polite behavior, or of logic, or of chess, or of counterpoint; also such things as scientific publications (and other publications); appeals to our sense of justice or generosity; or to our artistic appreciation; and so on, almost *ad infinitum*.

I believe that what I have here called Compton's problem is one of the most interesting problems of philosophy, even though few philosophers have seen it. In my opinion it is a real key problem, and more important than the classical body-mind problem which I am calling here "Descartes's problem."

In order to avoid misunderstandings I may perhaps mention that by formulating his problem in behavioristic terms, Compton certainly had no intention of subscribing to a full-fledged behaviorism. On the contrary, he did not doubt either the existence of his own mind or that of other minds, or of experiences such as volitions, or deliberations, or pleasure, or pain. He would, therefore, have insisted that there is a *second* problem to be solved.

We may identify this second problem with the classical body-mind problem, or Descartes's problem. It may be formulated as follows: how can it be that such things as states of mind—volitions, feelings, expectations—influence or control the physical movements of our limbs? And (though this is less important in our context) how can it be that the physical states of an organism may influence its mental states?[43]

Compton suggests that any *satisfactory* or *acceptable* solution of either of these two problems would have to comply with the following postulate which I shall call *Compton's postulate of freedom*: the solution must explain freedom; and it must also explain how freedom is not just chance but, rather, the result of a subtle interplay between *something almost random or haphazard*, and *something like a restrictive or selective control*—such as an aim or a standard—though certainly not a cast-iron control. For it is clear that the controls which guided Compton back from Italy allowed him plenty of freedom: freedom, say, to choose between an American and a French or Italian boat; or freedom to postpone his lecture, had some more important obligation arisen.

We may say that Compton's postulate of freedom restricts the acceptable solutions of our two problems by demanding that they should conform to *the idea of combining freedom and control,* and also to *the idea of a "plastic control,"* as I shall call it in contradistinction to a "cast-iron control."

Compton's postulate is a restriction which I accept gladly and freely; and my own free and deliberate though not uncritical acceptance of this restriction may be taken as an illustration of that combination of freedom and control which is the very content of Compton's postulate of freedom.

XIII

I have explained our two central *problems*—Compton's problem and Descartes's problem. In order to solve them we need, I believe, a *new theory;* in fact, a new theory of evolution and a new model of the organism.

This need arises because the existing indeterministic theories are unsatisfactory. They are indeterministic; but we know that indeterminism is not enough, and it is not clear how they escape from Schlick's objection, or whether they conform to Compton's postulate of *freedom plus control.* Also, Compton's problem is quite beyond them: they are hardly relevant to it. And although these theories are attempts to solve Descartes's problem, the solutions they propose do not appear to be satisfactory.

The theories I am alluding to may be called "master-switch models of control" or, more briefly, "master-switch theories." Their underlying idea is that our body is a kind of machine which can be regulated by a lever or switch from one or more *central control points.* Descartes even went so far as to locate his control point precisely: it is in the pineal gland, he said, that mind acts upon body. Some quantum theorists suggested (and Compton very tentatively accepted the suggestion) that our minds work upon our bodies by influencing or selecting some quantum jumps. These are then amplified by our central nervous system which acts like an electronic amplifier: the amplified quantum jumps operate a cascade of relays or master-switches and ultimately effect muscular contractions.[44] There are, I think, some indications in Compton's books that he did not much like this particular theory or model, and that he used it for one purpose only: to show that human indeterminism (and even "freedom") does not necessarily contradict quantum physics.[45] I think he was right in all this, including his dislike of master-switch theories.

For these master-switch theories—whether the one of Descartes, or the amplifier theories of the quantum physicists—belong to what I may perhaps call *"tiny baby theories."* They seem to me to be almost as unattractive as tiny babies.

I am sure you all know the story of the unmarried mother who pleaded: "But it is only a *very* tiny one." Descartes's pleading seems to me similar: "But it is such a tiny one: it is only an unextended mathematical point in which our mind may act upon our body."

The quantum theorists hold a very similar tiny baby theory: "But it is only with *one* quantum jump, and just within the Heisenberg uncertainties—and these are very tiny indeed—that a mind can act upon a physical system." I admit that there is perhaps a slight advance here, insofar as the size of the baby is specified. But I still do not love the baby.

For however tiny the master-switch may be, the master-switch-*cum*-amplifier model strongly suggests that all our decisions are either snap-decisions (as I have called them in section X above) or else composed of snap-decisions. Now I admit that amplifier mechanisms are important characteristics of biological systems (for the energy of the reaction, released or triggered by a biological stimulus, usually exceeds greatly the energy of the triggering stimulus[46]); and I also admit, of course, that snap-decisions do occur. But they differ markedly from the kind of decision which Compton had in mind: they are almost like reflexes, and thus conform neither to the situation of Compton's problem of the influence of the universe of meanings upon our behavior, nor to Compton's postulate of freedom (nor to the idea of a "plastic" control). Decisions which conform to all this are as a rule reached almost imperceptibly through lengthy *deliberation*. They are reached by a kind of *maturing* process which is not well represented by the master-switch model.

By considering this process of deliberation, we may get another hint for our new theory. For deliberation always works by *trial and error* or, more precisely, by *the method of trial and of error-elimination*: by tentatively proposing various possibilities, and eliminating those which do not seem adequate. This suggests that we might use in our new theory some mechanism of trial and error-elimination.

I shall now outline how I intend to proceed.

Before formulating my evolutionary theory in general terms I shall first show how it works in a particular case, by applying it to our first problem, that is, to Compton's problem of the *influence of meaning upon behavior*.

After having in this way solved Compton's problem, I shall formulate the theory in a general way. Then it will be found that it also contains—within the framework of our new theory which creates a new problem-situation—a straightforward and almost trivial answer to Descartes's classical body-mind problem.

XIV

Let us now approach our first problem—that is, Compton's problem of the influence of meaning upon behavior—by way of some comments on *the evolution of languages from animal languages to human languages.*

Animal languages and human languages have many things in common, but there are also differences: as we all know, human languages do somehow transcend animal languages.

Using and extending some ideas of my late teacher Karl Bühler[47] I shall distinguish two functions which animal and human languages share, and two functions which human language alone possesses; or in other words, two lower functions and two higher ones which evolved on the basis of the lower functions.

The two lower functions of language are these. First, language, like all other forms of behavior, consists of *symptoms or expressions*; it is symptomatic or expressive of the state of the organism which makes the linguistic signs. Following Bühler, I call this the *symptomatic or expressive function of language.*

Secondly, for language or communication to take place, there must not only be a sign-making organism or a "sender," but also a reacting one, a "receiver." The symptomatic *expression* of the first organism, the sender, releases or evokes or stimulates or triggers a reaction in the second organism, which *responds* to the sender's behavior, thereby turning it into a *signal.* This function of language to act upon a receiver was called by Bühler the *releasing or signaling function of language.*

To take an example, a bird may be ready to fly away and may *express* this by exhibiting certain symptoms. These may then *release or trigger* a certain response or reaction in a second bird, and as a consequence it too may get ready to fly away.

Note that the two functions, the expressive function and the release function, are *distinct*; for it is possible that instances of the first may occur without the second, though not the other way round: a bird may express by its behavior that it is ready to fly away without thereby influencing another bird. So the first function may occur without the second; which shows that they can be disentangled in spite of the fact that, in any genuine instance of communication by language, they always occur together.

These two lower functions, the symptomatic or expressive function, on the one hand, and the releasing or signaling function, on the other, are common to the languages of animals *and* men; and these two lower functions are always present when any of the higher functions (which are characteristically human) are present.

For human language is very much richer. It has many functions, and dimensions, which animal languages do not have. Two of these new functions are most important for the evolution of reasoning and rationality: the *descriptive function* and the *argumentative function*.

As an example of the descriptive function, I might now describe to you how two days ago a magnolia was flowering in my garden, and what happened when snow began to fall. I might thereby express my feelings, and also release or trigger some feeling in you: you may perhaps react by thinking of *your* magnolia trees. So the two lower functions would be present. But *in addition* to all this, I should have described to you some facts; I should have made some *descriptive statements;* and these statements of mine would be factually *true,* or factually *false*.

Whenever I speak I cannot help expressing myself; and if you listen to me you can hardly help reacting. So the lower functions are *always* present. The descriptive function *need not* be present, for I may speak to you without describing any fact. For example, in showing or expressing uneasiness — say, doubt whether you will survive this long lecture — I need not describe anything. Yet description, including the description of conjectured states of affairs, which we formulate in the form of theories or hypotheses, is clearly an extremely important function of human language; and it is that function which distinguishes human language most clearly from the various animal languages (although there seems to be something approaching it in the language of the bees.[48] It is, of course, a function which is indispensable for science.

The last and highest of the four functions to be mentioned in this survey is the *argumentative function of language,* as it may be seen at work, in its highest form of development, in a well-disciplined *critical discussion*.

The argumentative function of language is not only the highest of the four functions I am here discussing, but it was also the latest of them to evolve. Its evolution has been closely connected with that of an argumentative, critical, and rational attitude; and since this attitude has led to the evolution of science, we may say that the argumentative function of language has created what is perhaps the most powerful tool for biological adaptation which has ever emerged in the course of organic evolution.

Like the other functions, the art in critical argument has developed by the method of trial and error-elimination, and it has had the most decisive influence on the human ability to think rationally. (Formal logic itself may be described as an "organon of critical argument.")[49] Like the descriptive use of language, the argumentative use has led to the evolution of ideal standards of control, or of *"regulative ideas"* (using a Kantian term): the main regulative idea of the descriptive use of language is *truth* (as distinct from *falsity*); and that of the argumentative use of language, in critical discussion, is *validity* (as distinct from *invalidity*).

Arguments, as a rule, are for or against some proposition or descriptive statement; this is why our fourth function — the argumentative function — must have emerged later than the descriptive function. Even if I argue in a committee that the University ought not to authorize a certain expenditure because we cannot afford it, or because some alternative way of using the money would be more beneficial, I am arguing not only for or against a *proposal* but also for and against some *proposition—for* the proposition, say, that the proposed use will not be beneficial, and *against* the proposition that the proposed use will be beneficial. So arguments, even arguments about proposals, as a rule bear on propositions, and very often on *descriptive* propositions.

Yet the argumentative use of language may be clearly distinguished from its descriptive use, simply because I can describe without arguing: I can describe, that is to say, without giving reasons for or against the truth of my description.

Our analysis of four functions of our language—the expressive, the signaling, the descriptive, and the argumentative functions—may be summed up by saying that, although it must be admitted that the two lower functions—the expressive and signaling functions—are *always* present whenever the higher functions are present, we must nevertheless distinguish the higher functions from the lower ones.

Yet many behaviorists and many philosophers have overlooked the higher functions, apparently because the lower ones are always present, whether or not the higher ones are.

XV

Apart from the new functions of language which have evolved and emerged together with man, and with human rationality, we must consider another distinction of almost equal importance, the distinction between the evolution of *organs* and of *tools or machines,* a distinction to be credited to one of the greatest of English philosophers, Samuel Butler, the author of *Erewhon* (1872).

Animal evolution proceeds largely, though not exclusively, by the modification of organs (or behavior) or the emergence of new organs (or behavior). *Human evolution* proceeds, largely, by developing new organs *outside our bodies or persons*: "exosomatically," as biologists call it, or "extra-personally." These new organs are tools, or weapons, or machines, or houses.

The rudimentary beginnings of this exosomatic development can of course be found among animals. The making of lairs, or dens, or nests, is an early achievement. I may also remind you that beavers build very ingenious dams. But man, instead of growing better eyes and ears, grows spectacles, microscopes, telescopes, telephones, and hearing aids. And instead of growing swifter and swifter legs, he grows swifter and swifter motor cars.

Yet the kind of extra-personal or exosomatic evolution which interests me here is this: instead of growing better memories and brains, we grow paper, pens, pencils, typewriters, dictaphones, the printing press, and libraries.

These add to our language—and especially to its descriptive and argumentative functions—what may be described as new dimensions. The latest development (used mainly in support of our argumentative abilities) is the growth of computers.

XVI

How are the higher functions and dimensions related to the lower ones? They do not replace the lower ones, as we have seen, but they establish a kind of *plastic control* over them—a control with feedback.

Take, for example, a discussion at a scientific conference. It may be exciting and enjoyable, and give rise to expressions and symptoms of its being so; and these expressions in their turn may release similar symptoms in other participants. Yet there is no doubt that up to a point these symptoms and releasing signals will be due to, and controlled by, the scientific *content* of the discussion; and since this will be *of a descriptive and of an argumentative nature,* the lower functions will be controlled by the higher ones. Moreover, though a good joke or a pleasant grin may let the lower functions win in the short run, what counts in the long run is a good argument—a valid argument—and what it establishes or refutes. In other words, our discussion is controlled, though plastically, by the regulative ideas of truth and of validity.

All this is strengthened by the discovery and development of the new dimensions of printing and publishing, especially when these are used for printing and publishing scientific theories and hypotheses, and papers in which these are critically discussed.

I cannot do justice to the importance of critical arguments here: it is a topic on which I have written fairly extensively,[50] and so I shall not raise it again here. I only wish to stress that critical arguments are *a means of control*: they are means of eliminating errors, a means of selection. We *solve our problems* by tentatively proposing various competing theories and hypotheses, as trial balloons, as it were; and by submitting them to critical discussion and to empirical tests, for the purpose of error-elimination.

So the evolution of the higher functions of language which I have tried to describe may be characterized as the evolution of new means for problem-solving, by new kinds of trials, and by new methods of error-elimination; that is to say, new methods for *controlling* the trials.

XVII

I can now give my solution to our first main problem, that is, Compton's problem of the influence of meaning upon behavior. It is this.

The higher levels of language have evolved under the pressure of a need for the *better control* of two things: of our lower levels of language, and our adaptation to the environment, by the method of growing not only new tools, but also, for example, new scientific theories and new standards of selection.

Now in developing its higher functions, our language has also grown abstract meanings and contents; that is to say, we have learned how to abstract from the various modes of formulating or expressing a theory, and how to pay attention to its *invariant content or meaning* (upon which its truth depends). And this holds not only for theories and other descriptive statements, but also for proposals, or aims, or whatever else may be submitted to critical discussion.

What I have called "Compton's problem" was the problem of explaining and understanding the controlling power of meanings, such as the contents of our theories, or of purposes, or aims; purposes or aims which in some cases we may have adopted after deliberation and discussion. But this is now no longer a problem. Their power of influencing us is part and parcel of these contents and meanings; for part of the function of contents and meanings is to control.

This solution of Compton's problem conforms to Compton's restricting postulate. For the control of ourselves and of our actions by our theories and purposes is a *plastic* control. We are not *forced* to submit ourselves to the control of our theories, for we can discuss them critically, and we can reject them freely if we think that they fall short of our regulative standards. So the control is far from one-sided. Not only do our theories control us, but we can control our theories (and even our standards): there is a kind of *feedback* here. And if we submit to our theories, then we do so freely, after deliberation; that is, after the critical discussion of alternatives, and after freely choosing between the competing theories, in the light of that critical discussion.

I submit this as my solution of Compton's problem; and before proceeding to solve Descartes's problem, I shall now briefly outline the more general theory of evolution which I have already used, implicitly, in my solution.

XVIII

I offer my general theory with many apologies. It has taken me a long time to think it out fully and to make it clear to myself. Nevertheless, I still feel far from satisfied with it. This is partly due to the fact that it is an *evolutionary* theory, and one which adds only a little, I fear, to existing evolutionary theories, except perhaps a new emphasis.

I blush when I have to make this confession; for when I was younger I used to say very contemptuous things about evolutionary philosophies. When twenty-two years ago Cannon Charles E. Raven, in his *Science, Religion and the Future*, described the Darwinian controversy as "a storm in a Victorian teacup," I agreed, but criticized him[51] for paying too much attention "to the vapours still emerging from the cup,'' by which I meant the hot air of the evolutionary philosophies (especially those which told us that there were inexorable laws of evolution). But now I have to confess that this cup of tea has become, after all, *my* cup of tea; and with it I have to eat humble pie.

Quite apart from evolutionary *philosophies,* the trouble about evolutionary *theory* is its tautological, or almost tautological, character: the difficulty is that *Darwinism* and natural selection, though extremely important, explain evolution by "the survival of the fittest" (a term due to Herbert Spencer). Yet there does not seem to be much difference, if any, between the assertion "those that survive are the fittest" and the tautology "those that survive are those that survive." For we have, I am afraid, no other criterion of fitness than actual survival, so that we conclude from the fact that some organisms have survived that they were the fittest, or those best adapted to the conditions of life.

This shows that Darwinism, with all its great virtues, is by no means a perfect theory. It is in need of a restatement which makes it less vague. The evolutionary theory which I am going to sketch here is an attempt at such a restatement.

My theory may be described as an attempt to apply to the whole of evolution what we learned when we analyzed the evolution from animal language to human language. And it consists of a certain *view of evolution* as a growing hierarchical system of plastic controls, and of a certain *view of organisms* as incorporating—or in the case of man, evolving exosomatically—this growing hierarchical system of plastic controls. The Neo-Darwinist theory of evolution is assumed; but it is restated by pointing out that its "mutations" may be interpreted as more or less accidental trial-and-error gambits, and "natural selection" as one way of controlling them by error-elimination.

I shall now state the theory in the form of twelve short theses:

(1) All *organisms* are constantly, day and night, *engaged in problem-solving;* and so are all those evolutionary *sequences of organisms*—the *phyla* which begin with the most primitive forms and of which the now living organisms are the latest members.

(2) These problems are problems in an objective sense: they can be, hypothetically, reconstructed by hindsight, as it were. (I will later say more about this.) Objective problems in this sense need not have their conscious counterpart; and where they have their conscious counterpart, the conscious problem need not coincide with the objective problem.

(3) Problem-solving always proceeds by the method of trial and error: new reactions, new forms, new organs, new modes of behavior, new hypotheses, are tentatively put forward and controlled by error-elimination.

(4) Error-elimination may proceed either by the complete elimination of unsuccessful forms (the killing-off of unsuccessful forms by natural selection) or by

the (tentative) evolution of controls which modify or suppress unsuccessful organs, or forms of behavior, or hypotheses.

(5) The single organism telescopes[52] into one body, as it were, the controls developed during the evolution of its *phylum*—just as it partly recapitulates, in its ontogenetic development, its phylogenetic evolution.

(6) The single organism is a kind of spearhead of the evolutionary sequence of organisms to which it belongs (its *phylum*): it is itself a tentative solution, probing into new environmental niches, choosing an environment and modifying it. It is thus related to its *phylum* almost exactly as the actions (behavior) of the individual organism are related to this organism: the individual organism, and its behavior, are both trials, which may be eliminated by error-elimination.

(7) Using '*P*' for problem, '*TS*' for tentative solutions, '*EE*' for error-elimination, we can describe the fundamental evolutionary sequence of events as follows:

$$P \to TS \to EE \to P$$

But this sequence is not a cycle: the second problem is, in general, different from the first: it is the result of the new situation which has arisen, in part, because of the tentative solutions which have been tried out, and the error-elimination which controls them. In order to indicate this, the above schema should be rewritten:

$$P_1 \to TS \to EE \to P_2.$$

(8) But even in this form an important element is still missing: the multiplicity of the tentative solutions, the multiplicity of the trials. Thus our final schema becomes something like this:

$$\begin{array}{c} \nearrow TS_1 \searrow \\ Ps_1 \to TS_2 \to EE \to P_2 \\ \searrow \quad \cdot \quad \nearrow \\ \cdot \\ \cdot \\ \cdot \\ \cdot \\ TS_n \end{array}$$

Background Knowledge

(9) In this form, our schema can be compared with that of Neo-Darwinism. According to Neo-Darwinism there is in the main *one* problem: the problem of survival. There is, as in our system, a multiplicity of tentative solutions—the variations or mutations. But there is only *one* way of error-elimination—the killing of the organism. And (partly for this reason) the fact that P_1 and P_2 will differ essentially is overlooked, or else its fundamental importance is not sufficiently clearly realized.

(10) In our system, not all problems are survival problems: there are many very specific problems and subproblems (even though the earliest problems may have been sheer survival problems). For example an early problem P_1 may be reproduction. Its solution may lead to a new problem, P_2: the problem of getting rid of, or of spreading, the offspring—the children which threaten to suffocate not only the parent organism but each other.[53]

It is perhaps of interest to note that *the problem of avoiding suffocation by one's offspring* may be one of those problems which was solved by the evolution of *multicellular organisms*: instead of getting rid of one's offspring, one establishes a *common economy*, with various new methods of living together.

(11) The theory here proposed distinguishes between P_1 and P_2, and it shows that the problems (or the problem situations) which the organism is trying to deal with are often *new*, and arise themselves as products of the evolution. The theory thereby gives implicitly a rational account of what has usually been called by the somewhat dubious names of *"creative evolution"* or *"emergent evolution."*[54]

(12) Our schema allows for the development of error-eliminating controls (warning organs like the eye; feedback mechanisms); that is, controls which can eliminate errors without killing the organism; and it makes it possible, ultimately, for our hypotheses to die in our stead.

XIX

Each organism can be regarded as a hierarchical system of *plastic controls*—as a system of clouds controlled by clouds. The controlled subsystems make trial-and-error movements which are partly suppressed and partly restrained by the controlling system.

We have already met an example of this in the relation between the lower and higher functions of language. The lower ones continue to exist and to play their part; but they are constrained and controlled by the higher ones.

Another characteristic example is this. If I am standing quietly, without making any movement, then (according to the physiologists) my muscles are constantly at work, contracting and relaxing in an almost random fashion (see T_1 and TS_n in thesis (8) of the preceding section), but controlled, without my being aware of it, by error-elimination (EE) so that every little deviation from my posture is almost at once corrected. So I am kept standing, quietly, by more or less the same method by which an automatic pilot keeps an aircraft steadily on its course.

This example also illustrates the thesis (1) of the preceding section—that each organism is all the time engaged in problem-solving by trial and error; that it reacts to new and old problems by more or less chance-like,[55] or cloud-like, trials which are eliminated if unsuccessful. (If successful, they increase the probability of the survival of mutations which "simulate" the solutions so reached, and tend to make the solution hereditary,[56] by incorporating it into the spatial structure or form of the new organism.)

XX

This is a very brief outline of the theory. It needs, of course, much elaboration. But I wish to explain *one* point a little more fully—the use I have made (in theses (1) and (3) of section XVIII) of the terms "*problem*" and "*problem-solving* and, more particularly, my assertion that *we can speak of problems in an objective, or nonpsychological sense.*

The point is important, for evolution is clearly not a conscious process. Many biologists say that the evolution of certain organs solves certain problems; for example, that the evolution of the eye solves the problem of giving a moving animal a timely warning to change its direction before bumping into something hard. Nobody suggests that this kind of solution to this kind of problem is consciously sought. It is not, then, just a metaphor if we speak of problem-solving?

I do not think so; rather, the situation is this: when we speak of a problem, we do so almost always from hindsight. A man who works on a problem can seldom say clearly what his problem is (unless he has found a solution); and even if he can explain his problem, he may mistake it. And this may even hold of scientists—though scientists are among those few who consciously try to be fully aware of their problems. For example, Kepler's conscious problem was to discover the harmony of the world order; but we may say that the problem he solved was the mathematical description of motion in a set of two-body planetary systems. Similarly, Schroedinger was mistaken about the problem he had solved by finding the (time-independent) Schroedinger equation: he thought his waves were charge-density waves, of a changing continuous field of electric charge. Later Max Born gave a statistical interpretation of the Schroedinger wave amplitude, an intepretation which shocked Schroedinger and which he disliked as long as he lived. He had solved a problem—but it was not the one he thought he had solved. This we know now, by hindsight.

Yet clearly it is in science that we are most conscious of the problems we try to solve. So it should not be inappropriate to use hindsight in other cases, and to say that the amoeba solves some problems (though we need not assume that it is in any sense aware of its problems): from the amoeba to Einstein is just one step.

XXI

But Compton tells us that the amoeba's actions are not rational,[57] while we may assume that Einstein's actions are. So there should be some difference, after all.

I admit that there is a difference: even though their methods of almost random or cloud-like trial and error movements are fundamentally not very different,[58] there is a great difference in their attitudes toward error. Einstein, unlike the amoeba, consciously tried his best, whenever a new solution occurred to him, to fault it and detect an error in it: he approached his own solutions *critically*.

I believe that this consciously critical attitude toward his own ideas is the one really important difference between the method of Einstein and that of the amoeba. It made it possible for Einstein to reject, quickly, hundreds of hypotheses as inadequate before examining one or another hypothesis more carefully, if it appeared to be able to stand up to more serious criticism.

As the physicist John Archibald Wheeler said recently, "Our whole problem is to make the mistakes as fast as possible."[59] This problem of Wheeler's is solved by consciously adopting the critical attitude. This, I believe, is the highest form so far of the rational attitude, or of rationality.

The scientist's trials and errors consist of hypotheses. He formulates them in words, and often in writing. He can then try to find flaws in any one of these hypotheses, by criticizing it, and by testing it experimentally, helped by his fellow scientists who will be delighted if they can find a flaw in it. If the hypothesis does not stand up to these criticisms and to these tests at least as well as its competitors,[60] it will be eliminated.

It is different with primitive man, and with the amoeba. Here there is no critical attitude, and so it happens more often than not that natural selection eliminates a mistaken hypothesis or expectation by eliminating those organisms which hold it, or believe in it. So we can say that the critical or rational method consists in letting our hypotheses die in our stead: it is a case of exosomatic evolution.

XXII

Here I may perhaps turn to a question which has given me much trouble, although in the end I arrived at a very simple solution.

The question is: Can we show that plastic controls exist? Are there inorganic physical systems in nature which may be taken as examples or as physical models of plastic controls?

It seems that this question was implicitly answered in the negative by many physicists who, like Descartes or Compton, operate with master-switch models, and by many philosophers who, like Hume or Schlick, deny that anything intermediate between complete determinism and pure chance can exist. Admittedly, cyberneticists and computer engineers have more recently succeeded in constructing computers made of hardware but incorporating highly plastic controls; for example, computers with a built-in mechanism for chance-like trials, checked or evaluated by feedback (in the manner of an automatic pilot or a self-homing device) and eliminated if erroneous. But these systems, although incorporating what I have called plastic controls, consist essentially of complex relays of master-switches. What I was seeking, however, was a simple physical model of

Peircean indeterminism; a purely physical system resembling a very cloudy cloud in heat motion, controlled by some other cloudy clouds—though by somewhat less cloudy ones.

If we return to our old arrangement of clouds and clocks, with a cloud on the left and a clock on the right, then we could say that what we are looking for is something intermediate, like an organism or like our cloud of gnats, but not alive: a pure physical system, controlled plastically and "softly," as it were.

Let us assume that the cloud to be controlled is a gas. Then we can put on the extreme left an uncontrolled gas which will soon diffuse and so cease to constitute a physical *system*. We put on the extreme right an iron cylinder filled with gas: this is our example of a "hard" control, a "cast-iron" control. In between, but far to the left, are many more or less "softly" controlled systems, such as our cluster of gnats, and huge balls of particles, such as a gas kept together by gravity, somewhat like the sun. (We do not mind if the control is far from perfect, and many particles escape.) The planets may perhaps be said to be cast-iron controlled in their movements—comparatively speaking, of course, for even the planetary system is a cloud, and so are all the milky ways, star clusters, and clusters of clusters. But are there, apart from organic systems and those huge systems of particles, examples of any "softly" controlled small physical systems?

I think there are, and I propose to put in the middle of our diagram a child's balloon or, perhaps better, a soap bubble; and this, indeed, turns out to be a very primitive and in many respects an excellent example or model of a Peircean system *and* of a "soft" kind of plastic control.

The soap bubble consists of two subsystems which are both clouds and which control each other: without the air, the soapy film would collapse, and we should have only a drop of soapy water. Without the soapy film, the air would be uncontrolled: it would diffuse, ceasing to exist as a system. Thus the control is mutual; it is plastic, and of a feedback character. Yet it is possible to make a distinction between the controlled system (the air) and the controlling system (the film): the enclosed air is not only more cloudy than the enclosing film, but it also ceases to be a physical (self-interacting) system if the film is removed. As against this, the film, after removal of the air, will form a droplet which, though of a different shape, may still be said to be a physical system.

Comparing the bubble with a 'hardware' system like a precision clock or a computer, we should of course say (in accordance with Peirce's point of view) that even these hardware systems are clouds controlled by clouds. But these 'hard' systems are built with the purpose of minimizing, so far as it is possible, the cloud-like effects of molecular heat motions and fluctuations: though they are clouds, the controlling mechanisms are designed to suppress, or compensate for, all cloud-like effects as far as possible. This holds even for computers with mechanisms simulating chance-like trial-and-error mechanisms.

Our soap bubble is different in this respect and, it seems, more similar to an organism: the molecular effects are not eliminated but contribute essentially to the working of the system which is enclosed by a skin—a permeable wall[61] that leaves the system "open," and able to "react" to environmental influences in a manner which is built, as it were, into its "organization": the soap bubble, when struck by a heat ray, absorbs the heat (much like a hot-house), and so the enclosed air will expand, keeping the bubble floating.

As in all uses of similarity or analogy we should, however, look out for limitations; and here we might point out that, at least in some organisms, molecular fluctuations are apparently amplified and so used to release trial-and-error movements. At any rate, amplifiers seem to play important roles in all organisms (which in this respect resemble some computers with their master-switches and cascades of amplifiers and relays). Yet there are no amplifiers in the soap bubble.

However this may be, our bubble shows that natural physical cloud-like systems which are plastically and softly controlled by other cloud-like systems do exist. (Incidentally, the film of the bubble need not, of course, be derived from organic matter, though it will have to contain large molecules.)

XXIII

The evolutionary theory here proposed yields an immediate solution to our second main problem—the classical Cartesian body-mind problem. It does to (without saying *what* "mind" or "consciousness" is) by saying something about the evolution, and thereby about the functions, of mind or consciousness.

We must assume that consciousness grows from small beginnings; perhaps its first form is a vague feeling of irritation, experienced when the organism has a problem to solve such as getting away from an irritant substance. However this may be, consciousness will assume evolutionary significance—and increasing significance—when it begins to *anticipate* possible ways of reacting: possible trial-and-error movements, and their possible outcomes.

We can say now that conscious states, or sequences of conscious states, may function as systems of control, of error-elimination: the elimination, as a rule, of (incipient) behavior, that is, (incipient) movement. Consciousness, from this point of view, appears as just one of many interacting kinds of control; and if we remember the control systems incorporated, for example, in books—theories, systems of law, and all that constitutes the "universe of meanings"—then consciousness can hardly be said to be the highest control system in the hierarchy. For it is to a considerable extent controlled by these exosomatic linguistic systems—even though they may be said to be *produced* by consciousness. Consciousness in turn is, we may conjecture, *produced* by physical states; yet it controls them to a considerable extent. Just as a legal or social system is produced by us, yet controls us, and is in no reasonable sense "identical" to or "parallel" with us, but *interacts* with us, so states of consciousness (the "mind") control the body, and *interact* with it.

Thus there is a whole set of analogous relationships. As our exosomatic world of meanings is related to consciousness, so consciousness is related to the behavior of the acting individual organism. And the behavior of the individual organism is similarly related to its body, to the individual organism taken as a physiological system. The latter is similarly related to the evolutionary sequence of organisms — the *phylum* of which it forms the latest spearhead, as it were: as the individual organism is thrown up experimentally as a probe by the *phylum* and yet largely controls the fate of the *phylum,* so the behavior of the organism is thrown up experimentally as a probe by the physiological system and yet controls, largely, the fate of this system. Our conscious states are similarly related to our behavior. They anticipate our behavior, working out, by trial and error, its likely consequences; thus they not only control but they try out, *deliberate.*

We now see that this theory offers us an almost trivial answer to Descartes's problem. Without saying what *"the mind" is,* it leads immediately to the conclusion that our *mental states control (some of) our physical movements,* and that there is some give-and-take, some feedback, and so some *interaction,* between mental activity and the other functions of the organism.[62]

The control will again be of the "plastic" kind; in fact all of us — especially those who play a musical instrument such as the piano or the violin — know that the body does not always do what we want it to do; and that we have to learn, from our ill-success, how to modify our aims, making allowances for those limitations which beset our control: though we are free, to some considerable extent, there are always conditions — physical or otherwise — which set limits to what we can do. (Of course, before giving in, we are free to try to transcend these limits.)

Thus, like Descartes, I propose the adoption of a dualistic outlook, though I do *not* of course recommend talking of *two kinds of interacting substances.* But I think it is helpful and legitimate to distinguish *two kinds of interacting states* (or events), physio-chemical and mental ones. Moreover, I suggest that if we distinguish only these two kinds of states we still take too narrow a view of our world: at the very least we should also distinguish those artifacts which are products of organisms, and especially the products of our minds, and which can interact with our minds and thus with the state of our physical environment. Although these artifacts are often "mere bits of matter," "mere tools" perhaps, they are even on the animal level sometimes consummate works of art; and on the human level, the products of our minds are often very much more than "bits of matter" — marked bits of paper, say; for these bits of paper may represent states of a discussion, states of the growth of knowledge, which may transcend (sometimes with serious consequences) the grasp of most or even all of the minds that helped to produce them. Thus we have to be not merely dualists, but pluralists; and we have to recognize that the great changes which we have brought about, often unconsciously, in our physical universe show that abstract rules and abstract ideas, some of which are perhaps only partially grasped by human minds, may move mountains.

XXIV

As an afterthought, I should like to add one last point.

It would be a mistake to think that, because of natural selection, evolution can only lead to what may be called "utilitarian" results: to adaptations which are useful in helping us to survive.

Just as in a system with plastic controls the controlling and controlled subsystems interact, so our tentative solutions interact with our *problems* and also with our *aims*. This means that our aims can change and that *the choice of an aim may become a problem;* different aims may compete, and new aims may be invented and controlled by the method of trial and error-elimination.

Admittedly, if a new aim clashes with the aim of surviving, then this new aim may be eliminated by natural selection. It is well known that many mutations are lethal and thus suicidal; and there are many examples of suicidal aims. Others are perhaps neutral with respect to survival.

Many aims that at first are subsidiary to survival may later become autonomous, and even opposed to survival; for example, the ambition to excel in courage, to climb Mount Everest, to discover a new continent, or to be the first on the moon; or the ambition to discover some new truth.

Other aims may from the very beginning be autonomous departures, independent of the aim to survive. Artistic aims are perhaps of this kind, or some religious aims, and to those who cherish them they may become much more important than survival.

All this is part of the superabundance of life — the almost excessive abundance of trials and errors upon which the method of trial and error-elimination depends.[63]

It is perhaps not uninteresting to see that artists, like scientists, actually use this trial-and-error method. A painter may put down, tentatively, a speck of color, and step back for a critical assessment of its effect[64] in order to alter it if it does not solve the problem he wants to solve. And it may happen that an unexpected or accidental effect of his tentative trial — a color speck or brush stroke — may change his problem, or create a new subproblem, or a new aim: the evolution of artistic aims and of artistic standards (which, like the rules of logic, may become exosomatic systems of control) proceeds also by the trial-and-error method.

We may perhaps here look back for a moment to the problem of physical determinism, and to our example of the deaf physicist who had never experienced music but would be able to "compose" a Mozart opera or a Beethoven symphony, simply by studying Mozart's or Beethoven's bodies and their environments as physical systems, and predicting where their pens would put down black marks on lined paper. I presented these as unacceptable consequences of physical determinism. Mozart and Beethoven are, partly, controlled by their "taste," their system of musical evaluation. Yet this system is not cast-iron but rather plastic. It responds to new ideas, and it can be modified by new trials and errors — perhaps even by an accidental mistake, an unintended discord.[65]

In conclusion, let me sum up the situation.

We have seen that it is unsatisfactory to look upon the world as a closed physical system — whether a strictly deterministic system or a system in which whatever is not strictly determined is simply due to chance: on such a view of the world human creativeness and human freedom can only be illusions. The attempt to make use of quantum-theoretical indeterminacy is also unsatisfactory, because it leads to chance rather than freedom, and to snap-decisions rather than deliberate decisions.

I have, therefore, offered here a different view of the world — one in which the physical world is an open system. This is compatible with the view of the evolution of life as a process of trial and error-elimination; and it allows us to understand rationally, though far from fully, the emergence of biological novelty and the growth of human knowledge and human freedom.

I have tried to outline an evolutionary theory which takes account of all this and which offers solutions to Compton's and Descartes's problems. It is, I am afraid, a theory which manages to be too humdrum *and* too speculative at the same time; and even though I think that testable consequences can be derived from it, I am far from suggesting that my proposed solution is what philosophers have been looking for. But I feel that Compton might have said that it presents, in spite of its faults, a possible answer to his problem — and one which might lead to further advance.

Notes

These notes were not, of course, delivered with the text of the lecture, although most of them existed when the lecture was delivered. The text of the lecture, as here printed, has been revised, and a number of passages have been restored (especially sections VIII to X) which had to be omitted in order to keep to the allotted time. Much of this additional material was used in the Seminar which I conducted after the lecture.

1. When I came to Berkeley early in February 1962, I was eagerly looking forward to meeting Compton. He died before we could meet.

2. A. H. Compton and A. W. Simon, *Phys. Rev.*, 25, 1925, 309ff. (See also W. Bothe and H. Geiger, *Zeitschr. f. Phys.*, 26, 1924, 44ff., and 32, 1925, 639ff.; *Naturwissenschaften*, 13, 1925, 440.)

3. N. Bohr, H. A. Kramers, and J. C. Slater, *Phil. Mag.*, 47, 1924, 785ff., and *Zeitschr. f. Phys.*, 24, 1924, 69ff. See also A. H. Compton and S. K. Allison, *X-Rays in theory and experiment*, 1935; for example, pp. 211–227.

4. See chapter I, section 19, of Compton and Allison (note 3).

5. A. H. Compton, *The freedom of man*, 1935 (third edition, 1939). This book was based mainly on the Terry Foundation Lectures, delivered by Compton at Yale in 1931, and in addition on two other series of lectures given soon after the Terry Lectures.

6. A. H. Compton, *The human meaning of science*, 1940.

7. For the imperfections of the solar system see notes 11 and 16 below.

8. See section 23 of my book *The poverty of historicism* (1957 and later editions), where I criticize the "holistic" criterion of a "whole" (or "*Gestalt*") by showing that this criterion ("a whole is more than the mere sum of its parts") is satisfied even by the favorite holistic examples of non-wholes, such as a "mere heap" of stones. (Note that I do not deny that there exist wholes; I only object to the superficiality of most "holistic" theories.)

9. Newton himself was not among those who drew these "deterministic" consequences from his theory; see notes 11 and 16 below.

10. The conviction that determinism forms an essential part of any rational or scientific attitude was generally accepted, even by some of the leading opponents of "materialism" (such as Spinoza, Leibniz, Kant, and Schopenhauer). A similar dogma which formed part of the rationalist tradition was that all knowledge begins with *observation* and proceeds from there by induction. See my remarks on these two dogmas of rationalism in my book *Conjectures and refutations*, 1963, 1965, 1969, 1972, pp. 122ff.

11. Newton himself may be counted among the few dissenters, for he regarded even the solar system as *imperfect* and, consequently, as likely to perish. Because of these views he was accused of impiety, of "casting a reflection upon the wisdom of the author of nature" (as Henry Pemberton reports in his *A view of Sir Isaac Newton's philosophy*, 1728, p. 180).

12. *Collected papers of Charles Sanders Peirce*, 6, 1935, 6.44, p. 35. There may, of course, have been other physicists who developed similar views, but apart from Newton and Peirce I know of only one: Professor Franz Exner of Vienna. Schroedinger, who was his pupil, wrote about Exner's views in his book *Science, theory and man*, 1957, pp. 71, 133, 142ff. (This book was previously published under the title *Science and the human temperament*, 1935, and Compton referred to it in *The freedom of man*, see also note 25 below.

13. C. S. Peirce, *Collected papers*, 6, 6.47, p. 37 (first published 1892). The passage, though brief, is most interesting because it anticipates (note the remark on fluctuations in explosive mixtures) some of the discussion of macro-effects which result from the amplification of Heisenberg indeterminacies. This discussion begins, it appears, with a paper by Ralph Lillie, *Science 46*, 1927, pp. 139ff., to which Compton refers in *The freedom of man*, p. 50. It plays a considerable part in this work, pp. 48ff. (Note that Compton delivered the Terry Lectures in 1931.) Note 3 on pp. 51ff. contains a very interesting quantitative comparison of chance effects owing to molecular heat motion (the indeterminacy Peirce had in mind) and Heisenberg indeterminacy. The discussion was carried on by Bohr, Pascual Jordan, Fritz Medicus, Ludwig von Bertalanffy, and many others; more recently especially also by Walter Elsasser, *The physical foundations of biology*, 1958.

14. I am alluding to Paul Carus, *The Monist*, 2, 1892, 560ff. and 3, 1892, pp. 68ff.; Peirce replied in *The Monist*, 3, 1893, 526ff. (See his *Collected Papers*, 6, Appendix A, pp. 390ff.)

15. The sudden and complete transformation of the problem-situation may be gauged by the fact that to many of us old fogies it does not really seem so very long ago that empiricist philosophers (see for example Moritz Schlick, *Allgemeine Erkenntnislehre*, second edition, 1925, p. 277) were physical determinists, while nowadays physical determinism is being dismissed by P. H. Nowell-Smith, a gifted and spirited defender of Schlick's, as an "*eighteenth-century bogy*" (*Mind, 63*, 1954, p. 331; see also note 37 below). Time marches on and no doubt it will, in time, solve all our problems, bogies or non-bogies. Yet oddly enough we old fogies seem to remember the days of Planck, Einstein, and Schlick, and have much trouble trying to convince our puzzled and muddled minds that these great determinist thinkers produced their bogies in the eighteenth century, together with Laplace who produced the most famous bogy of all (the "super-human intelligence" of his *Essay* of 1819, often called

"Laplace's demon"; see Compton, *Freedom of man*, pp. 5ff., and *Human meaning of science*, p. 34, and Alexander, note 35 below. Yet a still greater effort might perhaps recall even to our failing memories a similar eighteenth-century bogy produced by a certain Carus (not the nineteenth-century thinker P. Carus referred to in note 14, but T. L. Carus, who wrote *Lucretius de rerum naturae*, ii, 251–260, quoted by Compton in *Freedom of man*, p. 1).

16. I developed this view in 1950 in a paper "Indeterminism in Quantum Physics and in Classical Physics," *British Journal for the Philosophy of Science, 1*, 1950, No. 2, 117–133, and No. 3, 173–195. When writing this paper I knew nothing, unfortunately, of Peirce's views (see notes 12 and 13). I may perhaps mention here that I have taken the idea of opposing *clouds* and *clocks* from this earlier paper of mine. Since 1950, when my paper was published, the discussion of indeterminst elements in classical physics has gathered momentum. See Leon Brillouin, *Scientific uncertainty and information*, 1964 (a book with which I am by no means in full agreement), and the references to the literature there given, especially on pp. 38, 105, 127, 151ff. To these references might be added in particular Jacques Hadamard's great paper concerning geodetic lines on "horned" surfaces of negative curvature, *Journal de mathématiques pures et appliquées*, 5th series, *4*, 1898, 27ff.

17. See also my book *The logic of scientific discovery*, especially the new Appendix *xi; also Chapter ix, which contains criticism that is valid in the main, though in view of Einstein's criticism in Appendix *xii, I had to withdraw the thought experiment (of 1934) described in section 77. This experiment can be replaced, however, by the famous thought experiment of Einstein, Podolsky, and Rosen, discussed in Appendixes *xi and *xii. See also my paper "The propensity interpretation of the calculus of probability, and the quantum theory," in *Observation and intepretation*, edited by S. Körner, 1957, pp. 65–70 and 83–89.

18. The last sentence is meant as a criticism of some of the views contained in Thomas S. Kuhn's interesting and stimulating book *The structure of scientific revolutions*, 1963.

19. See Werner Heisenberg, *The physical principles of the quantum theory*, 1930.

20. I am alluding to Compton's refutation of the theory of Bohr, Kramers, and Slater, *Phil. Mag.*, 47, 1924; see also Compton's own allusion in *Freedom of man*, p. 7 (last sentence), and *Human meaning of science*, p. 36.

21. See Compton's preface in Heisenberg's *Physical principles of quantum theory*, pp. iiiff.; also his remarks on the *incompleteness* of quantum mechanics in *Freedom of man*, p. 45 (with a reference to Einstein) and in *Human meaning of science*, p. 42. Compton approved of the incompleteness of quantum mechanics, while Einstein saw in it a weakness of the theory. Replying to Einstein, Niels Bohr (like J. von Neumann before him) asserted that the theory was *complete* (perhaps in another sense of the term). See, for example, A. Einstein, B. Podolsky, and N. Rosen, *Physical Review, 42*, 1935, 777–780; and Bohr's reply in *48*, 1935, 696ff.; also A. Einstein, *Dialectica, 2*, 1948, 320–324; Bohr, pp. 312–319 of the same volume; further, the discussion between Einstein and Niels Bohr in P. A. Schilpp (ed.), *Albert Einstein: Philosopher-scientist*, 1949, pp. 201–241, and especially 668–674, and a letter of Einstein's, published in my *Logic of scientific discovery*, pp. 457–464; see also pp. 445–456.

22. See the history of its discovery as told by N. R. Hanson, *The Concept of the Positron*, 1963, chapter ix.

23. See especially the passages on "emergent evolution" in *Freedom of man*, pp. 90ff.; *Human meaning of science*, p. 73.

24. *Freedom of man*, p. 1.

25. Ibid., pp. 26ff.; see also pp. 27ff. (the last paragraph beginning on p. 27). I may perhaps remind the reader that my views differ a little from the quoted passage because like Peirce I think it logically possible that the *laws* of a system be Newtonian (and so *prima facie* deterministic) and the system nevertheless indeterministic, because the system to which the laws apply may be intrinsically unprecise, in the sense, for example, that there is no point in saying that its coordinates, or velocities, are rational (as opposed to irrational) numbers. The following remark (see Schroedinger, *Science*,

theory and man, p. 143) is also very relevant: "the energy-momentum theorem provides us with only *four* equations, thus leaving the elementary process to a great extent undetermined, even if it complies with them." See also note 16 above.

26. *Human meaning of science*, p. ix.

27. Ibid., p. 42.

28. *Freedom of man*, p. 27.

29. Assume that our physical world is a *physically closed* system containing chance elements. Obviously it would not be deterministic; yet purposes, ideas, hopes, and wishes could not in such a world have any influence on physical events; assuming that they exist, they would be completely redundant: they would be what are called "epiphenomena." (Note that a deterministic physical system will be closed, but that a closed system may be indeterministic. Thus "indeterminism is not enough," as will be explained in section X, below; see also note 40 below.)

30. Kant suffered deeply from this nightmare and failed in his attempts to escape from it; see Compton's excellent statement on "Kant's avenue of escape" in *Freedom of man*, pp. 67ff. (In line 2 on p. 68 the words "*of Pure Reason*" should be deleted.) I may perhaps mention here that I do not agree with everything Compton has to say in the field of the philosophy of science. Examples of views I do not share are: Compton's approval of Heisenberg's positivism or phenomenalism (*Freedom of man*, p. 31), and certain remarks (note 7 on p. 20) which Compton credits to Carl Eckart: although Newton himself was, it seems, not a determinist (see note 11 above). I do not think that the fairly precise idea of *physical determinism* should be discussed in terms of some vague "law of causalty"; nor do I agree that Newton was a phenomenalist in a sense similar to that in which Heisenberg may be said to have been a phenomenalist (or positivist) in the 1930s.

31. David Hume, *A treatise of human nature*, 1739 (ed. L. A. Selby-Bigge, 1888 and reprints), p. 174; see also, for example, pp. 173 and 187.

32. Hume, ibid., pp. 408ff.

33. Ibid., pp. 403ff. It is interesting to compare this with pp. 404ff. (where Hume says, "I define necessity two ways") and with his ascription to "matter" of "that intelligible quality, call it necessity or not" which, as he says, everybody "must allow to belong to the will" (or "to the actions of the mind"). In other words, Hume tries here to apply his doctrine of custom or habit, and his association psychology, to "matter," that is, to physics.

34. See especially B. F. Skinner, *Walden two*, 1948, a charming and benevolent but utterly naïve Utopian dream of omnipotence (see especially pp. 246–250; also 214ff.). Aldous Huxley, *Brave new world*, 1932 (see also *Brave new world revisited*, 1959), and George Orwell, *1984*, 1948, are well-known antidotes. I have criticized some of these Utopian and authoritarian ideas in *The open society and its enemies*, 1945, fourth edition, 1962, and in *Poverty of Historicism*, e.g., p. 91. (See in both books especially my criticism of the so-called sociology of knowledge.)

35. My deaf physicist is, of course, closely similar to Laplace's demon (see note 15 above); and I believe that his achievements are absurd, simply because nonphysical aspects (aims, purpose, traditions, tastes, ingenuity) play a role in the development of the physical world; or in other words, I believe in *interactionism* (see notes 43 and 62 above). Samuel Alexander, *Space, time and deity*, 1920, vol. ii, p. 328, says of what he calls the "Laplacean calculator": "Except in the limited sense described, the hypothesis of the calculator is absurd." Yet the "limited sense" *includes* the prediction of *all* purely physical events, and would thus *include* the prediction of the position of all the black marks written by Mozart and Beethoven. It *excludes* only the prediction of mental experience (an exclusion that corresponds closely to my assumption of the physicist's deafness). Thus what I regard as absurd, Alexander is prepared to admit (I may perhaps say here that I think it preferable to discuss the problem of freedom in connection with the creation of music or of new scientific theories or technical inventions, rather than with ethics and ethical responsibility.)

36. Hume, *Treatise of human nature*, p. 609 (the italics are mine).

37. See note 15 above, and Gilbert Ryle, *The concept of mind*, 1949, pp. 76ff. ("The Bogy of Mechanism").

38. N. W. Pirie, "The meaninglessness of the terms life and living," *Perspectives in biochemistry*, 1937 (ed. J. Needham and D. E. Green), pp. 11ff.

39. See, for example, A. M. Turing, "Computing machinery and intelligence," *Mind, 59*, 1950, 433–460. Turing asserted that men and computers are in principle indistinguishable by their observable (behavioral) performance, and he challenged his opponents to *specify* some observable behavior or achievement of man which a computer would in principle be unable to achieve. But this challenge is an intellectual trap: by *specifying* a kind of behavior we would lay down a specification for building a computer. Moreover, we use, and build, computers because they can do many things which we cannot do; just as I use a pen or pencil when I wish to tote up a sum I cannot do in my head. "My pencil is more intelligent than I," Einstein used to say. But this does not establish that he is indistinguishable from his pencil. (See the final paragraphs, p. 195, of my paper "Indeterminism in quantum physics," and chapter 12, section 5, of my *Conjectures and meditations*.)

40. See M. Schlick, *Erkenntnis, 5*, p. 183 (extracted from the last eight lines of the first paragraph).

41. Hume, *Treatise of human nature*, p. 171. See also, for example, p. 407: "liberty . . . is the very same thing with chance."

42. *Freedom of man*, pp. 53ff.

43. A critical discussion of what I call here Descartes's problem will be found in chapters 12 and 13 of my book *Conjectures and refutations*. I may say here that, like Compton, I am almost a Cartesian, insofar as I reject the thesis of the physical completeness of all living organisms (considered as physical systems), that is to say, insofar as I conjecture that in some organisms mental states may *interact* with physical states. (I am, however, less of a Cartesian than Compton: I am even less attracted than he was by the master-switch models; see notes 44, 45, and 62 below.) Moreover, I have no sympathy with the Cartesian talk of a mental *substance* or thinking *substance*—no more than with his material *substance* or extended *substance*. I am a Cartesian only insofar as I believe in the existence of both physical *states* and mental *states* (and, besides, in even more abstract things such as states of a discussion).

44. Compton discussed this theory in some detail, especially in *Freedom of man*, pp. 37–65. See especially the reference to Ralph Lillie, *Science, 46*, in *Freedom of man*, p. 50. See also *Human meaning of science*, pp. 47–54. Of considerable interest are Compton's remarks, in *Freedom of man*, pp. 63ff., and *Human meaning of science*, p. 53, on *the character of individuality of our actions*, and his explanation of why it allows us to avoid what I may call the second horn of the dilemma (whose first horn is pure determinism), that is, the possibility that our actions are due to *pure chance;* see note 40 above.

45. See especially *Human meaning of science*, pp. viiiff., and p. 54, the last statement of the section.

46. This is a point of great importance, so much so that we should hardly describe any process as typically biological unless it involved the release or triggering of stored energy. But the opposite is, of course, not the case: many nonbiological processes are of the same character; and though amplifiers and release processes did not play a great role in classical physics, they are most characteristic of quantum physics and, of course, of chemistry. (Radioactivity with a triggering energy equal to zero is an extreme case; another interesting case is the—in principle adiabatic—tuning in to a certain radio frequency, followed by the extreme amplification of the signal or stimulus.) This is one of the reasons why such formulae as "the cause equals the effect" (and, with it, the traditional criticism of Cartesian interactionism) have long become obsolete, in spite of the continuing validity of the conservation laws. See note 43 below and the *stimulating or releasing* function of language, discussed in section XIV below; see also my *Conjectures and refutations*, p. 381.

47. The theory of the functions of language is due to Karl Bühler (*The mental development of the child*, 1919, English translation 1930, pp. 55, 56, 57; also *Sprachtheorie*, 1934). I have added to his three functions the argumentative function (and some other functions that play no role here, such as a hortative and a persuasive function). See, for example, my paper "Language and the body-mind problem," in *Conjectures and refutations*, p. 295, note 2 and text. (See also pp. 134ff.) It is not impossible that there exist in animals, especially in bees, transition stages to some descriptive language; see K. von Frisch, *Bees: their vision, chemical senses, and language*, 1950; *The dancing bees*, 1955; and M. Lindauer, *Communication among social bees*, 1961.

48. See the books by Frisch and Lindauer, note 47 above.

49. See my *Conjectures and refutations*, chapter 1, especially the remark on p. 64 on formal logic as "the *organon of rational criticism*"; also chapters 8 to 11, and 15.

50. See note 49 above and my book *Open society*, especially chapter 24 and the *Addendum* to volume ii (fourth edition, 1962); and *Conjectures and refutations*, especially the preface and introduction.

51. See p. 106, note 1, of my *Poverty of historicism*.

52. The idea of "telescoping" (though not this term, which I owe to Alan Musgrave) may perhaps be found in chapter vi of Charles Darwin's *The origin of species*, 1859 (I am quoting from the Mentor Book Edition, p. 180; italics mine): "every highly developed organism has passed through many changes; and . . . each modified structure tends to be inherited, so that each modification will not . . . be quite lost. . . . Hence, the structure of each part [of the organism] . . . is the sum of many inherited changes, through which the species has passed." See also E. Baldwin in *Perspectives in biochemistry*, pp. 99ff., and the literature there quoted.

53. The emergence of a new problem-situation could be described as a change or a differentiation of the "ecological niche," or the significant environment, of the organism. (It may perhaps be called a "habitat selection"; see B. Lutz, *Evolution, 2*, 1948, 29ff.) The fact that *any* change in the organism *or* its habits *or* its habitat produces new problems accounts for the incredible wealth of the (always tentative) solutions.

54. See note 23 for reference to Compton's remarks on "emergent evolution."

55. The method of trial and error-elimination *does not operate with completely chance-like or random trials* (as has been sometimes suggested), even though the trials may look pretty random; there must be at least an "after-effect" (in the sense of my *Logic of scientific discovery*, pp. 162ff.). For the organism is constantly learning from its mistakes, that is, it establishes *controls* which suppress or eliminate, or at least reduce the frequency of, certain *possible* trials (which were perhaps *actual* ones in its evolutionary past).

56. This is now sometimes called the "Baldwin Effect"; see, for example, G. G. Simpson, "The Baldwin Effect," *Evolution, 7*, 1953, 110ff., and C. H. Waddington, the same volume, p. 118ff. (see especially p. 124), and pp. 386ff. See also J. Mark Baldwin, *Development and evolution*, 1902, pp. 174ff., and H. S. Jennings, *The behaviour of the lower organisms*, 1906, pp. 321ff.

57. See *Freedom of man*, p. 91, and *Human meaning of science*, p. 73.

58. See H. S. Jennings, *Behavior of lower organisms*, pp. 334ff., 349ff. A beautiful example of problem-solving fish is described by K. Z. Lorenz, *King Solomon's ring*, 1952, pp. 37ff.

59. John A. Wheeler, *American Scientist, 44*, 1956, 360.

60. That we can only choose the "best" of a set of competing hypotheses—the "best" in the light of a critical discussion devoted to the search for truth—means that we choose the one which appears, in the light of the discussion, to come "nearest to the truth"; see my *Conjectures and refutations*, chapter 10. See also *Freedom of man*, pp. viiff., and especially p. 74 (on the principle of conservation of energy).

61. Permeable walls or membranes seem to be characteristic of all biological systems. (This may be connected with the phenomenon of biological individuation.) For their prehistory of the idea that membranes and bubbles are primitive organisms, see C. H. Kahn, *Anaximander*, 1960, pp. 111ff.

62. As hinted in several places, I conjecture that the acceptance of an *"interaction"* of mental and physical states offers the only satisfactory solution of Descartes's problem; see also note 43 above. I wish to add here that I think we have good reason to assume that there exist mental states, or conscious states (for example, in dreams) in which the consciousness of the ego (or of one's spatiotemporal position and identity) is very weak, or absent. It seems, therefore, reasonable to assume that full consciousness of the ego is a late development, and that it is a mistake to formulate the body-mind problem in such a way that this form of consciousness (or conscious "will") is treated as if it were the only one.

63. See, for example, my *Conjectures and refutations*, especially p. 312.

64. See, for example, Ernst H. Gombrich, *Meditations on a hobby horse*, 1963, especially p. 10; and the same author's *Art and illusion*, 1960, 1962 (see the index under "trial and error"). See also note 65 below.

65. For the close similarity of scientific and artistic production see *Freedom of man*, preface, pp. viiff., and the remark in *Freedom of man*, p. 74, referred to in note 60 above; further E. Mach, *Warmelehre*, 1896, pp. 440ff., where he writes: "The history of art . . . teaches us how shapes which arise accidentally may be used in works of art. Leonardo da Vinci advises the artist to look for shapes of clouds or patches on dirty or smokey walls, which might suggest to him ideas that fit in with his plans and his moods. . . . Again, a musician may sometimes get new ideas from random noises; and we may hear on occasion from a famous composer that he has been led to find valuable melodic or harmonic motifs by accidentally touching a wrong key while playing the piano."

The Placebo Concept in Medicine
and Psychiatry
Adolf Grünbaum

Just what is the problem of identifying an intervention or treatment *t* of one sort or another as a placebo for a target disorder *D*? One set of circumstances, among others, in which the need for such an identification may arise is the following: After the administration of *t* to some victims of *D*, some of them recover from their affliction to a significant extent. Now suppose that there is cogent evidence that this improvement can indeed be causally attributed at all to some factors or other among the spectrum of constituents comprising the dispensation of *t* to a patient. Then it can become important to know whether the therapeutic gain that ensued from *t* in the alleviation of *D* was due to *those particular factors* in its dispensation that the advocates of *t* have theoretically designated as deserving the credit for the positive treatment outcome. And one aim of this paper is to articulate in detail the bearing of the answer to this question on whether *t* qualifies generically as a placebo or not. For, as will emerge, the medical and psychiatric literature on placebos and their effects is conceptually bewildering, to the point of being a veritable Tower of Babel.

The proverbial sugar pill is hardly the sole placebo capable of producing ther-

Reprinted from M. Shepherd and N. Sartorius (Eds.). *Non Specific Aspects of Treatment.* Toronto, Lewiston, New York, Bern, Stuttgart: Hans Huber Publishers, 1989, pp. 7–38. Previously published in the same or similar form in *Psychological Medicine, 16,* 1986, pp. 19–38, and in *Placebo: Theory, Research and Mechanisms,* edited by L. White, B. Tursky, and G. E. Schwartz. New York: Guilford Press, 1985, pp. 9–36. Copyright (c) 1986 Adolf Grünbaum.

I thank Dr. Thomas Detre and Dr. Arthur K. Shapiro for useful expository comments on the first draft of this paper. And I am indebted to the Fritz Thyssen Stiftung, Cologne, West Germany, for the support of research. Furthermore, I am grateful to Dr. Jennifer Worrall, as well as to Dr. John Worrall, who offered some perceptive suggestions for clarifying some of the formulations in one of my early publications on this subject (Grünbaum, 1981). Sections from this earlier paper are used by permission of Pergamon Press, Ltd.

apeutic benefits for ailments other than hypoglycemia and other glucose deficits. Indeed, the long-term history of medical treatment has been characterized as largely the history of the placebo effect (A. K. Shapiro & Morris, 1978). After all, it is not only the patients who can be unaware that the treatments they are receiving are just placebos for their disorders; the physicians as well may mistakenly believe that they are administering nonplacebos for their patients' ailments, when they are actually dispensing placebos, while further enhancing the patients' credulity by communicating their own therapeutic faith. For example, as we shall see, surgery for angina pectoris performed in the United States during the 1950s turned out to be a mere placebo. Unbeknown to the physicians who practiced before the present century, most of the medications they dispensed were at best pharmacologically ineffective, if not outright physiologically harmful or even dangerous. Thus, during all that time, doctors were largely engaged in the unwitting dispensation of placebos on a massive scale. Even after the development of contemporary scientific medicine some 80 years ago, "the placebo effect flourished as the norm of medical treatment" (A. K. Shapiro & Morris, 1978, p. 371).

The psychiatrist Jerome Frank (1973) has issued the sobering conjecture that those of the roughly 200 psychotherapies whose gains exceed those from spontaneous remission do *not* owe such remedial efficacy to the *distinctive* treatment factors credited by their respective therapeutic advocates, but succeed for other reasons. Nonetheless, Frank admonishes us not to disparage such placebogenic gains in therapy, at least as long as we have nothing more effective. And even in internal medicine and surgery, a spate of recent articles has inveighed against downgrading placebogenic benefits, the grounds being that we should be grateful even for small mercies. Yet the plea not to forsake the benefits wrought by placebos has been challenged on ethical grounds: the injunction to secure the patient's informed consent is a demand whose fulfilment may well render the placebo ineffective, though perhaps not always (Park & Covi, 1965).

The physician Arthur K. Shapiro is deservedly one of the most influential writers in this field of inquiry. He has been concerned with the history of the placebo effect (1960) and with the semantics of the word "placebo" (1968), no less than with current empirical research on placebogenic phenomena in medical and psychological treatments (A. K. Shapiro & Morris, 1978). Thus, in his portion of the last-cited paper, he refined (1978, p. 371) his earlier 1971 definition of "placebo" in an endeavor to codify the current uses of the term throughout medicine and psychiatry. The technical vocabulary employed in A. K. Shapiro's earlier and most recent definitions is standard terminology in the discussion of placebo therapies and of experimental placebo controls, be it in pharmacology, surgery, or psychiatry. Yet just this standard technical vocabulary, I submit, generates confusion by being misleading or obfuscating, and indeed cries out for conceptual clarification. Thus, it is my overall objective to revamp Shapiro's definitions substantially so as to provide a clear and rigorous account of the placebo notion appropriate to current medicine and psychiatry.

Critique, Explication, and Reformulation
of A. K. Shapiro's Definition

Critique

While some placebos are known to be such by the dispensing physician—though presumably not by the patient—other placebo therapies are mistakenly believed to be nonplacebos by the physician as well. Mindful of this dual state of affairs, A. K. Shapiro's definition of a placebo therapy makes it clear that, at any given stage of scientific knowledge, a treatment modality actually belonging to the genus placebo can be of the latter kind rather than of the traditionally recognized first sort. To capture both of these two species of placebo therapy, he casts his definition into the following general form, in which the expression " $=_{def.}$" stands for the phrase "is definitionally equivalent to":

Therapy t is a placebo therapy

$=_{def.}$ t is of kind A OR t is of kind B.

Any definition of this "either-or" form is called a "disjunctive" definition, and *each* of the two independent clauses connected by the word "or" is called a "disjunct." For example, suppose we define a "parent" by saying:

Person X is a parent

$=_{def.}$ X is a father OR X is a mother.

This is clearly a *disjunctive* definition. And it is convenient to refer to each of the separate clauses "X is a father" and "X is a mother" as a "disjunct." Thus, the sentence "X is a father" can obviously be regarded as the first of the two disjuncts, while the sentence "X is a mother" is the second disjunct. Hence, for brevity, I thus refer respectively to the corresponding two parts of Shapiro's actual disjunctive definition (A. K. Shapiro & Morris, 1978):

> A *placebo* is defined as any therapy or component of therapy that is deliberately used for its nonspecific, psychological, or psychophysiological effect, or that is used for its presumed specific effect, but without specific activity for the condition being treated. (p. 371)

Shapiro goes on to point out at once that the term "placebo" is used not only to characterize a treatment modality or therapy, but also a certain kind of experimental control:

> A *placebo*, when used as a control in experimental studies, is defined

as a substance or procedure that is without specific activity for the condition being evaluated [*sic*]. (p. 371)

And then he tells us furthermore that

A *placebo effect* is defined as the psychological or psychophysiological effect produced by placebos. (p. 371)

All of the conceptual puzzlement warranted by these three statements arises in the initial disjunctive definition of a "placebo therapy." For it should be noted that this definition employs the tantalizing words "nonspecific effect," "specific effect," and "specific activity" in unstated *technical* senses. Once these terms are elucidated, the further definitions of a "placebo control" and of a "placebo effect" become conceptually unproblematic. Hence let us now concentrate on the disjunctive definition of a "placebo therapy," and see what help, if any, Shapiro gives us with the technical terms in which he has expressed it. Contrary to the belief of some others, I make bold to contend that his explicit comments on their intended construal still leaves them in an unsatisfactory logical state for the purposes at hand.

In their joint 1978 paper, A. K. Shapiro and Morris elaborate quite vaguely on the key concept of "specific activity" as follows:

Specific activity is the therapeutic influence attributable solely to the contents or processes of the therapies rendered. The criterion for specific activity (and therefore the placebo effect) should be based on scientifically controlled studies. (p. 372)

They provide this characterization as part of a longer but very rough delineation of the complementary notions denoted by the terms "specific" and "nonspecific," locutions that are as pervasive as they are misleading or confusing in the literature on placebos. Thus, they make the following comment on the definition of "placebo" given above, which I amplify within brackets:

Implicit in this definition is the assumption that active treatments [i.e., nonplacebos] may contain placebo components. Even with specific therapies [i.e., nonplacebos] results are apt to be due to the combination of both placebo and nonplacebo effects. Treatments that are devoid of active, specific components are known as pure placebos, whereas therapies that contain nonplacebo components are called impure placebos . . . Treatments that have specific components but exert their effects primarily through nonspecific mechanisms are considered placebo therapies . . .

The key concept in defining placebo is that of "specific activity." In nonpsychological therapies, specific activity is often equated with nonpsychological mechanisms of action. When the specific activity of a

treatment is psychological [i.e., in psychotherapies that derive therapeutic efficacy from those particular factors in the treatment that the pertinent theory singles out specifically as being remedial] this method of separating specific from nonspecific activity is no longer applicable. Therefore, a more general definition of specific activity is necessary. Specific activity is the therapeutic influence attributable solely to the contents or processes of the therapies rendered [i.e., the therapeutic influence, if any, that derives solely from those component factors of the therapy that are specifically singled out by its advocates as deserving credit for its presumed efficacy]. The criterion for specific activity (and therefore the placebo effect) should be based on scientifically controlled studies. . . . In behavior therapy, some investigators have utilized "active placebo" control groups whereby some aspects of the therapy affect behavior but those aspects differ from the theoretically relevant ingredients of concern to the investigator.
(pp. 371–372)

This passage urgently calls for clarification beyond what I have supplied within brackets. In particular, the terms "specific activity" and "nonspecific effect," though standard, are anything but clear. Yet, as the authors emphasize further on, it is by virtue of a treatment's *lack* of so-called "specific activity" for a given target disorder that this treatment *objectively* qualifies as a placebo, regardless of whether the dispensing physician believes the treatment to have actual placebo status or not. They import this emphasis on the irrelevance of belief to generic placebo *status* into their definition. There, in its first paragraph, a disjunction makes explicit provision for the presence of such belief on the part of the dispenser, as well as for its absence. In the first disjunct, it is a placebo that the physician *believes* himself or herself to be giving the patient, and the doctor is right in so believing. In the second disjunct, the physician believes himself or herself to be administering a *non*placebo, but he or she is definitely mistaken in so believing.

In either case, a placebo is actually being dispensed, be it wittingly or unwittingly. For brevity, I distinguish between the two situations to which these disjuncts pertain by saying that the treatment is an "intentional placebo" in the former case, while being an "inadvertent placebo" in the latter. Note that if a treatment *t* is actually not a placebo generically while its dispenser or even the whole professional community of practitioners believes *t* to be one, then *t* is precluded from qualifying as a "placebo" by the definition. To earn the label "intentional placebo," a treatment not only must be *believed* to be a placebo by its dispenser, but must also actually *be* one generically. Thus, therapists have administered a nonplacebo in the erroneous belief that it is a placebo. For example, at one time, some psychoanalysts used phenothiazines to treat schizophrenics in the belief that these drugs were mere (anger-reducing, tranquilizing) placebos;

they presumed them to be ineffective for the psychic dissociation and the pa-thognomonic symptoms of schizophrenia. But controlled studies showed that these medications possessed a kind of therapeutic efficacy for the disorder that was not placebogenic (Davis & Cole, 1975 a, b).

Incidentally, besides not being placebos for schizophrenia, the phenothiazines turned out to be capable of inducing the negative side effects of parkinsonism, at least transiently (Blakiston's *Gould Medical Dictionary,* 1972, p. 1130). But the motor impairment manifested in parkinsonism is attributed to a deficiency of brain dopamine. Thus the unfavorable parkinsonian side effect of the phenothia-zine drugs turned out to have *heuristic* value because it suggested that these drugs block the dopamine receptors in the brain. And since the drugs were also effec-tive nonplacebos for schizophrenia, the parkinsonian side-effect raised the pos-sibility that an excess of dopamine might be implicated in the etiology of schizo-phrenia. In this way, a *biochemical* malfunction of the brain was envisioned quite specifically as causally relevant to this psychosis (Kolata, 1979).

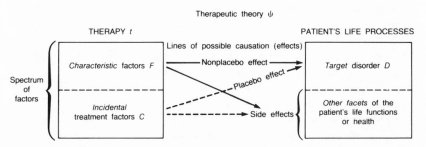

Figure 1. Illustration of therapeutic theory Ψ, used in clarifying the definition of "placebo."

Let me now specify the terminology and notation that I employ in my recti-fying explication of "placebo," using the diagram shown in Figure 1. Overall, there is some stated or tacit therapeutic theory, which I call "Ψ." Now Ψ de-signs or recommends a particular treatment or therapy *t* for a particular illness or target disorder *D*. In the left-hand box of Figure 1, I generically depict a treat-ment modality or therapy *t*. Note that it contains a spectrum of ingredients or treatment factors. For example, the theory Ψ may insist that if it is to recommend surgery for the treatment of gallstones, then the surgical process must obviously include the removal of the gallstones, rather than a mere sham abdominal inci-sion. I want a name for those treatment factors that a given theory Ψ thus *picks out* as the defining characteristics of a given type of therapy *t*. And I call these factors the "characteristic factors *F*" of *t*. But Ψ recognizes that besides the characteristic factors *F,* the given therapy normally also contains other factors which it regards as just incidental. For example, a theory that deems the removal of gallstones to be therapeutic for certain kinds of pains and indigestion will assume that this abdominal surgery includes the administration of anesthesia to the patient. To take a quite different example, when Freud recommended psychoanalytical treatment, he insisted on the payment of a hefty fee, believing it to be perhaps a catalyst for the patient's receptivity to the therapeutic task. Furthermore, a therapeutic theory may well allow that a given therapy includes not only known incidental factors, but also others that it has failed to recognize. And the letter C in the diagram, which labels "incidental treatment factors," is intended to apply to both known and unknown factors of this type.

Turning to the right-hand box in Figure 1, we note that the patient's life functions and activities are generically subdivided into two parts: the target disorder D at which the therapy t is aimed, and then the rest of his or her functions. But there may well be some vagueness in the circumscription of D. Both its pathognomonic symptoms and the presumed etiological process responsible for them will surely be included in the syndrome D. Yet some nosologists might include, while others exclude, certain accessory manifestations of D that are quite secondary, because they are also present in a number of other, nosologically distinct syndromes. Somewhat cognate conceptual problems of taxonomic circumscription arose in chemistry upon the discovery of isomerism, and even in the case of chemical isotopy.

Finally, in the middle of Figure 1, arrows represent some of the interesting possible causal influences or effects that may result from each of the two sets of treatment factors. Thus, one or more of the characteristic factors F may be remedial for the target disorder D, or the F factors may have no effect on D, or the F factors conceivably could make D even worse. By the same token, these factors F may have these three kinds of influence on other facets of the patient's health. And any of these latter effects—whether good or bad—will be called "side-effects." Now *if (and only if) one or more of the characteristic factors do have a positive therapeutic effect on the target disease D, then the therapy as a whole qualifies generically as a nonplacebo for D.* This is the situation that is depicted in the diagram by the words "nonplacebo effect" in the horizontal solid arrow from F to D.

It is vital to realize that, in Figure 1, the causal arrows are intended to depict *possible* (imaginable) effects, such that the given treatment factors may have various sorts of positive *or* adverse effects on the target disorder, or on other facets of the patient's health. Thus, the diagram can be used to depcit a nonplacebo therapy as well as a placebo therapy. In the former case, there is an actual beneficial causal influence by the characteristic factors on D, whereas in the latter case such an influence does not—as a matter of actual fact—exist, though it is imaginable (logically possible).

Similarly, the incidental treatment factors C may or may not have positive or negative effects on D. Furthermore, these factors C may have desirable or undesirable effects *outside of D,* which we again call side-effects. If the incidental factors do have an effect on D, we can refer to that effect as a "placebo effect," even if the therapy qualifies overall as a generic nonplacebo by containing therapeutically effective characteristic factors. For example, suppose that the characteristic factors in a certain chemotherapy are effective against a given kind of cancer, at least for a while, so that this chemotherapy is a nonplacebo for this affliction. Then this therapeutic effectiveness may well be *enhanced*, if the dispensing physician communicates his or her confidence in this therapy to the patient. And if there is such enhancement, the treatment factors C do indeed produce a positive placebo effect on D, a situation depicted in the diagram by the broken diagonal arrow. Thus we can say that *whether a given positive effect on D is or is not a placebo effect depends on whether it is produced by the incidental treatment factors or the characteristic ones*. (For *other* placebo effects see p. 160.)

Let me now use the preceding informal preliminary account to give a more systematic and precise characterization of the genus placebo as well as of two of its species, thereby also revamping A. K. Shapiro's definitions.

A treatment process normally has a spectrum of constituent factors as well as a spectrum of effects when administered for the alleviation of a given target disorder D. Effects on the patient's health not pertaining to D are denominated "side-effects." Though the term "side-effects" often refers to *undesirable* effects outside D, there is neither good reason nor general agreement to restrict it in this way. As I soon illustrate, the therapeutic theory Ψ that advocates the use of a particular treatment modality t to remedy D demands the inclusion of certain characteristic constituents F in any treatment process that Ψ authenticates as an application of t. Any such process, besides qualifying as an instance of t according to Ψ, will typically have constituents C other than the characteristic ones F singled out by Ψ. And when asserting that the factors F are remedial for D, Ψ *may* also take cognizance of one or more of the noncharacteristic constituents C, which I denominate as "incidental." Thus, Ψ may perhaps attribute certain side-effects to either F or C. Indeed, it may even maintain that one or another of the incidental factors affects D—say, by enhancing the remedial effects that it claims for F. In short, if a doctor is an adherent of Ψ, it may well furnish him or her with a therapeutic rationale for administering t to a patient afflicted by D, *or* for refraining from doing so.

For instance, consider pharmacological treatment, such as the dispensation of digitoxin for congestive heart dysfunction or of nitroglycerin for angina pectoris. Then it is perfectly clear that the water with which such tablets are swallowed, and the patient's awareness of the reputation of the prescribing cardiologist, for example, are incidental treatment factors, while the designated chemical ingredients are characteristic ones. But Freud also specified these two different sorts of treatment factors in the nonpharmacological case of psychoanalytical treatment, while recognizing that some of the incidental factors may serve initially as catalysts or icebreakers for the operation of the characteristic ones. Thus, he identified the characteristic constituents as the educative and affect-discharging lifting of the patient's presumed repressions, effected by means of overcoming ("working through") the analysand's resistance to their conscious recognition in the context of "resolving" his or her "transference" behavior towards the doctor. And Freud depicted the patient's faith in the analyst, and the derivation of emotional support from that authority figure, as mere catalysts or icebreakers in the initial stage of treatment—factors that are incidental, because they are avowedly quite incapable of extirpating the pathogenic causes, as distinct from producing merely cosmetic and temporary relief.

Hence Freud stressed tirelessly that the patient's correct, affect-discharging insight into the etiology of his or her affliction is the one quintessential ingredient that distinguishes the remedial dynamics of his treatment modality from any kind of treatment by suggestion. Treatments by suggestion, he charged, leave the pathogenic repressions intact, and yield only an ephemeral cosmetic prohibition of the symptoms (see Grünbaum, 1984). In the same vein, Freud came to maintain early in his career that the characteristic factors of Erb's electro-therapy for nervous disorders were therapeutically unavailing, and that any gains from treatment with that electric apparatus were achieved by its incidental factors.

Explications and Reformulations

The schematic diagram in Figure 1 can serve as a kind of glossary for the notations Ψ, t, F, and C that I have introduced. Using this notation, I shall offer several explications, which supersede those I have offered earlier (Grünbaum, 1981). In the first of these explications, which pertains to the "intentional" species of placebo, the fourth condition (d) is somewhat tentative:

(1) A treatment process t characterized by a given therapeutic theory Ψ as having constituents F, but also possessing other, perhaps unspecified incidental constituents C, will be said to be an "intentional placebo" with respect to a target disorder D, suffered by a victim V and treated by a dispensing practitioner P, just when the following conditions are jointly satisfied: (a) none of the characteristic treatment factors F are remedial for D; (b) P believes that the factors F indeed all *fail* to be remedial for D; (c) but P also believes that—at least for a certain type of victim V of D—t is nonetheless therapeutic for D by virtue of containing some perhaps even unknown incidental factors C different from F; and (d) yet—more often than not—P abets or at least acquiesces in V's belief that t has remedial efficacy for D by virtue of some constituents that belong to the set of characteristic factors F in t, provided that V is aware of these factors.

Note that the first of these four conditions explicates what it is for a treatment type t to have the objective generic property of being a placebo with respect to a given target disorder D. The objective property in question is just that the characteristic constituents F of t are actually not remedial for D. On the other hand, the remaining three of the four conditions describe the property of belonging to the species of intentional placebo, over and above being a placebo generically. And, clearly, these three further conditions pertain to the beliefs and intentions of the practitioners who dispense t and of the patients who receive it. In particular, they render whether the therapist is *intentionally* administering a generic placebo to the patient, rather than unaware of the placebo status of the treatment. But notice that the fourth condition would require modification, if there were enough cases, as has been suggested, in which a patient may benefit therapeutically even after being *told* that he or she is receiving a generic placebo. On the other hand, the fourth condition apparently still suffices to cover those cases in which surgeons perform appendectomies or tonsillectomies solely at the behest of their patients, who, in turn, may be encouraged by their families. The need to accommodate such interventions has been stressed by Piechowiak (1982, 1983).

The caveat regarding the fourth condition (d) is occasioned by a report (Park & Covi, 1965) on an exploratory and "paradoxical" study of 15 adult neurotic outpatients, who presented with anxiety symptoms. The treating therapists did provide support and reassurance, yet "the responsibility for improvement was thrown back to the patient by means of the paradoxical statement that he needed treatment but that he could improve with a [placebo] capsule containing no drug" (p. 344). Of the 14 patients who remained willing to receive the capsules for a week, six *disbelieved* the purported pharmacological inertness of the capsules, and three of them even experienced "side-reactions," which they attributed to the pills (p. 342). But the three patients who did firmly believe in the doctor's candid disclosure of inertness improved after 1 week, no less than the "sceptics," who thought they were receiving an effective nonplacebo after all. Hence Park and Covi concluded that "unawareness of the inert nature of the placebo is not an indispensable condition for improvement on placebo" (p. 342). Yet, as these authors acknowledged at once, in so small a sample of patients, improvement may have occurred "in spite of" the disclosure as a matter of course, under *any* sort of treatment or even as a matter of spontaneous remission. And since it is quite unclear whether the moral drawn by Park and Covi is at all generalizable beyond their sample, I have let the fourth condition stand.

Piechowiak (1983) also calls attention to uses of diagnostic procedures (e.g., endoscopy, stomach X-rays) when deemed unnecessary by the physician, but demanded by the anxious patient suffering from, say, cancerphobia, who may even believe them to be therapeutic. In the latter sort of instance, the gastroenterologist may justify an invasive procedure to himself or herself and the patient, because when the expected negative finding materializes, it may alleviate the patient's anxiety as well as the vexatious somatic effects of that anxiety. In some cases (e.g., Wassermann test for syphilis), the patient may be under no illusions as to the dynamics by which this relief was wrought, any more that the doctor.

But Piechowiak is concerned to point out that in other cases (e.g., angiography), the patient may well conceptualize the diagnostic intervention as *itself* therapeutic. And hence this author suggests the assimilation of these latter cases to intentional placebos. In this way, he suggests, account can be taken of the cognizance taken by doctors of the therapeutic beliefs of their patients—beliefs that are psychological realities, even if they are scientifically untutored.

As we have seen, a particular treatment modality *t* derives its identity from the full set of its characteristic treatment factors, as singled out by the therapeutic theory that advocates the use of *t* in stated circumstances. Hence therapies will be distinct, provided that they differ in at least one characteristic factor. By the same token, therapies whose distinct identities are specified in each case by two or more characteristic factors can have at least one such factor in common without detriment to their distinctness, just as they can thus share one or more incidental factors. Indeed, as I illustrate later, a shared factor that counts as characteristic of one therapy may qualify as merely incidental to another. And clearly these statements concerning factors common to distinct therapies hold for somatic medicine and psychotherapy alike.

Thus, in *either* of these two classes of healing interventions, a therapy that qualifies as a nonplacebo for a certain target *D* derives precisely this therapeutic status from the remedial efficacy of some or all of its characteristic factors. Yet it may share these efficacious ingredients with other, distinct therapies that differ from it in at least one characteristic factor. In fact, one or all of the common factors may count as only incidental to some of the other therapies. And it is to be borne in mind that a therapy having at least one remedial characteristic ingredient is generically a nonplacebo, even if the remaining characteristic factors are otiose. Hence a therapy *t* can be a nonplacebo with respect to a particular *D*, even if all of its efficacious characteristic treatment ingredients are common to both *t* and distinct other therapies!

Unfortunately, Critelli and Neumann (1984) run foul of this important state of affairs by concluding incorrectly that "the common-factors criterion . . . appears to be the most viable current definition of the placebo for the study of psychotherapy" (p. 35). They see themselves as improving on A. K. Shapiro's explication of the placebo concept, at least for psychotherapy. Yet they actually impoverish it by advocating the so-called common-factors definition (for psychotherapy), which they do not even *state*, and by altogether failing to render the two species of placebo adumbrated in the 1978 definition given by Shapiro and Morris. Besides, Critelli & Neumann contend that Shapiro's explication of the notion of a generic placebo suffers from his abortive attempt to encompass somatic medicine and psychotherapy simultaneously. But once I have completed my thorough recasting of Shapiro's pioneering definition below, it will be clear that—contrary to Critelli and Neumann—his endeavor to cover medicine and psychotherapy with one definitional stroke is *not* one of the defects of his explication.

Turning now to placebo *controls*, we must bear in mind that to assess the remedial merits of a given therapy t^* for some D, it is imperative to disentangle from each other two sorts of possible positive effects as follows: (1) those desired effects on D, if any, actually wrought by the characteristic factors of t^*; and (2) improvements produced by the expectations aroused in both the doctor and the patient by their belief in the therapeutic efficacy of t^*. To achieve just such a disentanglement, the baseline measure (2) of expectancy effect can be furnished by using a generic placebo t in a control group of persons suffering from D. For ethical reasons, informed consent has presumably been secured from a group of such patients to be "blindly" allocated to either the control group or the experimental group.

Ideally, this investigation should be a triply blind one. To say that the study is triply blind is to say the following: (*a*) the patients do not know to which group they have been assigned; (*b*) the dispensers do not know whether they are administering t^* or t; and (*c*) the outcome assessors do not know which patients were the controls. But there are treatment modalities — such as surgery and psychotherapy — in which the *second* of these three sorts of blindness obviously cannot be achieved.

By subtracting the therapeutic gains with respect to D in the control group from those in the experimental group, investigators can obtain the sought-after measure (1) of the incremental remedial potency of the characteristic factors in t^*. And, for brevity, one can then say that with respect to D, the generic placebo t functions as a "placebo control" in the experimental evaluation of the therapeutic value of t^* as such. More briefly, the placebo served in a controlled clinical trial of t^*.

As will be recalled, the relevant definition of that term given by A. K. Shapiro and Morris (1978, p. 371) reads as follows: "A placebo, when used as a control in experimental studies, is defined as a substance or procedure that is without specific activity for the condition being evaluated." But just this characterization of a "placebo control," as used in experimental studies in medicine or psychotherapy, is in dire need of emendation. As they would have it, "the condition" D is "being evaluated" in an experimental study employing a placebo control. But surely what is being evaluated instead is the conjectured therapeuticity of a designated treatment t^* (substance, procedure) for D. And I suggest that their definition of a placebo control be recast as follows. A treatment type t functions as a "placebo control" in a given context of experimental inquiry, which is designed to evaluate the characteristic therapeutic efficacy of another modality t^* for a target disorder D, just when the following requirements are jointly satisfied: (1) t is a *generic placebo* for D, as defined under the first condition (*a*) in the definition above of "intentional placebo"; (2) the experimental investigator conducting the stated controlled trial of t^* believes that t is not only a generic placebo for D, but also is generally quite harmless to those victims of D who have been chosen for the control group. And, as I have noted, the investigator's reason for using t as a placebo control when evaluating the characteristic therapeutic value of t^* for D is as follows: especially if t^* is expensive or fraught with negative side-effects, clinicians wish to know to what extent, if any, the benefical effects on D owing to its characteristic treatment factors *exceed* those produced by its incidental ones.

When schematized in this way, some of the complexities inherent in the notion of a placebo control are not apparent. To their credit, Critelli and Neumann (1984) have perceptively called attention to some of the essential refinements in psychotherapy research:

[I]t is imperative that test procedures be compared to realistic placebo controls. Too often in the past, false claims of incremental effectiveness have resulted from the experimental use of placebos that even the most naive would not mistake for genuine therapy. There appears to be a tendency for experimental placebos to be in some sense weaker, less credible, or applied in a less enthusiastic manner than treatments that have been offered as actual therapies. At a minimum, placebo controls should be equivalent to test procedures on all major recognized common factors. These might include induced expectancy of improvement; credibility of rationale; credibility of procedures; demand for improvement; and therapist attention, enthusiasm, effort, perceived belief in treatment procedures, and commitment to client improvement. (p. 38)

Having issued this salutary caveat, these authors claim that "current [psycho] therapies have yet to meet the challenge of demonstrating incremental effects" (p. 38). Yet one of the reasons they go on to give for posing this challenge relies on their belief that treatment factors common to two or more therapies *must* be — in my parlance — incidental rather than characteristic ingredients. As I have pointed out, however, formulations invoking this belief tend to darken counsel. Here too, placebo controls cannot be *doubly* blind.

Suedfeld (1984) likewise addresses methodological (and also ethical) problems arising in the employment of placebo controls to evaluate psychotherapy. As he sees it, "the necessity for equating the expectancy of the active [nonplacebo] and placebo treatment groups implies the acceptance of the null hypothesis, a position that is better avoided" (p. 161). To implement this avoidance, he advocates the use of a "subtractive expectancy placebo," which he describes as follows:

It consists of administering an active, specific therapeutic procedure but introducing it with the orientation that it is inert with respect to the problem being treated. In other words, the client is led to expect less of an effect than the treatment is known to produce. The Subtractive Expectancy Procedure avoids the need to invent or find an inert technique, attempts to create initial differences in expectancy which can be substantiated by the rejection of the null hypothesis, and also makes it feasible to assess the specific effect of an active treatment in a design with one treated and one untreated (control) group. (p. 161)

Here I am not concerned with the pros and cons of the subtractive expectancy placebo procedure advocated by Suedfeld, *qua* alternative to the null hypothesis on which my definition above of a "placebo control" is implicitly predicated. Whatever that balance of investigative cogency, there can be little doubt that some of the ideas in Suedfeld's paper are illuminating or at least suggestive. Besides, I appreciate his several citations of my initial paper, "The placebo concept" (Grünbaum, 1981). There I made concrete proposals for the replacement of the standard technical vocabulary used in the placebo literature, precisely because of the Tower of Babel confusion that is engendered by it.

Alas, in criticism of Suedfeld, I must point out that his exposition is genuinely marred by just the penalties of ambiguity, obscurity, and confusion exacted by the received placebo vocabulary, because he unfortunately chooses to retain that infelicitous terminology for the formulation of his ideas. As we shall see in due course, the terms "active," "specific," and "nonspecific" are especially insidious locutions in this context. Yet these ill-fated terms, and their cognates or derivatives, abound in Suedfeld's presentation. In any case, so much for the notion of a placebo control.

Recently there have been interesting conjectures as to the identity of the incidental constituents C that confer somatic remedial potency on medications qualifying as intentional placebos for some Ds with respect to certain therapeutic theories. It has been postulated (J. Brody, 1979) that, when present, such therapeutic efficacy derives from the placebo's psychogenic activation of the secretion of substances as follows: (1) pain-killing endorphins, which are endogenous opiate-like substances; (2) interferon, which counters viral infections; and (3) steroids, which reduce inflammations. Indeed, the physiological mechanisms involved are believed to be operative as well in the so-called miracle cures by faith healers, holy waters, and so-called quacks. As an example, there is evidence from a study of dental postoperative pain (Levine et al., 1978) that endorphin release does mediate placebo-induced analgesia. And this suggests analgesic research focusing on variables that affect endorphin activity (Levine et al., 1979).

So far I have explicated only one of the two species of placebo *therapy* adumbrated in the disjunctive definition given by A. K. Shapiro and Morris (1978). Hence let me now explicate their second disjunct, which pertains to the second species of placebo.

(2) A treatment process t characterized by a given therapeutic theory Ψ as having constituents F will be said to be an "inadvertent placebo" with respect to a target disorder D, suffered by a victim V and treated by a dispensing practitioner P, just when each of the following three conditions is satisfied: (a) none of the characteristic treatment factors F are remedial for D; (b) but—at least for a certain type of victim V of $D-P$ credits these very factors F with being therapeutic for D, and indeed he or she deems at least some of them to be causally *essential* to the remedial efficacy of t; also (c) more often than not, V believes that t derives remedial efficacy for D from constituents belonging to t's characteristic factors, provided that V is aware of these factors.

It is to be clearly understood that, as before, the first condition (a) codifies the *generic* property of being a placebo. The second condition (b) of this second explication renders the following: P denies that t's efficacy, if any, might derive mainly from its incidental constituents. Here the third condition (c) is subject to the same caveat (Park & Covi, 1965) that I have issued for the fourth condition (d) in my first explication above.

Clarifying Comments

Let me now add four sets of clarifying comments on my explications, because of questions put to me by Edward Erwin (personal communication, 1981), a philosopher of psychology.

(1) Clearly, it was the intentional species of placebo that was denoted by the term "placebo" in its original pharmacological use. And its use in A. K. Shapiro's definition to denote as well what I have called the inadvertent species constitutes a *generalization* of the genus placebo, prompted by the sobering lesson of the history of medicine that most treatments were inadvertent rather than intentional placebos, and often harmful to boot! But the tacit intuitions of many people as to what a placebo is are strongly geared to its original status in pharmacology. No wonder that these intuitions call for identifying the intentional species of placebo with the entire genus. Consequently, some people will be ruffled by the fact that, in my explication of the *generalized* use of the term, the generic property of being a placebo is, of course, considerably less restrictive than the property of being an intentional placebo. For, as is clear from the codification of the generic placebo property in the first condition (a) of both of my explications, any treatment t qualifies generically as a placebo for a given target disorder D merely on the strength of the failure of *all* of its characteristic factors F to be remedial for D.

But once the source of the counterintuitiveness is recognized, it should be dispelled and should occasion no objection to my explication of the generic property. Furthermore, in the generalized generic sense of "placebo," a treatment t does belong to the genus placebo even if its characteristic factors exacerbate

D, since exacerbation is a particularly strong way of failing to be remedial for D. Surely, it is the failure of the *characteristic* treatment factors to be *remedial* for D that is at the heart of the notion of a placebo therapy, *not* their failure to have an *effect* on D, either bad or good. And the failure of a practitioner who dispenses a harmful inadvertent placebo t to be cognizant of its ill effect hardly detracts from t's objective status as a generic placebo. Nor does the malaise of those who would invoke the favorable *etymological* significance of the term "placebo" in order to forbid a generalized generic concept that fails to exclude the envisaged untoward case. Either species of placebos can *undesignedly* exacerbate D! History teaches that many well-intended treatments were *worse than useless*.

Finally, note that if one were to define a generic placebo therapy t *alternatively* as one whose characteristic factors are *without effect* on D, it would have the consequence that a *non*placebo t would either exacerbate D or be remedial for it, or would have a merely neutral effect on it. But in my definitional scheme, one or more of the characteristic factors of a *non*placebo must be positively therapeutic.

(2) There are treatments only *some* of whose characteristic factors F are therapeutic for a given D, while the therapeutic theory Ψ that advocates their dispensation claims that *all* of the factors F are thus remedial. For example, it has recently been claimed (Kazdin & Wilson, 1978) that in the systematic desensitization brand of behavior therapy, which is an effective treatment for certain phobias, only one of its three F factors is thus therapeutic, while the other two appear unavailing. What, it might be asked, is the classificatory verdict of my explication as to whether a therapy whose characteristic factors comprise both efficacious and otiose members qualifies generically as a nonplacebo?

To answer this question, note that within the class of treatments for any given D, any member t will belong to the genus placebo exactly when *none* of its characteristic factors are remedial for D. Therefore any therapy whose characteristic factors include *at least one* that is therapeutic for D will pass muster as a nonplacebo. Evidently it is not necessary for being a nonplacebo that all of the F factors be remedial. It follows that, in the absence of further information, the designation of a given therapy—such as desensitization in the example above—as a nonplacebo does not tell us whether only some of its characteristic factors are remedial or whether all of them are. But this fact hardly militates against either my explication or the usefulness of the concept of nonplacebo as rendered by it.

Upon recalling A. K. Shapiro and Morris's cited characterizations of "pure" and "impure" placebos (1978, p. 372), we see that my construal of the generic placebo notion explicates what they call a "pure placebo." Their "impure placebos" are, as they put it vaguely, "treatments that have specific components but exert their effects primarily through nonspecific mechanisms" (p. 372). This sort of treatment does count as a nonplacebo, according to my formulation. But my parlance can readily characterize their so-called impure placebos by saying the following. Although the characteristic ingredients of these therapies do make some therapeutic contribution, this remedial effect is exceeded by the therapeutic benefit deriving from the *incidental* treatment factors. This quantitative vagueness is, of course, not my problem but theirs.

(3) It must not be overlooked that my explication of "placebo" is relativized not only to a given target disorder D, but also to those characteristic factors that are singled out from a particular treatment process by a specified therapeutic theory Ψ. It is therefore not my explication but a given theory Ψ that determines which treatment factors are to be classified as the characteristic factors in any one case. And by the same token, as I illustrate presently, the given therapeutic theory Ψ (in medicine or psychiatry) rather than my explication determines whether any factors in the physician-patient relationship are to count as only "incidental." Clearly, for example, a particular psychiatric theory might well designate some such factors as being characteristic. And just this sort of fact prompted A. K. Shapiro and Morris to disavow the common restriction of "specific activity" to "nonpsychological mechanisms of action," and to offer their "more general definition of specific activity" cited above.

An example given to me in a discussion at Maudsley Hospital in London called my attention to allowing for the possible *time-dependence* of the effects of *incidental* treatment factors. In pharmacological research on rats, it was noticed that the effects of injected substances were enhanced after a while, via Pavlovian conditioning, by the continued presence of blue light. That light can be deemed an incidental treatment factor throughout, I claim, although its effects will vary as time goes on. Hence I reject the suggestion that once the blue light has begun to potentiate the effects of the injected substances, the light must be reclassified to become a characteristic treatment factor, after starting out as a merely incidental one.

The divergence between Jerome Frank's (1973) theory of healing as persuasion on the one hand, and such psychotherapeutic theories as Freud's or Hans Eysenck's on the other, will now serve to illustrate three important points as follows. (a) As is evident from my explication, it is the given therapeutic theory Ψ rather than my explication of "placebo" that decides *which* treatment factors are to be respectively classified as "characteristic" and as "incidental." (b) Precisely because my analysis of the placebo concept does make explicit provision for the dependence of the memberships of these classes on the particular theory Ψ at hand, it allows for the fact that rival therapeutic theories can *disagree* in regard to their classification of particular treatment factors as "characteristic," no less than in their attribution of significant therapeutic efficacy to such factors. (c) Hence, the relativization of the classification of treatment factors to a given theory Ψ that is built into my explication prevents seeming inconsistencies and confusions, generated when investigators want to assess the generic placebo status of a therapy *t* across rival therapeutic theories, and without regard to whether these theories use different characteristic factors to identify *t*.

In the language and notions of my explications, Jerome Frank's (1973, pp. xv–xx) view of the therapeutic status of the leading rival psychotherapies can now be outlined. For *each* of these treatment modalities *t* and its underlying theory Ψ, he hypothesizes that *t* is as follows:

1. A generic placebo with respect to the characteristic treatment factors singled out by *its own* particular Ψ.

2. An inadvertent placebo with respect to the beliefs of those dispensers of *t* who espouse Ψ.

3. Therapeutically effective to the extent that the patient's hope is aroused by the doctor's healing symbols, which mobilize the patient's sense of mastery of his or her demoralization.

As is clear from the third item, Frank credits a treatment ingredient *common* to the rival psychotherapies with such therapeutic efficacy as they do possess. But his categorization of each of these therapies as a generic placebo rather than as a nonplacebo is now seen to derive just from the fact that he is tacitly classifying as "incidental," rather than as "characteristic," all those treatment factors that he deems to be therapeutic. In adopting this latter classification, he is speaking the classificatory language employed by the theories underlying the various therapies, although he denies their claim that the treatment ingredients they label "characteristic" are actually effective.

Yet in a language suited to Frank's own therapeutic tenets, it would, of course, be entirely natural to label as "characteristic" just those treatment factors that his own theory *T* deems remedial, even though these same ingredients count as merely incidental within each of the psychotherapeutic theories rejected by him. And if Frank were to couch his own *T* in that new classificatory language, then he would no longer label the leading psychotherapies as generic placebos, although he would be holding the same therapeutic beliefs as before. It should now be clear that by explicitly relativizing to a given Ψ the classification of particular treatment factors as "characteristic" or "incidental," no less than by relativizing their respective therapeutic efficacy to a particular *D*, my explication obviates the following sort of question, which is being asked across unspecified, tacitly presupposed therapeutic theories: If the effectiveness of a placebo modality depends on its symbolization of the physician's healing power, should this ingredient not be considered a *characteristic* treatment factor?

(4) In a paper devoted mainly to the ethical complexities of using placebo control groups in psychotherapy research, O'Leary & Borkovec (1978) write: "Because of problems in devising a theoretically and practically inert placebo, we

recommend that the term *placebo* be abandoned in psychotherapy research'' (p. 823). And they propose to ''circumvent the ethical concerns inherent in placebo methodology'' (p. 825) by devising alternative methods of research control. In this way, they hope to assure as well that ''the confusion associated with the term *placebo* would be avoided'' (p. 823).

But I hope it will become clear from my comparison of my explication above with the usual parlance in the literature that these confusions indeed can be avoided without abandoning the placebo concept in any sort of therapeutic research. Nor do I see why the theoretical identification of a particular incidental treatment factor that is effective for *D* rather than ''inert'' ever has to be detrimental to therapeutic research.

Logical Defects of Received Vocabulary

On the basis of my explications, I can now make two sets of comments on the logical defects of the key locutions commonly employed as technical terms throughout the medical and psychiatric literature on placebos.

(1) We are told that any effect that a placebo has on the target disorder *D* is ''nonspecific.'' But a placebo can have an effect on *D* that is no less sharply defined and precisely known than the effect of a nonplacebo. To take a simple example, consider two patients *A* and *B* suffering from ordinary tension headaches of comparable severity. Suppose that *A* unwittingly swallows the proverbial sugar pill and gets no relief from it, because it is indeed pharmacologically ''inert'' or useless for such a headache *qua* mere sugar pill. *A* stoically endures his or her discomfort. Assume further that *B* consults his or her physician, who is very cautious. Mindful of the potential side-effects of tranquillizers and analgesics, the doctor decides to employ a little benign deceit and gives *B* a few lactose pills, without disabusing *B* of his or her evident belief that he or she is receiving a physician's sample of analgesics. Posit that shortly after *B* takes the first of these sugar pills, the headache disappears altogether. Assume further that *B*'s headache would not have disappeared just then from mere internal causes. Both of these conditions might well apply in a given case. Thus *B* assumedly received the same headache relief from the mere sugar pill as he or she would have received if a pharmacologically *non*inert drug had been slipped into his food without his knowledge.

Clearly, in some such situations, the therapeutic effect of the sugar pill placebo on the headache can have attributes fully as sharply defined or ''specific'' as the effect that would have been produced by a so-called active drug like aspirin (Frank, 1973). Moreover, this placebogenic effect can be just as precisely described or known as the nonplacebogenic effect of aspirin. In either case, the effect is complete headache relief, even though the sugar pill as such is, of course, pharmacologically inert for headaches whereas aspirin as such is pharmacologically efficacious. It is therefore at best very misleading to describe as "nonspecific" the *effect* that the placebo produces on the target disorder, while describing the at least qualitatively like effect of the nonplacebo as "specific." Yet just such a use of the terms "nonspecific" and "specific" as modifiers of the term "effect" is made in A. K. Shapiro's above-cited definition of "placebo," in a leading treatise on pharmacological therapeutics (Goodman & Gilman, 1975), in a German work on psychoanalysis (Möller, 1978), in a German survey article on placebos (Piechowiak, 1983), and in a fairly recent article on treatments to reduce high blood pressure (A. P. Shapiro et al., 1977). Equally infelicitously, Schwartz (1978, p. 83) speaks of a "nonspecific placebo response." Why describe a treatment effect as "nonspecific" in order to convey that the incidental treatment factors, rather than the characteristic elements, were the ones that produced it? Relatedly, Klein (1980) points out that when a placebo counteracts demoralization in a depressed person, it is wrong-headed to describe this therapeutic outcome as a "nonspecific" effect. After all, the demoralization and the effect on it are quite specific in the ordinary sense.

Worse, as it stands, the locution "specific effect" is quite ambiguous as between the following two very different senses: (a) the therapeutic effect on D is wrought by the characteristic ("specific") factors F of the therapy t; or (b) the remedial effectiveness of t is specific to a quite small number of disorders, to the exclusion of a far more multitudinous set of nosologically different afflictions and of their respective pathognomonic symptoms. Most writers on placebos, though not all, intend the first construal when speaking of "specific effect." But others use the term "specific" in the second of these senses. Thus, as we shall see in greater detail further on, according to whether the effects of a given therapy are or are not believed to be "specific" in the *second* sense above, H. Brody (1977, p. 40–43) classifies that *therapy* as a "specific therapy" or as a "general therapy." And he wishes to allow for the fact that the placebogenic remedial efficacy of the proverbial sugar pill is presumed to range over a larger number of target ailments than the nonplacebogenic efficacy of widely used medications (e.g., penicillin). In an endeavor to make such an allowance, he uses the belief in the ability of a therapy to engender "specific effects" in the second sense above as the touchstone of its being a nonplacebo. In addition, Shepherd (1961) has pointed out yet another ambiguity in the loose use of "specific" and "nonspecific" to designate treatment factors in psychopharmacology. And Wilkins (1985, p. 120) speaks of "non specific events" not only to refer to treatment-factors *common* to rival therapies, but also to denote life events outside the treatment process altogether. How much better it would be, therefore, if students of placebo phenomena banished the seriously ambiguous use of "specific" as a technical term altogether.

As if this degree of technical confusion were not enough, the misleading use of "specific" in the sense of "nonplacebo" is sometimes encountered alongside the use of "specific" in the usual literal sense of "precise" or "well defined." Thus, when Miller (1980) writes that "placebo effects can be quite specific" (p. 476), the illustrations he goes on to give show that here "specific" has the force of "quantitatively precise." But in the very next paragraph, he uses the term "specific" as a synonym for "nonplacebo" when reporting that "it is only in the past 80 years that physicians have been able to use an appreciable number of treatments with specific therapeutic effects" (p. 476).

Indeed, the placebo research worker Beecher (1972), who is renowned for investigating the role of placebos in the reduction of pain, entitled one of his essays "The placebo effect as a non-specific force surrounding disease and the treatment of disease." But even metaphorically and elliptically, it seems inappropriate to speak of the placebo *effect* as being a nonspecific *force*, as Beecher (1972) does repeatedly.

On the basis of the explications I have given, it is appropriate to speak of an *effect* as a "placebo effect" under two sorts of conditions: (*a*) even when the treatment *t* is a *non*placebo, effects on *D*—be they good, bad, or neutral—that are produced by *t*'s *incidental* factors count as placebo effects, precisely because these factors wrought them; and (*b*) when *t* is a generic placebo whose characteristic factors have harmful or neutral effects on *D*, these effects as well count as placebo effects (see pp. 154–155). Hence if *t* is a placebo, then *all* of its effects qualify as placebo effects.

(2) A. K. Shapiro & Morris (1978) tell us in their definition that a placebo "is without specific activity for the condition being treated." And, as we recall, they contrast "active treatments" with placebos by saying that "active treatments may contain placebo components" (p. 371). Yet they also tell us that "in behavior therapy, some investigators have utilized 'active placebo' control groups" in which "some aspects of the therapy affect behavior but those aspects differ from the theoretically relevant ingredients of concern to the investigator" (p. 372). Furthermore, in the common parlance employed by two other investigators, even placebos that are acknowledged to be "potently therapeutic" or "effective" (for angina pectoris) are incongruously dubbed "inactive" just because they are placebos (Benson & McCallie, 1979). And Beecher (1972) emphasizes that some placebos "are capable of *powerful action*" (p. 178; italics in original), while contrasting them with treatments that he and others call "active" to convey that they are indeed nonplacebos.

By contrast to Beecher's use of "active," Bok (1974) tells us that any medical procedure, "whether it is active or inactive, can serve as a placebo whenever it has no specific effect on the condition for which it is prescribed" (p. 17). Thus, in Bok's parlance, placebos may be said to be "active" (p. 17) and "placebos can be effective" (p. 18), but they must be devoid of so-called specific effect. Yet just what is it for a placebo to be "active"? Clearly, a placebo therapy as a whole *might* be productive of (remedial or deleterious) effects on the target disorder while being devoid of significant (negative or positive) side-effects, or it may have only side-effects. On the other hand, it might have both kinds of effects. And it matters therapeutically, of course, which of these effects—if either—is produced by any particular placebo. Hence clarity will be notably served by explicitly indicating the *respect* in which a given placebo intervention is being said to be "active." Yet such explicitness is lacking when Bok tells us, for example, that there is a clear-cut "potential for damage by an active drug given as a placebo" (p. 20). Thus it is only a conjecture just what she intends the term "active" to convey in the latter context. Is it that there are pharmacologically induced side-effects in addition to placebogenic effects on the target disorder D? By the same token, her usage of "inactive" is unclear when she reports that "even inactive placebos can have toxic effects" (p. 20), even though she goes on to give what she takes to be an illustration. Bok's concern with placebos focuses, however, on ethically questionable dispensations of intentional placebos. But if a treatment is truly remedial, why should it matter to the patient that the treatment is *technically* a placebo relative to the therapist's theory?

Evidently there are divergences among writers on placebos in regard to the usage of the term "active." But they tell us in one voice, as Bok does, that a placebo procedure "has no specific effect on the condition for which it is prescribed" (p. 17). To this conceptually dissonant discourse, I say: in the case of a placebo it is, of course, recognized that incidental treatment factors *may* be potently remedial for D, although the characteristic ones by definition are not. And if some of the incidental constituents are thus therapeutic, then the actual specificity of their activity—in the ordinary sense of "specificity"—clearly does *not* depend on whether the pertinent therapeutic theory Ψ is able either to specify their particular identity or to afford understanding of their detailed mode of action. Hence if some of the incidental constituents of t are remedial but presently elude the grasp of Ψ, the current inability of Ψ to pick them out from the treatment process hardly lessens the objective specificity of their identity, mode of action, or efficacy. A theory's current inability to spell out certain causal factors and to articulate their mode of action because of ignorance is surely not tantamount to their being themselves objectively "nonspecific" as to their identity, over and above being unknown! At worst, the details of the operation of the incidental factors are left unspecified.

Hence, despite the assumed present inability of the pertinent theory Ψ to spell out which particular incidental constituents render the given placebo remedial for D, it is at best needlessly obscure to say that these constituents are "without specific activity" for D and are "nonspecific." A *fortiori*, it is infelicitous to declare of any and every placebo treatment modality as a whole that, *qua* being a placebo, it must be devoid of "specific activity." It would seem that, when speaking generically of a placebo, the risk of confusion as well as outright unsound claims can be obviated by steadfast avoidance of the term "nonspecific activity."

Instead, as I have argued earlier, the objective genus property of being a placebo should be codified as follows. With respect to the target disorder D, the treatment modality t belongs to the genus placebo just when its characteristic constituents *fail* to be remedial for D. Furthermore, clarity is served by using the term "incidental" rather than "nonspecific" when speaking of those treatment constituents that differ from the characteristic ones. In short, the generic distinction between placebos and nonplacebos has nothing whatever to do with the contrast between nonspecificity and specificity, but only with whether the characteristic treatment factors do play a therapeutic role for D or not. So much for my proposed rectifications of the misleading conceptualizations conveyed by the standard locutions whose confusion I have laid bare.

Clarifying Ramifications of My Explications

As is clear from my formulation, the genus property of being a placebo is altogether independent of the belief of the dispensing practitioner as to whether the treatment in question is a placebo. But, equally clearly, the species property of being an inadvertent placebo is explicitly relativized to this belief, no less than the species property of being an intentional one. Thus, a placebo treatment t that qualifies as inadvertent with respect to one school of therapeutic thought may be explicitly avowed to have intentional placebo status in the judgment of another school. By the same token, advocates of t who do not even entertain the possibility of its being a placebo will be preoccupied with its characteristic constituents, to the likely disregard of incidental factors in t that may turn out to be remedially potent for D. Consequently, if patients who received treatment t register gains, such advocates will erroneously discount any remedial efficacy actually possessed by these incidental factors. Moreover, these theoreticians will give undeserved credit to the characteristic factors for any successful results that issue from t. As recounted in Beecher's classic (1961) paper "Surgery as placebo," which is summarized by Benson and McCallie (1979), the history of surgical treatment for angina pectoris in the United States during the mid-1950s furnished a clear case in point.

Proponents of ligating the internal mammary artery claimed that this procedure facilitated increased coronary blood flow through collateral vessels near the point of ligation, thereby easing the ischemia of the heart muscle to which angina pectoris is due. And these enthusiasts then credited that ligation with the benefits exhibited by their surgical patients. But well-controlled, though ethically questionable, studies by sceptical surgeons in the late 1950s showed the following. When a mere sham bilateral skin incision was made on a comparison group of angina patients, then ligation of the internal mammary artery in randomly selected other angina patients yielded only equal or even less relief from angina than the sham surgery. Furthermore, the quality of the results achieved by the intentional placebo surgery was dramatic and sustained. Apart from subjective improvement, the deceived recipients of the sham surgery had increased exercise tolerance, registered less nitroglycerin usage, and improved electrocardiographically. Moreover, a similar lesson emerges from the use of a related surgical procedure due to Vineberg, in which the internal mammary artery was implanted into a tunnel burrowed into the myocardium. The results from this Vineberg operation (Benson & McCallie, 1979) suggest that placebogenic relief occurred even in a sizable majority of angina patients who had angiographically verified coronary artery disease. This history has a sobering moral. It bears further monitoring to what extent the positive results from coronary artery bypass surgery are placebogenic (Detre et al., 1984).

Now consider those who allow that such beneficial efficacy as a therapy t has could well be placebogenic. This group may thereby be led to draw the true conclusion that the characteristic factors do not merit any therapeutic credit. On the other hand, the therapeutic efficacy of a nonplacebo is enhanced if its incidental factors *also* have a remedial effect of their own. Thus, it has been found (Gallimore & Turner, 1977) that the attitudes of physicians toward chemotherapy commonly contribute significantly to the effectiveness of nonplacebo drugs. Again, Wheatley (1967) reported that in the treatment of anxiety by one particular nonplacebo drug, enthusiastic physicians obtained better results than unenthusiastic ones, although enthusiasm did not enhance the positive effect of tricyclic antidepressants on depression. Indeed, there may be synergism between the characteristic and incidental treatment factors, such that they potentiate each other therapeutically with respect to the *same* target disorder.

On the other hand, one and the same treatment may be a placebo with respect to the target disorder and yet may function as a nonplacebo for a secondary ailment. For example, when a viral cold is complicated by the presence of a secondary bacterial infection, a suitable antibiotic may serve as an intentional placebo for the viral cold while also acting as a nonplacebo for the bacterial infection. This case spells an important moral. It serves to discredit the prevalent stubborn refusal to relativize the placebo status of a medication or intervention to a stated target disorder, a relativization I have explicitly built into my definitions. For example, in the misguided effort to escape such relativization, Piechowiak (1983, p. 40) is driven to classify antibiotics as "false placebos." As he sees it, they are placebos because they are not pharmacologically effective for the typical sort of upper respiratory viral infection; but what makes them "false" placebos, in his view, is that they *are* pharmacologically potent (genuine medications, or in the original German, *"echte Pharmaka"*) for other diseases (e.g., bacterial pneumonia).

But, according to this reasoning, "false" placebos are quite common. A telling illustration is provided by the following story reported by Jennifer Worrall, a

British physician (personal communication, 1983). One of her patients, a middle-aged woman, complained of a superficial varicose leg ulcer. Worrall relates:

[The patient] was very demanding and difficult to please and claimed to suffer continuous agony from her ulcer (although there were none of the objective signs of pain, such as sleep disturbance, increased heart rate and blood pressure, pallor and sweating). All of the many mild-to-moderate analgesics were "useless" [according to the patient] and I did not feel opiates were justified, so I asked the advice of my immediate superior. The superior [here referred to as "W."] saw the patient, discussed her pain and, with a grave face, said he wanted her to try a "completely different sort of treatment." She agreed. He disappeared into the office, to reappear a few minutes later, walking slowly down the ward and holding in front of him a pair of tweezers which grasped a large, white tablet, the size of [a] half-dollar. As he came nearer, it became clear (to me, at least) that the tablet was none other than effervescent vitamin C. He dropped the tablet into a glass of water which, of course, bubbled and fizzed, and told the patient to sip the water carefully when the fizzing had subsided. It worked—the new medicine completely abolished her pain! W. has used this method several times, apparently, and it always worked. He felt that the single most important aspect was holding the tablet with *tweezers,* thereby giving the impression that it was somehow too powerful to be touched with bare hands!

Some may find this episode amusing. Yet it has a devastating moral for the not uncommon claim that without regard to the *specified* target disorder, a pharmacological agent can qualify as a generic and even as an intentional placebo. Assume that, for the varicose leg ulcer that afflicted the given patient, vitamin C is a generic placebo even in high doses; this assumption allows that, in such large doses, it may have negative side-effects. And furthermore, relying on W.'s findings, grant that for at least some patients suffering from a superficial leg ulcer, the administration of vitamin C as an intentional placebo in W.'s ceremonious manner ("with tweezers"!) is therapeutic for such an ulcer. Then surely such a placebo status for leg ulcer hardly detracts from the fact that, at least in sufficient doses, vitamin C is a potent nonplacebo for scurvy. And if Linus Pauling is to be believed, sufficiently high doses of this vitamin can even afford prophylaxis for certain cancers. In short, only conceptual mischief results from the supposition that the property of being a (generic) placebo is one that a treatment—be it pharmacological or psychiatric—can have *per se,* rather than only with respect to a stated target disorder.

Ironically, none other than the much-maligned proverbial sugar pill furnishes a *reductio ad absurdum* of the notion that a medication can be generically a placebo *simpliciter,* without relativization to a target disorder. For even a lay person knows that the glucose in the sugar pill is anything but a generic placebo if given to a victim of diabetes who is in a state of insulin shock, or to someone suffering from hypoglycemia. But if an antibiotic were a ''false placebo'' on the strength of the properties adduced by Piechowiak (1983), then—by parity with his reasoning—so also is the notorious sugar pill, the alleged paradigm of a ''true'' nonrelativized placebo. Even the diehards among the believers in intrinsic, non-relativized placebos will presumably regard this consequence of their view as too high a price to pay. Nor would they ever think someone's Uncle Charlie to be a ''false'' uncle merely because Charlie is not also somebody else's uncle!

Suppose that, for specified types of diseases, a certain class of afflicted victims does derive placebogenic remedial gain from the use of a particular set of therapeutic interventions. Then it may become important, for one reason or another, to ascertain—*within* the classes of incidental treatment factors picked out by the pertinent set of therapeutic theories—which particular kinds of factors are thus remedial. And this quest for identification can proceed across various sorts of treatment modalities (e.g., chemotherapy, radiation therapy, surgery), or may be focused more narrowly on factors within such modalities (e.g., surgery). Research during the past three decades has envisioned (1) that such placebogenic treatment gain may require a so-called placebo reactor type of victim of disease, characterized by a specifiable (but as yet unspecified) personality trait or cluster of such traits; or (2) that the therapeutic success of placebos may depend on certain kinds of characteristics or attitudes possessed by the treating physician. It should be noted that my explications of both the intentional and inadvertent species of placebo have made provision for these two possibilities. Both explications are relativized to disease victims of a specifiable sort, as well as to therapists (practitioners) of certain kinds. As it turns out, for some two dozen or so of proposed patient-trait correlates of placebo responsiveness, the first hypothesis named above—that of placebo reactivity—has been largely unsuccessful empirically, except for the following: generalized chronic anxiety has been frequently and reliably found to correlate with placebo responsivity, notably in the treatment of pain (Gallimore & Turner, 1977). Yet in a 25-year series of studies of placebo responsiveness in psychotherapy, Frank (1974) found reason to discount the role of enduring personality factors in the patient (see also Liberman, 1964). As for the second hypothesis, which pertains to the therapeutic relevance of the physician's communicated attitudes, I have already commented on the demonstrated role of physician's variables among incidental treatment factors in enhancing the therapeutic efficacy of nonplacebo drugs.

Having explicated the placebo concept by reference to A. K. Shapiro and Morris's proposed definition, I ought to comment on the divergences between theirs and the one offered by H. Brody (1977), which I have mentioned earlier.

Shapiro and Morris's definition appeared in 1978 in the *second* edition of the Garfield and Bergin *Handbook of Psychotherapy and Behavior Change*. But in the first edition of this *Handbook,* which appeared in 1971, Shapiro alone had published an only slightly different definition. This 1971 definition is not discussed by Brody (1977). But Brody claims rough consistency between Shapiro's (1968) definition of "placebo effect" and his own account of that notion. Hence I am concerned to point out that there are several important divergences between the construals of "placebo" given by Shapiro and Morris on the one hand, and Brody on the other. And these differences are such, I claim, that Shapiro and Morris render the generic placebo concept implicit in the medical and psychiatric literature far more adequately than Brody, notwithstanding the important respects in which I have found Shapiro and Morris's definition wanting.

The reader is now asked to recall my earlier remarks as to the consideration that seems to have prompted Brody's introduction of his notion of a "specific therapy": the putative fact that the placebogenic remedial efficacy of the proverbial sugar pill is presumed to range over a larger number of target ailments than the nonplacebogenic efficacy of widely used medications (e.g., of penicillin). Then the essence of his account becomes quite clear from his proposed definitions of the following terms: "therapy;" "specific therapy," which Brody avowedly contrasts with "general therapy" (1977, p. 41); and finally, "placebo." Let me first cite these definitions and Brody's comment on them. (For the sake of consistency, I am substituting the abbreviations used up to this point in this article for Brody's here.)

1) [*t*] is a therapy for condition [*D*] if and only if it is believed that administration of [*t*] to a person with [*D*] increases the empirical probability that [*D*] will be cured, relieved, or ameliorated, as compared to the probability that this will occur without [*t*]. (Brody, 1977, p. 38)

2) [*t*] is a specific therapy for condition [*D*] if and only if:
   (1) [*t*] is a therapy for [*D*].
   (2) There is a class *A* of conditions such that [*D*] is a subclass of *A*, and for all members of *A*, [*t*] is a therapy.
   (3) There is a class *B* of conditions such that for all members of *B*, [*t*] is not a therapy; and class *B* is much larger than class *A*.

For example, consider how the definition applies to penicillin used for pneumococcal pneumonia. Penicillin is a therapy for this disease, since it increases the empirical probability of recovery. Pneumococcal pneumonia is one of a class of diseases (infectious diseases caused by penicillin-sensitive organisms) for all of which penicillin is a therapy; but there is a much larger class of diseases (noninfectious diseases and infectious diseases caused by penicillin-resistant organisms) for which penicillin is not a therapy. (Brody, 1977, pp. 40–41)

It will be noted that Brody presumably intends the third requirement in the second definition to implement his stated objective of contrasting "specific therapy" with "general therapy"—an aim that, as we have seen, does *not* govern Shapiro & Morris's construal of "specific." For Brody's third requirement here makes the following demand. The membership of the class *B* of disorders for which *t* is believed to be *ineffective* has to be numerically greater than the membership of the class *A* of target disorders for which *t* is deemed to be remedial. But clearly, Shapiro and Morris's cited account of what it is for *t* to possess "specific activity" for *D* does *not* entail logically Brody's third restriction on the relative number of disorders for which *t* is (believed to be) therapeutic! For example, just think of how Shapiro and Morris would analyze the claim that aspirin is not a placebo for arthritis or tension headaches and that it affords nonplacebogenic prophylaxis for blood clotting and embolisms. Nor would Brody's third restriction seem to be often implicit in the medical and psychiatric usage of "specific therapy."

Yet Brody does deserve credit for pointing out, in effect, that the placebogenic efficacy of intentional placebos is believed to range over a larger number of target ailments, as a matter of empirical fact, than the nonplacebogenic efficacy of such medications as penicillin. This is *much less significant,* though, than he thinks: after all, the old sugar pill and penicillin alike have *placebogenic* efficacy, such that the sugar pill does not excel in regard to the number of target disorders!

The third of Brody's definitions reads:

3) A placebo is:

(1) a form of medical therapy, or an intervention designed to simulate medical therapy, that at the time of use is *believed* not to be a specific therapy for the condition for which it is offered and that is used for its psychological effect or to eliminate observer bias in an experimental setting.

(2) (by extension from (1)) a form of medical therapy now believed to be inefficacious, though believed efficacious at the time of use.

Clause 2 is added to make sense of a sentence such as, "Most of the medications used by physicians one hundred years ago were actually placebos." (Brody, 1977, p. 43; italics added)

A further major divergence between Brody's and Shapiro & Morris's definitions of "placebo" derives from the multiple dependence of Brody's generic placebo concept on therapeutic *beliefs,* in contrast to Shapiro & Morris's explicit repudiation of any such dependence of the generic notion of placebo. As shown by Brody's definition of "therapy" above, what renders a treatment a "therapy" in his construal is that "it is believed" to be remedial (by its advocates or recipients). Consequently, this dependence on therapeutic belief enters into Brody's definition of "specific therapy" via each of the three requirements that he lays down in his definition of that term above. On the other hand, no such belief-dependence is present in Shapiro and Morris's counterpart notion of "specific activity." As if this were not enough, Brody's definition of "placebo" invokes yet another layer of belief by requiring that "at the time of use," a placebo treatment be "believed not to be a specific therapy" for the target disorder, presumably by the doctor but not by the patient.

It is patent, therefore, that Shapiro and Morris's construal of the *generic* placebo notion, which we have seen to be objective rather than dependent on therapeutic beliefs, makes incomparably better sense than Brody's of such claims as "most of the medications used by physicians a century ago were actually placebos," a claim that Brody avowedly hopes to accommodate via the second requirement of his definition of "placebo." For on Shapiro & Morris's construal, physicians can in fact be *objectively* mistaken in deeming a treatment modality to be a nonplacebo. But on Brody's definition, it is merely a matter of a change in their therapeutic beliefs. For this reason alone, I have made Shapiro and Morris's definition rather than Brody's the focus of my explication.

Note that each of the two species of placebo therapy I have considered is defined by a *conjunction* of two sorts of statement: (1) an assertion of *objective fact* as to the therapeutic failure of *t*'s characteristic constituents with respect to *D;* and (2) claims concerning the *beliefs* held by the therapist and/or the patient in regard to *t*. Clearly, the belief-content of (2) does not lessen the objectivity of (1). Yet, in a reply to me, Brody (1985, p. 45) runs afoul of this point. For he thinks incorrectly that the belief-content of (2) negates the greater objectivity I have claimed for my definitions *vis-à-vis* his own *entirely belief-ridden* renditions of the pertinent concepts.

I hope it is now apparent that the customary notions and terminology of placebo research foster conceptual confusion, and that the adoption of the conceptualizations and vocabulary I have proposed would obviate the perpetuation of such confusion. Yet the perceived obfuscations die hard.

References

Beecher, H. K. (1961). Surgery as placebo. *Journal of the American Medical Association, 176,* 1102–1107.

Beecher, H. K. (1972). The placebo effect as a non-specific force surrounding disease and the treatment of disease. In R. Janzen, J. P. Payne & R. A. T. Burt (Eds.), *Pain: Basic principles, pharmacology, therapy* (pp. 176–178). Stuttgart: Thieme.

Benson, H., & McCallie, D. P. (1979). Angina pectoris and the placebo effect. *New England Journal of Medicine, 300,* 1424–1429.

Blakiston's *Gould medical dictionary* (3rd ed.) (1972). New York: McGraw-Hill.

Bok, S. (1974). The ethics of giving placebos. *Scientific American, 231* (November), 17–23.

Brody, H. (1977). *Placebos and the philosophy of medicine.* Chicago: University of Chicago Press.

Brody, H. (1985). Placebo effect: An examination of Grünbaum's definition. In L. White, B. Tursky & G. E. Schwartz (Eds.), *Placebo: Theory, research and mechanisms* (pp. 37–58). New York: Guilford Press.

Brody, J. (1979). Placebos work, but survey shows widespread misuse. *New York Times* April 3, p. C. 1.

Critelli, J. W., & Neumann, K. F. (1984). The placebo. *American Psychologist, 39,* 32–39.

Davis, J. M., & Cole, J. O. (1975a). Antipsychotic drugs. In S. Arieti (Ed.), *American handbook of psychiatry, Vol. 5* (2nd ed.) (pp. 444–447). New York: Basic Books.

Davis, J. M., & Cole, J. O. (1975b). Antipsychotic drugs. In A. M. Freedman, H. T. Kaplan & B. J. Sadock (Eds.), *Comprehensive textbook of psychiatry, Vol. 2* (2nd ed.) (pp. 1922–1930). Baltimore: Williams & Wilkins.

Detre, K. M., Peduzzi, P., Takaro, T., Hultgren, N., Murphy, M. L., & Kroncke, G. (1984). Eleven-year survival in the Veterans Administration randomized trial of coronary bypass surgery for stable angina. *New England Journal of Medicine, 311,* 1333–1339.

Frank, J. D. (1973). *Persuasion and healing* (rev. ed.). Baltimore: Johns Hopkins University Press.

Frank, J. D. (1974). Therapeutic components of psychotherapy. *Journal of Nervous and Mental Disease, 159,* 325–342.

Gallimore, R. G., & Turner, J. L. (1977). Contemporary studies of placebo phenomena. In M. E. Jarvik (Ed.), *Psychopharmacology in the practice of medicine* (pp. 51–52). New York: Appleton-Century-Crofts.

Goodman, L. S., & Gilman, A. (Eds.) (1975). *The pharmacological basis of therapeutics* (5th ed.). London: Macmillan.

Grünbaum, A. (1981). The placebo concept. *Behaviour Research and Therapy 19,* 157–167.

Grünbaum, A. (1984). *The foundations of psychoanalysis: A philosophical critique.* Berkeley: University of California Press.

Kazdin, A. E., & Wilson, G. T. (1978). *Evaluation of behavior therapy.* Cambridge, MA: Ballinger.

Klein, D. V. (1980). *Diagnosis and drug treatment of psychiatric disorders* (2nd ed.). Baltimore: Williams & Wilkins.

Kolata, G. B. (1979). New drugs and the brain. *Science, 205,* 774–776.

Levine, J. D., Gordon, N. C., & Fields, H. L. (1978). The mechanism of placebo analgesia. *Lancet, ii,* 654–657.

Levine, J. D., Gordon, N. C., Bornstein, J. C., & Fields, H. L. (1979). Role of pain in placebo analgesia. *Proceedings of the National Academy of Sciences USA, 76,* 3528–3531.

Liberman, R. (1964). An experimental study of the placebo response under three different situations of pain. *Journal of Psychiatric Research, 2,* 233–246.

Miller, N. E. (1980). Applications of learning and biofeedback to psychiatry and medicine. In A. M. Freedman, H. T. Kaplan & B. J. Sadock (Eds.), *Comprehensive textbook of psychiatry, Vol. 1* (3rd ed.) (pp. 468–484). Baltimore: Williams & Wilkins.

Möller, H. J. (1978). *Psychoanalyse.* Munich: Wilhelm Fink.

O'Leary, K. D., & Borkovec, T. D. (1978). Conceptual, methodological and ethical problems of placebo groups in psychotherapy research. *American Psychologist, 33,* 821–830.

Park, L. C., & Covi, L. (1965). Nonblind placebo trial. *Archives of General Psychiatry, 12,* 336–345.

Piechowiak, H. (1982). Die namenlose Pille. Über Wirkungen und Nebenwirkungen im therapeutischen Umgang mit Plazebopräparaten. *Internistische Praxis, 22,* 759–772.

Piechowiak, H. (1983). Die Schein-Heilung: welche Rolle spielt das Placebo in der ärztlichen Praxis? *Deutsches Ärzteblatt, 4,* March, 39–50.

Schwartz, G. E. (1978). Psychobiological foundations of psychotherapy and behavior change. In S. L. Garfield & A. E. Bergin (Eds.), *Handbook of psychotherapy and behavior change* (2nd ed.) (pp. 63–99). New York: Wiley.

Shapiro, A. K. (1960). A contribution to a history of the placebo effect. *Behavioral Science, 5,* 109–135.

Shapiro, A. K. (1968). Semantics of the placebo. *Psychiatric Quarterly, 42,* 653–696.

Shapiro, A. K., & Morris, L. A. (1978). The placebo effect in medical and psychological therapies. In S. L. Garfield & A. E. Bergin (Eds.), *Handbook of psychotherapy and behavior change* (2nd ed.) (pp. 369–410). New York: Wiley.

Shapiro, A. P., Schwartz, G. E., & Ferguson, D. C. (1977). Behavioral methods in the treatment of hypertension. *Annals of Internal Medicine, 86,* 626–636.

Shepherd, M. (1961). Specific and non-specific factors in psychopharmacology. In E. Rothlin (Ed.), *Neuropsychopharmacology, Vol. 2* (pp. 117–129). Amsterdam: Elsevier.

Suedfeld, P. (1984). The subtractive expectancy placebo procedure: a measure of non-specific factors in behavioural interventions. *Behaviour Research and Therapy, 22,* 159–164.

Wheatley, D. (1967). Influence of doctors' and patients' attitudes in the treatment of neurotic illness. *Lancet, ii,* 1133–1135.

Wilkins, W. (1985). Therapy credibility is not a non-specific event. *Cognitive Therapy and Research, 9,* 119–125.

Clinical versus Statistical Prediction

Human Mind versus Regression Equation: Five Contrasts

Lewis R. Goldberg

> *Why should people have been so surprised by the empirical results in my summary chapter? Surely we all know that the human brain is poor at weighting and computing. When you check out at a supermarket, you don't eyeball the heap of purchases and say to the clerk, "Well it looks to me as if it's about $17.00 worth; what do you think?" The clerk adds it up. There are no strong arguments, from the armchair or from empirical studies of cognitive psychology, for believing that human beings can assign optimal weights in equations subjectively or that they apply their own weights consistently.*
>
> (Meehl, 1986, p. 372)

It has been said that the single most difficult thing to do in the world is to write with clarity and style. (It has also been said that fine writing is easy: One simply stares at the blank paper until the sweat on one's brow turns to blood.) Paul Meehl writes with the elan of no one else in our field, and to read him is to experience

The preparation of this chapter was supported by Grant MH-39077 from the National Institute of Mental Health, U. S. Public Health Service. The author is indebted to W. Scott Armstrong, Thomas Bezembinder, Berndt Brehmer, Matthias Burisch, William F. Chaplin, Lee J. Cronbach, Robyn M. Dawes, Adriaan D. de Groot, David Faust, Baruch Fischhoff, David C. Funder, Janice C. Goldberg, Kenneth R. Hammond, Sarah E. Hampson, Paul Herzberg, Willem K. B. Hofstee, Robert Hogan, John Horn, Irving L. Janis, Oliver P. John, Daniel Kahneman, Henry F. Kaiser, Kevin Lanning, Sarah Lichtenstein, John C. Loehlin, Robert R. McCrae, Warren T. Norman, Daniel Ozer, Dean Peabody, Leonard G. Rorer, Tina K. Rosolack, Myron Rothbart, Paul Slovic, Ross Stagner, Auke Tellegen, Amos Tversky, and Jerry S. Wiggins for their thoughtful reactions to previous drafts. All of the remaining errors in this chapter are the fault of those who were invited to correct them but have neglected to do so.

an aesthetic rush along with the inevitable intellectual jolt. Indeed, while waiting for my own sweat to congeal, I sometimes engage in a peculiar form of biblio-therapy: I read a piece or two (or seven if the blood feels thin) by Meehl. The particular piece does not seem to matter all that much, although I have my favor-ites. Any section of *Clinical versus statistical prediction* (Meehl, 1954) will do the job, so that monograph was always near at hand throughout the 1960s. Later, Meehl concocted an even stronger tonic, "Why I do not attend case confer-ences," and therefore the book in which that chapter appeared (Meehl, 1973) soon took its turn as my security blanket. Reprinted in that 1973 collection is the classic, "When shall we use our heads instead of the formula?" (Meehl, 1957), in which Meehl tried to provide a logical analysis of the conditions favoring hu-man over actuarial predictions.

Meehl has frequently expressed disappointment in his readers' near-exclusive focus on the clinical versus statistical box-score of the moment, rather than on the merits of his logical analyses. In the latter, he posited some characteristics of pre-diction problems in applied settings that might lead the human mind to triumph over typical actuarial procedures. Such possibilities included open-ended predic-tion tasks, unanalyzed stimulus equivalences, empty cells, theory mediation, in-sufficient time, and highly configural prediction functions (Meehl, 1959). The last of these, the only one of the set that was later to be studied empirically, con-cerns the nature of the relations between predictor and criterion variables. Meehl assumed that for many important prediction problems these relations would be nonlinear and/or interactive in character. If so, he reasoned, the linear additive assumptions incorporated into the multiple regression model would severely at-tenuate the predictive accuracy of any regression equation. On the other hand, if professional experts have learned these complex relations and can use them in diagnostic decision-making, then the human predictions should be superior to those generated by a regression equation.

Were it only so. As it has turned out, research findings suggest that highly configural predictor-criterion relations may be quite rare (e.g., Goldberg, 1965, 1969) and the human's ability to learn such complex relations, when they do oc-cur, is far from optimal (e.g., Brehmer, 1979, 1980; Goldberg, 1968). As a con-sequence, it now appears that Meehl's initial concern about the limitations of the regression model no longer need be considered so seriously. Indeed, this highly popular and versatile technique could well be considered a prototypical example of standard actuarial methodology. In the present chapter, I will compare the fea-tures of multiple regression analysis with those of human numerical predictions. Specifically, I will ask: What does the regression equation do, and what would the human mind have to be able to do, in order for both mind and equation to forecast with equal accuracy? I will assume that readers share my understanding of the by-now-overwhelming empirical evidence favoring the use of actuarial methods (e.g., the regression equation) over unaided human intuition (the mind, however labeled) for predicting a diverse array of important human outcomes, and consequently I will not review that literature here. I will also assume that readers share my appreciation for the quite remarkable powers of the human mind over a wide range of contexts in which multiple-regression analyses are not appropriate, the prototypical example being that of pattern recognition.

In this chapter, I will describe five key features of a multiple-regression analysis, five problems in prediction that are automatically solved when one employs a regression algorithm. Specifically, a regression equation takes into account, and optimally[1] adjusts for, (a) differential *validities* within a set of predictors, (b) differences in *metrics* between the criterion and each of the predictors, (c) *consistency* of the forecasts from identical predictor patterns, (d) differential degrees of *redundancy* within sets of predictors, and (e) all *regression* effects associated with imperfect predictor-criterion associations. Historically, proponents of statistical predictions focused our attention on the first of these features, and perhaps as a consequence investigators of human decision-making explored them in roughly this order, as will I.

Adjusting for Differential Validities among the Predictors

The most obvious feature of a multiple-regression analysis is its optimal weighting of the predictors as a function of their differential validities: Other things being equal, the stronger the relation between a predictor and the criterion, the more weight that predictor is given in the regression equation. Clearly, humans cannot do this task perfectly, and perhaps they do it quite poorly. To discover the weights that experts implicitly assign to predictor information, Hammond (1955) and Hoffman (1960) suggested that we try to capture those weights by constructing a regression equation to predict each individual's judgments. Hoffman (1960), who labeled these equations "paramorphic representations" of the judgment process, assumed that "the regression weights signify, with certain limitations, the emphasis or importance attached to each of the predictor variables by the judge. Large coefficients mean, empirically, that the corresponding predictors can account for large proportions of the variance of judgment; and a predictor with a small beta coefficient contributes little beyond the contribution of other predictors" (p. 120). Later, Hammond, Hursch, and Todd (1964) and Tucker (1964) mathematically formulated some of the components of clinical inference within this multiple-regression framework. For more complete accounts of this analytical strategy and the research it spawned, see Hammond, McClelland, and Mumpower (1980).

All of this early work was based on the assumption that a major—if not the major—difference between human and equation was non-optimal versus optimal weighting of the predictor validities. Not until a decade later were we told that this difference may not be as critical as we had assumed. Dawes and Corrigan

(1974; see also Dawes, 1979) showed that equations with unit weights (sometimes even with random weights) produced predictions similar to those produced by models based on regression weights under three conditions: (a) a *correlational* index is used as the standard of comparison among the prediction methods, (b) the *signs* of the predictor-criterion relations are correctly identified, and (c) the *metrics* of the predictors have been transformed so as to eliminate any differences in predictor variances (e.g., they are all standardized in z-score form). Because the widely cited findings of Dawes and Corrigan (1974) have frequently been overgeneralized, it is important to try to clarify some of the basic issues they raise.

First of all, as has been brilliantly articulated by Cronbach and Gleser (1953) in another context, there are different statistical standards that can be used to index the accuracy of numerical predictions. Within the present context two standards have been invoked, those based on *relational* indices such as the correlation coefficient and those based on an average *discrepancy* between predicted and criterion values such as the standard error of prediction (i.e., the square root of the mean squared error). Dawes and Corrigan (1974) showed that under certain conditions the predictions generated by unit-weighted and regression-weighted models may be highly correlated. Indeed, as demonstrated some time ago by Gulliksen (1950, pp. 312–327) and more recently by Einhorn and Hogarth (1975) and von Winterfeldt and Edwards (1987), the size of the expected correlation between the predictions from any two models is a negative function of the number of predictors and a positive function of their average intercorrelation. Moreover, whereas the predictions from two models may be highly related, one could still relate positively and the other negatively with any other variable, including a criterion variable. For example, even when the predictions from two models correlate .80, one of them could correlate as high as .32 and the other as low as − .32 with the same criterion. In addition, correlations do not reflect any constant or systematic errors that affect the means and/or variances of the predictions. In the remainder of this chapter, I will assume the use of some accuracy measure that is so affected, such as the standard error of prediction.

Using such a standard, what do we know about the accuracy with which people can learn to assess the relative validity of different predictors? The classic work on this problem was carried out by Chapman and Chapman (1967) and subsequently replicated and extended by Golding and Rorer (1972). In a nutshell, they showed that we can rather easily be led to see what we expect to see, even when what we expect is not there. Specifically, when people expect to find predictor-criterion relations in a stimulus set in which those relations are absent, they "find" them anyway. What this suggests is that our ability to learn the differential validities of predictors is far from perfect (see Brehmer, 1980; Gaeth & Shanteau, 1984). Unlike the regression equation, which performs this chore optimally, the human mind does not. Perhaps the most pessimistic assessment of the powers of the human mind in this regard has been provided by Nisbett and Ross (1980), who concluded that the evidence shows that people are poor at detecting many sorts of covariation: "The layperson apparently does not understand intuitively the basic logic of covariation assessment underlying the 2 × 2 contingency table. Perception of covariation in the social domain is largely a function of preexisting theories and only very secondarily a function of true covariation. In the absence of theories, people's covariation detection capacities are extremely limited" (p. 111).

Aligning the Metrics of the Predictors with That of the Criterion

In the studies by Dawes and his colleagues, both the "improper" and the "proper" weights under study were always applied to standardized (z-scored) predictors. Indeed, the very notion of "unit" or equal weights makes no sense unless applied to predictors scaled in the same metric. Other things being equal, the contribution of each part to a composite is a direct function of the relative variances of the parts; specifically, the larger the variance of a part, the more it contributes to the variance of the composite. One function of a regression equation is to align the metrics of each of the predictors with that of the criterion, and it does this in an optimal manner. Clearly, humans will not align diverse metrics so keenly, and this cognitive limitation could result in their intuitive weights differing from those they intended.

Some studies of the effects of differing predictor metrics were carried out by Paul Hoffman in the early 1960s. In the one published report of this work (Knox & Hoffman, 1962), judgments based on predictor scores expressed in T-score metric were compared with judgments based on the same scores expressed in percentiles. College students rated the intelligence or sociability of (fictitious) target persons on two occasions, using eight potential predictors of sociability and nine of intelligence. Each profile was displayed in either T-score or percentile format. Within each of the eight cells generated by three experimental conditions (T score vs. percentile, intelligence vs. sociability, test vs. retest), a regression model was fitted to the judgments of each subject. Of the two metrics under study, the percentile format was associated with greater variance of the judgments (and therefore higher test-retest reliability and higher predictability by the paramorphic representations), leading the investigators to conclude that "judgments from profiles are influenced not only by the underlying meaning of the plotted scores but by their graphical location as well" (Knox & Hoffman, 1962, p. 14). On the other hand, differences in metric were not associated with different patterns of relative weights of the predictors. Moreover, because the profiles were fictitious, no assessment of differential accuracy was possible. Finally, within each of the eight conditions all predictors were scaled in the same metric, thus rendering impossible any analyses of potential difficulties in aligning diverse metrics within the same task.

Such difficulties were hypothesized, and investigated indirectly, in one of the five studies reported by Slovic and MacPhillamy (1974). In these studies, sets of stimuli were compared on features, some of which are common to all stimuli and some of which are unique to each one. The major hypothesis was that people would tend to weight the common features more highly than the unique ones. Subjects compared pairs of hypothetical high school students on their potential college success. Scores were available for both students in each pair on one common attribute (e.g., English skills) and for each student on one unique attribute. For half of the subjects, scores on the three (one common and two unique) attributes were all in the same metric, whereas for the other half of the subjects each of the three attributes was scored in a different metric. Unfortunately, all analyses were focused on the effects of common vs. unique attributes, rather than on the comparison between same and different metrics (labeled "equal vs. unequal" units). The investigators concluded that the "common-dimension effect was as strong in the equal as in the unequal-units conditions, contrary to the expectation that it would be easier to use the unique information in the equal-units condition since there was less data transformation for the judge to consider" (Slovic & MacPhillamy, 1974, p. 180).

Additional indirect evidence about human limitations in aligning different metrics comes from some recent studies by Tversky, Sattath, and Slovic (1988) that focused on individuals' judgments about their preferences. Based on the initial findings of Slovic (1975), these investigators showed that attributes that are scaled in a metric that is compatible with that of the judgmental response format will be weighted more highly than are attributes scaled in any other metric. Said another way, in intuitive decision-making the weight of an attribute is enhanced by its compatibility with the output format or metric. The probable reason for this effect is that the incompatibility between input and output requires additional mental transformations, which in turn demand increased effort, which can lead to strain and to errors. For example, in one study subjects were asked to predict the decisions of a college admissions committee from applicants' *ranks* on one attribute (e.g., an ability test) and from *categorical* values on another (e.g., a strong versus a weak pattern of extracurricular activities). Subjects were told that the committee ranked all applicants and accepted the top quarter, and they were randomly assigned to predict either the rank or the acceptance decision for each applicant. As hypothesized, subjects asked to predict the rankings weighted the attribute scaled in ranks more highly than the attribute presented categorically, whereas the reverse pattern characterized subjects asked to predict the categorical decisions.

In summary, then, although none of the studies to date has focused directly on numerical predictions in applied settings, all of the indirect evidence suggests that the task of aligning attributes scaled in different metrics is not likely to be a forte of the human mind. Regression equations, on the other hand, handle this aspect of prediction tasks as facilely as they handle other aspects.

Forecasting with Consistency

In the quotation with which this chapter begins, Meehl noted that "There are no strong arguments . . . for believing that human beings can . . . apply their own weights consistently." Hubris demands that I now finish that sentence: "the query from which Lew Goldberg derived such fascinating and fundamental results" (Meehl, 1986, p. 372). The results to which Meehl alludes (Goldberg, 1970) have been cited frequently enough, and have now been replicated in enough new contexts, that I can describe them here quite briefly. When a paramorphic representation of a person's judgments is substituted for that person in the same predictive context, the person's model typically turns out to be more accurate than the person's own judgments. How can that be? The paramorphic model is a regression equation, and one crucial feature of all such equations is that their test-retest reliabilities are perfect. Given the same pattern of predictor values, the equation must generate identical predictions. Humans, on the other hand, are not like equations: Their repeated judgments of the same predictor configurations are often different. Indeed, one can be almost completely unreliable in a predictive situation in which one expects to be perfectly reliable, as was revealed in an intensive study of an experienced graphologist whose test-retest reliability turned out to be near zero (Goldberg, 1986). Because unreliability inherently limits potential validity, it is undesirable in any predictive context.

Over the past decade, there have been frequent demonstrations that seemingly innocuous and normatively inconsequential changes in the formulation of prediction problems can produce substantial inconsistencies when persons respond to two or more forms of the same problem. These inconsistencies are referred to as "framing" effects, and they have now been obtained across a quite diverse set of judgmental tasks. Because superb reviews of framing effects are readily available (e.g., Kahneman & Tversky, 1984; Slovic, Fischhoff, & Lichtenstein, 1982), I will say no more about them here other than to point to their relevance for any comparisons between the human mind and the regression equation.

Accounting for Predictor Redundancies

Not all of the attributes we use as predictors come packaged independently of each other; indeed, most attributes covary in nature to some extent. Such covariation implies information redundancy, and redundant predictor information adds no zest to the predictive punch. A multiple regression equation automatically takes the intercorrelations among the predictors into account in deriving the

Table 1. Types of Predictor-Criterion Correlational Patterns

Correlation	Redundancy Strong	Weak	Independence	Enhancement Weak	Strong
Validity of the first predictor (r_{yx_1})	.50	.50	.50	.50	.50
Validity of the second predictor (r_{yx_2})	.40	.40	.40	.40	.40
Correlation between the two predictors $(r_{x_1x_2})$	.60	.30	.00	−.30	−.60
Multiple Correlation $(R_{y.x_1x_2})$	.52	.56	.64	.76	1.00

predictor weights. Humans are unlikely to do this optimally. Even worse, they tend to value redundancy for its own sake, because redundancy leads them to have increased confidence in their predictions (Slovic, 1966).

Other things being equal, predictive accuracy is increased when all predictors are mutually orthogonal, and accuracy is enhanced even more when the predictors are correlated with each other in ways other than the ways they are correlated with the criterion. Table 1 provides examples in the most simple case — two predictors (x_1 and x_2) and one criterion (y) — of three types of information configurations: redundancy, independence, and enhancement. In all cases, the validity of one predictor is .50 and that of the other is .40. When the predictors are redundant, use of them both does not improve predictive accuracy much beyond what can be attained by the best of them alone. When the predictors are unrelated, predictability is increased considerably. When the sign of the correlation between the predictors is the oppposite of the signs of their validity coefficients, predictability is enhanced substantially. Indeed, when the two predictors are correlated approximately −.60, multiple prediction is perfect.

Given sets of stimulus materials corresponding to each of these configurations in a learning task, humans much prefer redundancy to either of the other two conditions, even though they should be able to predict most accurately in their least preferred configuration. To demonstrate this effect, Kahneman and Tversky (1973) asked subjects to predict grade-point average on the basis of two pairs of aptitude tests. Subjects were told that one pair of tests (e.g., creative thinking and symbolic ability) was highly related, whereas the other pair of tests (e.g., mental flexibility and systematic reasoning) was unrelated. The scores they encountered conformed to these expectations. Subjects were told that "all tests were found equally successful in predicting college performance." Although in this situation higher predictive accuracy can be achieved with the unrelated than with the related pair of tests, subjects were significantly more confident in predicting from the related pair. Specifically, "they were more confident in a context of inferior predictive validity" (Kahneman & Tversky, 1973, p. 249).

Other things being equal, the more certain we are of being correct, the more extreme are the numerical values we give; when we are in doubt, we tend to respond more cautiously, and thus more neutrally. As a consequence, any increment in redundancy within a predictor set tends to increase the variance of intuitive predictions. And, to the extent to which our confidence is misplaced—that is, we are "more confident in a context of inferior predictive validity"—we are doing the opposite of what we should do under the circumstances. What we should do is covered in the next section.

Adjusting for Regression Effects

Regression to the mean is like the weather: Everybody talks about it, but few of us do anything about it. However, it is unlike the weather, because most of us fail to recognize it, even when it hits us on the nose. Consider the following regression axiom: In the context of numerical prediction problems, the variance of our predictions should never be larger than that of the criterion we seek to predict. (Never, not just hardly ever.) Indeed, virtually always the variance of our predictions should be much smaller than that of the criterion. As their name implies, regression equations are specifically constructed to handle regression effects optimally. Like the other four features of this analytic method, the fifth just comes with the territory.

Although it has long been known, at least by statistics instructors, that the concept of regression was not part of our human intuitions, it remained for Kahneman and Tversky (1973) to document the extent of this cognitive limitation, to analyze some conditions under which this failing is particularly severe, and to provide a theoretical rationale to explain both how we make intuitive predictions and why they tend to be nonregressive in character. Briefly, these investigators have shown that intuitive predictions are often based on a heuristic called "representativeness"—specifically, that we tend to assess outcomes by the extent to which the outcomes resemble or "represent" the main features of the evidence. Predictions based on resemblance are not regressive, whereas all predictions should be.

The best summary of the evidence on the use and misuse of the representativeness heuristic in making intuitive predictions has been provided by Nisbett and Ross (1980; see especially chapter 7), who argued that the tendency to be insufficiently regressive has two causes. On the one hand, people may often over-estimate the degree of covariation among events in the social domain, at least when such events can be linked by plausible causal theories, scripts, or stereotypes. More important, however, is the fact that people fail to make regressive predictions even when they recognize that the available predictor variables are only weakly related to the criterion. That is, incorrect theories about the strength of relations lead to exaggerated beliefs about the utility of potential predictors, and intuitive prediction strategies result in nonregressive predictions even when the weakness of the relations is recognized. Nisbett and Ross (1980) concluded that "when it comes to predictions, a little knowledge (that is, knowledge of the target's score on a weakly related predictor variable) is a dangerous thing" (p. 153).

Summary

Of the five types of problems solved automatically by the regression equation, which is the most troublesome for the human mind? In a first draft of this chapter, I questioned whether the relative importance of the five problems in differentiating human from equation was not the very opposite of their historical order of investigation (and the opposite of their order of presentation here). I speculated that the most obvious limitation of the human mind as compared to the regression equation—failure to give proper weight to differences in the validities of the predictors—may not turn out to be the key villain in this mystery story. Rather, the very feature of the regression equation that gives it its name may be the most important of the five contrasts. Now older and wiser (see the note on the first page of this chapter), I lean toward reversing my initial importance ranking. In so doing, I thereby demonstrate the very deficiencies that I have been chronicling—an inability to figure out the relative validities of each of the five features, confusion stemming from the incommensurability of their metrics, obvious inconsistency in my forecasting, difficulty combining nonredundant features, and finally a failure to regress to the mean, which in this case would amount to a prediction that all the features are quite similar in their importance. Indeed, all that is clear to me at this point is that as humans we do none of them optimally.

In the 1950s, it was Paul Meehl who brought to the attention of both the clinical and the scientific communities in psychology the necessity of comparing the accuracy of intuitive and actuarial procedures so as to better understand "what can the clinician do well?" In so doing, he forced us to become aware of our cognitive limitations, and he led us to think more carefully about the logic of the predictive enterprise. During the 1960s and 1970s, his name was primarily associated with his summaries of the empirical comparisons between intuitive and actuarial predictions. Now in the 1990s, we should be ready to appreciate his contributions for what *he* valued most in them, his extraordinarily prescient insights into the assets and the liabilities associated with human intuitions. To the extent to which we do so, we will begin to attentuate his anguish about his readers' reactions, or lack thereof, to his 1954 monograph:

People sometimes ask me whether I am disappointed by the relatively feeble impact of that book and of the many studies that were stimulated by it. . . . I have learned to develop a certain Buddhistic detachment about the matter. Suppose a social worker confidently tells me that of course we can predict how this delinquent will do on probation by reflecting on psychodynamic inferences and subjective impressions, recorded in a 10-page presentence investigation, despite the malignant rap sheet record and acting-out psychometrics, and the officer's comment that "he's a real mean, tough street kid." Well, I remind myself that Omniscient Jones has not put me in charge of reforming the world (Meehl, 1986, p. 375).

Note

1. The coefficients in a multiple-regression equation are "optimal" only in the sample in which they were derived, and consequently the validity of a regression equation will tend to shrink when it is applied in new samples. In general, the robustness of the equation is negatively related to the number of predictor variables used to derive it, and positively related to the size of the derivation sample and its representativeness of the population to which the equation is to be applied.

References

Brehmer, B. (1979). Effects of practice on utilization of nonlinear rules in inference tasks. *Scandinavian Journal of Psychology, 20,* 141–149.

Brehmer, B. (1980). In one word: Not from experience. *Acta Psychologica, 45,* 223–241.

Chapman, L. J., & Chapman, J. P. (1967). Genesis of popular but erroneous psychodiagnostic observations. *Journal of Abnormal Psychology, 72,* 193–204.

Cronbach, L. J., & Gleser, G. C. (1953). Assessing similarity between profiles. *Psychological Bulletin, 50,* 456–473.

Dawes, R. M. (1979). The robust beauty of improper linear models in decision making. *American Psychologist, 34,* 571–582.

Dawes, R. M., & Corrigan, B. (1974). Linear models in decision making. *Psychological Bulletin, 81,* 95–106.

Einhorn, H. J., & Hogarth, R. M. (1975). Unit weighting schemes for decision making. *Organizational Behavior and Human Performance, 13,* 171–192.

Gaeth, G. J., & Shanteau, J. (1984). Reducing the influence of irrelevant information on experienced decision makers. *Organizational Behavior and Human Performance, 33,* 263–282.

Goldberg, L. R. (1965). Diagnosticians vs. diagnostic signs: The diagnosis of psychosis vs. neurosis from the MMPI. *Psychological Monographs, 79,* (9, Whole No. 602).

Goldberg, L. R. (1968). Simple models or simple processes? Some research on clinical judgments. *American Psychologist, 23,* 483–496.

Goldberg, L. R. (1969). The search for configural relationships in personality assessment: The diagnosis of psychosis vs. neurosis from the MMPI. *Multivariate Behavioral Research, 4,* 523–536.

Goldberg, L. R. (1970). Man versus model of man: A rationale, plus some evidence, for a method of improving on clinical inferences. *Psychological Bulletin, 73,* 422–432.

Goldberg, L. R. (1986). Some informal explorations and ruminations about graphology. In B. Nevo (Ed.), *Scientific aspects of graphology* (pp. 281–293). Springfield, IL: Charles C. Thomas.

Golding, S. L., & Rorer, L. G. (1972). Illusory correlation and subjective judgment. *Journal of Abnormal Psychology, 80,* 249–260.

Gulliksen, H. (1950). *Theory of mental tests.* NY: Wiley.

Hammond, K. R. (1955). Probabilistic functioning and the clinical method. *Psychological Review, 62,* 255–262.

Hammond, K. R., Hursch, C. J., & Todd, F. J. (1964). Analyzing the components of clinical inference. *Psychological Review, 71,* 438–456.

Hammond, K. R., McClelland, G. H., & Mumpower, J. (1980). *Human judgment and decision making: Theories, methods, and procedures.* NY: Praeger.

Hoffman, P. J. (1960). The paramorphic representation of clinical judgment. *Psychological Bulletin, 57,* 116–131.

Kahneman, D., & Tversky, A. (1973). On the psychology of prediction. *Psychological Review, 80,* 237–251.

Kahneman, D., & Tversky, A. (1984). Choices, values, and frames. *American Psychologist, 39,* 341–350.

Knox, R. E., & Hoffman, P. J. (1962). Effects of variation of profile format on intelligence and sociability judgments. *Journal of Applied Psychology, 46,* 14–20.

Meehl, P. E. (1954). *Clinical versus statistical prediction: A theoretical analysis and review of the evidence.* Minneapolis: University of Minnesota Press.

Meehl, P. E. (1957). When shall we use our heads instead of the formula? *Journal of Counseling Psychology, 4,* 268–273.

Meehl, P. E. (1959). A comparison of clinicians with five statistical methods of identifying psychotic MMPI profiles. *Journal of Counseling Psychology, 6,* 102–109.

Meehl, P. E. (1967). What can the clinician do well? In D. N. Jackson & S. Messick (Eds.), *Problems in human assessment* (pp. 594–599). NY: McGraw-Hill.

Meehl, P. E. (1973). *Psychodiagnosis: Selected papers.* Minneapolis: University of Minnesota Press.

Meehl, P. E. (1986). Causes and effects of my disturbing little book. *Journal of Personality Assessment, 50,* 370–375.

Nisbett, R., & Ross, L. (1980). *Human inference: Strategies and shortcomings of social judgment.* Englewood Cliffs, NJ: Prentice-Hall.

Slovic, P. (1966). Cue-consistency and cue-utilization in judgment. *American Journal of Psychology, 79,* 427–434.

Slovic, P. (1975). Choice between equally valued alternatives. *Journal of Experimental Psychology: Human Perception and Performance, 1,* 280–287.

Slovic, P., Fischhoff, B., & Lichtenstein, S. (1982). Response mode, framing, and information-processing effects in risk assessment. In R. Hogarth (Ed.), *New directions for methodology of social and behavioral science: Question framing and response consistency: No. 11* (pp. 21–35). San Francisco: Jossey-Bass.

Slovic, P., & MacPhillamy, D. (1974). Dimensional commensurability and cue utilization in comparative judgment. *Organizational Behavior and Human Performance, 11,* 172–194.

Tucker, L. R. (1964). A suggested alternative formulation in the developments by Hursch, Hammond, and Hursch, and by Hammond, Hursch, and Todd. *Psychological Review, 71,* 528–530.

Tversky, A., Sattath, S., & Slovic, P. (1988). Contingent weighting in judgment and choice. *Psychological Review, 95,* 371–384.

von Winterfeldt, D., & Edwards, W. (1987). *Decision analysis and behavioral research.* NY: Cambridge University Press.

What If We Had Really Listened?
Present Reflections on Altered Pasts
David Faust

In stories on time travel, writers often lead us to wonder what one who alters the past would find upon one's return to the present. One can reverse this mental exercise; if the present were different, how would antecedent events have differed? In 1986, Paul Meehl said:

> People sometimes ask me whether I am disappointed by the relatively feeble impact of that book [clinical versus statistical prediction] and the many studies that were stimulated by it. . . . I really didn't expect people to think rationally about it. (p. 375)

Imagine now the events that would have preceded a statement that instead read:

> People sometimes ask me whether I am pleased by the impact of that book. Well, yes, I was surprised that most people could think rationally about it.

What Fisbee Would Have Said:
Fisbee's 1990 Presidental Address to the Society for Probabilistic Personality Assessment

Those who forget the past are doomed to omit the prior odds when predicting the future. Today I will review past events, often forgotten or taken for granted, which reshaped the personality-assessment landscape. As a practicing diagnostician, I believe that the recognition and description of critical problems may in-

My sincere thanks to Hal R. Arkes, Robyn M. Dawes, Lewis R. Goldberg, and Barry Nurcombe who reviewed an initial draft of this manuscript (no small undertaking) and offered many helpful comments.

185

deed stimulate crisis, but that such crises may be required to jar us from out-moded thinking and to initiate self-correction. It was not fortuitous that a book devoted to Karl Popper was titled *Criticism and the Growth of Knowledge*. Of course, criticism requires an open audience, one willing to take risks and subor-dinate self-interest to the abstract good of scientific advance.

Overview of Meehl (1954) and Meehl and Rosen (1955)

About 35 years ago, Paul Meehl published his book on clinical versus statistical prediction, following within a year by an article with Albert Rosen on antecedent probability and cutting scores. Meehl's book compared the clinical method, or conclusions based on data processing "in the head," to the actuarial method, or data combination that eliminates the human judge and rests on empirical relations or frequencies. Meehl mainly addressed the philosophical underpinnings of the two approaches and their potential advantages and disadvantages. He did review the scientific comparisons available at the time, which could not resolve many of the issues but clearly favored the actuarial or statistical approach. Meehl took special pains to outline circumstances in which the clinician might beat the ac-tuary. He also addressed practical implications. For example, actuarial ap-proaches save time and costs, which can free clinicians to pursue tasks at which they are uniquely qualified, such as psychotherapy. Even today, service needs exceed availability, and time savings permit at least some of those who are de-serving but would otherwise go unserved to be served.

In 1955, Meehl and Rosen described what later came to be called the "rela-tivity of validity" principle. Meehl and Rosen showed that the validity of diag-nostic or predictive signs is never absolute or constant, but must be interpreted in relation to the prior odds or the base rates, that is, the frequency of the things to be identified or predicted. For example, compared to predictions founded on the base rates, a sign (or set of signs) that achieves 75% accuracy will exceed base-rate predictions if the event of interest occurs 65% of the time (and thus one achieved 65% accuracy by always guessing "yea"). However, the sign will fall below base-rate accuracy if the event occurs 85% of the time (and one could thereby achieve 85% accuracy by always guessing "yea").

Meehl and Rosen thus established a necessary hurdle for diagnostic or predic-tive signs. Demonstrations of validity were not enough, for the use of a valid sign could still *decrease* accuracy relative to that achieved by base-rate predictions. The sign(s) must also exceed base-rate accuracy. Meehl and Rosen provided pro-cedures (based on Bayes's Theorem) for analyzing the utility of signs, and they offered constructive suggestions. For example, base-rate accuracy is hard to beat with high- and low-frequency events (because highly accurate base-rate predic-tions are possible in both cases by always saying "yea" or "nay," respectively). They suggested that we might increasingly focus our diagnostic methods on clinically meaningful phenomena with about even (50–50) distributions. Base-rate predictions are least accurate when things occur half the time, and thus there is the greatest chance (and need) for deriving tests or signs that exceed base-rate accuracy.

Meehl and Rosen

I will deal with the impact of Meehl and Rosen first, for the basic issues were pretty straightforward. Meehl and Rosen's central points rested on fundamental principles of probability and logic — were essentially self-evident — hence there could be little dispute about their accuracy. Some clinicians argued that the methods Meehl and Rosen described did not help to distinguish between different possible disorders. Others argued that the overall hit-rate was not necessarily of the utmost concern. Even signs that reduced overall accuracy (relative to the base rates) could favorably alter the *ratio* of false-positive and false-negative errors. For example, an increase in overall error might be acceptable if one lowered false-negative error — less frequently missed potentially serious psychiatric conditions. Further, many psychiatric conditions are infrequent, which might lead the base-rate player to say uniformly, "no such disorder," and thereby to miss all cases of disorder.

These objections were largely superfluous. Meehl and Rosen's points applied equally to disorder present-disorder absent distinctions as to the differential between alternate diagnostic possibilities. Whichever distinction was sought, the value of diagnostic signs still varies depending on the base rate(s) of the thing(s) to be identified, whether this is the frequency with which a disorder is present versus absent, or the relative frequency of different disorders.

Suppose a diagnostic sign is related to both Disorder A and Disorder B, but that the strength of association is twice as strong for A versus B. Within the population of interest, if disorders A and B occur with equal frequency, then the presence of the sign should lead one to diagnose A over B. However, suppose disorder B is much more frequent, e.g., within a clinical population the base rate for major depression is ten times greater than that for anorexia nervosa. Suppose further that a sign (e.g., weight loss) is associated twice as strongly with anorexia nervosa than with major depression. Nevertheless, because depression is so much more frequent, when the sign occurs and one or the other disorder is present, depression is usually the right choice.

Nor did Meehl and Rosen argue that when base rates proved most accurate overall, one should always rely upon them, even if serious and frequent false-negative errors resulted. Meehl and Rosen instead provided a means for analyzing the actual impact of a sign or test on diagnostic accuracy, which offered informed guidance for the decision-maker. Decisions based on known consequences of alternate actions are more likely to fulfill our aims than judgments that ignore or misappraise consequences. The purpose is not to replace good intention with blind adherence to probabilities but to increase the chances that our decisions will achieve what we value.

The merit of informed judgment became apparent upon finding that base-rate analysis often produced decision guides that hardly necessitated subtle distinctions or elaborate value appraisals. Of interest is the fact that these guides often pointed in the opposite direction to that expected. Many of our popular clinical signs produced so many more false-positive errors than valid-positive identifications that their use was indefensible. For example, many "signs" of schizophrenia produced 10 to 20 times more false-positive errors than correct identifications. False labeling of this sort had such potential for harm that the trade-off was obviously not worth the price, and use of the signs was discontinued.

Even when the costs of false-negative identifications were potentially dreadful (e.g., missing suicidal intent), base-rate analysis often produced startling results. For example, in settings with exceedingly low rates of suicide, such as general hospitals, certain signs for identifying suicidal intent (e.g., those based on the Rorschach) resulted in *hundreds* of times more false-positive than valid-positive identifications. How could one justify such methods? Consider the potential harm and cost of false diagnoses and unnecessary preventive measures; the alternate and more productive uses to which wasted resources could be directed, which surely would save lives (e.g., feeding the starving); and the limits in the effectiveness of preventive measures, even if undertaken.

As it turned out, signs that decreased overall accuracy (relative to the base rates) rarely altered the ratio of false-negative to false-positive errors in a sufficiently robust manner to support their use. Lack of information had also handicapped attempts to appraise trade-offs between overall accuracy and ratio of error types. For example, we knew almost nothing about the relative costs or actual consequences of false-positive and false-negative errors. Almost no research had examined the impact of false-positive diagnoses on individuals. We did not know how often false-positive diagnoses were later corrected. We could not know, when a label of disorder was falsely applied and an individual refused to participate in treatment, how much harm we might have done.

The analogy we drew to medicine, in which false-positive error is often considered far less serious than false-negative error (i.e., missing actual disorders), offered poor guidance for the mental-health field. At the time of Meehl and Rosen's work, the ratio of successful to unsuccessful treatment was perhaps two to one. "Spontaneous" cure rate was considerable for certain conditions, and the cost of false-positive errors (e.g., falsely diagnosing brain damage) was unknown but may have been appreciable. Thus, could we say with surety that false-negative errors were far more wicked than false-positive ones? These concerns stimulated efforts to obtain scientific information on the impact of varying errors, and to build utility models that incorporated the likelihood of different error types and adjusted decision-making guides in relation to human costs and benefits. The whole point of this enterprise was rather obvious. A greater awareness of the trade-off stemming from different decision policies allows one to better identify the best "deal."

One of the more substantive reactions to Meehl and Rosen went as follows: Base-rate predictions reduce error but also accept some, or even considerable, error. Perhaps error could be further decreased if clinicians tried to identify instances in which to countervail base-rate predictions. Some asserted that clinicians were ethically *obligated* to make this attempt, for intelligent efforts to identify exceptions would "undoubtedly" improve upon "blind" adherence to base-rate predictions. Thus, one must seek out exceptions to protect individuals' interests.

However, most clinicians considered this assertion dubious. They pointed out that all of our predictors, even in combination, relate imperfectly to the criteria of interest, and error is thus inevitable. Further, the scientific enterprise has shown us all too often that what appears obvious can be flat-out wrong. Categorical assumptions were unwarranted and best framed as empirical questions. The question here was whether select disregard of base-rate predictions produced more "saves" (mistaken base-rate predictions caught and corrected) than "spoils" (correct base-rate predictions inadvertently overturned). The question was put to test and the answer was no. I will say more about this when I return to the work on clinical versus statistical methods.

A more refined approach to a related issue did prove helpful. Perhaps the choice was not always one of deciding whether to use measures depending on their satisfaction of the base-rate hurdle. Even should the base rates achieve greater accuracy across all cases, perhaps in a subset of cases the test results could beat the base rates. One might not be able to know beforehand when an individual would obtain a test score that proved more useful than the base rates, but there still might be sufficient grounds to proceed anyway and find out. For example, although many patients might obtain intermediate test scores of less predictive validity than the base rates, some might obtain extreme scores that would prove useful for purposes of diagnosis or prediction.

Thus, there might be good reason to administer a test, even if one could not guarantee its usefulness (i.e., satisfaction of the base-rate hurdle), without one's conscience dictating that because the test was administered, the information *had* to be used. Professionals agreed that even low-yield procedures could be acceptable so long as informed consent was obtained—that clients knew the expense and possible risk of diagnostic procedures, and the odds that they would facilitate decision-making. As a result, clinicians felt less compelled to perform "salvage operations"—to use data whether they were truly useful or not, or to try to somehow, some way, decipher something from the data to justify its collection. Such practices, of course, had only hindered clinical decision-making, because even partial reliance on poor data when better data or decision guides are available reduces accuracy. The rational but difficult thing to do is to not use something (e.g., a test result), no matter the cost involved in obtaining it, if it turns out that one would be better off not using it. Clinicians found it much easier to explain to clients, and themselves, why the time and expense involved in psychological testing had not proved productive. Sometimes the best one can do is to estimate beforehand, rather than foresee, a procedure's likely payoff.

The realization that many tests surpassed the base-rate hurdle in only a subset of cases with extreme scores stimulated the development of what we now call "stop-go" procedures. We recognized that it might be possible to determine, early on, whether sufficiently extreme (i.e., valuable) scores would be obtained on a test to justify its continuation. This led to a variation of adaptive testing in which items most predictive of extreme (useful) scores were administered first; by using simple tables the examiner could determine, on an item-by-item basis, the probability of a useful final result. It sometimes required but a few items to discover that the probabilities were too low to continue, the result being considerable savings in time and expense.

Meehl and Rosen's work was also the initial impetus for what became one of our key standards for psychological and educational testing. How many of you have read our national association's ethical standards since you had them at your side while completing your SSACKC modules (Standard, Simulated Appraisal of Clinical Knowledge and Competencies) for purposes of licensing? I don't see too many heads nodding. In any case, you might recall that Principle 1.3, adopted in 1958, starts by drawing a rough analogy between the formation of ideas or hypotheses about the client and the context of discovery, and the formulation of diagnostic and predictive conclusions and the context of verification. The clinician is under few restraints in the selection of methods or tools when generating hypotheses. However, as Principle 1.3 dictates, in the context of diagnosis and prediction:

> A valid relation between a test score and the criterion of interest is not sufficient, by itself, to justify its use for purposes of diagnosis or prediction. It must also be shown that the test surpasses base-rate accuracy or, when compared to the use of base rates, favorably influences the ratio of false-negative to false-positive errors to an extent that justifies inflation of the opposing error type.
>
> Comment: Any decision to sacrifice overall accuracy for reduction in one or another type of error demands careful examination of both the actual change in frequency with which false-negative and false-positive errors occur and the relative costs of *both* error types. Although scientific analysis will often point to a clear course of action, decision policies ultimately rest on value judgments and thus require the client's informed participation. When the human cost of false-negative and

false-positive errors is approximately equal, consideration of overall accuracy should prevail. When a sign or test score produces far more frequent errors than does base-rate prediction, the latter predictive mode should almost always prevail. In between are circumstances in which discretion and judgment must determine the course of action.

The clinician should periodically review research on base rates, test accuracy, and the consequences of false-positive and false-negative errors. The clinician must keep abreast of research on these topics in order to make truly informed decisions and to help the client do so as well. Lack of familiarity with available knowledge does not relieve responsibility for improper decision practices or the communication of erroneous information to clients.

Principle 1.3 has been widely supported within and outside our profession, and its violation is a potential basis for remedial action, expulsion, and malpractice suits. You are probably familiar with the Kramner versus Kramner custody case of 1961, in which a psychologist advised the family court that a parent was unlikely to provide adequate child care. The conclusion was based partly on test results which were not validated for use in determining parental suitability, and without demonstration that the predictions so founded exceeded base-rate accuracy. In a successful countersuit, the psychologist was shown to have violated his own professional organization's ethical guidelines. Specifically, he had used a test to reach conclusions on a matter of vital human importance for which its efficacy was not established and, as base-rate estimates showed, likely decreased accuracy. The defense argued that the psychologist proceeded on the basis of his professional judgment and experience, and that there was no definitive proof the test lacked merit or failed to surpass base-rate predictions. This line of defense failed, however. One does not *justify* a procedure with a claim that it has not been proven to be no good, particularly in the absence of evidence supporting its satisfaction of the base-rate hurdle and, hence, usefulness. As a result of this suit, the policy of "use and then prove" was replaced by "prove and then use."

It was soon recognized that the base-rate hurdle was insufficient by itself, and Principle 1.4 was added in 1962, which addressed incremental validity. It was noted that a test or sign could be valid and exceed base-rate accuracy, but when combined with already developed predictors it might still yield no increase (increment), or even a *decrease,* in overall accuracy. For example, when combined via means of clinical judgment, the addition of a relatively weak predictor to even a few stronger predictors can decrease accuracy. Even when combined statistically, the additional sign, particularly if highly correlated with already available predictors, might not add to overall accuracy.

According to the standards, the clinician was on safest grounds if a test was of demonstrated incremental validity, or, more specifically, produced a meaningful increase in the accuracy of diagnosis or prediction achieved by already available predictors. Alternatively, the use of a test could be justified if it did *not* lead to a meaningful decrease in overall accuracy and either saved time or cost, reduced risk, or favorably altered the ratio of false-negative and false-positive errors. The use of additional or substitute measures short of incremental validity or the application of these alternate factors was deemed potentially unethical. Further, because there was little to be gained by replacing modestly accurate measures with equally modest ones—we needed to bolster current levels of accuracy, not just match them—incremental validity was described as a "highly desirable" quality.

The standards further stated that incremental validity could not be assumed but required empirical demonstration. Judgments or impressions about incremental validity often rested on seemingly plausible but erroneous assumptions (e.g., that validity was *necessarily* cumulative or was greatly enhanced by additional "confirmation" from closely related measures). Nor is the unaided human mind geared to perform the operations or computations needed for accurate appraisal. Scientific tests were required because impressions about incremental validity too often proved wrong.

The addition of these dual hurdles to the standards left clinicians in the lurch. Lacking data on base rates and incremental validity, they often could not evaluate satisfaction of the hurdles and thus could not use many popular measures. Clinicians also complained, quite rightly, of a double standard—they were now often prohibited from practicing their trade with no corresponding responsibilities or limitations placed on others. For example, tests were marketed that neglected the hurdles. Many researchers, who were capable of producing the data needed by clinicians to evaluate assessment devices, also ignored the hurdles without penalty. These researchers could continue publishing and, unlike the clinician, get on with their careers just fine. Further, if application was a major goal of test development and of considerable ongoing research, it made little sense to ignore fundamental tests of applied usefulness.

Hence, the APA Ethics Committee formed a working subcommittee in 1963, BOLDER (Bound Operations: Linking clinical Developments, Ethics, and Research), which eventually gained permanent status. By its composition alone, this group was a groundbreaker. It included "pure" academicians, "pure" clinicians, clinician-researchers, and representatives from editorial policy boards, the testing industry, and consumer-advocacy groups. The committee's charge was to "unify scientific, clinical, and ethical concerns in test development and use." According to BOLDER, tools which helped decide human fates must be carefully harnessed, given their potential for benefit and harm. BOLDER argued strenuously for rigorous, internal regulation of quality control. As BOLDER noted, the ultimate choice was not between internal control and no control. We could implement internal controls that incorporated proper checks and balances and that regulated practices on the basis of informed awareness and scientific knowledge. Alternatively, we could await failures in self-regulation, the result being reactionary external constraints, embedded in a complex bureaucracy and driven by political concerns.

The group members were hardly naïve. They recognized the need for compromise but maintained that clinical, research, and consumer interests were fundamentally harmonious and that cooperative effort was best for all involved. If high-quality scientific effort yielded high-quality assessment instruments which were applied wisely by clinicians, the "products" would sell themselves, enhance the field's professional status, and build positive sentiment among funding agencies. It was an article of faith (later proven correct) that the considerable intellectual firepower within psychology, if aimed properly, would yield quality accomplishments that excluded the need for gimmicks or premature applications. In contrast, worthless procedures implemented on the basis of erroneous hopes or false optimism, rather than adequate scientific foundations, would eventually be laid bare and produce a disastrous backlash. We would one day enter the age of accountability, a development we could welcome or fear depending on our preparation.

BOLDER's foremost accomplishment was to persuade test developers and testing firms to adopt standards which paralleled those guiding clinical practice. Tests were not to be marketed for applied use as diagnostic or predictive aids unless shown to satisfy the clinical standards addressing base rates and incremental validity. Lack of data on these matters became the responsibility of test developers and firms. These guides increased the cost of test development. Firms which did not conform ordained their own demise, for clinician/consumers would not purchase their unproven products. Firms with serious commitments to quality control thrived, for their products were preferred. Further, these better firms no longer feared the loss of market shares to competitors who rushed to publish and publicize highly touted but inferior products. Keep in mind that the quality of goods reflects consumers' discernment. If garbage sells like gold, but more profitably, whose mess is it?

A corresponding alteration was made in the editorial policies of those APA journals which handled research on assessment devices. Research on tests and diagnostic signs which claimed usefulness or criterion-based validity (as opposed to construct validity) now had to distinguish between statistical and clinical significance. Claims for the latter could not be made unless base-rate analyses were conducted and incremental validity demonstrated (where competing procedures were available). Work that included analyses of base rates *and* incremental validity was strongly preferred. Lacking such data, the researcher had to state clearly that clinical utility was unknown. Even some well-known researchers were jolted by such reviewer's comments as: "The work done is exemplary, but short of at least a base-rate analysis the utility of the author's test is unknown. I strongly recommend against acceptance unless this problem is addressed or resolved.'' Researchers are an adaptive lot, and given a little feedback of this type, analyses of base rates and incremental validity soon became standard fare.

Thus, in less than ten years, analyses of base rates and incremental validity were incorporated into test development, marketing, and clinical application, all stemming initially from the little article by Meehl and Rosen. Indeed, you "new-timers" out there might wonder how a test could have been rationally justified or evaluated before these modifications. But remember, the problem was nearly invisible before Meehl and Rosen's work.

Three Additional Benefits of Meehl and Rosen

Identifying False Associations

The intense focus on the base-rate problem had a series of unanticipated benefits. As base-rate information was collected, particularly among normal populations, it became painfully obvious that we held many false notions about disturbed conduct and mental content. Much of what we thought was specific or limited to the disordered, or what we considered rare or deviant, was just not so; rather, it was characteristic of the human condition. Exposure to select, nonrepresentative samples within the clinic had promoted false associations between our patients' characteristics and the presence of disorder. Many "patient" characteristics are frequent in general and, being so, they also happen to be common among our clientele but are not specific to them, i.e., they are not reliable "signs" of aberrance.

Unlearning false associations between (pseudo)signs and disorder decreased the rate of false-positive diagnosis. To our abhorrence, we came to recognize that we had frequently mislabeled those with normal behaviors, conflicts, and problems as abnormal. Indeed, we had often attempted to persuade individuals who "resisted corrective" input that they were indeed disordered when, unbeknownst to us, they were not. We had inadvertently conspired in the formation of false and malignant self-beliefs. We can only guess about the full consequences of our well-intended but misguided actions, for the ultimate effects can never be known. One does not know, for example, how much better off a person might have been had we not made the damaging mistake we did make.

Before base-rate analyses, the tendency to overpathologize was largely uncontrolled. Our impressions guided our actions, and our actions created self-fulfilling prophecies—events that precluded the receipt or proper interpretation of corrective feedback. Therapy was prescribed and positive outcome attributed to treatment effects. Yet individuals might have been initially misdiagnosed as disordered; the good outcome was merely consistent with actual pretreatment status. Other victims of mislabeling resisted entry into treatment and were judged irrational, thereby supporting our initial impressions no matter their accuracy.

Absent any further involvement with these individuals, we could not learn when we had been mistaken.

Similarly, we uncovered false associations between specific types of mental disorders and their etiological "explanations." The identified precipitants for certain acquired mental aberrations (e.g., trauma-induced disorders) could not be sufficient, because the postulated causal events were no more common among those with than without the affliction. Some of you may recall an earlier error of this type that compounded the mental anguish of already suffering souls. We believed that maternal aloofness caused autism, until we found that the mothers of autistic children were no more or less aloof than mothers of those with other psychiatric afflictions, or indeed parents in the general population (once one considered normal parental reactions to a nonresponsive child).

How did we form so many false associations between signs and disorders, and between supposedly precipitating events and disorders? Consider the great variability of human behavior over situation and time, and the tremendous overlap between the behavior and histories of the normal and abnormal. Further, given the select sample to which we are exposed within the clinic, we often cannot determine the sample's fit with the overall population. Thus, we could select just about any proposed environmental cause for almost any aberration and find some "support" for its existence. Knowledge of base rates or relative frequencies among the full range of individuals with *and* without the disorder protects us against such seductive mental traps. The human mind's predilection to identify causal agents necessitates such restraints or safeguards.

We learned to exercise far greater caution before linking "signs" to disorder or antecedents (causes) to specific dysfunctions. How could one justify either burdening individuals with loose conjectures about the presence or cause of a disorder that failed to withstand even base-rate analysis, or straining taxpayers' pockets to support intensive research on hopeless leads? It hurt to discard long-held beliefs about the childhood traumas, child-parent relations, or family structures that "produce" specific disorders, but we learned to eliminate many false leads *before* undertaking fruitless efforts. This is sometimes the most that rationality can do for us: It cannot tell us the right answer but it can reveal mistaken ones. And the time we do not waste chasing foreseeable dead ends can be spent on leads that might pan out. Scientific advance itself is partly probabilistic, and even under the best of conditions the chances of productive outcome in social-science research are not particularly favorable. Channeling efforts more intelligently ultimately accelerates scientific advance.

The gains achieved through the careful collection and analysis of base-rate information recalled a simple but profound lesson. Attention to the fundamentals or basics first, rather than to the spectacular or "penetrating," provides the foundation often needed to pursue more exciting achievements. One should not attempt advanced math before working out the number tables. Such "drab" information as base rates can create the required underpinnings for addressing more far-reaching questions. Short of such fundamentals, exploring the greater issues provides immediate thrill without ultimate fulfillment. Reach for the stars by building methods of flight, not flights of fancy.

Empirical Test Selection and Combination

The focus on base rates and incremental validity had a second major benefit—the development of empirical methods for test selection and combination. Believe it or not, test selection and combination once rested almost entirely on subjective, unvalidated methods. Think about what you might experience if you had to select and combine tests primarily on the basis of your impressions, rather than on scientifically based guides and decision aids? Of course, you'd be lost in a maze of speculations.

Upon discovering that many signs and tests did not beat the base rates or achieve incremental validity, we were struck by a seemingly easy solution—further lengthen test batteries. If a few modestly valid tests could not do the job, perhaps six or seven or more could, for validity was surely cumulative. Now a little reflection could have shown this belief to be fallacious. Taken to its natural extension, one must conclude that 15 tests which each account for 10% of the variance, when combined, will account for 150% of the variance. If our powers of reflection sometimes failed us, careful examination of outcome did not.

Research demonstrated an immense gap between the results we expected to occur when we lengthened test batteries and actual outcomes. As one added more test data, a point of diminishing returns was reached much sooner than expected, particularly when clinical judgment guided the selection or expansion of test batteries. Rarely did the third or fourth test add more than negligibly to the variance accounted for, particularly if one started with the best available measures. If one wanted to identify depression or to predict rehospitalization, one or two tests or subtests would often do as well as five or six or more, once one included certain demographic and historical variables in the mix and incorporated frequency data. It became apparent that test selection and combination was no easy enterprise and, if based upon clinical experience and impression, defied even the most adept intellects.

It was again necessary to uncover error and to penetrate its source to achieve correction. Clinicians tended to expand batteries by selecting related measures. If the results on one measure of depression (e.g., Scale 2 on the MMPI) were ambiguous, one might add a depression inventory, regardless of the relation between the two measures, or indeed because they were closely aligned. This is exactly the opposite of what needs to be done. One wants to select a second measure that is also validly related to the criterion of interest (e.g., depression) but as independent of the first measure as possible, or even better, negatively correlated with the first measure. Adding additional measures is useful to the extent that these measures are valid and *nonredundant*, not to the extent that they (re)measure common variance. In contrast to adding highly redundant measures or tests as a whole, which is often nearly or completely useless, adding even five or ten test items that contribute unique variance can produce a meaningful gain in validity. There is little relation per se between the number of tests one uses and diagnostic or predictive validity. Rather, it all depends on what one adds. The quip goes: "More of the same, no gain. Seek the unique."

One rude awakening led to another as we examined for other possible discrepancies between perceived and actual outcomes in test selection/combination. One main finding emerged: decisions about the selection and extension of test batteries rested mainly on a few overly global cues that held limited, or even negative, relations to the criteria of interest. Thus, the actual combinations formed, or the test additions made, almost always failed to produce the most useful information. In fact, more comprehensive test batteries often yielded no better, or even less valid, clinical interpretations than less "complete" batteries. The main finding was explained thus.

First, when designing or tailoring batteries, most clinicians started with a core set of test favorites. If dissatisfied with the results, clinicians then added a subset, or subsets, of additional tests. Thus, most everybody received tests A, B, C, and D; a subgroup also received tests e, f, and g, or perhaps h, i, and j. Rarely did individuals receive just A, or A, f, h, i, and z. "Flexible" test selection was less flexible than we thought.

Clinicians' selection of core tests and their addition of subsets of tests rested mainly on the questions of interest and the perceived ambiguity of initial test results. These considerations are theoretically appropriate, but their application was problematic. For example, ambiguous results on the core tests might lead to the administration of additional tests. These tests often seemed to produce sufficiently "clear" scores to diagnose or predict, which "reinforced" such decisions. If an initial depression inventory yielded borderline scores, a second or third depression inventory might yield an elevated score that "confirmed" the suspected diagnosis. In truth, however, if an initial test produces borderline results and it is the best available measure, one typically should not add another measure but instead defer to the base rates. Recall that it is often just a subset of extreme scores that satisfies the base-rate hurdle.

Further, clinicians often made suboptimal choices when selecting specific tests to address specific referral questions. The selections did not incorporate anywhere near the full range of available measures and were overly determined by extraneous factors. Too often the added tests focused upon intrapsychic processes that defied accurate measurement, and though the examinee's responses fostered great inferential excursions, the results were minimally predictive of behavior. Suppose an intelligence test is the best predictor of occupational potential. If one attempts to "refine" predictions based on the IQ score by adding measures of achievement motivation that are dubiously related to the criterion of interest, and overlooks alternate and more useful predictive sources, one will usually do worse, not better.

In actuality, clinicians' test usage was overly determined by the idiosyncratic preferences of their past mentors, theoretical orientations and biases, and a host of considerations other than the only important one—informational value for the task at hand. There were also so many tests already on the market, and so much research conducted, that clinicians could not possibly keep up with all of this information. Even the most dedicated clinicians lacked detailed knowledge about more than a small percentage of available tests. It was more difficult still to remember just what test was useful for what purpose and, given the lack of available evidence, almost impossible to know what tests and test combinations were optimal for different populations and questions of interest.

Test selection and combination were also exceedingly prone to problematic judgment habits. Information obtained during the initial phases of assessment tended to exert a far greater influence on judgment than information obtained later, regardless of its value. Salient data were often accorded greater weight than less salient but more valuable data. One dramatic response on the Rorschach could overshadow a far more predictive—but unexciting—history of steady employment. Clinicians tended to form rapid impressions of clients and then attempted to confirm these possibilities, which biased their subsequent data collection. An individual who focuses on confirmation also biases hypothesis-testing, for supportive data are weighted more heavily than negative evidence. Rarely did clinicians select the tests more likely to disconfirm false hypotheses, a more efficient and less ambiguous method of hypothesis testing.

The same research which exposed clinicians' reliance on a restricted range of measures and their problems with test selection also exploded its main ideological base—the myth of "general-purpose" tests. Tests were used too broadly and often applied to purposes they could not serve. Test validity was surely not an omnipresent quality. Even "general-purpose" tests had a narrow range of application for which they were truly useful, much less for which they were optimal (when compared to alternative measures). Seemingly trivial changes in the questions of interest, population parameters, or base rates might considerably alter interpretive rules (e.g., cutting scores) or negate the test's value. Put simply, our general-purpose tests were misnamed and misused: there were no general-purpose tests. There being no general-purpose tests, proper selection required familiarity with hundreds of measures.

It was difficult enough to determine range of application for a single test or to identify the best test for a particular question or circumstance, but these complications were minor compared to those involved in the construction of optimal test batteries or the combination of results across tests. In truth, test selection and combination create complexities far beyond what we had imagined at the time. It demands access to vast amounts of information and the capacity for nearly instantaneous, repeated alterations in selection as one proceeds. Data must be combined continually to guide the selection process, not just at the endpoint of testing. Data combination itself involves vexing problems. One must separate artifactual and true contrasts in level of performance across tests. One must combine information from tests that differ in their level of measurement, the shape of their distributions, etc. All this was much too much for the mind to manage.

And so our grand schemes collapsed under their own crushing weight. Recognizing that tests could not answer all questions, we were forced to ask what questions we most wanted answered. Applied questions involving treatment planning seemed most pressing. Clearly, we had not, and still have not, approached formal theories that incorporate intrapsychic processes into refined postulates of the form that permit accurate point predictions. We realized that our aims and approach must be more modest. Could our tests help with basic distinctions that, absent a decision-making technology, were much more difficult than we thought? Could we distinguish between those who would or would not benefit from treatment? Those who might be harmed by treatment? Could we form rudimentary matches between client presentation and basic treatment modality, such as pharmacological, versus psychological, versus both? Within these basic modalities, could we make a few additional distinctions, e.g., whether "supportive" versus "insight-oriented" psychotherapy was preferable? Alternatively, did certain information often emerge "late" in the psychotherapy process that, if recognized earlier, could shorten treatment time (e.g., that gentle handling of the client was not really necessary and a direct approach would quickly resolve complaints)?

There was considerable skepticism about our return to basics. Some sophisticated studies supported the argument that treatment effectiveness was accounted for by general, not specific factors. If treatment choice mattered little, why attempt irrelevant distinctions? It took us some time to catch on. Indeed, various dysfunctions are equally responsive to various treatments, but there are also many potential choices or (mis)matches that tend to produce poor outcome. Gestalt and rational-emotive treatment might be equally likely to help, but both are better than a verbal assault on the client's self-worth. (We had again gotten ahead of ourselves by attempting refined distinctions that assumed theoretical accomplishments more imagined than real. Most therapies required the clinician to make overly complex and difficult judgments, which often precluded accurate interpretations and diluted any specific treatment effects—we were generally incapable of delivering the treatments as specifically designed.) What to omit was much more important, and specifiable, than what to provide. The key, then, was not to find *the* best match but to avoid a mismatch, a relevant concern because mismatching commonly occurred.

Most existent assessment methods and tests helped little with the basic distinctions sought, or in the prediction of undesirable treatment matches and conditions. Both "depth" psychology and behavioral assessment had led us astray. Depth psychology postulated that the assessment of intrapsychic processes permitted useful inferences about treatment approaches—that the "theories" were sufficiently powerful to assist in pragmatic decision-making. Behavioral psychology had assumed that there was only one treatment of choice—itself—and thus it could not help in selecting among possibilities. One approach was too deep and the other too shallow.

We had overlooked a viable alternative. Given the state of our science, direct sampling of relevant behavior is generally more efficacious (although less esteemed) than indirect sampling of postulated mediating entities or behavioral traits and characteristics. Perhaps we could derive brief but representative samples of the contrasts or divergencies across alternate treatment approaches (what we now call "distinguishing instances") and directly assess clients' reactions to them. We could gradually refine our sampling and our methods of appraising clients' reactions to enhance predictive power. Such assessment was amenable to computer simulation, which permitted the needed blend of standardization, flexible interaction with the examinee, and objective measurement.

We also found it useful to simply ask clients what they preferred. Even disturbed individuals can usually describe their treatment preferences, if two conditions are satisfied. First, alternatives must be clearly described and illustrated through exemplars or samples (e.g., brief simulations). Second, one must substitute a more neutral, nonreactive, and standardized presentation format for therapists' overly personalized descriptions of treatment alternatives. Inadvertently or otherwise, therapists' descriptions come loaded with suggestions about the choices that will gain their approval.

The initial attempts to link the selection and order of measures to a sequence of clinically relevant distinctions utilized a decision-tree or branching format. One began by entering certain sociodemographic and frequency data (e.g., local base rates) and the criterion of interest. One then learned whether any assessment device might be useful (could beat the base rates). If so, one administered the test or procedure best suited to the first distinction sought. One then proceeded sequentially, entering results at each step and learning whether or how to proceed further. One continued along the decision points until informed that further information would not enhance discriminative power or validity.

This sequential approach was a vast improvement over subjective methods for selecting and expanding test batteries. The computer could access detailed information on virtually all available tests, often could administer and score these tests, and could rapidly combine and "interpret" the data (derive actuarial statements) as one proceeded. Further, given the proper programming, computerized data combination avoided such nasty human judgment habits as overweighting initial impressions, which also biases subsequent test selection, and formulating expectations about additional test results, which biases test administration, scoring, and interpretation. Nor was the computer swayed by non-predictive information. Stated differently, by allowing the data and empirical relations to "decide," the computer avoided such judgment frailties as premature closure, confirmatory bias, and dependence on false associations. However, the approach was not particularly efficient.

It dawned on us that branches could be represented as dimensions, which in turn could be arranged in multidimensional space. The procedure or sequence could now be guided by the information that moved one most efficiently toward the single point that best captured multiple discriminations. One could thereby address multiple dimensions simultaneously and move along much more quickly. This approach required far more flexible and rapid shifts in the selection of measures, properties partly realized by decomposing tests into their elements and combining elements from other tests into new combinations. Often, what one added to an initial test (or one or more of its elements) were nonredundant item clusters from one or more other tests. This was much more efficient than adding tests as a whole, and it permitted much finer matching between the information needed and the means used to obtain it. As you all know, intensive work continues on the development of these methods, and major challenges remain (e.g., the range of combinations is infinite), but surely we have made great strides. We can often accomplish in 30 minutes what used to require hours and do a much higher quality job of it at that.

Predicting the Predictable

Meehl and Rosen's work produced a third benefit. As base-rate information came in, we could no longer resist a simple, inescapable conclusion. Some important behaviors were so rare that even with a refined assessment technology and a bar-no-expenses workup, a satisfactory outcome was quite unlikely—the base rates posed an almost insurmountable obstacle. Given finite resources, it was more sensible to direct our efforts toward other important behaviors with much more favorable frequency distributions, where the chances of payoff were so much greater.

Meehl and Rosen's initial suggestion to focus assessment efforts on behaviors with more favorable frequency distributions was henceforth incorporated into research and clinical practice. Predicting the esoteric or rare, mystique and all, became less attractive. Rare events not only resisted accurate prediction but, being less frequent, they were of less overall consequence than more common but still important events. Predicting the more commonplace gained appeal because one could be reasonably optimistic of success. As one of my colleagues commented, "I liked being a man of magic, but I was taken in by my own illusions. The magic often didn't work so good. To my astonishment, the simple but dependable success following my conversion to science remarkably increased my internal comfort and prestige."

Meehl's "Little" Book

Clinical versus Statistical Judgment

Unlike the self-evident validity of Meehl and Rosen's basic points, Meehl's work on the clinical versus actuarial method posed empirical questions. Meehl's review of the issues and evidence had convinced most of us that the actuarial method generally could or would outperform the clinical method. There seemed little point in pursuing comparisons where the odds were stacked against the clinician, although a small flurry of work appeared which confirmed the actuarial method's superiority. Rather, it would be more efficient to study conditions that seemed to most favor the clinician. If these conditions did not produce a clinical advantage, the implications for less favorable circumstances would be clear.

Meehl had outlined possible advantages of the clinical method, in particular instances in which the clinician recognized patterned relationships that did not seem amenable to actuarial analysis, or in which the clinician processed information through theoretical mechanisms that resisted reduction to input and output variables. An example of the first might be the detection of thematic dream content, and of the second the prediction of behavior based on an analysis of the patient's dynamics.

We proceeded to compare actuarial methods to expert clinicians who made predictions common to their everyday practices and for which they claimed particular expertise. Clinicians collected information in their preferred manner. In contrast, the actuarial methods were among the simplest available, involving linear combinations of equally weighted variables.

This work produced two startling findings. The first related to the performance of the judges. Even under the conditions described, experts often disagreed with each other (which had obvious implications in and of itself), and thus one had to compare each judge to the particular actuarial method. In absolute terms, the judges often performed poorly, with misses sometimes far exceeding hits. Further, the judges' accuracy was neither consistent nor general. For example, if one repeated the study with fresh cases of the same type, the judges who initially performed best tended not to do so again. In significant part, performance levels were a matter of chance. Second, even these exceedingly simple actuarial methods consistently equaled or outperformed the clinical judges. Thus, after a relatively brief period of intensive work, comparative studies of this kind ceased.

Meehl himself suggested that there was little point in further comparisons. He conceded that his pro-actuarial arguments were not strong enough and that his pro-clinician possibilities were still conceptually sound but not practically viable. In practice, what remained of the pro-clinical argument if clinicians who claimed to depend on patterned relationships or theory-mediated judgments could rarely agree with one another, if clinical predictions were of such low absolute validity, and if actuarial methods actually could incorporate configural relations? Meehl himself had said that one could not expect a miraculous mutation of mental processes when we entered the clinic and began appraising patients. But even Meehl had failed to fully appreciate that clinical observation is just as dangerous a basis for appraising psychological theory. Clinical appraisals of theory are equally bounded by human cognitive limitations and processed through cognitive mechanisms that nurture unwarranted faith. Meehl admitted, "I should have known that my pro-clinician arguments depended on a state of theory we have not yet approached, or are likely to approach, for many years. For unless one has a well-corroborated theory, which has high verisimilitude and includes nearly all of the important variables, an accurate technology of measurement, and access to the initial and boundary conditions of the system, one cannot use theoretical concepts to formulate accurate predictions."

And so our 1962 ethical standards, which already included the principles addressing base rates and incremental validity, also incorporated the scientific findings on actuarial versus clinical prediction. Principle 1.5 read:

> Except in unusual circumstances, diagnosis and prediction should not stray from actuarial conclusions when such analysis is available and applicable to the judgment(s) of interest. It is inappropriate to substitute less valid means of appraisal or data interpretation for more valid means.
>
> Comment: Principle 1.5 does not eliminate the need for clinical judgment, knowledge, or skill. However, when viable actuarial methods exist, the attempt to selectively countervail actuarial conclusions, except in very unusual circumstances, represents an abuse of reason. Rather, knowledge and judgment are needed to determine whether an actuarial method is applicable to the question of interest and the particular client. Further, because the conditions under which actuarial formulae are applied in new cases never duplicate exactly the conditions under which they were derived, generalization is usually of concern. Changes in local norms, client characteristics, and the precise nature of the question addressed may alter the trustworthiness of actuarial conclusions.
>
> When actuarial procedures are judged appropriate for use but generalization is in doubt, reduced confidence should be placed in the findings, with the reduction proportionate to the degree of doubt. For example, although previous research may show that a particular method identifies a particular condition with 80% accuracy, a lower level of

accuracy or confidence should be assumed when generalization is uncertain. Adjustments in confidence are best founded on empirical study, but sufficient data may be lacking, and it is not possible to examine every possible application. No matter what procedure is used, the clinician should explain to clients in clear terms the meaning of results and the degree of confidence they merit.

Test Construction and Interpretation: Of Mind and Never-Mind

Our discovery that reliance on "mere" frequency data proved consistently superior to clinically based, theory-mediated judgments led us to reconsider the role of theory in test development and use, and forced us to make finer distinctions. What was useful in test construction and development was not necessarily useful in test interpretation.

What I will now present is a somewhat exaggerated dichotomy, but it helps to illustrate the intended points. One brand of test construction rested mainly on psychodynamic, projective assumptions. This approach dictated the selection of face-valid items (face valid within the theoretical framework), selection which need not be further burdened or restrained by formal scientific study. So long as items elicited material from which to infer intrapsychic processes or states, the test would supposedly facilitate understanding and prediction. There was but one true "test" of these tests—clinicians' perceptions of their usefulness on the clinical firing line. Neither rain, nor sleet, nor "foul" research precipitation of any kind, no matter the quality of the work, could override this mode of evaluation.

On the other side of the fence was the strict empirical approach to test development. This approach was presumably exemplified by the development of the MMPI, although I fear that we formed a gross stereotype of the process. The legend grew and grew until some storytellers wove the tale that the Minnesota contingent first generated every possible combination of words in the English language and then pared down this infinite pool to a mere 500+ based strictly on numerical indicators.

The face-valid approach, lacking empirical checks and standard procedures for test scoring and analysis, led to inter-interpreter agreement coefficients that were typically closer to .00 than 1.00, and to highly individualistic test interpretations. The approach proved nearly useless on the clinical firing line, where indeed the task often involved pragmatic decision-making. In fact, the tests were often worse than useless, failing to even approach the accuracy of base-rate predictions.

The super-empirical approach, or at least its description, *was* a grossly exaggerated stereotype. There is no way to design test items, much less measures, in the absence of human thought, conceptualization, and guiding principles. If one examines the actual evolution of the MMPI, using the K-correction as an example, conceptualization tempered by clinical experience and observation, and just plain educated guesswork were essential. Further, when the stereotypic, super-empirical approach was taken literally and test items developed almost blindly, interpretive rules were overly sensitive to chance relations and the idiosyncrasies of local population parameters. We had become engulfed by a form of statistical madness. Complex multivariate procedures produced classification rules that were as remarkable for their success within the derivation sample as for their failure anywhere beyond it.

The design of measures and items falls mainly within the context of discovery, but one constrained by principles of test construction. Theory, or at least conceptualization, is pertinent at two levels. First, one needs ideas about human characteristics, and about what one wants to measure and how to go about doing so. For example, assumptions about the human mind and human characteristics are essential. When constructing an intelligence test, one does not assume that: (1) all individuals are capable of solving advanced problems in theoretical physics; (2) these skills are core requirements for everyday functioning; and (3) the test will thus contain only such items, with a title that reads: "The General Intelligence Scale of Everyday Problem-Solving Capacities in Theoretical Physics." Second, we must consider principles of test design and construction. If one ignores certain rules of the game, failure is certain. If the first version of a test yields a test-retest reliability of .17, one does not conclude that there is really nothing to worry about because, after all, the big fuss about reliability is just the invention of uptight academics.

Notions about human beings and principles of measurement are essential in the design stage. However, even today, psychological theories usually offer little help in test interpretation and, not infrequently, impede optimal utilization. As shown by the clinical versus actuarial comparisons, test "interpretation" or data combination based on straightforward empirical frequencies is superior to theory-mediated, inferentially based approaches. Our personality theories are still insufficiently developed to successfully "refine" or modify actuarial conclusions. Theory-driven modifications rarely enhance accuracy and often make things worse.

We also gained a related insight. The accuracy achieved by available measures primarily depends on the extent to which they decrease subjectivity and variability in administrative and interpretive procedures. Perhaps this should have been obvious, because it holds in virtually all scientific fields. The geneticist does not map genes by the seat of his pants but follows set procedures; the physicist does not determine velocity by subjective impression but reads her instruments. We had recognized the need for standardization, but not completely. Many of our tests included standardized instructions for administration and scoring. Actuarial methods of interpretation were also sometimes available. However, we did not realize that what one gains through standardization, or loses for lack of it, applies equally to evaluation as a whole and not just to single tests. Thus, the clinician might follow standard procedures for some, or even most, components of an evaluation. However, when it came to combining the data, these considerations were scrapped. We freely marched to our own interpretive drumbeat, no matter how subjective, "creative," or idiosyncratic, blithely disregarding the complete lack of scientific foundations. It was when we finally realized that such practices undermine the advantages gained by any standardization of the components that we moved quickly toward prespecified procedures for the full evaluative process.

Even today, standardized procedures are often confused with inflexible procedures that disregard "qualitative" observations. But flexibility and standardization are perfectly compatible, so long as choices are determined by set decision rules. Further, almost all qualitative observations can be coded in some quantitative form that captures their informational value and permits their use in formal decision-making procedures. How else could we have standardized interviewing procedures without losing, and rather better capitalizing upon, the human capacity to make unique observations?

Clinicians do possess observational advantages over the computer. However, lacking the needed decision aids, clinical observations were rarely utilized optimally. What the clinician thought was important often was not, and vice versa, and balancing and combining interview and test results was challenging, to say the least. These problems have been reduced by coding clinical observations and incorporating the data into decision models, with these models then determining whether to assign any weights at all and, if so, in what direction. For example, the clinician's decided advantage over the computer in the observation of facial expressions need not be disregarded. Meehl, then, was partly right. Individuals do have certain unique observational skills. However, the actuarial method makes far better use of these observations than the clinical method.

Learning from Experience?

In the initial comparative studies, clinicians' experience varied somewhat but, surprisingly, showed no relation to diagnostic or predictive accuracy. The studies were extended to include highly contrasting groups, with similar results obtained—the less experienced often performed as well as, or better than, the more experienced. Furthermore, if expertise was defined solely by accuracy, the most "expert" of all was almost always the actuarial method (the output of which even relative beginners could interpret readily). The same results were obtained again and again across varying diagnostic and predictive tasks, and even in studies of treatment effectiveness. Beyond minimal levels, additional experience rarely produced a discernible advantage. One of our most treasured prizes— experience—had to be reappraised.

We now know, of course, that the conditions under which clinicians typically practiced were not at all conducive to experiential learning. Although lack of gain was initially attributed to inadequate feedback, this was but a small part of the problem. Even when feedback was obtained, it often misled. For example, therapists frequently used treatment response to evaluate the accuracy of their judgments or the validity (utility) of their interventions. However, treatment feedback is not representative of the phenomena (e.g., the effectiveness of interventions) the clinician wishes to appraise. For example, past clients who send Christmas cards are rarely those who doubt our virtues. Stated more generally, the probability of feedback is confounded with outcome, or unequal across the varieties of outcome that make up the whole. Also, as previously mentioned, our initial appraisals produce self-fulfilling prophecies. If we "know" we would not work well with a client and refer her elsewhere, we will never learn when we were wrong. It is also exceedingly difficult to identify just what accounts for a specific outcome. Did the patient get better because he was misdiagnosed initially and was really okay to start with? Did he recover spontaneously? Was it really the treatment? If so, what specific treatment components?

Further, like human beings in general, clients can be sincere but grossly inaccurate when evaluating their therapist's interpretations. Tell a person she has a problem with self-esteem and she will agree. Alternatively, say that everyone is somewhat insecure and she is no more insecure than most, and she will probably also agree. Thus, agreement (or disagreement) with our statements are poor markers of their accuracy, and yet we relied on this feedback to "fine-tune" our diagnostic skills.

I will mention just one more of the many hindrances to the productive use of feedback. We often fail to recognize instances of disconfirmation. The human mind is remarkably adept at concocting plausible explanations for discrepant outcomes that align with our preconceptions. For example, we predict that a client is a poor candidate for antidepressant medication. He later tells us that he did well on this medication, and we then conclude that he experienced a placebo effect, or that his report is false, or that his status had changed, or something of the sort. Rarely do we first think of the simple, but plausible, conclusion that we were just plain wrong.

Feedback is necessary for self-correction, but it often will not result in learning unless it is obtained under conditions and constraints that are difficult to achieve in clinical practice but common in formal research. Do not forget that research is a form of accumulated "experience" that can add to the record. Further, scientific "experiences" or observations are usually far more systematic, controlled, and representative than those gathered in the course of clinical practice. The experiences may not be ours directly, which has its disadvantages. However, in contrast to personal experience, science is a public enterprise, which facilitates the careful scrutiny of ideas and the dissemination of results.

Our increased awareness of the impediments to experiential learning led us to design some simple, helpful procedures. For example, if one made predictions ahead of time and specified possible outcomes that might support one's initial impressions, and also those that might refute them, instances of disconfirmation were better recognized. Even such basic steps as keeping actual count of our hits and misses helped reduce the tendency to overestimate confirmatory instances and to underestimate disconfirmatory ones.

Training programs made good use of such corrective procedures. Simulations became commonplace. Students working from delineated data sets formulated specific diagnoses or predictions, and then obtained immediate feedback about their success. One resourceful professor, finding that this feedback, by itself, rarely altered problematic practices, changed the basis for assigning grades in her assessment seminar. She disregarded the creativity that students displayed in inventing new ways to alter validated procedures. Rather, grades were determined solely in relation to the gap between students' accuracy and that achieved by the best available, prespecified means of data collection and interpretation. There was one easy way to obtain that coveted "A": Follow the established procedures. Inventiveness was welcomed in the context of research but not in the context of pragmatic decision-making. Students learned quickly under these conditions.

As this professor knew, learning to do one's own thing as a psychotherapist (within restraints) might have advantages, but the personal touch or idiosyncrasies reduce diagnostic and predictive accuracy. Indeed, experience creates dangers. In particular, it fosters the false conviction that one knows enough to modify set decision rules and that doing so improves upon overall results. Our clinical observations almost inevitably convince us that we know things we do not know, and know better than "mindless" procedures which ignore our clients' unique features or our accumulating, special knowledge.

Experience surely teaches, but often the wrong things when obtained under the typical conditions of clinical practice. Consider our select exposure to deviant populations, the limited and distorted feedback we receive, and the extensive scientific efforts needed to develop predictors of even modest validity. Given all this, it is mistaken, if not downright foolish to believe that we can regularly invent our own procedures or devices and, without so much as one true scientific check, expect improved results. Do not misunderstand me. Experience is irreplaceable, but the purposes it best serves differ from those commonly assumed. Experience has no peer or substitute in the formation of ideas and hypotheses. Experience helps us to uncover the limits of our procedures and possible directions for their improvement. However, experience is no substitute for the scientific testing of our ideas or hypotheses.

Conclusions

In summary, our contemporary diagnostic and predictive practices were substantially reshaped by the realizations, events, and research initially triggered by Meehl's work in the '50s. In hindsight, it may seem as if the events could not have been otherwise, and that the same gains would have been made regardless of anything Meehl did or did not write or say. I believe, however, that had Meehl *not* been taken seriously, we might have continued to wander along many of the nonproductive lines we were pursuing, wasting the better part of many promising research careers and available dollars, while maintaining diagnostic practices that all too often had profound iatrogenic effects. Further, although it may seem like a wild possibility, we might, even today, still be relying upon assessment methods that fall well short of base-rate predictions or that contribute nothing to incremental validity. I am thankful I did not have to wait my lifetime for such rudimentary accomplishments.

We still face many challenges, and much of what we currently believe will undoubtedly be altered and refined in the future. If and when we develop a more powerful theory of human behavior, almost all the rules of the game will change, and we will no longer be restricted to the type of decision-making technology upon which we must now depend. Such a theory still seems many years away, and our current methods can be improved in various ways. We are still plagued by the sensitivity of decision procedures to local parameters. Thus, we must continue our attempts to increase the generalization of decision rules. Nor do our methods help us to make anything but the most basic decisions. More refined discriminations would prove most useful. The cost and efficiency of our procedures can always be improved.

If there is a moral in my story, it is this: No matter how distressing we may initially find it, we must know what *not* to do in order to channel human intelligence and effort most productively. Ultimately, there is perhaps nothing more important and productive than uncovering and clearly illuminating essential, previously unrecognized constraints and problems, as Meehl did in the '50s. To maintain ignorance despite its revelation degrades human intelligence. Rather, when we embrace the revelation of obstacles to human progress, so too do we celebrate human genius.

A Closing Note of Personal Interest

By the way, you may ask what Paul Meehl is doing now? By the mid-60s, at which time the basic issues regarding base rates and clinical versus actuarial methods had been pretty well settled, Meehl turned his efforts elsewhere. There was no longer a need to persuade anyone about these matters, and he has not written on either topic in over 20 years. Meehl took up other scientific problems within psychology, such as the genetic basis of schizophrenia. He also wrote a paper titled "Why I Now Attend Case Conferences," which commended practitioners for their improved mental habits in the decade following incorporation of base rates and actuarial methods into clinical practice and education. However, Meehl increasingly drifted to other pursuits. He dabbled with empirical comparisons of the ontological claims found within religious systems versus branches of science. An example was his effort to determine the completeness of the fossil record and its compatibility with modern evolutionary theory. Meehl bowed out of the formal academic setting in the early '90s and became a beekeeper in England, where he still sees an occasonal psychotherapy client and continues his philosophical and theoretical writing.

Reference Note and Acknowledgments

The liberal use of imagination in this chapter creates two particular complications. First, readers less familiar with the judgment literature or psychological assessment may sometimes find it difficult to distinguish descriptions based on imagination versus actual research. Second, I am unsure about the sources for some of my ideas. For example, some of the material that I think is original may duplicate published work.

The following description of source material is intended to properly credit others and to distinguish the research findings and developments described in the chapter that rest on established work, not imagination. My application of research may differ somewhat from the author's original work, which can be consulted to determine whether the blame is mine alone. I sincerely apologize to those whose work I unknowingly relied upon and have failed to properly credit. I welcome correspondence that requests further clarification about real versus imaginary developments or that corrects my oversights.

Two papers by Rorer and colleagues address the incorporation of utilities into base-rate analyses and consideration of error types (Rorer, Hoffman, & Hsieh, 1966; Rorer, Hoffman, LaForge, & Hsieh, 1966). I was unaware of these excellent papers when I wrote this section of the chapter, and I thank Lewis Goldberg for bringing them to my attention.

The problem of false-positive diagnosis (overpathologizing) is well captured in a classic study by Temerlin and Trousdale (1969). Faust, Guilmette, Hart, Arkes, Fishburne, and Davey (1988) describe the rate of false-positive diagnosis across studies on neuropsychologists' judgments. Extended discussion of overpathologizing appears in a number of sections of Ziskin and Faust (1988). Discussions with Elizabeth Seebach and Robyn M. Dawes stimulated my own thinking about the problem, and Dr. Dawes pointed out the near impossibility of determining iatrogenic effects secondary to misdiagnoses of dysfunction.

My conjectures about the direct assessment of client response to contrasting therapeutic interventions were partly based on Mischel's (1972) paper on direct versus indirect assessment of personality.

Various researchers have examined outcome when judges selectively countervail set decision rules. Einhorn (1986) provides an eloquent discussion of the issues, Sawyer's (1966) earlier review of the evidence remains a landmark, and Goldberg (1968), and Arkes, Dawes, and Christensen (1986) have conducted distinguished research on the topic.

My imaginary ethical standards emerged from discussions with Robyn M. Dawes. Dawes (1988) also provides an excellent overview of work on the "sunk cost effect," a basis for my discussion of the salvage operations that may sometimes characterize clinicians' attempts to use psychological test data that are better disregarded.

Discussions of incremental validity and their incorporation into clinical practice and editorial policy can be found in Faust (1986 a&b). Moreland (1985) describes disturbing trends in quality-control standards for computer-based test interpretation.

Chapman and Chapman (1967, 1969) conducted the seminal studies on the formation of false associations, or illusory correlations, work extended by Kurtz and Garfield (1978). Nisbett and Ross (1980) provide an excellent overview of illusory correlation and problems analyzing co-variation. Noteworthy work in this area has been conducted by Arkes and Harkness (1983), and by Smedslund (1963).

The overlap between normal and disordered individuals is described magnificently by Gardner (1975), and highlighted by the research of Renaud and Estes (1961). Overviews of confirmatory bias are provided by Greenwald, Pratkanis, Leippe, and Baumgardner (1986), and by Nisbett and Ross (1980). Turk and Salovey (1985) describe the operation of confirmatory bias within clinical practice, and a unique experiment by Mahoney (1977) demonstrates its occurrence among scientists.

Sines (1959) conducted a classic study on clinicians' use of additional information, a partial basis for my discussion of the limited gains realized by lengthening test batteries. Slovic and Lichtenstein (1971) provide an extremely detailed and scholarly review of cue utilization, in which they describe individuals' restricted capacity to manage or decipher complex data and patterned relations among cues. Fisch, Hammond, and Joyce (1982) provide a more recent demonstration of clinicians' reliance on a few variables in drawing conclusions, despite their belief that they have integrated many cues. Such research demonstrates substantial differences between subjective impressions and objective measures of cue utilization. Goldberg (this volume) discusses the disadvantages of positively correlated measures.

Tversky and Kahneman (1974; Kahneman & Tversky, 1982) deserve much of the credit for uncovering many of the problematic judgment practices described in this chapter. Dailey (1952) was among the earlier researchers to address premature closure. Nisbett and Ross (1980) provide a clear and detailed overview of problematic judgment habits and the heuristics upon which they may reset.

Sawyer (1966) provides a thorough review of research on clinical versus actuarial judgment, and Wiggins (1981) a more recent update. (I will save references to Meehl's work until later but will mention here his own recent reviews on the topic: Meehl, 1986; Dawes, Faust, & Meehl, 1989). For leading work on simple actuarial methods, including their superiority over clinical judgment and their capacity to duplicate purportedly complex decision processes, see Dawes (1971, 1979) and Goldberg (1965, 1968).

Hayek (1952 a&b) discusses the necessity for implicit models of human behavior and thinking in social-science research and measurement.

Wiggins (1973) summarizes studies which challenge the assumption that experience leads to more accurate clinical judgment. Smith and Glass (1977), and Berman and Norton (1985) summarize the studies which fail to show a relation between therapist experience and psychotherapy outcome. Faust et al. (1988) conducted a recent, detailed study on neuropsychologists' training, experience, and judgmental accuracy.

Rotter (1967) reviews impediments to experiential learning, and Brehmer (1980) and Dawes (1986) offer cogent comments on the topic. Failure to recognize disconfirming instances and the tendency to incorporate discrepant outcomes into already existing beliefs are covered by Einhorn and Hogarth (1978), Fischhoff (1975, 1977), and Slovic and Fischhoff (1977). Some of the possible means I describe for increasing the benefits of experience, in particular the consideration of alternative possibilities, are based on work by Arkes, Faust, Guilmette and Hart (1988), Fischhoff (1982), Koriat, Lichtenstein, and Fischhoff (1980), and Lord, Lepper, and Preston (1984). Work by Snyder (1974), and Snyder, Shenkel, and Lowery (1977) demonstrates and explains individuals' endorsement of overly general personality descriptors. Ziskin and Faust (1988, chapter 8, vol. 1) provide extensive coverage of the problems involved in using treatment response to gauge the validity of clinical judgments and theories.

Campbell (1974), Mahoney (1985), Popper (1959), and Weimer (1979) have described scientific advance or human intellectual growth as a self-corrective process that depends substantially on the detection and elimination of error. This general viewpoint is expressed throughout the chapter.

How much of this chapter and of the work I have cited above was stimulated by Paul Meehl or addressed issues he raised? Much of it and perhaps most of it. There is the obvious connection between the theme of this chapter and Meehl's

(1954) book on clinical versus actuarial judgment, and Meehl and Rosen's (1955) article. However, Meehl's thinking extends well beyond base rates or the clinical-actuarial debate and encompasses profound ideas about such topics as the cognitive activity of the clinician; the validation of psychological tests, constructs, and theories; the measurement of latent entities; classification; and philosophy of science and law. If one peruses Meehl's writing (e.g., 1957, 1960, 1972, 1973, 1978, 1979), one will find original expressions of ideas that subsequently captured the attention and effort of so many of the best contemporary psychologists. Many psychologists, to a lesser or greater degree, are Paul Meehl protégés. There is perhaps no greater compliment or achievement than to have one's ideas consummated in wide-scale scholarly debate and research activities that have produced, and will continue to produce, lasting gains.

References

Arkes, H. R., Dawes, R. M., & Christensen, C. (1986). Factors influencing the use of a decision rule in a probabilistic task. *Behavior and Human Decision Processes, 37,* 93–110.

Arkes, H. R., Faust, D., Guilmette, T. J., & Hart, K. (1988). Eliminating the hindsight bias. *Journal of Applied Psychology, 73,* 305–307.

Arkes, H. R., & Harkness, A. R. (1983). Estimates of contingency between two dichotomous variables. *Journal of Experimental Psychology: General, 112,* 117–135.

Berman, J. S., & Norton, N. C. (1985). Does professional training make a therapist more effective? *Psychological Bulletin, 98,* 401–407.

Brehmer, B. (1980). In one word: Not from experience. *Acta Psychologica, 45,* 223–241.

Campbell, D. T. (1974). Evolutionary epistemology. In P. A. Schlipp (Ed.), *The philosophy of Karl Popper.* Vol. 14. *The library of living philosophers* (pp. 413–463). LaSalle IL: Open Court Publishing Co.

Chapman, L. J., & Chapman, J. P. (1967). Genesis of popular but erroneous psychodiagnostic observations. *Journal of Abnormal Psychology, 72,* 193–204.

Chapman, L. J., & Chapman, J. P. (1969). Ilusory correlation as an obstacle to the use of valid psychodiagnostic signs. *Journal of Abnormal Psychology, 74,* 271–280.

Dailey, C. A. (1952). The effects of premature conclusions upon the acquisition of understanding of a person. *Journal of Psychology, 33,* 133–152.

Dawes, R. M. (1971). A case study of graduate admissions: Application of three principles of human decision making. *American Psychologist, 26,* 180–188.

Dawes, R. M. (1979). The robust beauty of improper linear models in decision making. *American Psychologist, 34,* 571–582.

Dawes, R. M. (1986). Representative thinking in clinical judgment. *Clinical Psychology Review, 6,* 425–441.

Dawes, R. M. (1988). *Rational choice in an uncertain world.* New York: Harcourt Brace Jovanovich.

Dawes, R. M., Faust, D., & Meehl, P. E. (1989). Clinical versus actuarial judgment. *Science, 243,* 1668–1674.

Einhorn, H. J. (1986). Accepting error to make less error. *Journal of Personality Assessment, 50,* 387–395.

Einhorn, H. J., & Hogarth, R. M. (1978). Confidence in judgment: Persistence of the illusion of validity. *Psychological Review, 85,* 395–416.

Faust, D. (1986a). Research on human judgment and its application to clinical practice. *Professional Psychology: Research and Practice, 17,* 420–430.

Faust, D. (1986b). Learning and maintaining rules for decreasing judgment accuracy. *Journal of Personality Assessment, 50,* 585–600.

Faust, D., Guilmette, T. J., Hart, K., Arkes, H. R., Fishburne, J., & Davey, L. (1988). Neuropsychologists' training, experience, and judgment accuracy. *Archives of Clinical Neuropsychology, 3,* 145–163.

Fisch, H. U., Hammond, K. R., & Joyce, C. R. B. (1982). On evaluating the severity of depression: An experimental study of psychiatrists. *British Journal of Psychiatry, 140,* 378–383.

Fischhoff, B. (1975). Hindsight ≠ foresight: The effect of outcome knowledge on judgment under uncertainty. *Journal of Experimental Psychology: Human Perception and Peformance, 1,* 288–299.

Fischhoff, B. (1977). Perceived informativeness of facts. *Journal of Experimental Psychology: Human Perception and Performance, 3,* 349–358.

Fischhoff, B. (1982). Debiasing. In D. Kahneman, P. Slovic, & A. Tversky (Eds.), *Judgment under uncertainty* (pp. 422–444). New York: Cambridge University Press.

Gardner, H. (1975). *The shattered mind: The person after brain damage.* New York: Alfred A. Knopf.

Goldberg, L. R. (1965). Diagnosticians vs. diagnostic signs: The diagnosis of psychosis vs. neurosis from the MMPI. *Psychological Monographs* 79 (9, Whole No. 602).

Goldberg, L. R. (1968). Simple models or simple processes? Some research on clinical judgments. *American Psychologist, 23,* 483–496.

Goldberg, L. R. (1990). Human mind versus regression equation: Five contrasts. Chapter 7 this volume.

Greenwald, A. G., Pratkanis, A. R., Leippe, M. R., & Baumgardner, M. H. (1986). Under what conditions does theory obstruct research progress? *Psychological Review, 93,* 216–229.

Hayek, F. A. (1952a). *The sensory order.* Chicago: University of Chicago Press.

Hayek, F. A. (1952b). *The counter-revolution of science: Studies on the abuse of reason.* New York: Free Press.

Kahneman, D., & Tversky, A. (1982). Intuitive prediction: Biases and corrective procedures. In D. Kahneman, P. Slovic, and A. Tversky (Eds.), *Judgment under uncertainty: Heuristics and biases* (pp. 414–421). New York: Cambridge University Press.

Koriat, A., Lichtenstein, S., & Fischhoff, B. (1980). Reasons for confidence. *Journal of Experimental Psychology: Human Learning and Memory, 6,* 107–118.

Kurtz, R. M., & Garfield, S. L. (1978). Illusory correlation: A further exploration of Chapman's paradigm. *Journal of Consulting and Clinical Psychology, 46,* 1009–1015.

Lord, C. G., Lepper, M. R., & Preston, E. (1984). Considering the opposite: A corrective strategy for social judgment. *Journal of Personality and Social Psychology, 47,* 1231–1243.

Mahoney, M. J. (1977). Publication prejudices: An experimental study of confirmatory bias in the peer review system. *Cognitive Therapy and Research, 1,* 161–175.

Mahoney, M. J. (1985). Open exchange and epistemic progress. *American Psychologist, 40,* 29–39.

Meehl, P. E. (1954). *Clinical vs. statistical prediction: A theoretical analysis and a review of the evidence.* Minneapolis: University of Minnesota Press.

Meehl, P. E. (1957). When shall we use our heads instead of the formula? *Journal of Counseling Psychology, 4,* 268–273.

Meehl, P. E. (1960). The cognitive activity of the clinician. *American Psychologist, 15,* 19–27.

Meehl, P. E. (1972). Reactions, reflections, projections. In J. Butcher (Ed.), *Objective personality assessment: Changing perspectives* (pp. 131–189). New York: Academic Press.

Meehl, P. E. (1973). *Psychodiagnosis: Selected papers.* Minneapolis: University of Minnesota Press.

Meehl, P. E. (1978). Theoretical risks and tabular asterisks: Sir Karl, Sir Ronald, and the slow progress of soft psychology. *Journal of Consulting and Clinical Psychology, 46,* 806–834.

Meehl, P. E. (1979). A funny thing happened to us on the way to latent entities. *Journal of Personality Assessment, 43,* 564–581.

Meehl, P. E. (1986). Causes and effects of my disturbing little book. *Journal of Personality Assessment, 50,* 370–375.

Meehl, P. E., & Rosen, A. (1955). Antecedent probability and the efficiency of psychometric signs, patterns, or cutting scores. *Psychological Bulletin, 52,* 194–216.

Mischel, W. (1972). Direct versus indirect personality assessment: Evidence and implications. *Journal of Consulting and Clinical Psychology, 38,* 319–324.

Moreland, K. L. (1985). Validation of computer-based test interpretations: Problems and prospects. *Journal of Consulting and Clinical Psychology, 53,* 816–825.

Nisbett, R. E., & Ross, L. (1980). *Human inference: Strategies and shortcomings of social judgment.* Englewood Cliffs, NJ.: Prentice-Hall.

Popper, K. R. (1959). *The logic of scientific discovery.* New York: Harper & Row.

Renaud, H., & Estes, F. (1961). Life history interview with one hundred normal American males: "Pathogenicity" of childhood. *American Journal of Orthopsychiatry, 31,* 786–802.

Rorer, L. G., Hoffman, P. J., & Hsieh, K. (1966). Utilities as base-rate multipliers in the determination of optimum cutting scores for the discrimination of groups of unequal size and variance. *Journal of Applied Psychology, 50,* 364–368.

Rorer, L. G., Hoffman, P. J., LaForge, G. E., & Hsieh, K. (1966). Optimum cutting scores to discriminate groups of unequal size and variance. *Journal of Applied Psychology, 50,* 153–164.

Rotter, J. B. (1967). Can the clinician learn from experience? *Journal of Consulting Psychology, 13,* 12–15.

Sawyer, J. (1966). Measurement *and* prediction, clinical *and* statistical. *Psychological Bulletin, 66,* 178–200.

Sines, L. K. (1959). The relative contribution of four kinds of data to accuracy in personality assessment. *Journal of Consulting Psychology, 23,* 483–492.

Slovic, P., & Fischhoff, B. (1977). On the psychology of experimental surprises. *Journal of Experimental Psychology: Human Perception and Performance, 3,* 544–551.

Slovic, P., & Lichtenstein, S. C. (1971). Comparison of Bayesian and regression approaches to the study of information processing in judgment. *Organizational Behavior and Human Performance, 6,* 649–744.

Smedslund, J. (1963). The concept of correlation in adults. *Scandinavian Journal of Psychology, 4,* 154–173.

Smith, M. L., & Glass, G. V. (1977). Meta-analysis of psychotherapy outcome studies. *American Psychologist, 32,* 752–760.

Snyder, C. R. (1974). Why horoscopes are true: The effect of specificity on acceptance of astrological interpretation. *Journal of Clinical Psychology, 30,* 577–580.

Snyder, C. R., Shenkel, J. R., & Lowery, C. R. (1977). Acceptance of personality interpretations: The "Barnum Effect" and beyond. *Journal of Consulting and Clinical Psychology, 45,* 104–114.

Temerlin, M. K., & Trousdale, W. W. (1969). The social psychology of clinical diagnosis. *Psychotherapy: Theory, Research and Practice, 6,* 24–29.

Turk, D. C., & Salovey, P. (1985). Cognitive structures, cognitive processes, and cognitive-behavior modification: I. Judgments and inferences of the clinician. *Cognitive Therapy and Research, 9,* 19–33.

Tversky, A., & Kahneman, D. (1974). Judgment under uncertainty: Heuristics and biases. *Science, 183,* 1124–1131.

Weimer, W. B. (1979). *Notes on the methodology of scientific research.* Hillsdale, NJ.: Erlbaum.

Wiggins, J. S. (1973). *Personality and prediction: Principles of personality assessment.* Reading, MA: Addison-Wesley.

Wiggins, J. S. (1981). Clinical and statistical prediction: Where are we and where do we go from here? *Clinical Psychology Review, 1,* 3–18.

Ziskin, J., & Faust, D. (1988). *Coping with psychiatric and psychological testimony* (vols. 1–3) (4th ed.). Marina Del Ray, CA: Law and Psychology Press.

Recent Developments in
Computerized Clinical Judgment
Benjamin Kleinmuntz

More than 30 years ago Meehl (1957) posed an important question in the form of a paper with the catchy title "When Shall We Use Our Heads Instead of the Formula?" His answer was that if we have a formula, then we should use our heads only "very, *very* seldom." The "head" in the title of the paper refers to the processing of clinical data intuitively, the "formula" to any form of nonjudgmental, mathematical, statistical, or mechanical handling of the same information.

Meehl's main objective in his paper was to alert clinical psychologists to the idea that in making predictions about patients, "we are not as good as we thought we were" (p. 272). He has often reiterated this counterintuitive theme (e.g., Meehl, 1959, 1960, 1967), usually in the context of urging clinical psychologists to use the time freed from diagnostic chores to pursue the more creative endeavors of clinical research and psychotherapy. This urging was based on existing empirical evidence showing the superiority of formal over subjective clinical information processing, a superiority which has continued to be supported by subsequent and current studies (see, for example, Goldberg, 1965; B. Kleinmuntz & Szucko, 1984; Szucko & B. Kleinmuntz, 1981; Wiggins, 1973, p. 172). However, if we extend Meehl's query beyond clinical psychology to, let us say, complex information processing in clinical psychology and in medicine, then the evidence favoring the formula is less impressive, as we shall see.

Without attempting to pit the head against the formula, my purpose in this chapter is to critically trace the historical and current efforts at replacing the head with formal procedures whose goals are to outperform clinical decision-makers.

The preparation and writing of this review were supported in part by the National Library of Medicine Grant No. 1-R01 LMO4583-05 to whom I am grateful. I also want to express thanks to Arthur S. Elstein and Don N. Kleinmuntz who reviewed this paper at various stages of its writing.

The road has been interesting but rocky, and, as I have argued elsewhere (B. Kleinmuntz, 1990), the head is still the best game in town. However, two recent articles and an editorial in the *Journal of the American Medical Association* (Barnett, Cimino, Hupp, & Hoffer, 1987; Shortliffe, 1987) suggest that major efforts and much funding are currently being expended in replacing the head with the formula, at least in medicine.

I begin with a review of Meehl's important contribution to this development (see Blois, 1980); I proceed with a look at Bayesian decision theory, decision analysis, behavioral decision theory, and information-processing psychology; and I conclude with a note on the progress of expert systems research and a review of the importance of the computer as an information rather than as a number-crunching machine. All of these developments had their origins in the early and mid-1950s (see B. Kleinmuntz, 1984; Kleinmuntz & Elstein, 1987 for more complete descriptions).

Clinical versus Statistical Prediction

One of the most important steps toward the scientific study of the clinician as a variable in the decision process occurred when Meehl wrote his influential polemic monograph *Clinical versus Statistical Prediction* (1954). In it, he argued that many clinical judgments are best made by statistical or actuarial rather than intuitive means. He reviewed 20 empirical studies in which predictions made intuitively were compared with those made more formally and showed that in 11 of these instances the latter outperformed human clinical judgment. Only in one case was the clinical method better. Eight studies showed equivalence of the two methods. He later increased this boxscore tally to 35 studies, none of which favored the clinical approach. Twelve studies demonstrated "approximate equality" (see Wiggins, 1973, p. 172).

Meehl's analysis spawned many other studies, mainly in clinical psychology, that further verified the importance of formal or mechanical methods. Most of these dealt with predictions made from psychological test data in a variety of applied judgment tasks including predicting college success, aviator school dropout rates, psychodiagnosis, and prison parolee recidivism.

But Meehl's actuarial stance did not go unchallenged. The most forceful argument on the clinical side of the controversy was that of Robert R. Holt (1958, 1978), also a clinical psychologist. Over the years Holt has steadfastly maintained that persons could not be understood or measured meaningfully without including the subjective judgments of the clinician, who perceives, empathizes, intuits, integrates, and synthesizes information while constructing a theory of the patient being studied. Holt's main argument with Meehl's and others' boxscore tallies was that the outcomes being predicted (i.e., college grades, diagnostic labels, job success, parole violation) put the clinician at a considerable disadvantage vis-à-vis statistics because the clinician usually makes considerably more complex decisions using softer data.

Commenting directly on the limitations of computers, Holt (1978, pp. 14–15) had this to say: "What I have been opposing all these years is not formal methods . . . but attempts to denigrate and eliminate judgment. . . . Attempts to computerize diagnosis in internal medicine have been going on for some years, but they still fail to yield definite results in many cases, so that the physician still has to fall back on his judgment. If that judgment is constantly derogated . . . will he be able to accept the responsibility of using it when it is most needed?"

Thus, we see that Meehl's analysis of the empirical evidence supporting formal methods for studying clinical judgment was disconcerting to Holt because it challenged the dignity and worth of human intelligence. Unfortunately, the counterintuitive fact of the matter is that much of what clinicians do requires an optimal combination of hard and/or soft data according to learned rules and facts. This is precisely where intuitive strategies are most flawed, regardless of our opinions about the dignity of human judgment. Consequently, it is here that the computer's memory and information manipulation capabilities should be of greatest value.

But it must also be noted that Meehl's (1957) position does not differ radically from that of Holt's notion that the clinician will excel in certain predictive tasks. For example, Meehl (1954, p. 24) gives the following illustration: "If a sociologist were predicting whether Professor X would go to the movies on a certain night, he might have an equation involving age, academic specialty, and introversion score. The equation might yield a probability of .90 that Professor X will go to the movie tonight. But if . . . Professor X had just broken his leg, no sensible sociologist would stick with the equation." Here Meehl emphasizes, with several caveats, the importance of "special cases." Meehl then goes on to cite several other instances in which the clinician has to process novel patterns where the head might excel; and in his 1954 book he describes a number of psychodynamic and ongoing therapeutic productions that do not easily lend themselves to formalization. Hence, Meehl is not the wicked actuary that Holt portrays in his writings.

What is not clear from this controversy, however, is that Meehl's main contribution was to place clinical judgment center stage. He did not deal with it at a general philosophical level, nor did he provide just another tool for the "statistical" side of the argument. Rather, Meehl produced empirical evidence that clinical intuition was flawed. Hence, he inspired researchers to attend directly to how the clinician processes data in order to arrive at predictions. In fact, at one point in his classic monograph (Meehl, 1954, p. 38), he anticipated the computer's imminent importance for clinical decision-making when he predicted that "Hollerith Machines" will someday take over the clinicians' mundane decision chores, especially those decisions for which the machine is better equipped than humans. Unfortunately, for the vast majority of clinical prediction in clinical psychology and in medicine, Meehl's anticipation has yet to be realized.

Bayesian Decision Theory and Decision Analysis

At about the same time that Meehl was writing his treatise, L. J. Savage (1954, 1972) wrote about statistical decision theory, which in his later writing he applied to clinical prediction in medical diagnosis and prognosis. This approach provides a method of combining data and beliefs in the form of subjective probabilities. The idea of subjective probability was first presented by Ramsey (1931) and later by de Finetti (1937) in the 1930s but was not widely known among researchers in decision-making until Savage wrote his 1954 book *The Foundations of Statistics*. The Bayesian approach was then communicated in 1959 to businessmen by Schlaifer (1959) and, during the same year, to medical diagnosticians by Ledley and Lusted (1959), who embarked on an ambitious attempt to formalize what Sir William Osler a half-century earlier had called "a science of uncertainty and art of probability."

Lusted's later book, *Introduction to Medical Decision Making* (1968), provided a theoretical foundation for analyzing the statistical properties of clinical data and clinical inference. The clinical domain selected for this exploration was diagnostic radiology, but the general principles could have been applied equally well to any psychological or medical domain that requires clinical reasoning. Lusted did not attempt to develop the empirical data needed to implement a Bayesian approach to diagnosis, but rather to demonstrate that such an approach was, in principle, logical and possible.

By the mid-1970s interest in applying statistical decision theory to medical problems began to grow rapidly. For example, a midsummer issue of the *New England Journal of Medicine* (e.g., Ingelfinger, 1975; Lusted, 1975) was devoted entirely to formal approaches to medical decision-making, thus effectively heralding the arrival of this form of inquiry into medicine.

Decision analysis (Fryback & Thornbury, 1976; Keeney, 1982; Raiffa, 1968), a variant of Bayesian decision theory, consists of a set of techniques for decision-making under uncertainty. These techniques are appropriate for situations in which choices must be made and where the outcomes of actions are predictable only on the average (in the long run) but not for individual cases. Decision analysis is a tool for analyzing situations where some chance of a poor or less desired outcome exists even if the "right" decision has been made, and where one would wish to distinguish between employing a rational coherent *process* to reach a decision and achieving a good *outcome*. The theory can also incorporate problems of optimal allocation of scarce resources and deciding if the incremental benefit of obtaining additional information is worth the cost. This is accomplished by weighing the costs and risks associated with data collection against the presumed quality of the information once it is in hand.

The theoretical foundation of decision analysis is the theory of expected utility (von Neumann & Morgenstern, 1947; also see Schoemaker, 1982), a way of ordering preferences for outcomes of action that follows logically and coherently from a few axioms. Because expected utility theory has an axiomatic base, it has had great appeal as the foundation for a rational theory of decision-making and choice under uncertainty.

Decision analysis decomposes decision problems into discrete components and provides a procedure for synthesizing these components into an overall measure of the attractiveness of alternatives so that the optimal strategy can be selected. Data required are of two types—measures of uncertainty and measures of values. In the vocabulary of decision theory, uncertainties are expressed as probabilities and values as utilities. The criterion for choice is to act so as to maximize expected utility.

The possible application of Bayesian statistics to medicine was illustrated in several demonstrations (Edwards, 1954, 1972; Weinstein & Fineberg, 1980) and an outstanding example of a probabilistic system for computer-assisted diagnosis is that developed over more than a dozen years by de Dombal and his co-workers (1972, 1975, 1984a). The system is designed for the differential diagnosis of acute abdominal pain and proceeds by probabilistic (i.e., Bayesian) analysis of prior and conditional probabilities. A data matrix stored in the computer provides conditional probabilities of a variety of clinical findings given each of a family of disorders and the prior probability of each disorder. These probabilities were developed by means of an international survey of some 6000 cases obtained between 1976 and 1982, all presenting with acute abdominal pain. Each patient's examination was conducted according to a highly structured form developed by the research team. Thus, errors in the clinical inputs into the aggregation system (the computer) were minimized.

The system constitutes a fine example of expert measurement (of clinical parameters) and mechanical combination. By 1975, de Dombal and his co-workers were able to report that an early version of this system reached 91% accuracy and outperformed senior clinicians (de Dombal, et al., 1975). Extensive testing was then undertaken in a number of countries, and it proved to be largely generalizable, although some of the probabilities had to be adjusted to better match the local population. In one country, the system proved to be unsuccessful. De Dombal attributes this failure to departures from a structured system for entering the clinical findings, not to variations in clinical pictures or to a failure of the Bayesian combination rule.

This computer-aided diagnosis system, which is comparable to many studies in clinical psychology where the formula was shown to outperform the head has, in principle, several advantages over human judgment. First, the number of cases in the data bank may be taken as a rough approximation of the "clinical experience" available to whatever rule system is used for inference. It can be readily seen that the computer's "clinical experience" of the varieties of abdominal pain is several times greater than that of all but the most senior clinical specialists; further, a case will never be forgotten nor will it be overweighted owing to recency or other cognitive biases. Second, all data available on a clinical case are aggregated by a simple form of Bayes's rule, which assumes conditional independence. While it is unlikely that this assumption is met across the entire spectrum of findings, the system's diagnostic accuracy is remarkably insensitive to any violations of this assumption. Third, the probabilities are data-based, not subjective, and hence free of estimation biases such as availability and representativeness (Tversky & Kahneman, 1974).

However, despite these virtues, computer-assisted differential diagnosis of acute abdominal pain is still not routine clinical practice in most settings, perhaps because of the developers' overly cautious view of the first-rate excellence of their program for serious physical disorders (see de Dombal, 1984b). This caution, it should be noted, about the use of a formula before it has been thoroughly validated to meet the highest possible degree of excellence is commendable, especially when viewed in light of the premature practical application of such unvalidated clinical psychology tools as computer-based personality test interpretation programs. This is a topic I address later.

Behavioral Decision Theory

Decision theory as a representation of human thinking was, as indicated earlier, introduced to psychologists by Edwards (1954, 1961), who coined the term behavioral decision theory. Psychological research on behavioral decision-making (Einhorn & Hogarth, 1981; Hogarth, 1987; Slovic, Lichtenstein, & Fischhoff, 1986) describes and analyzes the cognitive processes and principles employed in decision-making under uncertainty. It is concerned with what people *actually do* (descriptive theory), not with what *they should do* (normative theory). Studies conducted in this area typically use normative decision theory as the standard of comparison.

Elstein and Bordage (1979) raise two important questions of immediate concern to the clinician who formalizes decision-making in this way: "How accurate are clinical subjective probabilities? What difference do any errors in these estimates make in the process of clinical decision-making?" In answering these questions, they refer to three heuristic principles used to estimate subjective probabilities as first described by Tversky and Kahneman (1974): (1) representativeness, which refers to erroneous estimates of the frequency of an event because it resembles another event in certain essential features; (2) availability, when the probability of an event is misjudged because of its salience in the clinician's memory; and (3) anchoring and adjustment, in which clinicians first estimate subjectively and then adjust insufficiently to arrive at a final diagnostic opinion.

In addition, people tend to be more confident about the accuracy of their guesses than is warranted, which Szucko and B. Kleinmuntz (1981) and B. Kleinmuntz and Szucko (1984) found endemic among polygraphers, and Fischhoff and his colleagues (1982) found among college students who estimated the frequency of a variety of causes of death in America. To compound this difficulty inherent in estimating probabilities there is evidence cited in the research of Einhorn and Hogarth (1978), and from a review by Einhorn and Hogarth (1981), who suggest that humans tend to ignore nonoccurrences of events in favor of those that confirm their hypotheses, and that attempts to alter this tendency have been generally unsuccessful. Similar reasoning errors have been reported in problem-solving tasks by Wason and Johnson-Laird (1972).

It is worth noting at this point that the role of the computer in the development of behavioral decision theory as well as in Bayesian and decision analysis is the same as in any scientific field that deals with large amounts of quantitative data. The use of computers has been as a number-crunching device that helped analyze, coordinate, store, retrieve, and compute as well as compile at rapid rates the vast amounts of information that become the knowledge-base of any clinical specialty that uses diagnoses. Without the computer, many of the studies reviewed here would not have been feasible. But the use of computers *as information machines,* as Newell and Simon use the terms (see below), played no role in these studies, nor in any of the other work already discussed.

Information-Processing Psychology

One of the first scientists to recognize the computer as more than a quantitative data-processing tool was the physicist L. N. Ridenour (1952), who observed that the name given these machines obscured the fact that they were called computers because computation was the only significant chore that had been assigned to them. He proposed that computers be given a new name — information machines — to better describe their noncomputational potential. This information function of computers was soon thereafter also recognized by Newell (1955), who published a paper on "The Chess Machine." In that paper he proposed the possibility of building computer programs to deal with such complex cognitive tasks as playing chess. This was followed by a paper, published in 1957 together with Shaw (Newell & Shaw, 1957), on "Programming the Logic Theory Machine." In turn, this line of thinking culminated in the now classic *Psychological Review* paper, "Elements of a Theory of Human Problem Solving," written in collaboration with Simon (Newell, Shaw, & Simon, 1958), which laid the groundwork for information-processing psychology and for much of what is now called expert systems.

Together, these papers proposed that one can construct theories about thinking and reasoning using an information-processing computer language, just as theories of chemical or physical phenomena can be constructed using systems of differential equations, or models of genetic processes can be built using probabilistic assumptions and mathematics. Continuing along these lines, Newell and Simon over the years have argued and demonstrated that the human problem-solver can articulate his or her reasoning strategies by producing "thinking aloud" protocols while solving problems. When these verbal protocols were articulated in sufficient detail to permit the programming of computers to "simulate" the human problem-solver, then the computer-program statements become the software facsimiles of the problem-solver's thinking, thus providing the elements of a theory of problem-solving (Newell & Simon, 1961, 1972; Simon, 1979, 1981).

For example, an information-processing theory of chess playing was constructed on the basis of detailed information obtained from the player. The program was sufficiently complete and detailed to predict the actual moves a particular human player will consider, given certain positions of the pieces on the board. Newell and Simon then showed that a chess program based on a single subject can be generalized to playing the game of chess by others.

Among the first forays of information-processing psychology into the sphere of clinical judgment occurred with B. Kleinmuntz's studies at Carnegie-Mellon (1963, 1968, 1969), which set out to model a clinician's interpretations of the graphic plots obtained from the scores on the Minnesota Multiphasic Personality Inventory (MMPI). This test yields a multivariate profile and was designed to help identify persons with known personality disorders. Profile interpretation is a complex task resembling the reading of EEG or EKG wave tracings.

In these studies, an expert clinician's problem-solving strategies were "captured" by asking him to think aloud while interpreting the MMPIs of 126 subjects, of which roughly one-half were emotionally unstable and the other half not. The expert's task was simply to indicate whether a particular MMPI profile was that of an emotionally adjusted or maladjusted person. The procedure yielded about 30 hours of tape recording. The material was then edited for redundancies, next compiled, flow charted, and then programmed for the computer. The computer program thus became a simulation of the MMPI expert's reasoning strategies, which, incidentally, functioned about as well as the best clinician's head (see, especially, B. Kleinmuntz, 1967, 1969) and better than the average clinician's head. However, the expert's task was exceedingly simple in that it required only a binary decision. Current uses of the computer in automated personality test interpretations is considerably more complex and, correspondingly, considerably less successful, as I indicate later.

Another set of Carnegie-Mellon studies then focused on the cognitive activities of clinical neurologists diagnosing central nervous system disorders (B. Kleinmuntz, 1972). To encourage the neurologists to think aloud, pairs of clinicians played games of Twenty Questions with each other. One neurologist (the experimenter) was a constant presence over a set of about 25 games. The other player, the diagnostician, was given a set of symptoms and the presenting complaints of a patient to be diagnosed. The problem-solving consisted of the latter clinician asking about the presence or absence of other symptoms, signs, or biographical facts, as well as requesting the results of specific laboratory tests and inquiring about their results. Again, as in the MMPI studies, a clinician's thinking was tape-recorded and subsequently modeled. But unlike the relatively simple binary decision-making of the MMPI studies, neurologists' decision-making tends to be highly complex and, consequently, their heads are still the best bets in town for accurate clinical diagnoses. In other words, there are as yet no automated neurology systems available that approximate the clinician's expertise.

Expert Systems Research

In this section, we review several computer expert systems that are partially based on information obtained from clinicians as well as on textbook knowledge, and several others that are still experimental and deal with the more fundamental questions of how clinicians' reasoning strategies influence the outcomes of their problem-solving.

An example of a computer program under development for the past 15 years that attempts to replace the clinician's head with the formula uses expert protocols as well as case-history data, and an extensive understanding of the clinical literature as a knowledge base, is INTERNIST/CADUCEUS. This program is designed to diagnose complaints in the entire domain of internal medicine. Its designers (Miller, Pople, & Myers, 1982) attempted to equip the program with some human or heuristic rules of thumb by borrowing these from observations of a human clinician.

One version of the program, INTERNIST-I, has a knowledge base that includes more than 500 individual disease profiles and about 3550 manifestations of disease. Its disease profiles originated from a review of the literature and consultations with an expert physician. Following construction of a problem space, one of three questioning strategies is used to gather further data—pursuing a particular diagnosis, ruling out one or more, and discriminating a best fit from among two- to- four competing diagnoses.

The INTERNIST-I program was heralded as among the most ambitious attempts to simulate human clinical reasoning by Blois (1980) and more recently by Banks (1986); but its designers as well as prospective users are more concerned with its deficiencies than its abilities. Among these they list its inability to attribute findings to their proper causes and to reason anatomically or temporally. In short, the work of Miller and his associates has reinforced their impression that medical diagnosis is a complex process yet to be approximated by formal approaches. Politser's (1981) concern with those aspects of the program that rely on the simulation of human clinicians is that the success of the approach depends considerably on the competence of the clinician who is being simulated. In other words, so far, judging from the evidence now available, there is little reason to believe that the expert's use of the head in arriving at diagnostic decisions in internal medicine has been adequately simulated so that one might use INTERNIST as a formula for diagnostic purposes (also see Barnett, et al., 1987).

Another ambitious attempt to use a process-tracing or simulation approach to diagnostic problem solving is Shortliffe's (1976, 1986, 1987) and his colleagues' (Clancey, Shortliffe, & Buchanan, 1979) efforts to build instructional computer programs that prescribe antimicrobial treatment. One of Shortliffe's programs is called MYCIN (1976), and it is intended to assist and educate physicians who need advice about appropriate antimicrobial therapy. Its rationale is that the basis of infectious-disease therapy is identification of the offending micro-organisms. MYCIN consists of three subprograms. The first subprogram is a consultation system that uses information about a patient plus MYCIN's stored data base or knowledge of bacterial infectious diseases. Such knowledge permits MYCIN to decide whether the patient needs to be treated, what is the likely identity of the offending organisms, what are the possible drugs for use against these organisms, and what drugs are best for the particular patient, given his or her current clinical condition.

The second subprogram is an explanation subsystem. This component attempts to answer questions from the user both during and after a consultation session. It attempts to do so in terms designed to convince the physician that it reaches decisions in much the same way as human clinicians. The user may ask MYCIN to explain the reason for a question during the consultation or may demand explanations of decisions that the program has reached. In an effort to make such explanations easy to obtain, subprogram 2, as it is called, has been given limited ability to understand simple English. Subprogram 3 is a rule-acquisition system designed for use by experts in infectious-disease therapy. The capabilities of these components are intended to permit an expert to teach MYCIN certain simple rules that will then be incorporated into the system's knowledge base for use in future consultations.

A more recent version of these programs, ONCOCIN (Shortliffe, 1986), which is an oncology protocol management system, is an extension of MYCIN that assists physicians with the management of outpatients in cancer chemotherapy programs. Essentially ONCOCIN helps the physician sort out from within complex 40–60 page protocols information regarding proper drug dosages and laboratory tests to order. Physicians are frequently confronted by 50 such protocols in a major cancer center, and they are not likely to remember all the details in one of the protocol documents. ONCOCIN assists (not replaces) them in this and has been operative at several treatment centers and recognized as useful.

Finally, a series of recent studies on modeling clinical judgment are interesting for the light they shed on human judgment that have implications that extend beyond clinical reasoning in a specific domain such as clinical psychology or medicine (D. N. Kleinmuntz, 1982, 1985; D. N. Kleinmuntz & Thomas, 1987). These studies differ from the foregoing in that they deal with hypothetical symptoms, signs, treatments, and environments rather than real ones. In the first stage of these studies, simulated task environments resembling medical-decision problems were created. For each "case" the probabilistic relations between all of its symptoms, diseases, and laboratory tests, and the effects of various treatments of these hypothetical diseases were specified. Three experimental decision strategies for the solution to these relations were developed: (1) an expected utility (EU) maximizer, using Bayes's theorem to combine new data with previous observations; (2) a heuristic strategy that searches for satisfactory solutions using informal decision rules; and (3) a generate-and-test search approach, which is a random trial-and-error procedure. Each strategy was applied to diagnose 100 hypothetical cases. Generally, expected utility performed slightly better than the heuristic strategy, with both performing better than the generate-and-test method but to a lesser extent than one might expect from such a random decision procedure. The results only weakly supported the contention, often heard among judgment and decision researchers, that more formal quantitative strategies are superior.

Among major insights gained from these analyses was the apparent trade-off between effort and decision quality. While the complex EU strategy performed better, the modest performance gain was offset by the increase in complexity. These results indicate that there are diminishing returns to performance from increased computational effort and rule complexity. This emphasizes the need for some cost-benefit considerations when assessing the efficacy of decision rules and raises a question about the conditions under which quantitative models will improve upon heuristic strategies enough to justify the extra effort. Information-processing models of expertise that capture heuristic rule strategies may serve us well here.

The second stage of the studies investigated a variety of decision strategies across variations in the structure of the medical tasks, using computer simulations to assess the strategies' performance. The results indicated that (1) certain task variables had a very large impact on performance, and these variables were related to dynamic aspects of tasks that often confront clinicians, like time pressure and treatment risk; (2) other task variables, like the diagnosticity of symptoms and the distribution of base rates, had some influence on performance of the strategies, but much less than might be predicted from previous research; and

(3) the success rates of different strategies were directly related to their use of task-specific knowledge. This confirms previous findings of Newell and Simon about the important role of task structure and task knowledge in determining performance. The results demonstrated as well that both accurate task knowledge and a favorable task structure are required for heuristics to do well, suggesting a need for more research with human problem-solvers on how task knowledge is acquired and how heuristics are selected.

In a third, more recent study (D. N. Kleinmuntz & Thomas, 1987), naïve decision-makers (i.e., no clinical training) were observed performing the simulated medical decisions under varying task conditions. A comparison of their performance to the simulated strategies indicated that the cognitive effort expended on decision-making was only sometimes rewarded by an increase in performance. In particular, the decision-makers demonstrated a strong predilection toward strategies that emphasized diagnosis even in circumstances where immediate treatment would have been warranted. It remains for future investigations to establish how experienced clinicians differ in their perceptions of the value of different strategies.

Conclusions

Let us begin by noting that in medicine, at least, the head is still a more effective mode of proceeding than the use of a formula. The main limiting factor here, of course, is the lack of a proper formula for medical diagnosis. It is also important to note that computer modeling has had less impact on medicine than it has had on some other spheres, an observation with which G. Octo Barnett (1982) of Massachusetts General Hospital seems to be in agreement. He indicated that the optimism of 20 years ago that "computer technology would . . . play an important part in clinical decisions" has not been realized. Can this be explained on the basis of the complexity of medical decision processes vis-à-vis other areas in which similar intelligent judgment is needed? Probably not. For, if we broadly define clinical reasoning to include any human intelligent activity that entails the processing of complex data to arrive at decisions, then we can point to a number of the computer's resounding successes in other areas. Let us briefly mention these successes and then attempt to account for the computer's (read formula's) difficulties in medicine.

One is the computer's ability to play masters level chess. Although grandmaster level computer programs are not yet available, the information-processing group at Carnegie-Mellon and others are making substantial headway toward that goal. As Herbert A. Simon (1981) noted, a good chess player needs to know some 1300 patterns of chess pieces and their positions to play well; masters and grandmasters must know some 50,000 patterns and configurations. These estimates of the number of patterns and their complexity seem equivalent to those that exist in most clinical specialities of medicine. But this analogy should not be pushed too far because there are important differences between chess and medicine. Compared to medicine, chess is well structured, the moves of each piece are well defined, and less is at stake if one loses. Moreover, the "opponent" in medicine is nature, about which there is more uncertainty than about a chess opponent.

Another nonmedical, and perhaps better, example is the thriving industry of automated personality-test interpretation. There are currently no fewer than two dozen computer programs commercially available to interpret the complex configural patterns of personality test profiles. Most of them, to be sure, despite their vendors' and some users' testimonials to the contrary, have not been found to be as good as the best available clinicians for making complex decisions (Adair, 1972; Butcher, 1978; Eyde 1985; Sundberg, 1985); but some are routinely used and, although their narrative productions have yet to be properly validated, do perform classification and descriptive tasks seemingly as well as some clinicians. (For a scathing critique of contemporary uses of computers in psychological testing, and the ethical and legal implications of rendering such unvalidated automated interpretive services, see Matarazzo [1983, 1985, 1986a] as well as his detractors' reply [Fowler & Butcher, 1986] and Matarazzo's rejoinder to them [1986b].) It should be noted in this regard that although the available commercial programs aim to render predictions and decisions that are a good deal more complex than the binary decision program described earlier, the main deterrent to proper validation is motivational rather than the complexity of the task being formalized (see Hartman, 1986a, 1986b). In other words, the technology is available for validating these systems, but the time necessary for conducting validation studies seems, at least from the standpoint of many commercial enterprises, too costly. An outstanding exception is one MMPI interpretive program (see Sundberg, 1985), whose publisher is willing to invest the necessary wherewithal to produce a validated system.

Psychological testing aside, the professional domains in which computer-assisted problem-solving is carried on more extensively and successfully than in clinical psychology and medicine are in such game-playing problem-solving domains as chess, Go, and cryptarithmetic as well as in engineering and many other sciences in which the variables are quantifiable. One obstacle that accounts for the computer's relatively poorer performance in clinical psychology and medicine than in game-playing and the quantitative sciences, as mentioned earlier, is the comparatively greater complexity of reasoning needed in clinical diagnosis.

Another obstacle to computerized decision support is that it works best with well-structured problems. Computerized MMPI profile, EEG, and EKG interpretation works in many instances because the problem domain is not too complex and because the end-point scores provide a general problem structure applicable to all cases.

A third obstacle to broadening the role of computers in psychological and medical diagnosis is that existing programs are not good enough to warrant broad acceptance. This argument rests on the firm foundation that there is a vast qualitative difference when applying technology to humans between a decision being "good enough" and one that is the "best possible" available. In the case of decision-making about humans, close approximations are inherently unacceptable.

The idea of "best possible" is similar to the objections raised by Holt (1978), quoted earlier, in which he is wary of dehumanizing or denigrating clinicians qua clinical decision-makers. The other side of this coin is Holt's deeper belief that one does not tamper with the lives or dignity of humans, be they patients or clinicians.

But Holt's and my own reservations regarding the future of computerized clinical decision-making or consultation notwithstanding, one fact stands out clearly: the literature on artificial intelligence in medicine (AIM) and automated test interpretation is proliferating. Thus, researchers and prospective users continue to be interested in these areas. With this amount of interest, it is plausible to speculate that something of value may emerge and that in the foreseeable future the formula may be used instead of the head for a whole host of clinical predictions. The question "When shall we use our heads instead of the formula?"—alas 35 years after Meehl posed the question—remains to be answered. Meanwhile, as I indicate elsewhere (B. Kleinmuntz, 1972; B. Kleinmuntz, 1987, 1990; B. Kleinmuntz & Elstein, 1987), one should not despair about the formula's past and current disappointments. Time is on the side of those who wager that the formula in the form of the computer will play an essential role in clinical reasoning. For one reason, much effort is presently being invested in AI research. No doubt there will be spin-offs from this. This has been the trend so far. Finally, the best reason is that clinicians are increasingly becoming frighteningly aware that they are, in the last analysis, not as good as they thought they were.

References

Adair, F. L. (1972). Re MMPI computerized scoring and interpreting services. In O. K. Buros (Ed.), *Seventh mental measurements yearbook.* Highland Park, NJ: Gryphon Press.

Banks, G. (1986). Artificial intelligence in medical diagnosis: The Internist/Caduceus approach. *Critical Reviews in Medical Informatics, 1,* 23–54.

Barnett, G. O. (1980). The computer and clinical judgment. *New England Journal of Medicine, 307,* 493–494.

Barnett, G. O., Cimino, J. J., Hupp, J. A., & Hoffer, E. P. (1987). DXplain: An evolving diagnostic decision-support system. *Journal of the American Medical Association, 258,* 67–74.

Blois, M. S. (1980). Clinical judgment and computers. *New England Journal of Medicine, 303,* 192–197.

Buros, O. K. (1978) (Ed.). *Eighth mental measurements yearbook.* Highland Park, NJ: Gryphon Press.

Butcher, J. N. (1978). Review of computerized scoring and interpreting services. In O. K. Buros (Ed.), *Eighth mental measurements yearbook*. Highland Park, NJ: Gryphon Press.

Chandrasekaran, B., & Mittal, S. (1983). Deep versus compiled knowledge approaches to diagnostic problem-solving. *International Journal of Man-Machine Studies, 19*, 425–442.

Clancey, W. J., Shortliffe, E. H., & Buchanan, B. G. (1979). Intelligent computer-aided instruction for medical diagnosis. *Proceedings of the Third Annual Symposium on Computer Applications in Medical Computing*. Silver Spring, MD, October, pp. 175–183.

de Dombal, F. T. (1984a). Future progress for computer aids as gastroenterology. *Frontiers of Gastrointestinal Research, 7*, 186–198.

de Dombal, F. T. (1984b). Clinical decision making and the computer: Consultant, expert, or just another test? *British Journal of Health Care Computing, 1*, 7–12.

de Dombal, F. T., Horrocks, J. C., Walensley, A., et al. (1975). Computer-aided diagnosis and decision-making in the acute abdomen. *Journal of the College of Physicians* (London), *9*, 211–223.

de Dombal, F. T., Leaper, D. J., Stanilaud, J. R., McCann, A. P., & Horrocks, J. C. (1972). Computer-aided diagnosis of acute abdominal pain. *British Medical Journal, 2*, 9–18.

de Finetti, B. (1937). La prévision: Ses lois logique, ses source subjectives. *Annals de Institute Henri Poincaré, 7*, 1–68.

Edwards, W. (1954). The theory of decision making. *Psychological Bulletin, 51*, 380–417.

Edwards, W. (1961). Behavioral decision theory. *Annual Review of Psychology, 12*, 473–498.

Edwards, W. (1972). N = 1: Diagnosis in unique cases. In J. A. Jacquez (Ed.), *Computer diagnosis and diagnostic methods*. Springfield, IL: Charles Thomas, pp. 139–151.

Einhorn, H. J., & Hogarth, R. M. (1978). Confidence in judgment: Persistence of the illusion of validity. *Psychological Review, 85*, 395–406.

Einhorn, H. J., & Hogarth, R. M. (1981). Behavioral decision theory: Processes of judgment and choice. *Annual Review of Psychology, 32*, 53–88.

Einhorn, H. J., Kleinmuntz, D. N., & Kleinmuntz, B. (1979). Linear regression *and* process tracing models of judgment. *Psychological Review, 86*, 465–485.

Elstein, A. S., & Bordage, G. (1979). Psychology of clinical reasoning. In G. C. Stone (Ed.), *Health psychology: A handbook*. San Francisco: Jossey-Bass.

Elstein, A. S., Shulman, L. S., & Sprafka, S. A. (1978). *Medical problem solving: An analysis of clinical reasoning*. Cambridge: Harvard University Press.

Eyde, L. D. (1985). Review of the Minnesota Report: Personnel selection system for the MMPI. In J. V. Mitchell, Jr. (Ed.), *Ninth mental measurements yearbook*. Lincoln, NE: University of Nebraska Press.

Fischhoff, B. (1980). Clinical decision analysis. *Operations Research, 28*, 28–43.

Fischhoff, B., Goitein, B., & Shapira, Z. (1982). The experienced utility of expected utility approaches. In N. T. Feather (Ed.), *Expectations and actions: Expectancy value models in psychology*. Hillsdale, NJ: Erlbaum.

Fowler, R. D., & Butcher, J. N. (1986). Critique of Matarazzo's views on computerized testing: All sigma and no meaning. *American Psychologist, 41*, 94–96.

Fryback, D. G., & Thornbury, J. R. (1976). Evaluation of a computerized Bayesian model of renal cyst versus tumor versus normal variant from excretory urogram information. *Investigations in Radiology, 11*, 102–111.

Goldberg, L. R. (1965). Diagnosticians vs. diagnostic signs: The diagnosis of psychosis vs neurosis from the MMPI. *Psychological Monographs, 79*, (9, Whole No. 602).

Hartman, D. E. (1986a). On the use of clinical psychology software: Practical, legal and ethical concerns. *Professional Psychology: Research and Practice, 17*, 462–465.

Hartman, D. E. (1986b). Artificial intelligence or artificial psychologist? Conceptual issues in clinical microcomputer use. *Professional Psychology: Research and Practice, 17*, 528–534.

Hogarth, R. M. (1987). *Judgement and choice: The psychology of decision*. London: Wiley.

Holt, R. R. (1958). Clinical and statistical prediction. *Journal of Abnormal and Social Psychology,* *56,* 1–12.

Holt, R. R. (1978). *Methods in clinical psychology: Predictions and research* (vol. 2). New York: Plenum.

Kahneman, D., Slovic, P. M., & Tversky, A. (Eds.) (1982). *Judgment under uncertainty: Heuristics and biases.* New York: Cambridge University Press.

Ingelfinger, F. J. (1975). Decision in medicine. *New England Journal of Medicine, 293,* 244–245.

Keeney, R. L. (1982). Decision analysis: An overview. *Operations Psychology, 3,* 803–833.

Kleinmuntz, B. (1963). Personality test interpretation by digital computer. *Science, 139,* 416–418.

Kleinmuntz, B. (1967). Sign and seer: Another example. *Journal of Abnormal Psychology, 72,* 163–165.

Kleinmuntz, B. (1968). The processing of clinical information by man and machine. In B. Kleinmuntz (Ed.), *Formal representation of human judgment.* New York: John Wiley, pp. 149–186.

Kleinmuntz, B. (1969). Personality test interpretation by computer and clinician. In J. N. Butcher (Ed.), *MMPI: Research developments and clinical applications.* New York: McGraw-Hill, pp. 97–104.

Kleinmuntz, B. (1972). Medical information processing by computer. In J. A. Jacquez (Ed.), *Computer diagnosis and diagnostic methods.* Springfield, IL: Charles C. Thomas, pp. 45–72.

Kleinmuntz, B. (1984). The scientific study of clinical judgment in psychology and medicine. *Clinical Psychology Review, 4,* 111–126.

Kleinmuntz, B. (1987). Automated interpretation of neuropsychological test data: Comment on Adams and Heaton. *Journal of Consulting and Clinical Psychology, 55,* 266–267.

Kleinmuntz, B. (1990). Why we still use our heads instead of formulas: Toward an integrated approach. *Psychological Bulletin, 107,* 296–310.

Kleinmuntz, B., & Elstein, A. S. (1987). Computer modeling of clinical judgment. *Critical Reviews in Medical Informatics, 1,* 3, 209–228.

Kleinmuntz, B., & Szucko, J. J. (1984). A field study of the fallibility of polygraphic lie detection. *Nature, 308,* 349–350.

Kleinmuntz, D. N. (1982). *The relative performance of decision strategies: Heuristics and task structure.* Unpublished doctoral dissertation. University of Chicago, Chicago, Illinois.

Kleinmuntz, D. N. (1985). Cognitive heuristics and feedback in a dynamic decision environment. *Management Science, 31,* 680–702.

Kleinmuntz, D. N. (1987). Human decision processes: Heuristics and task structure. In R. A. Hancock (Ed.), *Human factors psychology* (pp. 123–154) Amsterdam: Elsevier-North Holland.

Kleinmuntz, D. N., & Kleinmuntz, B. (1981). Decision strategies in simulated environments. *Behavioral Science, 26,* 294–305.

Kleinmuntz, D. N., & Thomas, J. B. (1987). The value of action and inference in dynamic decision making. *Organizational Behavior and Human Decision Processes, 39,* 341–364.

Ledley, R. S., & Lusted, L. (1959). Reasoning foundations of medical diagnosis. *Science, 130,* 9–22.

Lusted, L. (1968). *Introduction to medical decision making.* Springfield, IL: Charles C. Thomas.

Lusted, L. B. (1975). In the process of solution. *New England Journal of Medicine, 293,* 255–256.

Matarazzo, J. D. (1983). Computerized psychological testing (Editorial), *Science, 221,* 323.

Matarazzo, J. D. (1985). Clinical psychological test interpretations by computer: Hardware outpaces software. *Computers and Human Behavior, 1,* 235–253.

Matarazzo, J. D. (1986a). Computerized clinical psychological test interpretations: Unvalidated plus all mean and no sigma. *American Psychologist, 41,* 14–24.

Matarazzo, J. D. (1986b). Response to Fowler and Butcher on Matarazzo. *American Psychologist, 41,* 96.

Meehl, P. E. (1954). *Clinical versus statistical prediction*. Minneapolis: University of Minnesota Press.

Meehl, P. E. (1957). When shall we use our heads instead of the formula? *Journal of Counseling Psychology, 4*, 268–273.

Meehl, P. E. (1959). A comparison of clinicians with five statistical methods of identifying psychotic MMPI profiles. *Journal of Counseling Psychology, 2*, 102–109.

Meehl, P. E. (1960). The cognitive activity of the clinician. *American Psychologist, 15*, 19–27.

Meehl, P. E. (1967). What can the clinician do well? In D. N. Jackson & S. Messick (Eds.), *Problems in human assessment*. New York: McGraw-Hill, pp. 594–599.

Miller, R. A., Pople, H. E., & Myers, J. D. (1982). INTERNIST-I: An experimental computer-based diagnostic consultant for general internal medicine. *New England Journal of Medicine, 307*, 486–476.

Mitchell, J. V., Jr. (Ed.) (1985). *Ninth mental measurements yearbook*. Lincoln, NE: University of Nebraska Press.

Newell, A. (1955). The chess machine: An example of dealing with a complex task by adaptation. *Proceedings of the Western Joint Computer Conference, 101*–108.

Newell, A., & Shaw, J. C. (1957). Programming the logic theory machine. *Proceedings of the Western Joint Computer Conference,* 230–240.

Newell, A., Shaw, J. C., & Simon, H. A. (1958). Elements of a theory of human problem solving. *Psychological Review, 65*, 151–166.

Newell, A., & Simon, H. A. (1961). Computer simulation of human thinking. *Science, 134*, 2011–2017.

Newell, A., & Simon, H. A. (1972). *Human problem solving*. Englewood Cliffs, NJ: Prentice-Hall.

Politser, P. (1981). Decision analysis and clinical judgment: A reevaluation. *Medical Decision Making, 1*, 363–389.

Raiffa, H. (1968). *Decision analysis: Introductory lectures on choice under uncertainty*. Reading, MA: Addison-Wesley.

Ramsey, F. P. (1931). Truth and probability. In F. P. Ramsey (Ed.), *The foundations of mathematics and other logical essays*. New York: Harcourt Brace.

Ridenour, L. N. (1952). Computers as information machines. *Scientific American, 187*, 116–118.

Savage, L. J. (1954). *The foundations of statistics*. New York: Wiley.

Savage, L. J. (1972). Diagnosis and the Bayesian viewpoint. In J. A. Jacquez (Ed.), *Computer diagnosis and diagnostic methods*. Springfield, IL: Charles C Thomas, pp. 131–138.

Schlaifer, R. (1959). *Probability and statistics for business decisions*. New York: McGraw-Hill.

Schoemaker, P. J. H. (1982). The expected utility model: Its variants, purposes, evidence and limitations. *Journal of Economic Literature, 20*, 529–540.

Shortliffe, E. H. (1976). *Computer-based medical consultations: MYCIN*. New York: Elsevier.

Shortliffe, E. H. (1986). Update on ONCOCIN: A chemotherapy advisor for clinical oncology. *Medical Informatics, 11*, 15–21.

Shortliffe, E. H. (1987). Computer programs to support clinical decision making. *Journal of the American Medical Association, 258*, 61–66.

Simon, H. A. (1979). Information processing models of cognition. *Annual Review of Psychology, 30*, 363–396.

Simon, H. A. (1981). *The sciences of the artificial* (2nd Ed.). Cambridge, MA: MIT Press.

Slovic, P., Lichtenstein, S., & Fischhoff, B. (1986). Decision making. In R. C. Atkinson, R. J. Herrnstein, G. Lindzey, and R. D. Luce (Eds.), *Stevens' handbook of experimental psychology* (2nd Ed.). New York: Wiley.

Sundberg, N. D. (1985). Reviews of Behaviordyne Psychodiagnostic Laboratory Service for the MMPI and Re MMPI IVPS Test Report. In J. V. Mitchell, Jr. (Ed.), *Ninth mental measurements yearbook*. Lincoln, NE: University of Nebraska Press.

Szucko, J. J., & Kleinmuntz, B. (1981). Clinical versus statistical lie detection. *American Psychologist, 36*, 488–496.

Tversky, A., & Kahneman, D. (1974). Judgment under uncertainty: Heuristics and biases. *Science, 185*, 1124–1131.

Tversky, A., & Kahneman, D. (1981). The framing of decisions and the psychology of choice. *Science, 211*, 453–458.

Tversky, A., & Kahneman, D. (1986). Rational choice and the framing of decisions. *Journal of Business, 6251–6278*.

von Neumann, J., & Morgenstern, O. (1947). *Theory of games and economic behavior*. Princeton: Princeton University Press.

Wason, P. C., & Johnson-Laird, P. N. (1972). *Psychology of reasoning: Structure and content*. Cambridge, MA: Harvard University Press.

Weinstein, M. C., & Fineberg, H. V. (1980). *Clinical decision analysis*. Philadelphia: Saunders.

Wiggins, J. S. (1973). *Personality and prediction: Principles of personality assessment*. Reading, MA: Addison-Wesley.

Wright, G. (1984). *Behavioral decision theory*. New York: Penguin Books.

Probabilistic versus Causal Thinking

Robyn M. Dawes

In my mind, I know what she was thinking and feeling at the time of her death — Dr. Douglas Jacob [Reported in the October 21, 1987, *New York Times*, p. A22, on the occasion of Dr. Jacob's "psychological autopsy" being allowed into testimony at the trial of Teresa Jackson for (psychological) child abuse following the suicide of her daughter, Fort Lauderdale, Florida.]

Overview

Following Hume's (1740, 1748) convincing argument that causal inferences based on everyday experience cannot be empirically verified, many philosophers have agreed with Mill that "observation, in short, without experimentation (supposing no aid from deduction) can ascertain sequences and co-existences, but cannot prove causation" (1843, p. 253). Others have been less restrictive and argued that causality can be inferred on a statistical basis granting certain assumptions—e.g., "that there is no third event that we can use to factor out the probability relationship between the first and second event" (Suppes, 1970, p. 10)—assumptions that are subject to empirical verification, or at least "falsifiability." As Glymour (1986), for example, points out, we believe genetic constitution to be a causal agent without manipulating it (e.g., by creating trisomy 21 on a random basis at a human conception and observing the subsequent incidence of Down's Syndrome). What is commonly agreed, however, is that causal assertions cannot be established without some *test* involving either manipulation or careful examination of potentially related variables and their pattern of covariation with the alleged "cause" and "effect." Such tests necessarily involve observations of equivalent ("substitutable") events as well as of the particular

235

events about which a causal inference is made. We experiment, or we conduct a careful statistical analysis. (Again, not all philosophers agree that the latter path is sufficient.)

The impact of Hume's analysis stems from the readily observable fact that most of us much of the time *do* make causal inferences from everyday experience, and do so without any ancillary tests of their validity. We ask ''what caused her to do that?'' We believe that unusual or particularly salient events ''demand explanation.'' We continually ask ''why''—e.g., ''why did he commit suicide?'' ''why did this twin get the schizophrenia when the other didn't?'' And we provide, or at least hypothesize, answers. As lay or professional psychologists observing the blooming, buzzing confusion of human behavior (perhaps even our own), we are particularly prone to seek causal explanations. We are rarely content with simply saying ''this happened and that followed'' (just as Hume was not content with the simple temporal connection between lighting a fire and feeling warm). We add a causal explanation (or at least a statement with a causal flavor—e.g., ''the Germans were particularly vulnerable to Nazi propaganda because the typical German upbringing fostered authoritarian attitudes and personality''), and we do so without embarking on a series of experimental or correlational tests of our ''analysis.'' (In fact, some interpreters of human life maintain that each person and event is so intrinsically ''unique'' that the substitutability assumptions underlying all such tests are untenable; ironically, many of these same people are apt to be free with causal explanations of human life—e.g., in a clinical setting.)

Are such causal attributions about unique events ever justifiable? Either the experimental or correlational approach implies three necessary conditions. First, the relationship must involve a cause (or causes) and an effect (or effects) that are *separately identifiable;* second, the link between cause and effect must be based on prior multiple observations of events that can be unambiguously identified with the hypothesized unique cause and unique effect; third, the conditional probability previously established between these sets of events must be close to 1 in at least one direction (from cause to effect for ''sufficient'' causes and from effect to cause for ''necessary'' causes). Consider, for example, the assertion that ''your particular headache is caused by your particular brain tumor.'' That statement is based on: (i) separate criteria for establishing the existence of the effect (self-report of headache) and the cause (X-ray of brain tumor), (ii) past observations of multiple headaches and multiple brain tumors, and (iii) a high probability of the type of headache reported given the type of brain tumor observed (fortunately for headache sufferers, not the reverse)—although a *few* people with identifiable tumors of the type may not experience headaches.

Compare the headache/tumor statement to: ''Your anxiety about your forthcoming divorce is caused by your mother's rejection of you when you were an infant.'' First, the mother's rejection is *not* identified separately from the anxiety;

both are based on the subject's self-report. Second, no clear conceptions of "rejection" or "anxiety" exist that would allow the multiple observations of equivalent events necessary for either an experimental or a correlational analysis of cause. Third, prospective studies that nevertheless do attempt to establish links (e.g., Parker & Asher, 1987) find low correlations whose proximity to zero cannot be attributed solely to fuzziness of conception or to measurement error; even mildly impressive predictability occurs only for subsets—most often characterized by their unusualness—of the supposedly equivalent events. (For example, children at the extremes of rejection by their peers—indicated both by few or no friends *and* by being disliked—have a clear *tendency* to have problems in adolescence, see p. 376.) Such predictability is presented positively in the research literature as confident rejection of the null hypothesis (that "there is not nothing," or more precisely that "if there is nothing, I sampled an unusual value of it"). But such mere rejection does *not* yield the degree of predictability required for a causal conclusion in the multiple observation context, hence provides no justification for such statements concerning unique events. Purportedly causal statements about unique events involving people, groups, organizations, societies, and nations suffer from these same three flaws.

I am not arguing that there is something about the subject matter of psychology and other social sciences that precludes causal explanations, even of unique events. Rather, I am maintaining that given the current state of the constructs employed and the degree of predictability discovered in using them, there is no *empirical* justification for causal analysis. (Whether such analysis can be justified in the future is itself an empirical matter.) Of course, it is possible to adopt "determinism" *re* human existence as a philosophical assumption, but given our *actual* ability to predict the course of that which is supposedly determined, such an assumption involves as much faith as does one of free will. An alternative justification is to postulate causal thinking as a "category of intuition" describing the way we humans attempt to order our worlds. If it were one with which we were "stuck," however, how could we accept Hume's arguments as valid?

A final alternative is to regard the "search for causes" as a motivating force in seeking knowledge that ultimately results in an understanding of experimental manipulations (perhaps under our control) or of valid statistical contingencies. ("The universe shows us nothing save an immense and unbroken chain of cause and effect"—P. H. D'Holbach [1770]; "All successful men have agreed in one thing—they were causationists"—R. W. Emerson [1860].) In this paper, I want to argue the reverse—that the "excess baggage" imposed by searching for causal explanations may in fact *obscure* statistical contingency—that even in attempting to change the world, we may be better off trying to understand what is related to what than what causes what. I am talking about "causal analysis" in its everyday sense of postulating causes and effects, without satisfying the three necessary criteria outlined above (which I am not maintaining are the only ones) for justi-

fying such an analysis. As curious humans we ask "why did he commit suicide?" and we tend to ask the same question as "scientists" studying the phenomenon suicide, or as "clinicians" attempting to make sense of a particular
individual's suicide. What I want to demonstrate—by example—is that in the
latter roles we may function better *without* asking such questions than with asking them. (I strongly suspect that we make better judgments in everyday life as
well, but that hypothesis is beyond the scope of this paper.) I will argue by example because assessing the utility of causal thinking is an empirical matter that
has not yet been investigated in a systematic manner. So I begin where we all
begin empirical quests: Unsystematic observations and anecdotes. These will,
quite naturally, involve instances where causal thinking is pernicious rather than
helpful; the case against causal as opposed to probabilistic (statistical) thinking is
thus far from proved. I hope these analyses will, however, stimulate some
thought and more systematic investigations of whether our penchant for causal
thought—which is so dubious on philosophical grounds—is useful, or of where
it impedes analysis and where it facilitates it.

A second purpose of this paper is to suggest that much of the schism[1] between
professional and academic psychology is linked to this intellectual difference between causal versus probabilistic thinking, as well as to political and financial
factors.

A Social Judgment Example

The point of this example—and subsequent ones—is to demonstrate that causal
versus probabilistic approaches to a problem are not just matters of framing, but
can result in profound differences in the way a problem is investigated, and in the
conclusions reached in this investigation. The problem is that of analyzing the
relationship between an individual's own response to a question, or willingness to
engage in a behavior, and that individual's estimation of the responses of others
in a specified group containing that individual. It is an important question because it involves the prediction of others' responses and behaviors (one of the
most important predictions we make in life), and the role of one's own predispositions and behaviors in making that prediction.

Literature addressed to this problem purportedly demonstrates what has been
termed a *false consensus effect,* which is described as an egoistic bias to over-
estimate the degree to which others are like us. The criterion for establishing this
existence of the effect is a positive correlation across subjects (within items) between their own endorsements of a behavior or attitude item and their estimates
of the endorsement frequencies in the specified group. To quote the authors of the
two most recent interviews:

False consensus refers to an egocentric bias that occurs when people estimate consensus for their own behavior. Specifically, the false consensus hypothesis holds that people who engage in a given behavior will estimate that behavior to be more common than it is estimated to be by the people who engage in the alternative behavior. (Mullen, Atkins, Champion, Edwards, Hardy, Story, & Venderklok, 1985, p. 262)

and

The paradigm for examining the false consensus bias is a simple one. Individuals are generally asked to indicate their attitude or behavior on a dichotomous measure (*yes* or *no, agree* or *disagree*). They are then asked to estimate the percentage of their peers who would respond one way or the other. (Sometimes the order of these two ratings is counterbalanced.) Individuals are said to perceive the false consensus when their estimate consensus for their own position exceeds the estimate for it made by those who endorse the opposite position. Thus, the bias is relative to the perception of those who endorse a position opposite or alternative to one's own view. (Marks & Miller, 1987, p. 74)

The effect is labeled "false"—and "egocentric"—on the grounds that because there is an actual endorsement rate in the group, estimates deviating from it in the direction of the subject's own response supposedly cannot result from accurate estimation procedures. "Not everyone can be right," in particular not both the group member endorsing the item who estimates a relatively high proportion of endorsement and the group member rejecting it who estimates a relatively low proportion. (See Ross & Sicoly [1979].) Because there is a true (but often unknown) endorsement frequency, "any naturally occurring association between subjects' own position and actual target position is defined away" (Hoch, 1987, p. 223).

The subject's own response, the argument runs, has no causal effect on others' responses. Given this lack of causality, any correlation between the subject's own endorsement and the group endorsement frequency is simply a part-whole correlation, which will dissipate the zero as the group size increases. Discovery of a nontrivial correlation, therefore, indicates that subjects are engaged in a *false* social inference procedure. For example, in the original study by Ross, Green, & House (1977), student subjects at Stanford University were requested to walk around campus for 30 minutes wearing a sandwich board that read, "Repent!" Those who agreed estimated on average that 63.5% of their fellow students would also agree, while those who disagreed estimated that figure to be 23.3% on average. The experimenters had no random sample from which to draw an inference about the actual proportion of Stanford students at that time who would agree, but—they argued—since it was clear that this proportion could not be both approximately two-thirds and approximately one-fourth simultaneously, these estimates in the direction of the subjects' own behavior clearly constituted a bias.

In contrast, view the problem as one in which the subject is asked to make a valid statistical inference about an unknown binomial probability or proportion. Each subject has a sample of size one about this proportion—his or her own endorsement or rejection of the statement or behavior being investigated. The subject who agrees has sampled a "success"; the subject who disagrees has sampled a "failure." Should their estimates of the desired probability or proportion be the same? Of course not. To understand this probabilistic analysis, consider the Ross, Green and House finding viewed within a Bayesian framework. Before reaching their own decisions, subjects undoubtedly have very little idea about the proportion of Stanford students who would be willing to carry around such a sign. Under such circumstances, it is not irrational to postulate a uniform prior. Now consider the subject who decides to carry the board. That subject has sampled a success. The probability of such a success if the proportion of successes is p is itself p. The posterior probability is therefore $pf(p)/.50$ because .50 is the mean of the prior distribution. The mean of the posterior distribution of belief about this probability is, therefore, the integral from zero to one of $p \times pf(p)/.50 = p^2/.50$, which is 2/3 when f(p) is uniform. Similar reasoning indicates that the subject who samples a "failure" (on the basis of refusing to carry the sign) should have a mean of the posterior distribution equaling 1/3. Those estimates are remarkably close to the average estimates actually attained from the subjects of the experiment.

Before abandoning this example, it should be noted that because Bayesian analysis is independent of the order of information, "prior" in this context can be interpreted simply as meaning "independent of the subject's response." Further, while the reader may have some objection to a prior distribution as extreme as the uniform one, *any* prior distribution not concentrated at a single point implies that a subject who agrees should have a higher mean for the distribution of posterior belief than the subject who disagrees. The result of a Bayesian inference is a positive correlation within items between the subjects' own endorsements and their estimates of the endorsement frequencies of others.

It is not even necessary to adopt an explicit Bayesian framework to reach the same conclusion. Unless each subject's response to every item is uncorrelated with the responses of all other subjects in the relevant group, there will be a correlation between endorsements and endorsement frequencies across items and people. For example, if 40 of 60 people endorse one item and only 20 endorse a second, this correlation across both items and people equals 1/3. Now consider a subject who knows that the two items have endorsement frequencies of 1/3 and 2/3 but doesn't know which item is which. If one applies the standard regression equation, such a subject should estimate the endorsement frequency to be 5/9 for an item to which he or she responds positively and 4/9 for an item to which he or she responds negatively. Two-thirds of such judgments will be in error by 1/9, which yields a squared error of 1/81. The remaining third of these estimates will be in error by 2/9, which yields a squared error of 4/81. The mean squared error of using such an estimation procedure is therefore $(2/3)(1/81) + (1/3)(4/81) = 6/243 = .0247$. In contrast, subjects who have paid no attention to their own responses should estimate that each item has an endorsement frequency of 1/2. All estimates will be in error by 1/6, yielding a mean square error of $1/36 = .0278$. That squared error is greater than .0247, which means that if subjects fall prey to the supposedly "false" consensus effect they are *more* accurate than if they don't.

In fact, I (1988b) have demonstrated that the Bayesian and the regression approaches yield exactly the same estimates, even though the Bayesian approach is framed in terms of a distribution of prior belief about a particular proportion while the regression approach is framed in terms of a distribution of endorsement probabilities for different items.[2]

Now, of course, this analysis assumes that subjects are either omniscient or have strong and specifiable prior beliefs. While subjects cannot be expected to be all-knowing or precisely accurate, surely they have *some* ideas about the domain of items used in the standard "false consensus" experiment (food preferences, political attitudes, willingness to engage in unusual behaviors, etc.), and some types of prior beliefs. Moreover, the general principle that one's own response should be correlated with those of others—which forms the basis of analyses—is not a particularly "egoistic" one. In fact, according to this analysis, it is people who *fail* to make this assumption who are less accurate than those who do. It is such a failure that constitutes an "egocentric bias," in direct opposition to the conclusion of earlier investigators that this assumption itself constitutes such a bias. It would, of course, be "magic" to believe that our own responses "cause" other people to respond in a similar manner. It is, in contrast, perfectly valid statistical reasoning to believe that when we are part of a group, what the group is likely to do we are likely to do as well. And estimate group propensities accordingly.

This analysis leads to the conclusion that there should be a *positive* relationship between the degree to which subjects show a 'false consensus effect" in their accuracy. What data there are support this inference. When Hoch (1987) related the degree of false consensus effect—defined as a correlation within persons across items between endorsement and estimates of endorsement frequency—to accuracy in a context in which such accuracy was readily assessed, he found that it was positively related ("averaging across all three target populations in which a majority of subjects [65% using the optimal weighting measure d'] can actually increase their predictive accuracy by relying on their own positioning to a greater extent than they actually did," p. 231). Van de Kragt and Dawes (in preparation) report the same finding in a study involving six different groups of subjects responding in seven item domains involving liberal-conservative attitudes, beliefs about urine tests for illegal drugs, beliefs about AIDS testing, and so on. Moreover, this probabilistic analysis implies that subjects should be equally influenced by their own responses and by the response of some other group member that is made available to them. In a unique study, Sherman, Presson & Chassin (1984) provided their subjects with just such a sample of size one of another group member's response; they found that their subjects' own responses had "no special status" in the resulting estimates, except in a domain involving threat to self-esteem. (Subjects told that they had answered an ability item incorrectly but some other group member had answered it correctly tended to give lower estimates for the success rate of other group members than did those subjects who were told that they had answered it correctly but that some other group member had answered it incorrectly.) While being neither a classical nor a Bayesian statistician, Emerson may have been essentially correct when he stated "to believe in your own thought, to believe what is true for you in your private heart, is true for all men — that is genius" (*Self Reliance*).

Before ending this example, I want to point out that believing that the consensus effect is necessarily false is *equivalent* to believing that base rates are irrelevant to individual predictions. One way of conceptualizing the importance of base rates is to note that there is a *correlation* between base rates and individual responses, as pointed out in the example of items with endorsement frequencies of 1/3 and 2/3. Hence, ignoring base rates is equivalent to ignoring an important predictive variable in a multiattribute prediction situation. Correlation is symmetric. Our poor research subjects fail to integrate the base-rate information in the famous blue/green bus problem — unless they are told 90% of the accidents in the area involve blue busses *because* . . . (Bar-Hillel, 1980). Our misguided clinical colleagues make horrific representative judgments without considering base rates — "this child's doll play is typical of those who have been abused, therefore she was abused" — and seemingly endless didactic efforts to get them to attend to base-rate information fail (Meehl & Rosen, 1955 to Melton, 1988). They are interested in what makes *this* individual "tick," and class membership doesn't provide a causal mechanism — just a probability (and some of us have even been told that we "fail to realize" that "statistics do not apply to the individual"). Well, my response made in isolation does not *cause* others to respond as I do, nor do their responses cause me to act as they do, but our responses *are* correlated; unless response rate is the same to all questions, there *is* a correlation between one response and another.

How do our own colleagues respond to simple hypothetical demonstrations of this correlation? I have many times heard the assertion that there is a correlation *because* a single subject "contributes" a lot to the base rate in these examples. "If the group got larger, the correlation would disappear." Of course it doesn't. The correlation remains constant, as is easily demonstrated by multiplying the number of hypothetical subjects in either the Bayesian or correlational demonstrations by 1,000. What is truly important is not group size, but variance of base rates.

We too do not appreciate contingency without causality.

I also want to point out that the statistically correct use of the consensus effect illustrates a principle expounded by Einhorn (1986) that often it is necessary "to make error in order to avoid error." The subjects who use their own responses in making their estimates will occasionally be quite wrong (e.g., off 4/9 in the two-item example as opposed to 1/6 if they always predict the overall average of 1/2). Nevertheless, their overall accuracy is enhanced—as demonstrated both by the statistical argument and by the data. While the example of probability matching referenced by Einhorn appears on the surface to be a contradictory one, in which subjects should always make the same response rather than different ones, it involves the same principle: behaving in a statistically valid way means accepting occasional "error." Consider, for example, the subject in the Tversky and Edwards (1966) experiment who was *explicitly* told that a left or right light would flash with a stationary probability for 1,000 trials and who is rewarded with a nickel for each correct prediction. By the end of the first 50 trials, the subject should have a very good idea of which light is more probable and in a 70/30 condition has an expectation of receiving $33.25 by predicting that light on each and every trial. In fact, subjects predict the more probable light on approximately 76% of the trials, obtaining about $25.27 instead. I present this example here because it is no different in kind from later examples involving very important outcomes in careers and clinical interactions.

Two "Clinical" Examples

The last Rorschach test I ever administered was to a sixteen-year old girl who had been hospitalized against her will by her parents. The presenting symptom was that she was dating a man almost twice her age. Quite mature appearing and acting, she responded well to the testing situation, except for occasional periods of crying. She explained that she felt quite depressed by her current situation and that her feelings of inadequacy were exacerbated whenever she could not answer a question "correctly." Despite her negative affect and the occasional long latencies, which I carefully timed with my stopwatch, she obtained a full score WAIS IQ of 126, and she gave 41 responses to the Rorschach, 40 of which were clearly "good form." The one exception was for ink blot card 8. "It looks like a bear to me." Upon inquiry, she stated that she could not explain why it looked like a bear to her, and began to cry. "It just looks like a bear. That's all. I can't explain."

At the subsequent staff meeting, the head psychologist displayed card 8 to everyone assembled and asked rhetorically "Does that look like a bear to you?" (I trust I am not violating the APA ethics rules by stating that card 8 does not look like a bear, and thereby jeopardizing the validity—if it had any—of a future Rorschach test used to psychodiagnose the reader.) Because card 8 did not look like a bear to anybody, there had to be a reason not apparent to them why she had seen a bear, a cause for such a striking misperception. The handiest one was hallucination, a plausible cause supported by the occasional long response latencies that I had so dutifully documented. When I protested that 40 good form of 41 responses was actually a higher percentage than the average found among normal individuals, the head psychologist responded that while I understood measurement, I failed to understand people. In particular, I failed to understand that "statistics do not apply to the individual." The patient was diagnosed "schizophrenic" and sent home to her parents, because that particular setting was not one appropriate to deal with schizophrenia. (I should point out in defense of this diagnosis that she also drew eyes looking to one side in the Draw-a-Person-Test, bit her nails, and occasionally rocked in her bed when she went to sleep.)

This anecdote indicates a clear contrast between a causal versus a statistical approach to an aberrant response. The causal approach is based on explaining it. The statistical approach views it as a single element in a sample of her potential responses to ink blots. (On another day, she may have seen something else.) This element is understood as providing information about those potential responses, but this information is derived from the characteristics of the sample *in toto*. In this example, the response of a bear to card 8 was embedded within a sample of 40 other responses all of which were "good form," and the most striking characteristic of the "form level" of this *sample* was that it was *higher* than the average found among normal people. Analyzed within the framework of normative statistical models, therefore, the bear response would lead to the conclusion that her potential responses to the ink blots *were not in the least* biased in the direction of "poor form." Even if we were to agree that a tendency to see poor form responses on the Rorschach was indicative of hallucination, we would conclude that there was no evidence for any such activity on her part. "Explaining" the response in causal terms leads to the exact opposite conclusion.[3] (There is an apparent, but not real, inconsistency between the false consensus example and the bear example. In the false consensus example, normative statistical principles imply placing great weight on a single response, in the bear example little weight. The reason is that in the false consensus example that single response is the only datum available, while in the bear example, the sample contains much more data: the other 40 responses. Moreover, both examples indicate how statistics *do* apply to individuals. A high proportion of endorsements from my group creates a high likelihood of my endorsement. The high form levels of normal people create a high likelihood that a normal person will have a high form level. Such likelihoods can then be combined with priors, and possibly other information, to make a valid statistical inference.)

My second example is a more informal one, concerning a causal inference an individual made for himself. Several years back, a university at which I was working sponsored an education program for prisoners who were first-time offenders and who otherwise qualified for admission. The prisoners lived in a "half-way house" near campus and took regular academic courses. While not supposed to frequent the local taverns as well as the classes, many did. I met one at such a tavern who after many beers began talking about how he had been arrested. A bartender in an establishment that sponsored illegal gambling, he had also been involved in collecting gambling debts, at gunpoint if that appeared necessary. One day a man from another state, Nevada, had come to the bar and had lost a substantial amount of money, for which he had written I.O.U.s on which he subsequently reneged. My friend had been sent to Nevada to collect the money. He tracked down the man and demanded it—at gunpoint. The man promised to have it that afternoon, and when my friend returned and drew out his gun again "there were cops behind every chair in the apartment." After expressing his moral outrage at somebody who would renege on a debt and con the police into helping, my friend announced he would never end up in jail again, "because I'll never go to Nevada again."

People laugh when I tell that story, but viewed in non-probabilistic terms, the enforcer's inference isn't that bad. He had collected debts at gunpoint many times without being arrested, and he had been in Nevada only once. To believe that there was something special about Nevada that "caused" his arrest is compatible with the "canons" of inductive inference.

An alternative—statistical—interpretation is that he always risked some small probability of being arrested each time he collected money at gunpoint. And it happened. The way to avoid being arrested for collecting money at gunpoint is to stop doing it, as opposed to trying to figure out what led to arrest on one particular occasion versus not being arrested on all the others. Certainly, there was a *sequence of events* preceding that incident that was not present in others, but is it productive to think of this sequence as a *"cause?"* In fact, the attempt to discover such causes may contribute to the maintenance of behavior that is self-defeating or socially pernicious, because once we decide "why" such a behavior led to bad consequences on one occasion but not on others, we may feel safe in repeating it.

The Efficacy of Psychotherapy

Meta-analysis is often criticized because it "combines apples and oranges." But apples and oranges are fruit, and the fuzzy category of activities that we term "psychotherapy" constitutes a category as broad as "fruit," and more amorphous. The first meta-analysis of psychotherapy outcomes by Smith and Glass (1977) demonstrated that when amalgamating across a variety of problems and measures of success of coping with them, the average score on these measures of people given psychotherapy is approximately .68 standard deviations above the mean of the measures for the control group—e.g., people given no treatment or put on wait-list. There were a few problems with the Smith and Glass analysis. For example, they amalgamated across measures rather than across studies (thereby "overweighting" studies with multiple redundant measures as opposed to those with fewer), and they included studies without real randomized selection, opting instead to evaluate the effect of quality of study by correlating an overall index of it with the strength of the effect. Landman and Dawes (1982) subsequently addressed these problems by scrutinizing a sample of the original studies (20%)—omitting those not subject to journal review (e.g., doctoral dissertations, approximately 20%) and those in which the assignment to therapy versus control groups was not truly random (approximately 33% of those remaining); moreover, Landman and Dawes averaged across studies rather than across measures. Despite these changes, Landman and Dawes arrived at virtually the same conclusion. Moreover, they later rejected selective publication as an explanation for the effect (the "file-drawer problem")—both by the standard Rosenthal (1979) technique and by their own "truncated normal" one, in which they demonstrated that the average effect size above z-scores values defining "significance" (e.g., 1.96, 2.34) was well above that predicted by sampling randomly from a normal distribution above that value (Dawes, Landman, & Williams, 1984).

The fact that the mean of the therapy groups on these measures is .68 standard deviations above the mean on the control group distribution is typically translated into the statement that the average subject of the therapy group is at the 75th percentile of those in the control group. There is another simple translation. If a randomly chosen person from the therapy group is compared to a randomly chosen one from the control group, the odds are 2 to 1 that the person from the therapy group has a higher score. Such odds are fairly impressive. For example, knowing that the odds are 2 to 1 that one treatment for cancer is more effective than another would lead most of us to choose the first treatment without much ambivalence. But odds of 2 to 1 are not 10 to 1, or 20 to 1, or 100 to 1. Some people will be better off without therapy than with it.[4]

If we accept the statistical nature of the outcome, the obvious next question is whether a statistical prediction can be made of *which* people are better off without therapy. Perhaps attempting such a prediction would be as fruitless as previous attempts to relate therapeutic efficacy to background of therapist, years of experience, type of therapy, and therapist personality. Perhaps not. (These attempts have, in my opinion, been horribly flawed by the practice of sampling patients rather than therapists, therapies, or settings—the typical study being one in which a "significant difference" between two to four therapists or two treatment procedures is to be established by treating the *patient* as the unit of measurement.) To the best of my knowledge, there have been no studies oriented toward determining who should *not* enter therapy. Instead, psychotherapy is recommended as a universal panacea—by sources ranging from Dear Abby (often on the basis of a two-sentence description of unhappiness) to the American Psychological Association Ethics Committee (which will mandate that an errant psychologist receive psychotherapy, as opposed to simply mandating that the undesirable behavior not be repeated).

The 2-1 odds are, in my view, lost in a sea of causality about social power in the deliberations of people concerned with the ethics of sexual, social, or business contacts between therapists and *former* clients. While many of us (e.g., Dawes, 1986b) argue that such contact between therapist and *current* client is a form of social fraud, the (apparent) majority view among the opinion leaders in clinical psychology is that it is unethical because of the "power differential" of therapist and patient, which can be presumed to extend beyond the termination of psychotherapy (incidentally, with or without the patient's concurrence or assent). That opinion was expressed in a 6-1 vote approving a proposal passed at the June 1986 meeting of the American Psychological Association (APA) Ethics Committee. It reads: "In adjudicating complaints of sexual intimacy under principle 6a of the ethical principles of psychologists, the Ethics Committee takes the position that 'once a person becomes a client, regardless of the termination of the professional relationship, all subsequent sexual intimacies with that client are unethical. This policy becomes effective upon the date of this notification of membership. Passed 6-1 (Dawes dissenting).' " While this proposal was subsequently put in abeyance by the APA Board of Directors because it had the effect of "setting down a new rule or principle"(Ennis, Friedman, Bersoff, & Ewing, letter dated 8/29/86), it clearly expressed the views of the committee members. Note that there was no specification of type of therapy or duration of contact; in fact, the prohibition was meant to refer to *all* "professional relationships," including, for example, administering and interpreting a Strong Vocational Interest Test.

The 2-1 odds suggest, in contrast, that psychotherapy may be more a matter of "nudging" than of controlling the client. For example, the statement of a well-known and politically active psychotherapist that "their [clients'] very existence often depends on the therapist," implies that there should be a rather striking difference between the outcomes for therapy and control groups. (Taken literally, that statement implies that a number of the potential patients randomly assigned to control groups should be dead.) The statistical analysis of psychotherapy outcomes simply does not match the hypothesized limitlessness of the therapist's power. In fact, the statistical analysis suggests that this hypothesis—rather than being a characterization of reality—expresses a belief that itself may be a phenomenon worthy of scientific investigation.[5]

Viewing the efficacy of psychotherapy in probabilistic terms does *not* mean that it cannot have profound effects. The client coming into psychotherapy is most usually in a very distressed state that has become increasingly severe in the period of time before he or she enters therapy. It is reasonable, therefore, to postulate that this distress involves positive feedback loops between behaviors and feeling—"*deviation amplifying*" loops in Maruyama's (1963) terminology—as opposed to cybernetic, i.e., "deviation counteracting," loops. As Maruyama so convincingly argues, it is precisely in such deviation-amplifying processes that "small" changes may have "large" effects; for example, feeling better about oneself may lead to more socially integrated behavior, which may in turn exacerbate positive self-regard.

Let me illustrate such a process by an example of the "Polya urn problem" discussed by J. E. Cohen (1982). An urn contains one red and one white ball. One of these balls is sampled at random, and both it and a new ball of the same color are placed back in the urn; the process is repeated. It is easily proved that as the number of balls in the urn increases, the proportion of red balls stabilizes. But this proportion is equally likely to stabilize *anywhere* in the 0-1 interval. The value this proportion "approaches" is very dependent upon the first few drawings, even though the balls involved in each such draw constitute a very small proportion of the total number of balls in the urn as the process is repeated. Figure 1 illustrates this dependency, in which I had simulated the proportion after 1,000 draws when the red ball is chosen first with the probability of .5, .6, .7, .8, .9, or 1.00. Such small changes have profound effects, owing to the deviation-amplifying nature of the process.[6]

Life is no more drawing a ball from an urn than it is a river. The point, however, is that there are many choices in life that are dependent upon pre-existing propensity, and even though the choice itself may be a probabilistically generated one, the result can be quite stable. It may, then, *appear* to the observer that such stability results from a stable beginning and that change can only be accomplished through the most radical intervention. Conversely, it may *appear* that if change is effected, the intervention must have been radical. As illustrated in figure 1, change at the *right point* that is fairly trivial, e.g., "nudging" the probability of choosing a red ball on the first trial from .6 to .7, can have a profound effect. The question is whether the point at which therapeutic intervention is attempted is the "right" one. A pessimist may claim that the analogy suggests that the only type of intervention that can have such an impact would be at a very early age; the optimist would point out that people come to psychotherapy in crisis situations in which the future is indeed problematic, unknown, and demarcated from the past. The point of the analogy is to suggest that psychotherapy can have highly profound consequences even though its effects are highly probabilistic, and even though the power of the therapist is often extraordinarily limited. The meta-analyses of therapeutic outcomes certainly support the former condition and imply the latter, the judgment of some therapists notwithstanding.

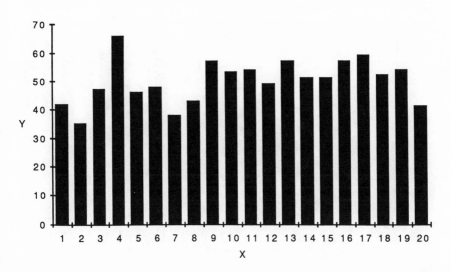

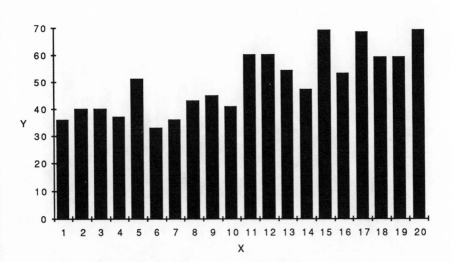

In concluding this section, I want to point out that this conclusion is not a particularly popular one. In fact, one suggestion of Meehl's that has received even less popular enthusiasm than his insistence that actuarial prediction is superior to clinical prediction is that *pure bad luck* may play an important role in the

p=.7

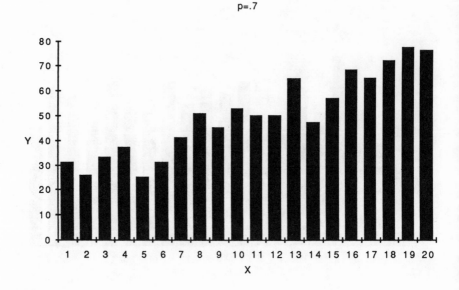

p=.8

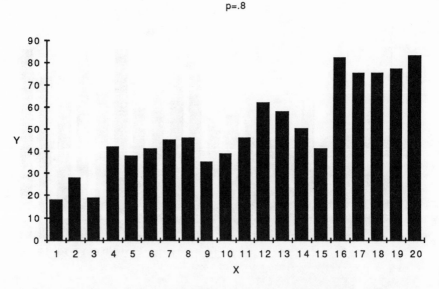

development and course (or even amelioration) of psychopathology. ''We see no inconsistency between our psychological analysis on the one hand and speculating that if the automobile had been functioning on that particular evening, the whole tragedy that gave rise to this paper may have been averted'' (Malmquist &

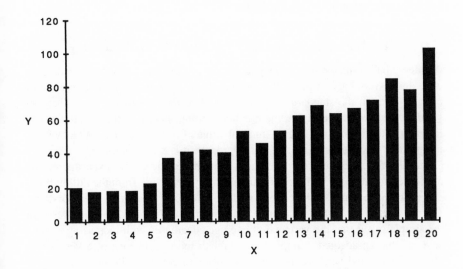

p=.9

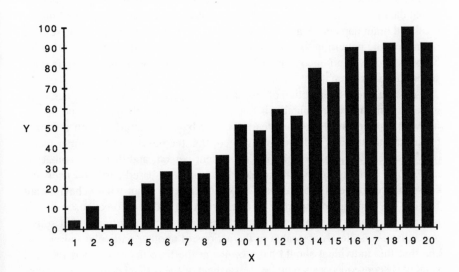

p=1

Meehl, 1978, p. 155). As I have attempted to point out, at least by analogy, there is *no* inconsistency between belief on the one hand that "pure luck" may play an important role in human life and on the other that psychotherapy may be of profound value. (It is!) There is no more contradiction between these conclusions than between accepting the wisdom of *Ecclesiastes* and simultaneously making an effort to change one's life for the better.

The Academic versus Professional Split in Psychology

As Meehl has pointed out in many places (e.g., 1978), the social sciences in general, and psychology in particular, are based on proving the mere existence of effects, through the standard significance test of the null hypothesis. That test yields a positive assertion that there is not nothing, based on the negative assertion that if there were nothing an unusual value of it was sampled. Whatever the merits, and obvious demerits, of this approach, it is a common one.

In the process of rejecting their null hypotheses, academic experimentalists are forced to compare variance accounted for by departure from the null hypothesis with unaccounted variance in their data—"error," uncontrolled factors, etc. *Unaccounted for variance is almost always larger.* Hypothesis testing rests on the simple result that the variance of averages decreases with increasing sample size, so that an adequate sample can establish the significance of a very small effect. This actual variance associated with the effect itself, however, is always small relative to the variance without the effect. Academicians' dearest theories predict systematic departures from null hypotheses, but they do not predict the actual data points very well, even in such areas as accessing the effects of highly localized brain damage. Statistics, the tool of the experimentalists, is the science of discovering pattern in the context of uncertainty (given the assumption that the chaos is additive and unconfounded with the pattern). Such uncertainty is quite salient to experimentalists.

Consider, then, the reaction of an academic experimentalist on an ethics committee when this experimentalist is told that a subsequent therapist found that an individual's current distress is clearly *caused* by a sexual affair with a former therapist after therapy had been terminated, that the motive of the former therapist was clearly one of exploiting a dependent person, and that such contact is *necessarily* bad. It is one thing to have a set of rules based partly on *probable* consequences of certain behaviors (or on convictions about what behaviors are "right" or "wrong" irrespective of consequences) and to enforce those rules. It is quite something else to base an ethical judgment on the certainty that someone's distress is clearly traceable to the actions of another particular individual, and that this individual should have *known* at the time the action was initiated what these consequences would be. Nevertheless, the official position of the current American Psychological Association Ethics Committee (*APA Monitor* 1987) is that "with cases involving post-termination patient sexual contact, [it] is currently adjudicating such complaints on a case-by-case basis. One important dimension in these matters is the nature and intent of the treatment termination. If, *upon examination,* it *seems* that the treatment ended in order to give the appearance of compliance with the ethical constrictions against psychologist-client sexual intimacies, the committee will find that behavior is a clear violation of principle 6.a'' (italics added). It turns out that even if the behavior is not in violation of 6.a it "may be found out to be inconsistent with the highest standards of the profession." To the experimentalist it may seem incomprehensible that someone can make a judgment of whether or not "treatment ended *in order to*" do or not do any one thing in particular. Moreover, the criterion for censure or expulsion from membership in the American Psychological Association is one of harm. How can it be determined that harm is caused by a particular action? Finally, the individuals on ethics committees wishing to make a positive judgment of harm in such cases face a particularly difficult problem because the complainant most often did not bring charges until the love affair with the former therapist had broken up *and* the complainant had subsequently become psychologically distressed *and* the complainant had subsequently entered therapy with somebody else—that is, not until years after the behaviors to be judged have occurred.

I was such an academic experimentalist on the American Psychological Association Ethics Committee, the academician who had replaced the previous one who had resigned in protest over such reasoning. When I objected to such judgments, as opposed to simply enforcing well-considered rules, the standard response was to analogize to the harm of asbestos. This analogy does not work. First, asbestos harm is not assessed by the victim himself or herself, but by an agent—a doctor—who bases a diagnosis on data (e.g., an X-ray) *independent of* the complainant's own statements (my first necessary condition for making a causal inference). Second, the "source" of the harm is not assessed on the basis of the individual case, but on the basis of an aggregation of cases that lead to a statistical conclusion (the substitutability criterion). Third, we understand the physiological mechanisms involved in the harm. Like it or not, our understanding of psychological factors that potentiate or ameliorate distress is not as well developed. What statistical studies there are relating harm to such contact are based on selective reporting self-evaluation, or that of a subsequent therapist. These assessments are not as unambiguous as that of the radiologist diagnosing lung cancer.

Certain behaviors, I maintain, *should* be considered unethical because they *do* have a sufficiently high *probability* of causing harm, or they violate our beliefs about right and wrong. The question is how to establish that. By a "case-by-case" analysis of something that happened between a particular former client and a particular former therapist four and a half years ago? or by using our knowledge to specify a set of reasonable rules that are then enforced? I emphasize the term "reasonable," because I believe that the simple rule ignoring reasons for contact and its duration passed on June 6, 1986, is not reasonable. Moreover, I believe a major impediment to creating reasonable rules is the deterministic thinking expressed in Keith-Spiegel and Koocher (1985). On page 14 we read that someone high in idealism and low in relativism, which is the position espoused by the authors, "assumes that the best possible outcome can always be achieved by following universal moral rules." *Always!?* that amounts to an assertion of a belief in "the just world." If, indeed, the best possible outcome could always be achieved in this way, then it *would* be reasonable to assess the ethics of a decision on the basis of the consequences that actually occurred, rather than on the probable consequences that could be reasonably foreseen by the decision-maker. Historically, however, both instrumentalists (e.g., J. S. Mill) and non-instrumentalists (e.g., E. Kant) have rejected such a view. That the consequences are probabilistic in nature is assumed both by those who view ethical rules to transcend consequences and by those who view them in a "utilitarian" manner. Even "rule utilitarians" do not maintain that the best possible consequences can be guaranteed by the best acts in the situation. Again, the experimentalist viewing deeply held beliefs validated only on a statistical basis cannot accept a *post hoc ergo propter hoc* policy for making ethical judgments. While the deterministic approach to human life leads to belief in the validity of very case-by-case analysis, a probabilistic one mandates rules.

In contrast, clinicians must act, not theorize. Whatever factors related to "deep" psychological needs or to cultural beliefs are involved, most people in our current society find it easier to act when they believe that the consequences of action are relatively certain than when they believe that the consequences are relatively uncertain. While both the rationality and the psychological necessity[7] of this preference for certainty are open to question (cf. Dawes, 1988), it appears to be a strong one, particularly among people who must make decisions that have profound effects on others' lives. (See, for example, March and Shapira's [1987] discussion of views of uncertainty expressed by business executives.) As indicated early in this chapter, it can extend to the point of "knowing" something one could not possibly know, or even postulating necessity. (At an administrative hearing in which I participated in 1982-83, a licensed psychologist condemning the behavior of a colleague whose license was in jeopardy was asked at one point whether "all psychologists would agree with you." Her response: "hum, yes, I believe they would. And if they don't, they should.")

The result? "Scientists lose respect for practitioners who seem to act without a word of uncertainty; practitioners lose respect for scientists who fail to produce the research they need [to eliminate that uncertainty]" (Fischhoff, Lichtenstein, Derby, Slovic, & Keeney, 1981, p. 67).

In addition, an amazing number of people want to be told what to do, what to think, and how to feel. In current American society, this desire is met through a hodgepodge of sources: Born-Again Christianity, traditional religion, Dear Abby, Dr. Ruth, and . . . psychologists. As the central office of the American Psychological Association was fond of pointing out, *Psychology Today,* before it was abandoned after a loss of $18 million over a 5-year period,[8] was the main communication between professional psychology and the lay public. However innoc-uous its contents had become (e.g., Americans love their automobiles, and pris-oners behave better when they believe they are monitored), its television commercials had conveyed a clear message: Professional psychology will tell you what to do, how to think, and how to feel. Moreover, within the organization itself, committees mandating how *psychologists* should think, feel, and behave have proliferated.

Telling people how to think, feel, and behave is predicated on three assump-tions: (1) You know how people do think, feel, and behave; (2) you know what change in thoughts, feelings, and behaviors is desirable; and (3) you know how to effect that change. Consider again academic experimenters. They collect data for the precise reason that they do *not* "know" how people think, feel, and behave. Instead, they propose and test hypotheses. Skepticism is at the core of academic psychology. In contrast, true belief is the core of advice-giving, publishing *Psy-chology Today,* and setting up "guidelines" committees *ad infinitum.*

One striking example of the difference based on the assumption of how much we know can be found in the struggle over "designation" of psychology pro-grams. In May 1984, the Task Force on Education confidentially distributed "recommendations for a designation system." The impetus for this task force came from a meeting of the Council of Graduate Departments of Psychology of the Council of Graduate Programs in Psychology (COGDOP) that I attended. The main focus of that meeting was on the ruling of a California judge named McKinnon that a Mr. Berger should be allowed to take the licensing exam to practice psychology despite not having a degree in it because "there is no corpus of knowlege in psychology." The way to prove that there was such a corpus was not by constructing an examination that an unqualified person would not pass, but by having a professional association set up a committee that would "desig-nate" what this corpus consisted of. The May 1984 report was the final result.

In the appendix of that report, the committee presented "feedback received on the task force on education credentials November 1983 revised recommendations for the designation system" (1984). In that appendix it referred to 248 commu-nications, most of which were evaluative. People were asked to respond to a 2-point rating scale running from "not helpful at all" to "extremely helpful" in which the middle category was "helpful." (!) Second, there is a great deal of inconsistency between the text and the listing of the communications; for ex-ample, I counted almost twice as many communications in the list specified as "representing the department" as were referred to in the text.

But despite these flaws, we can ask a simple question. Who supported desig-nation and who opposed it? The appendix included 20 communications from ac-ademic psychology departments. In 1983, the National Academy of Sciences in conjunction with the Associated Research Councils of the American Council of Learned Societies, American Council of Education, National Research Council, and Social Science Research Council rated 150 psychology programs on both "faculty quality" and "effectiveness of graduate research training" (1983). Categorizing the departments that responded to the request for feedback into top and bottom halves on the ratings[9] revealed that among those in the top category, 8 of the 10 opposed designation. In the bottom half, 8 favored designation and 2 opposed. This median split yields a phi-coefficient of .60 between quality of department and endorsement of the procedure, which even with this small sample is "significant" at the .01 level. Further, 10 state associations were referenced in both the text and the appendix; 8 favored and 2 opposed. The American Psychological Association ignored the input from the highly ranked departments and implemented the designation procedure.

If the question were simply one of academic versus professional 'turf," we would expect the departments responding to be opposed. But half are in favor. My interpretation, by contrast, is that the "academic skepticism" referred to earlier is more pronounced in the more highly ranked departments. What is being conveyed is a belief that we simply don't have well-established "first principles" of sufficient generality that a professional committee can designate a "corpus" of psychological knowledge. McKinnon is *correct* in distinguishing psychology from physics, biology, medicine, and engineering; he would be incorrect in concluding there is no knowledge. ("Corpus" is an ambiguous term.) What the communicators from the highly rated departments are conveying is skepticism that we can "designate" the very fuzzy set consisting of this knowledge.

Another main source of dispute between academicians and professionals is the role of "experience" — pure and simple — in making valid inferences. Most academicians believe with Ben Franklin that "experience is a dear teacher, and only fools will learn from no other" (*Poor Richard's Almanac*). After all, the point of conducting experiments and contrasting different possible hypotheses is that experience *per se* does *not* provide answers to our most important questions. The basic problem with experience is that you have no idea what *would* have happened *if* you or someone else had done what you or they didn't do. One way of viewing the whole enterprise of randomization in experiments is as a method for circumventing that problem.

Nevertheless, "it is my experience that . . . " has become a hallmark of the professional psychologists in court testimony (Faust, 1986), recommendations for social policy, and even in the intricate rules for judging the behavior of their colleagues. Of course, if causality existed and were clear and determinable, such grounds would be justified. Once again, a probabilistic as opposed to a deterministic view of human problems leads to the opposite conclusion.

The popular belief is that the schism in the American Psychological Association is due to the feeling on the part of academics that it doesn't do enough for them, particularly relative to the dues they must pay. I suggest that, in fact, much of the schism is based on the belief that the American Psychological Association does *too much,* particularly in the promulgation of dubious recommendations and strictures based on knowledge of causes that simply does not—in the academician's view—exist.

The Superiority of Probabilistic Thinking

I end this chapter by suggesting that causal versus probabilistic ways of thinking about life are not merely alternative modes of approaching its problems, but that the probabilistic way is superior. Inability to understand that when we are (slightly) representative of the groups of which we are members (section 2), belief that we can assess the cause of a single Rorschach response without considering the 40 others available (section 3), belief that we can figure out what led us to be arrested on one occasion but not on another (section 3), belief that efficacy as a therapist is equivalent to control (section 4), and belief that we know so much that we can tell others how to feel, think, and behave (section 5) are all—I suggest—fallacies. They are based on a deterministic view of life and the search for causes. My own response does not cause others to respond in a particular way, there must be some reason for seeing a bear on card 8, something must have caused me to be arrested this time but not other times, I can only influence if I can control, ethical behavior always leads to the best possible outcomes, others would be better off if they followed my advice, and on the basis of unsystematic experience I can figure out the important causal factors in life. By contrast, a probabilistic approach leads to opposite conclusions: if most people in the group of which I am a member endorse an item or behavior I am *likely* to as well, a single response embedded in those with an above average "form level" on the Rorschach is not indicative of hallucination, continued illegal activity has a high probability of resulting in arrest one way or another, psychotherapy increases only the probability of changing feelings and behavior in a favorable direction that may continue, the ethics of a decision should be judged on the basis of its probable consequences as assessed at the time it occurred rather than on "what happened," psychologists are not as omnipotent as might be inferred from their attempts to advise others, and experience is just that—experience.

Examples are easy. Where is the strong, systematic evidence for the superiority of probabilistic thinking? I believe that it comes from the finding that Meehl first studied in 1954 and recently summarized (1986)—the superiority of statistical to clinical prediction. As he maintains (1986, pp. 373-374, italics added), *"There is no controversy in social science which shows such a large body of qualitatively diverse studies coming out so uniformly in the same direction as this one."* Why?

Goldberg (this volume) has contributed an excellent analysis of the *structural* reasons we should expect clinical judgment to be inferior (here "reasons" referring to scientific principles rather than causes). I would like to suggest an additional one, concerning the substance of the prediction. *Clinical judges overestimate the degree to which it is possible to predict outcomes*. Knowing that the "simple" combinations (usually linear) of "simple" predictors—most often based on indices summarizing past behavior or total scores on carefully devised tests—do not predict, clinical judges add others, impressionistic "intuitive" ones. These others are added inconsistently, leading to the apparently paradoxical finding that even though linear models outperform judges they also describe the predictions of these same judges (Goldberg, 1968). These others are added when the outcomes are important, or when the clinical judges believe themselves to be experts (Arkes, Dawes, & Christensen, 1986). But because they are added inconsistently, they are very difficult to characterize and describe systematically, which is precisely what the clinicians themselves say about their departures from statistically valid prediction; such departures are based on vague, ineffable, "intuitive" judgments. One hypothesis I have presented elsewhere (Dawes, 1986a) is that these departures are based on representative thinking, but while we can devise experiments to demonstrate (quite strongly) the existence of such thinking, exactly when and how it will occur in particular judgment situations cannot be predicted. There is no way of forecasting that a particular head psychologist will "glom onto" a particular Rorschach response in order to make a "counterinductive" (Meehl, 1977) inference.

Such lack of predictability is, I suggest, exactly what is not appreciated in the deterministic thinking of many clinicians. The reality of this lack is, however, evidenced by the result that all the studies showing the superiority of statistical predictions are based on *simple* predictors. (See Dawes, 1979.) Undergraduate grades and GRE (or LSAT) scores are the best predictors of graduate performance. A point system based overwhelmingly on the incidence of past criminal behavior is the best predictor of staying out of jail on parole (Hoffman & Beck, 1974; Carroll, Wiener, Coates, Galegher, & Alibrio, 1982). Biopsy characteristics that could be as well coded by a laboratory technician as by the world's expert on Hodgkin's disease are the best predictors of survival time (Einhorn, 1972). Simple financial ratios are the best predictors of business bankruptcy (Beaver, 1966; Deacon, 1972; Libby, 1976)—the best of all being the ratio of assets to liabilities. The list goes on and on. The predictors are overwhelmingly of the type that people with the most minimal training in the relevant areas would choose. Highly trained Rorschach experts are sensitive to the presumed psychological nuances of CF responses (those determined primarily by color and secondarily by form) versus FC responses (those determined primarily by form and secondarily by color), but the ratio—or difference, or transformed difference—turns out to predict nothing at all. Even the tendency to see human movement turns out to predict nothing (McCall, 1959). "Depth psychology" has simply failed, or at least failed to lead to any principles of general applicability. (In his recent review of the irrelevance of depth psychology to matters of peace and security, Blight [1987] mentioned all its limitations except the most important one, which is that it is incapable of yielding the degree of predictability desired.)

The simplest principle is that: *past behavior is the best predictor of future behavior and it isn't very good.* Of course, it is far from a perfect predictor. People change. But when we deviate from that principle and from using other "obvious" predictors, our predictions degenerate. Because these predictors are not perfect, we will always make "errors," and we know in advance of prediction that such errors are inevitable. Nevertheless, such error is smaller than the error that abandoning them generates. Again, as Einhorn (1986) stated, we must "accept error to make less error."

One explanation for this degeneracy is that we have been too stupid to find the right predictors, or to combine those we have in just the right way. The dismal success rate of past attempts to make curvilinear, interactive, and other "configural" predictions argues against the latter possibility, but failure to find the right predictors remains as one good possibility. The other is that there are simply intrinsic limits on the predictability of human life. If so, probabilistic prediction and judgment *must* be superior to that based on deterministic searches, because probability theory and statistical analysis are those branches of human intellectual development specifically addressing the problem of finding structure in a context of uncertainty. More likely, there are limits, *and* we have been too stupid to find variables that push back those limits to make life more predictable. From the point of view of the current evaluator, however, who must make judgments and predictions on the basis of what is now known, the possibility of a future expansion in the degree of predictability is irrelevant. The course of life is probabilistic.

Many of our colleagues claim that a meta-assumption of "determinism" is, if not relevant to current applied problems, necessary for the development of a true science. Bertrand Russell challenged that claim in 1913, and questioned whether the concept of "cause" was even important in modern science. (While F = ma may have been motivated by finding a cause for accelerated movement, the equation is now used to define mass as the ratio of F to a.) His challenge was on philosophical grounds, while the challenge in this paper is on *empirical* grounds.

We can now also add an empirical example from social science itself: behavioral genetics. Even the most casual perusal of papers in this field or of standard texts (e.g., McCleary & DeFries, 1973) reveals its probabilistic basis. (In fact, all genetic analysis is probabilistic in nature, as evidenced by some of its most famous "laws," such as the Hardy-Weinberg, which is a probabilistic one developed by a probabilist.) Moreover, with the possible exception of the inheritance of intelligence (and that is open to some dispute), the findings of behavioral genetics always have the same characteristic referenced in my earlier discussion of experimental psychology: more outcome variance is unaccounted for than is accounted for. The probabilistic nature of the conclusions in no way invalidates behavioral genetics as a scientific field, in fact a rather successful one. As argued in this paper, a similar approach would facilitate other branches of psychology and the social sciences as well.

In closing, I would like to speculate that there are substantial resistances to probabilistic thinking that are common *both* to psychologists (and other social scientists) and to the lay public. If the course of the human life is probabilistic rather than deterministic, I am vulnerable. As a clinician, I am vulnerable to the same sort of disorders that affect my clients unless I can find unique causal factors that determine their behavior that would not determine mine. As an academician, I am vulnerable to being wrong. During the jury deliberations in the New Bedford rape trials presented on CNN, Doctor Lee Salk mentioned that victimization not only involves physical trauma but severely weakens the fundamental beliefs on which our daily functioning is based; that we are superior, that we are invulnerable, and that the world is just. "And it takes several years to reestablish these beliefs." If I accept the probabilistic view of life, I as a person come face to face with the conclusion that I am *not* superior, that I am *not* invulnerable, and that the world is *not* just. Moreover, I am apt to be at odds with my culture—which emphasizes optimism *per se* as a noble virtue. (Seligman, 1987, has made a persuasive *post hoc* argument that this emphasis on optimism may even have had a profound effect on the outcome of recent presidential elections.) To admit to a probabilistic view of outcomes even conflicts with the *summum bonum,* a belief in "internal control." Moreover, neither clinicians nor academicians are reinforced for failure to replicate or for proclaiming the *absence* of a factor or effect—e.g., "I can provide no particular reason why she saw that," or "I have no clear ideas about the future of the field of behavioral decision-making." "I don't know" is not a recipe for professional success.

The saving grace from a decision-theoretic point of view is that since alternatives should be chosen on the basis of their *expected* value, rather than on the certainty of their consequences, the degree which probabilities deviate from 0 and 1 is often totally irrelevant. In many—if not most—contexts belief that we can control 10% of the outcome variance leads us to choose the same options as would belief that we can control 100% of it. Conversely, uncertainty does have value. It gives us hope,[10] and that "cloud" of doubt that we're really as omniscient as we might like to be can make us kinder and more humane in our treatment of others.

Finally, understanding that the course of life is probabilistic and that consequently we often do not have control can be liberating. In an article otherwise arguing that belief in control is adaptive in adjusting to threatening situations, Taylor (1983, p. 1170) presents the following anecdote about a woman with breast cancer.

One of the women I interviewed told me that after detection of her breast tumor she believed that she could prevent future recurrences by controlling her diet. She had, among other things, consumed huge quantities of vitamin A through the singularly unappetizing medium of mashed asparagus. A year and a half later, she developed a second malignancy. This, of course, is precisely the situation all control researchers are interested in: a dramatic disconfirmation of efforts to control. I asked her how she felt when that happened. She shrugged and said she guessed she'd been wrong. She then decided to quit her dull job and use her remaining time to write short stories—something she always wanted to do. Having lost control in one area of her life, she turned to another area, her life work, that *was* controllable.

Taylor presents no evidence whatsoever that her subjects who attempted to achieve control over recurrence of breast cancer were better off than those who didn't, although the article itself contains throughout the clear implication that attempting such control is psychologically valuable. However, her anecdote can be interpreted in precisely the opposite way; it can be interpreted as an example in which *giving up* the attempt to control is valuable. Exactly why devoting one-self to one's "life work" should be interpreted as an effort at "control" is un-clear. By contrast, "shrugging" is clearly a communication that one does *not* have control. Perhaps if the shrug had occurred a year and a half earlier, a year and a half of this woman's life (and all our lives are finite) would have been de-voted to the work she desired rather than to a dull job and mashed asparagus.

Notes

1. Between drafts of this paper, the schism has widened considerably.

2. Analyzing the above example in a Bayesian framework, we note that the likelihood of an endorsement given we are sampling from the 2/3 item is just 2/3's, hence the posterior probability of sampling from that item given an endorsement is $(2/3)(1/2)/(1/2) = 2/3$, because the prior probability of sampling from it and the prior probability of an endorsement both equal 1/2. Therefore, the mean of the distribution of posterior belief about proportion equals $(2/3)(2/3) + (1/3)(1/3) = 5/9$, and similar reasoning indicates that this mean following a rejection equals 4/9.

3. "The view that recognition [sic], the act of construing an unfamiliar stimulus, taps central components of personality functions is one that will remain central in any psychology committed to the understanding of human experience" (Bernstein, 1972, p. 434). Note that Bernstein presents a *view*, not a finding—a view that is apparently resistant to overwhelming amounts of negative evidence (Dawes, 1988a, chapter 11).

4. Many clinicians with whom I discuss these findings counter that the type of therapy academics study is not oriented to the "real" type of problem they encounter in their practice; for example, systematic desensitization for snake phobias is easy to study, and its efficacy is amenable to simple evaluation (the degree to which the client will handle, or approach, a snake), but snake phobias are important only for clients whose jobs require crawling under buildings! Generalization to profes-sional practice, the argument runs, is more a matter of analogizing than of making a sound statistical inference. In response, I point out that the sample Landman and I investigated involved, among other problems: schizophrenia, alcoholism, recovery from heart attacks, and control of potentially fatal asthma attacks. Also, at least some practicing clinicians are aware of the probabilistic nature of psy-

chotherapy outcomes; for example, Gonsiorek writes (1987, p. 417): "If psychotherapy were a drug, it would be prohibited by the Food and Drug Administration because a 10% to 15% rate of adverse effects would be intolerable." (The meta-analyses indicate 33%.)

5. I personally would not like to be a client of the therapist quoted. If the analysis of the "false consensus" considered in the second section of this paper is valid, my personal repugnance for the attitude expressed may be an important datum for evaluating others' response to such an attitude.

6. I thank Eric Gold for conducting the simulation.

7. For starters, try to imagine the extreme of no uncertainty whatsoever. Life would be intolerable.

8. Letter to the Council of Representatives of the American Psychological Association from Raymond D. Fowler, President, 7/22/88.

9. Both "faculty quality" and "effectiveness" resulted in the same categorization.

10.   Prometheus: I stopped mortals from foreseeing their fate.

Chorus: What sort of remedy did you find for this plague?

Prometheus: I planted in them blind hope.

Chorus: That was the great advantage you gave mortals?

Prometheus: And besides I gave them fire.

Aeschylus, *Prometheus Bound*

References

APA Monitor (June 1987). Sex with ex-clients judged on intent of termination, p. 45.

Arkes, H. R., Dawes, R. M., & Christensen, C. (1986). Factors influencing the use of a decision rule in a probabilistic task. *Organizational Behavior and Human Judgment Processes, 37,* 93–110.

Bar-Hillel, M. (1980). The base rate fallacy in probability judgments. *Acta Psychologica, 44,* 211–233.

Beaver, W. H. (1966). Financial ratios as predictors of failure. In *Empirical research in accounting: Selected studies.* Chicago: University of Chicago, School of Business, Institute of Professional Accounting.

Bernstein, A. G. (1972). Rorschach review. In O. K. Burros, (Ed.), *Seventh mental measurements yearbook.* Highland Park, NJ: Gryphon Press.

Blight, J. G. (1987). Toward a policy-relevant psychology of avoiding nuclear war: Lessons from the Cuban missile crisis. *American Psychologist, 42,* 12–29.

Carroll, J. S., Wiener, R. L., Coates, D., Galegher, J., & Alibrio, J. J. (1982). Evaluation, diagnosis, and prediction in parole decision making. *Law and Society Review, 17,* 199–228.

Cohen, J. E. (1982). How is the future related to the past? *Annual Report 1982, Center for Advanced Study in the Behavioral Sciences,* 59–71.

Dawes, R. M. (1979). The robust beauty of improper linear models in decision making. *American Psychologist, 31,* 571–582.

Dawes, R. M. (1986a). Representative thinking in clinical judgment. *Clinical Psychology Review, 6,* 425–441.

Dawes, R. M. (1986b). The philosophy of responsibility and autonomy versus that of being one-up. Paper presented at the American Psychological Association, August 24.

Dawes, R. M. (1988a). *Rational choice in an uncertain world.* San Diego: Harcourt, Brace and Jovanovich.

Dawes, R. M. (1988b). Statistical criteria for establishing a truly false consensus effect. *Journal of Experimental Social Psychology.*

Dawes, R. M., Landman, J., & Williams, M. (1984). Reply to Kurosawa. *American Psychologist,* 74–75.

Deacon, E. B. (1972). A discriminant analysis of business failure. *Journal of Accounting Research, 10,* 167–179.

D'Holbach, P. H. (1770). *Le Système de la Nature,* I.

Einhorn, H. J. (1972). Expert measurement and mechanical combination. *Organizational Behavior and Human Performance, 13,* 387–395.

Einhorn, H. J. (1986). Accepting error to make less error. *Journal of Personality Assessment, 50,* 387–395.

Emerson, R. W. (1860). *The conduct of life,* II. New York: A. L. Burt Company.

Emerson, R. W. (1841). *Essays: Self reliance.* London: James Fraser.

Ennis, B., Friedman, P., Bersoff, D., & Ewing, M. (1986). Letter dated 8/29/86.

Faust, D. (1986). Declarations versus investigations: The case for the special reasoning abilities and capabilities of the expert witness in psychology/psychiatry. *The Journal of Psychiatry and Law, 13,* 33–59.

Fischhoff, B., Lichtenstein, S., Slovic, P., Derby, S. L., & Keeney, R. L. (1981). *Acceptable risk.* Cambridge, England: Cambridge University Press.

Glymour, C. (1986). Comment: Statistics and metaphysics. *Journal of the American Statistical Society, 81,* 964–966.

Goldberg, L. R. (1968). Simple models or simple processes? Some research on clinical judgment. *American Psychologist, 23,* 483–496.

Goldberg, L. R. (this volume). Human mind versus regression equation: Five contrasts.

Gonsiorek, J. C. (1987). Intervening with psychotherapists who sexually exploit clients. *Innovations in Clinical Practice: A Source Book, 6,* 417–426.

Hoch, S. J. (1987). Perceived consensus and predictive accuracy: The pros and cons of projection. *Journal of Personality and Social Psychology, 21,* 221–234.

Hoffman, P. B., & Beck, J. L. (1974). Parole decision-making: A salient factor score. *Journal of Criminal Justice, 2,* 195–206.

Hume, D. (1740). *A treatise in human nature.*

Hume, D. (1748). *An inquiry concerning human understanding.*

Keith-Spiegel, P., & Koocher, G. P. (1985). *Ethics in psychology.* Hillsdale, NJ: Lawrence Erlbaum.

Landman, J. T., & Dawes, R. M. (1982). Psychotherapy outcome: Smith and Glass' conclusions stand up under scrutiny. *American Psychologist, 37,* 504–516.

Libby, R. (1976). Man versus model of man: Some conflicting evidence. *Organizational Behavior and Human Performance, 16,* 1–12.

Malmquist, C. P., & Meehl, P. E. (1978). Barabas: A study in guilt-ridden homicide. *The International Review of Psychoanalysis, 5,* 149–174.

March, J. G., & Shapira, Z. (1987). Managerial perspectives on risk and risk taking. *Management Science, 11,* 1404–1408.

Marks, G., & Miller, N. (1987). Ten years of research on the false-consensus effect: An empirical and theoretical review. *Psychological Review, 102,* 72–90.

Maruyama, M. (1963). The second cybernetics: Deviation-amplifying mutual causal processes. *American Scientist, 51,* 164–179.

McCall, R. J. (1959). Rorschach review. In O. K. Burros, (Ed.), *Fifth mental measurements yearbook.* Highland Park, NJ: Gryphon Press.

McCleary, G. E., & DeFries, J. C. (1973). *Introduction to behavioral genetics.* San Francisco: W. H. Freeman.

Meehl, P. E. (1954). *Clinical versus statistical prediction: A theoretical analysis and review of the literature.* Minneapolis: University of Minnesota Press.

Meehl, P. E. (1977). Why I do not attend case conferences. In P. E. Meehl, (Ed.), *Psychodiagnosis: Selected Papers.* Minneapolis: University of Minnesota Press.

Meehl, P. E. (1978). Theoretical risks and tabular asterisks: Sir Karl, Sir Ronald and the slow progress of soft psychology. *Journal of Clinical Psychology, 46*, 806–834.

Meehl, P. E. (1986). Causes and effects of my disturbing little book. *Journal of Personality Assessment, 50*, 370–375.

Meehl, P. E., & Rosen, A. (1955). Antecedent probability and the efficacy of psychometric signs, patterns, or cutting scores. *Psychological Bulletin, 52*, 194–201.

Melton, G. B. (1988). Psychologists' involvement in cases of child maltreatment: Limits of roles and expertise. (Working paper, adopted as a policy statement by Division 37 [Child, Youth and Family Services] of the American Psychological Association.)

Mill, J. S. (1832). *A system of logic.*

Mullen, B., Atkins, J. L., Champion, D. S., Edwards, C., Hardy, D., Story, J. E., & Venderklok, M. (1985). The false consensus effect: A meta-analysis of 115 hypothesis tests. *Journal of Experimental Social Psychology, 21*, 262–282.

National Academy of Sciences. (1983). *An assessment of research: Doctorate programs in the United States.*

Parker, J. G., & Asher, S. J. (1987). Peer relations and later personal adjustments: Are low-acceptance children at risk? *Psychological Bulletin, 3*, 357–389.

Rosenthal, R. (1979). The "file drawer problem" and tolerance for null results. *Psychological Bulletin, 86*, 638–641.

Ross, L., Greene, D., & House, P. (1977). The "false consensus effect": An egocentric bias in social perception and attribution process. *Journal of Experimental Social Psychology, 13*, 279–301.

Ross, L., & Sicoly, F. (1979). Egocentric biases in availability and attribution. *Journal of Personality and Social Psychology, 37*, 322–336.

Russell, B. (1913). On the notion of cause. *Proceedings of the Aristotelian Society 13*, 1–26.

Seligman, M. P. E. (1987). Predicting depression, poor health and presidential elections. Edited transcript, *Science and public policy seminars*. Federation of Behavioral, Psychological and Cognitive Sciences.

Sherman, J. C., Presson, V. V., & Chassin, L. (1984). Mechanisms underlying the false consensus effect: The special role of threats to the self. *Personality and Social Psychology Bulletin, 10*, 127–138.

Smith, M. L., & Glass, G. V. (1977). Meta-analysis of psychotherapy outcome studies. *American Psychologist, 32*, 752–760.

Suppes, P. C. (1970). *A probabilistic theory of causality.* Amsterdam: North-Holland.

Task Force on Education and Credentialling. Recommendations for a Designation System: Final Report to the APA Board of Directors and the Council of Representatives. Washington, D.C. May, 1984.

Taylor, S. E. (1983). Adjustment to threatening events: A theory of cognitive adaptation. *American Psychologist, 38*, 1161–1173.

Tversky, A., & Edwards, W. (1966). Information versus reward in binary choice. *Journal of Experimental Psychology, 71*, 680–683.

van de Kragt, A. J. C., & Dawes, R. M. (in preparation). The consensus effect that's truly false: Failure to give enough weight to one's own response.

Contributors

Dante Cicchetti, professor, Departments of Psychology and Psychiatry; director, Mt. Hope Family Center, University of Rochester.

W. Grant Dahlstrom, professor, Department of Psychology, University of North Carolina at Chapel Hill.

Robyn M. Dawes, professor, Department of Social and Decision Science, Carnegie-Mellon University.

David Faust, professor, Department of Psychology, University of Rhode Island.

Paul Feyerabend, professor emeritus, Department of Philosophy, University of California at Berkeley.

Lewis R. Goldberg, professor, Department of Psychology, University of Oregon; research scientist, Oregon Research Institute.

William M. Grove, assistant professor, Department of Psychology, University of Minnesota.

Adolf Grünbaum, Andrew Mellon Professor of Philosophy; Research Professor of Psychiatry; chairman, Center for Philosophy of Science, University of Pittsburgh.

Benjamin Kleinmuntz, professor, Department of Psychology, University of Illinois at Chicago.

David T. Lykken, professor, Department of Psychology, University of Minnesota.

Sir Karl Raimund Popper, CH, FRS, FBA, professor of logic and scientific method, University of London.

Leonard G. Rorer, professor, Department of Psychology, Miami University.

William Schofield, professor emeritus, Departments of Psychiatry and Psychology, University of Minnesota.

Index

abstract meanings, universe of: affects physical universe, 116

accuracy: decreased by use of a valid sign, 186; and false consensus effect, relationship between, 241; of judges, neither consistent nor general, 202

accuracy, predictive: maximal when predictors are orthogonal, 180; unrelated to clinicians' experience, 206–207

actuarial prediction: vs. clinical prediction, 213; and denigration of human judgment, 219; less favored in complex information processing in clinical psychology and medicine, 217; outperformed clinical judges, 202; principle of very seldom contradicting, 203

acute abdominal pain: differential diagnosis of, 221

adaptation, control of: argumentative language as means for, 123

adaptive testing, 190

affirming the consequent: logical fallacy of, 75, 76

American Psychological Association (APA), 253, 256: Ethics Committee of, 247, 253

anchoring and adjustment: heuristic, 223

angina pectoris: surgical treatment of, 162

antecedent probability: and cutting scores, 186

antimicrobial therapy: MYCIN, computer program for, 226

anti-social personality: in *DSM-III*, 29. *See also* psychopathy

argument as means of control of adaptation efforts, 122–123

autism: maternal aloofness as putative cause of, 195

automated personality-test programs, 229

availability: heuristic, 222

bad luck, 249

ban, natural: as measure of change in evidence, 49

Barnett, G. O., 228

Barry, W., 9

Bartley, W. W., III, 69, 70

base rates, 194, 195, 196, 213: accuracy and intremental validity of, 192; and individual predictions, correlation between, 242

base-rate predictions, 186–191, 209: finding exceptions to superiority of, 189; incorporation of utilities into, 210

batteries, tests in: clinicians' choice of, 197

Bayes's Theorem, 80, 81, 82, 186, 227

Bayesian vs. regression analyses of false consensus effect, 241

Bayesian decision making, insensitivity of: in violation of conditional-independence-of-signs assumption, 222

Bayesian decision theory, 220

Bayesian inference, 61, 72: problem of radically differing prior probabilities, 82; in theory testing, 81

Bayesian probabilistic analysis: of false consensus effect, 240

Dr. Dante Cicchetti is professor in the departments of Psychology and Psychiatry at the University of Rochester and director of the Mt. Hope Family Center, University of Rochester. He obtained his doctoral degree in clinical and developmental psychology under Paul Meehl. Currently, Cicchetti's theoretical and research interests are focused on the area of developmental psychopathology. He is the author of numerous articles and books on normal and abnormal devleopment.

Dr. William M. Grove is assistant professor in the Department of Psychology at the University of Minnesota and was previously a researcher at the University of Iowa. He obtained his doctoral degree under Paul Meehl. Grove is the author of publications on the diagnosis, classification, and genetics of mental illness.